EARLY HISTORY

OF THE

UNIVERSITY OF VIRGINIA,

AS CONTAINED IN THE LETTERS OF

THOMAS JEFFERSON AND JOSEPH C. CABELL,

HITHERTO UNPUBLISHED;

WITH AN

APPENDIX,

CONSISTING OF

MR. JEFFERSON'S BILL FOR A COMPLETE SYSTEM OF EDUCATION, AND OTHER ILLUSTRATIVE DOCUMENTS;

AND AN

INTRODUCTION,

COMPRISING

A BRIEF HISTORICAL SKETCH OF THE UNIVERSITY, AND A BIOGRAPHICAL NOTICE OF JOSEPH C. CABELL.

J. W. RANDOLPH,
121 MAIN STREET, RICHMOND, VA.
1856.

C. H. WYNNE, PRINTER, RICHMOND.

TO THE

VISITORS, FACULTY AND ALUMNI

OF THE

UNIVERSITY OF VIRGINIA,

THIS WORK IS RESPECTFULLY DEDICATED

BY THE EDITOR,

ON BEHALF OF THE LATE

RECTOR.

PREFACE.

A few words are necessary to account for the appearance of this work at this time, and for the connection of the present Editor with its publication.

A Society of Alumni of the University of Virginia was formed in 1838. At their Annual Meeting in 1852, it was suggested, as a desideratum, that some fuller and more complete history of the Institution than any as yet extant should be compiled, and that the duty of its preparation might properly be assumed by the Society itself. In the discussion which arose they were told, that the least known but not the least interesting portion of such history would be *a narrative of the early efforts which led to its establishment;* and that this could not be written without the use of certain papers in the possession of the then Rector, who was himself a principal actor in those scenes. The correspondence between himself and Mr. Jefferson gave ample details of those efforts, and several judicious persons who had been favored with a perusal thought the letters worthy of separate publication. An informal request to that effect had heretofore been declined by Mr. Cabell, who thought that such a step would hardly be becoming in his life-time. On being again urged from this quarter, he gave a reluctant consent, with certain provisions. Not all of the letters related to the University. Some of them entire, and parts of others, were either confidential or touched on matters no longer of public interest. When these were separated from the mass, and a fair transcript made of the remainder, as also of certain other documents, both printed and manuscript, deemed pertinent to the main object, something, he thought, was yet wanting in the way of elucidation. This, Mr. Cabell had promised to supply at his leisure from his own reminiscences, aided by other papers in his possession and the contemporary public journals. Enquiry was occasionally made as to his progress, but he had never found time for entering on a task which was rather foreign to his then pursuits.

Feeling, at length, that he had incurred an obligation which, if to be fulfilled at all, must be attended to without further delay, he devolved the *editorial* duty proper on a friend, to whom for that purpose he gave free access to all his books and papers. Much time and labor were spent in examining these collateral sources, but with no corresponding result. Frequent and abundant confirmation of the statements of the text came under his notice, yet little that was new. The deficiency will, however, be slightly felt. *The letters, for the most part, explain themselves.* The Editor has therefore, in general, limited his task to the humble duty of explaining, by the use of notes or connecting narrative, such allusions to places, persons, or current events, as would otherwise be obscure or unintelligible to the general reader. Where he has deviated from this plan, the reason will either be obvious or expressly stated. The additional information contained in the Introduction, it was also thought, might be not unacceptable. Mr. Cabell's proposed contribution—in the form of Recollections of his intercourse with Mr. J. on this subject—was postponed until he was seized with the lingering indisposition which at length proved fatal. The Editor, who had occasionally heard from him characteristic anecdotes of Mr. J., cannot but regret this omission on the reader's account.

A few of the letters of Mr. Jefferson in the following series may also be found in the two editions of his works which have already appeared; but not enough to impair the interest of the reader in the Correspondence as a whole. He will also have made some progress in the perusal before he detects any reference to the University, which thereafter continues to be almost the sole topic. This earlier portion is retained as serving to shew how the relations between the parties grew up and were matured into confidence, and will thus prepare the reader for the sequel. The letters of Mr. Cabell, it need scarcely be said, were written without the remotest view to publication; many of them under the pressure of fatigue, or of other public duties, and with the sole purpose of giving his correspondent the earliest or most satisfactory intelligence of the progress of the cause which each had so much at heart. They will be read, of course, principally for their matter; yet will their unstudied character give them a present and life-like interest which often evaporates from more formal documents; and their style has been thought not wholly unworthy of the association in which they will be found. Those of Mr. Jefferson, it is believed, present certain traits of the patriot, and of the man, in as favorable, if not a more attractive light, than does any former publication.

July 4, 1856.

CONTENTS.

CONTENTS OF APPENDIX.

A.

B.

H.

I.

K.

L.

M.

N.

O. (*a*)

O. (*b*)

O. (*c*)

P.

Q.

INTRODUCTION.

The University of Virginia, which was opened for the reception of students in the spring of 1825, has now been in regular operation for more than thirty years. The body of those who have here received instruction, has varied with the state of the times and other circumstances, but has, on the whole, progressively increased, until for several years past it has exceeded five hundred in number. Of the thousands who have partaken of its advantages, many have acquitted themselves honorably in the various walks of private life; and not a few have been distinguished in the public service of this and other States. With a popularity already greater than that of any other institution of learning in the southern division of our Union, its capacities for usefulness have been recently enlarged and with improved prospects for the future.

While these and other considerations have of late years excited a renewed interest in its history, no detailed and connected narrative adequate to the present demand has as yet been supplied. The actors in its earliest scenes have nearly all left the stage; the traditions of their doings are fading away; the printed documents which would illustrate these, have been dispersed through volumes or pamphlets not generally accessible, and others of like character have remained in manuscript. To the two latter classes have heretofore belonged the following Correspondence and the papers appended. They are here embodied and offered to the public with the view of meeting a supposed want of the friends of education in our country. They may not, perhaps, in strictness be called a history of the University, but they do contain the most material facts which would go to the composition of such a work; and while it must be left to other hands to digest these into a regular form, it is believed that the volume possesses an interest of its own, independent of the fact that it sets before us the names and services of its more active friends during the era which it embraces.

That to THOMAS JEFFERSON the State of Virginia is principally indebted for her University, is generally known. As one of his chief titles to the remembrance of posterity, it is engraved on his tomb. But few are aware of the origin of the idea, of the successive steps in its realization, of the singular unity and tenacity of his purpose in relation thereto, and of the length of time during which it was maturing. But few of his contemporaries were apprised, and still fewer of the present generation have been informed of the labors necessary to prepare the public mind for such a measure.

The colonial annals of Virginia inform us that an University was contemplated by the early adventurers, with a liberal endowment of lands at least; but that the project, after an auspicious commencement, was defeated by the massacre of 1622, which threatened the extinction of the colony, and by other causes. It was not until 1692, that the college of William & Mary was established, which, having been endowed in part by public authority, in part by private benefactions, at home and from abroad, continued for several generations the sole seat of higher learning among us. In that capacity it was eminently useful, though distinguished less for the number than for the character and attainments of its alumni. The variety and extent of culture here received were, perhaps, as great as could have been expected when the utilitarian cast of the general pursuits of our citizens is regarded; though both of the former were outgrown in the progress of society before the needful changes and additions were made. It was probably owing to the peculiar constitution of that society, and to the fluctuating character of our population, that scholastic education other than collegiate, was left to private interest or individual enterprise. While a fortunate few received this part of their discipline abroad, we learn also from reliable authority, that there were a number of excellent classical schools within the colony. And, be it said to their honor, that many of these were conducted by clergymen of the Established Church, who, we may presume, were well qualified for this part of their function by their education in foreign Universities. Mr. Jefferson himself assures us, that the mass of education in Virginia before the Revolution, placed her with the foremost of her sister colonies,* though for a time afterwards it had much declined.

It was not that the importance of this matter was under-valued by the public authorities, who were well aware that the purity, nay the life and permanence of republican institutions must depend on the intelligence of the people. So early as 1776, a committee appointed by the Assembly for a general revision of the laws, took the subject into consideration; and Mr. Jefferson, who was one of that committee, proposed a general system of education for the whole State, including establishments of three grades; 1. Primary Schools; 2. Academies and Colleges; 3. An University. The measure was not acted on until 1796, when only the bill authorizing elementary schools to be established at public charge was passed, and even that became inoperative from its execution having been left optional with the county courts.† The attention of the Legislature was afterwards and repeatedly called to the subject by several incumbents of the Executive chair, in their annual messages: as by Governor Monroe, in 1801, and again 1802; by

---

* See Letters CIV. of the following series.

† Writings of T. Jefferson, I. 38, 40.

Governor Cabell in 1806 and 1808; and still more urgently by Governor Tyler in 1809 and 1810. In January of this latter year, it was that the Literary Fund of Virginia had originated in a "bill to appropriate certain escheats, penalties and forfeitures to the encouragement of learning." In a few years it had considerably increased from these and other sources, since when its administration has become a regular department of our State Government.

The Revisors in 1776 had suggested the adoption and further endowment of William & Mary College as the University of the State; which would have rendered more appropriate the title which it had before received by courtesy. An objection to this was its locality, somewhat eccentric, and believed to be unhealthy for natives of the upper country. It had, moreover, been ever in the hands of Episcopalians, and by its constitution was designed to propagate their system. To supersede these would have been of doubtful policy if equitable, and yet to favor them at public expense, would seem unjust to other sects. Mr. Jefferson, however, in 1779, being a Visitor of that institution, effected a desirable change in its curriculum of studies,* the influence of which has been felt to this day.

While Minister resident at Paris, he did not lose sight of the cause of education at home. Letters of his are extant, written from thence to several of his young countrymen, offering judicious counsel as to the course and conduct of their studies;† while others of his correspondents are kept advised as to the state of literature, and the progress of science and the arts.† From the

* Writings of T. Jefferson, I. 38, 40.

† See the Letters to J. Banister, Peter Carr, T. M. Randolph, Jr., and J. W. Eppes. Writings of Thomas Jefferson, I. 345, I. 285, II. 215, 325, II. 190, II. 180, and Works III. 145. See also the Letters to R. Izard and Mr. McAlister, Works II. 427, III 313. Of the latter kind were the letters to Bishop Madison, Dr. Styles, D. Rittenhouse, and Mr. Bellini. Writings I. 328, II. 335, I. 257, 431, 326.

former we learn, that, although of foreign Universities, he gave the palm to Edinburgh and Geneva, the result of his observations was a conviction that European discipline could not supply the peculiar wants of Americans, even if it failed to corrupt and pervert them; and especially that for Virginians a Southern education was preferable to such as was to be had at the North.

Hence the necessity of removing the temptation to go abroad in pursuit of such an object by supplying the means of its attainment at home. On the failure of that part of his scheme which related to William & Mary, he did not surrender his general purpose as hopeless. There is reason to believe that from an early period he looked forward to the ultimate establishment of a new institution, in a more eligible situation, on a novel and comprehensive plan, better suited to modern society, and to the wants of our own society in particular; untrammelled by prior engagements and antiquated prejudices; and that for years he was perfecting his ideas of such a plan. And at one time there appeared a hope of its early fulfillment. It is a somewhat remarkable fact, that in 1794, owing to some dissatisfaction with the political state of the canton, several of the leading professors of the college of Geneva proposed to Mr. Jefferson to transfer themselves in a body to Virginia, should the measure receive the countenance and patronage of the State. Mr. J. sounded the Legislature, or rather certain of its leading members, through his friend Col. Nicholas. The project was thought desirable, but attended with difficulties which made it premature if feasible at all, and so was dropped.*

Still the principal object was not forgotten, and he was content to hasten more slowly, and in another mode. In January, 1800, he thus writes to Dr. Priestly, who had come to the United States six years before, and settled in Pennsylvania:

---

* See Letters to M. D'Ivernois and Col. Nicholas. Writings III. 309. Works IV. 109, 113.

"How sincerely I have regretted that your friend, before he fixed his choice of a position, did not visit the valleys on each side of the ridge in Virginia, as Mr. Madison and myself so much wished......... But since you would not make it your country by adoption, you must now do it by your good offices—one of which I have to propose to you." After referring to the College of William & Mary, the causes which unfitted it for the chief seminary of the State, he adds: "We wish to establish, in the upper country, and more centrally for the State, an University on a plan so broad and liberal and *modern*,* as to be worth patronising with the public support, and be a temptation to the youth of other States to come and drink of the cup of knowledge, and fraternise with us. The first step is to obtain a good plan; that is, a judicious selection of the sciences, and a practicable grouping of some of them together, and ramifying of others, so as to adapt the professorships to our uses and our means. In an institution meant chiefly for use, some branches of science, formerly esteemed, may be now omitted; so may others now valued in Europe, but useless to us for ages to come."...... "Now there is no one to whom this subject is so familiar as yourself. ....To you, therefore, we address our solicitations."...... "We should propose that the professors follow no other calling, so that their whole time may be given to their academical functions; and *we should propose to draw from Europe the first characters in science, by considerable temptations, which would not need to be repeated after the first set should have prepared fit successors, and given reputation to the institution.* I do not propose to give you all this trouble of my own head: that would be arrogance. It has been the subject of consultation *among the ablest and highest characters of our State*, who only wait for a plan to make a joint, and, I hope, a successful effort to get the thing carried into effect." *Works*, IV. 311.

Again, in February, 1803, in a letter to M. Pictet, one of the Genevese professors, who had proposed the transfer to Virginia, we find the following:

"I rejoice that the opinion which I gave you on the removal

---

* Italics are Mr. J.'s.

hither proved useful. I knew it was not safe for you to take such a step until it could be done on sure ground. I hoped, at the time, that some canal shares, which were at the disposal of General Washington, might have been applied towards the establishment of a good seminary of learning; but he had already proceeded too far on another plan to change their direction. *I have still had constantly in view to propose to the Legislature of Virginia the establishment of one on as large a scale as our present circumstances would require or bear.* But, as yet, no favorable moment has occurred. In the meanwhile, I am endeavoring to procure materials for a good plan. With this view I am to ask the favor of you to give me a sketch of the branches of science taught in your college, and how they are distributed among the professors..........Your successful experience in the distribution of business will be a valuable guide to us who are without experience." *Works*, IV. 462.

In August, 1814, when, at length, success was nearer in prospect, he says, in a letter to Dr. Cooper:

"In my letter of January 16th, I mentioned to you that it had long been in contemplation to get an University established in this State, in which all the branches of science useful *to us*, and *at this day*, should be taught in their highest degree.......... But what are the sciences useful to us, and at this day thought useful to any body? A glance over Bacon's *Arbor Scientiæ* will shew the foundation for this question, and how many of his ramifications of science are now lopt off as nugatory. To be prepared for this new establishment, I have taken some pains to ascertain those branches which men of sense, as well as of science, deem worthy of cultivation. To the statements which I have obtained from other sources, I should highly value an addition of one from yourself. You know our country, its pursuits, its facilities, its relations with others, its means of establishing and maintaining an institution of general science, and the spirit of economy with which it requires that these should be administered.........To accommodate the sciences to our economy, it will be necessary further to distribute them into groups, each group comprehending as many branches as one industrious professor may competently teach, and, as much as may be, a duly associated family; or class of kindred sciences. The object of this is to bring the whole circle of useful science under the direction of the smallest number of professors possible, and that our means may be so frugally employed as to effect the greatest possible good. We are about to make an effort for the introduction of this institution." *Works,* VI. 371.

The germ of the University was an incorporated Academy, authorized by law to be established in the county of Albemarle, with funds to be raised by a lottery, and by private subscription. The contributions from this source, when once begun, having been both more speedy and liberal than was expected, it was enlarged by the same authority into an institution of higher grade, known as the Central College; and before either Academy or College had gone into operation, the latter was adopted by the State, liberally endowed and expanded into the seat of science, now known as the University of Virginia.

As these several steps were probably both foreseen and designed, it becomes a matter of some interest to trace the gradations by which they were reached. The earliest mention, by Mr. Jefferson, of such an Academy, as yet discovered, appears in the following extract of a letter to a friend in Albemarle, dated Annapolis, December 31st, 1783, which also throws a light on the then state of education in our country:

"Just before I left Albemarle, a proposition was started for establishing there a grammar school. You were so kind as to tell me you would write me the progress of the proposition; on my part I was to enquire for a tutor. To this I have not been inattentive. I enquired at Princeton, of Dr. Witherspoon, but he informed me that that college was but just getting together again, and that no such person could, of course, be had there. I enquired in Philadelphia for some literary character of the Irish nation in that city. There was none such; and in the course of my enquiries I was informed that learning is but little cultivated there, and that few persons have ever been known to come from that nation as tutors. I concluded, on the whole, then, if the scheme should be carried on and fixed on so firm a basis as that we might, on its faith, venture to bring a man from his own country, it would be best for me to interest some person in Scotland to engage a good one. From that country we are surest of having sober, attentive men. However, this must await your information."

It was not, however, until the year 1803, that a charter was granted for this purpose, which was amended by another act of the same or succeeding session. Still, from whatever cause, no efficient action seems to have been taken in the matter until the spring of 1814, when Mr. Jefferson, now again a private citizen, was elected one of the trustees, and Peter Carr was appointed their President. A part of these early proceedings may be found in our Appendix A. In the autumn of the same year, Mr. J. addressed to Mr. Carr a letter, suggesting a plan as proper to be pursued by them in the beginning, and giving, in some detail, his views of the general subject. As this letter was not only published and widely read, but is believed to have had no little influence on the fortunes of education in Virginia, it also appears in our Appendix B. The promptness and liberality with which the people of Albemarle seconded the trustees with their subscriptions, induced them at once to essay the enlargement of their academy into a college. Another favorable circumstance was, that shortly afterwards Mr. Say, the Political Economist, had intimated to Mr. Jefferson a willingness to remove to Virginia, and to Albemarle—in which case Mr. J. hoped he might be engaged as one of the professors, with other eminent men whom he had in view as his colleagues.*

A petition to the Legislature for the further endowment of

* See letter XX. *infra,* and Works VI. 405.

their academy with a specific public fund, and for its incorporation as a College, was accordingly prepared and sent down,* with other explanatory papers, but from some cause was withheld until the succeeding session. Mr. J. writing, in January, 1815, to Mr. Cabell, who was then the Senator from his district, commends the papers to his care, and the subject to his patronage, with this emphatic declaration: "*We had always counted on you as the main pillar of their support.*" His confidence was not misplaced. An act for establishing the Central College was passed February 14th, 1816.†

The Visitors first named by the Executive, in October of that year, were Thomas Jefferson, James Madison, James Monroe, Joseph C. Cabell, John H. Cocke, and David Watson. The 8th of April, 1817, had been proposed as the day of their first meeting. Only Mr. Jefferson, Mr. Cabell and General Cocke attended. These three having examined various sites, which had been proposed for the College in the vicinity of Charlottesville, made a conditional choice and purchase of the present location, which was approved and ratified by Messrs. Madison and Monroe, at their next meeting, on the 5th of May.‡ Measures were im-

---

* The original has not been found, but for a synopsis of its contents, see Appendix C.

† See Appendix D.

‡ These and other proceedings of the Visitors, with Mr. J.'s report of them to the Executive, may be found in Appendix E. It may here be mentioned, that contemporaneously with the petition of the trustees, given in Appendix C, another petition, signed by 147 citizens of Albemarle, was offered to the Assembly, praying the passage of a law authorizing a sum to be raised, by lottery, sufficient for the purchase of *the house then occupied by Triplett T. Estes, in the village of Charlottesville*, for the establishment and use of an Academy. This building, then called "the Stone Tavern," is now the older part of the Monticello House. This proposal, though favored at first, was finally rejected, lest it might conflict with the interests of the College. The purchase of it was left optional with the trustees, who preferred the present site, not as being the one most eligible, but the best that could then be obtained.

mediately taken for the erection of suitable buildings, according to a plan proposed by Mr. Jefferson, and the corner stone of the first pavillion was laid with appropriate ceremonies, on the 6th of October.* Additional subscriptions had been made in Albemarle, and papers were now circulated in other counties for the same object, and with considerable success.† There was, also, a hope of obtaining the funds of the Virginia Branch of the Society of Cincinatti; but in this they were disappointed, the preference having been given to Washington College.

We have seen above that enlightened individuals among us had long known the importance of having a University in fact as well as in name. The Legislature had now ordered an enquiry on the subject, as preliminary to action. Mr. Jefferson was desirous of having it located in his vicinity, and that the Central College should serve as its nucleus. This College had now attained a vantage ground, which would entitle it to enter into competition with other localities for the site. But were that attained, very much would yet remain to be done. The influence of Mr. Jefferson's name and opinions was great, but could not accomplish every thing. He had not only retired from public life, but, as he himself was well aware, there was yet remaining in the minds of certain classes of our citizens, a strong feeling against himself, individually, arising from political or other causes, which, united with local interests, might turn the scale; and he

---

* "We understand, that agreeably to appointment the first stone of the Central College was laid, at Charlottesville, on Monday last, (the 6th,) and that with all the ceremony and solemnity due to such an occasion. The society of Free Masons, and a large company of citizens, attended. The scene was graced by the presence of Thomas Jefferson and James Madison, late Presidents of the United States, and of James Monroe, the actual President." *Richmond Enquirer, of October 10th,* 1817.

† The names of subscribers, with the sums contributed, will be found in Appendix F.

could no longer combat these opposing influences by his personal presence and solicitation.

There were yet other and formidable obstacles to success. The mass of our people, and most of their representatives, had very inadequate ideas of the nature and requirements of such an institution. Virginia had already provided, in her literary fund, ample means for its establishment; but opinions were divided as to the proper direction of its proceeds, and the aid to be expected from this quarter might be doled out with grudging hand, by piece-meal, year after year, according to the varying temper and complexion of the Legislature. To enlighten the public mind as to the need of an institution on a larger scale than had before been known among us, and commensurate with the growing wants of the community: to show how much we had suffered for the want of it: to conciliate rival interests, or such as thought themselves likely to be injured: to allay the bitterness of ancient political animosities, and quiet sectarian distrust: to stimulate the luke-warm, and encourage the timid politician: to guide the willing and keep the friendly steadfast; all this, and more must be done. Enough, indeed, there was to require the co-operation of the liberal and patriotic of all parties. Nor could this be effected or maintained unless some one would accept or assume the duties of a leader, the proper discharge of which would demand a steadfast zeal and discretion not unlike those of Mr. Jefferson himself.

As Mr. Cabell was assigned to this post by express invitation of Mr. Jefferson, and the seeming concurrence of others, the reader may desire to know something of the antecedents of one who undertook the arduous enterprise, and conducted it to a successful issue.

Joseph Carrington Cabell, the third son and fourth child of his parents, was born December 28, 1778, at their residence, afterwards known as Liberty Hall, on James river, in Nelson county, then a part of Amherst. His father was Col. Nicholas Cabell, a gentleman who engaged in the military service of the State early in the Revolution, and at a later day sat during several terms in the Senate of Virginia. His mother was Hannah, daughter of Col. George Carrington, of Cumberland, several of whose sons were also known as public men of the Revolutionary era. Mr. Cabell's early education was received either in his father's house or at schools held in the immediate vicinity. His instruction in the classics and sciences was also commenced here, though continued at two other schools; the one on the northern border of the county, the other in the adjoining county of Albemarle, and not far from the present village of Warren. In 1795, he was sent to Hampden Sidney College; but this institution, from the want of a permanent head and other causes, being then in a depressed condition, he remained there but a single term. In the autumn of 1796, he betook himself to William & Mary, where he appears, from the first, to have attracted the regards of the venerable President, Bishop Madison, in an unusual degree. By his counsel and assistance, a comprehensive plan of culture was laid down, and most diligently pursued; and in 1798 he graduated with honor in a class, a large proportion of whose members afterwards rose to distinction.

Having selected the law as his profession, he studied during two years in Amherst, in the office of his elder brother, then a popular advocate, and who afterwards rose to the highest seat both in the Executive and Judiciary of Virginia. In the fall of 1800, he returned to Williamsburg, and attended the lectures of Judge Tucker, then Professor of Law in the College. At the expiration of the term, he came to Richmond, proposing to complete the course of reading preparatory in the office of the late Daniel Call. He had been here but a short time, when his health, which had latterly been delicate, suddenly failed, and all study was suspended.

A voyage to South Carolina, a winter's residence in Charleston, and return by land, a visit to the Virginia Springs, and several excursions on horseback to other parts of the State, were all tried without material benefit to his health. Friends and physicians now advised a winter's residence in the south of France. But a late embarkation and a long voyage brought the end of February, 1803, when he landed at Bordeaux, and with strength so impaired, that two other months were spent in recruiting, after which he proceeded directly to Paris. He remained three years abroad, instead of one, as he had proposed. Much of the time was spent in the metropolis or vicinity, and in the society of the American Embassy, from the several and successive chiefs of which he received the most kind and friendly attentions. He also traversed France in various directions, besides taking the tour of Switzerland and Italy, and a short excursion to Holland and England. His health was not yet such as to permit a return to regular study; but his thirst for knowledge being unabated, sought gratification in the society of learned and intelligent persons, with several of whom he was on terms of intimacy, as well as in general observation.

Particular circumstances also seemed to direct his attention to the subject of education, and the establishments provided for its maintenance in those countries. Thus the winter after his arrival was spent in Montpelier, where there was a University celebrated for its regard to the natural sciences. He here became favorably known to more than one of the professors, and through them to the savans and authorities of several of the Universities of Italy; as at Milan, Padua, Rome, and Naples, at all of which places he made some stay; the state of science and education being a principal subject of his enquiries. While in Switzerland he visited Yverdun, and on conference with the celebrated Pestalozzi, and examination of his system, he was so much struck with certain of his improvements in primary instruction, that long afterwards he sought to have them naturalized in Virginia. When in Holland and England, he did not fail to visit the Universities of Leyden, Oxford, and Cambridge. While in Montpelier he also attended a course of lectures on Botany, which stimulated his taste for the natural sciences generally, and the rather that, these being illustrated by experiments or collections of specimens, some knowledge of them might be obtained without a close application to books, which was still interdicted to him. He accordingly attended the lectures of Cuvier, Vanquelin, Thenard, and other professors of the college of France, during the latter part of his sojourn in Paris. The recollection of these things, no doubt, animated his zeal in after years when endeavoring to secure a home for the sciences in his native State.*

Mr. Cabell left France with renovated health, the 18th April, 1806, and landed in New York the 18th of May. After some stay in this and the intermediate cities, he came on to Washington, bringing letters to Mr. Jefferson, to whom he was now introduced for the first time, although he had cherished an hereditary admiration for his political principles. The manners and conversation of his young countryman seem to have left a favorable impression on the mind of the President, who, in the course of this and the next year, made him various offers of honorable employment, both at home and abroad, all of which, however, were declined.

---

* Several of the facts here mentioned, are referred to in the second Letter of the following series.

At the beginning of 1807, Mr. Cabell married in Williamsburg; and during a temporary residence in the ancient city which followed that event, an incident occurred, which, as it had a probable influence in hastening the advent of the University, is not unworthy of mention. A Mr. De La Coste, a foreign savant, had proposed a scheme for establishing there, by private subscription, a museum of Natural History in connexion with the college. Bishop Madison and some of the professors approved the object, though they feared that neither time nor place was the most suitable. Mr. Cabell, whom he had consulted, also doubted, but thought that an effort should be made, and that if not wholly successful then, it might serve as the foundation of something better in future. He accordingly assisted in maturing the plan, and applied to several of his friends for aid in the form of contributions. One of these, Mr. Isaac A. Coles, then private Secretary to Mr. Jefferson, in his reply, writes as follows:

"If I could bring myself to consider Williamsburg as the permanent seat of science; as the spot where the youth of our State for centuries to come would go to be instructed in whatever might form them for usefulness, my objections would, in a great measure, cease. But the old college is declining, and perhaps the sooner it falls entirely, the better, if it might be the means of pointing out to our legislative body the necessity of founding an institution on an extended and liberal scale. This is the point at which we ought to begin, *and this is what you ought to attempt if you are desirous of doing something which will be of permanent value.* This would indeed be an object worthy of your attention, and if the amelioration of education and the diffusion of knowledge be the favorite objects of your life, avail yourself of the favorable dispositions of your countymen, and consent to go into our legislative body. Instead of wasting your time in attempting to patch up a decaying institution, direct your efforts to a higher and more valuable object *Found a new one which shall be worthy of the first State in the Union.* This may, this certainly will one day be done, and why not now? *You may not succeed in one session, or in two, but you will succeed at last.* If you are disposed to think of this, as far as my little efforts or means will go, you will not find me wanting. I would contribute with pleasure to such an object, when I could feel confident that every little advance we made would not be lost, and that we should not be dependent on circumstances for the preservation of any collection which we might have it in our power to form."

He adds—"The President has been so engaged that I have had but little opportunity of conversing with him on this subject; but from what I have been able to draw from him, he thinks the attempt premature."*

A peculiar intimacy subsisted between these gentlemen, originating in boyhood, and continued without interruption through after years. We might infer, then, that such an appeal would not pass unheeded, or be hastily dismissed as the effusion of too partial friendship; and there is reason to believe that it was not forgotten when the day for action had arrived.

Mr. Cabell entered the House of Delegates in 1809, where he remained for two years, when he was transferred to the Senate, of which body he continued a member throughout the entire period embraced by the following correspondence. During the early years of his service, the foreign relations of the country were in a disturbed state, and the attention of the Legislature was called to subjects then deemed of more pressing interest than the endowment of a new institution for the purposes of education. The Literary Fund of Virginia, however, dates back to this era, and Mr. Cabell was of the committee which was ordered to bring in a bill for its establishment.†

---

* To a direct application of Mr. De La Coste, Mr. Jefferson made a similar reply. Works, V. 79.

† Ordered, that leave be given to bring in a bill "to appropriate certain escheats, penalties, and forfeitures, to the encouragement of learning;" and that Messrs. Noland, Preston, Peyton, Stevenson, Johnson, (of Isle of Wight) Claiborne, Jeffries, Blackburne, Stanard, (of Spottsylvania) Archer, (of Norfolk Borough) McCampbell, Laidley, Berkshire, and Cabell, do prepare and

We have seen above, when and how it was, that Mr. Cabell, on the overture of Mr. Jefferson, was enlisted in behalf of the Central College, and thence of the University. The following paragraphs from a paper drawn up by himself, pending an application for money to complete the buildings, furnish a summary of events relating thereto, and offer substantial reasons for an enlarged plan and a liberal and prompt endowment:

Session 1815–16. The balance of the debt due from the General Government, with certain exceptions, was appropriated to public education. And the President and Directors of the Literary Fund were required to report the plan of a University to the Assembly at its next session.

In the course of the year 1816, they addressed letters of enquiry as to a system of public education embracing a University, to literary men throughout the United States.

At the session of 1816–17, the President and Directors made an able report to the Assembly, with the answers of the learned men annexed. At the same session, a bill containing a complete system of native education, and embracing a University, passed the House of Delegates, and was lost in the Senate. The bill creating the Central College, containing the plan of a University in fact, but without giving adequate funds, had passed at a previous session. Both these circumstances presented the subject of a University fully before the public mind. But to draw forth the sense of the State, when the University bill failed in the Senate, at the session of 1816–17, the pamphlet entitled "Sundry documents on the subject of a system of public education," was ordered by the General Assembly to be printed and distributed. The pamphlet was circulated through the whole State in the course of the year 1817.

---

bring in the same." December 15th, 1809. Journal of House of Delegates, 1809–10, p. 25.

Mr. Noland presented, according to order, "A bill to appropriate certain escheats, penalties, and forfeitures, to the encouragement of learning." January 19, 1810. Ib. p. 74.

This bill, though presented by another, it now appears, was drawn by Mr. James Barbour.

At the session of 1817–18, the General Assembly passed the bill for the erection of a University, and for the education of the poor. After long and patient discussion and investigation, it was decided not to interfere with education, except in the points where it could not safely be left to individual enterprise, viz: in the case of persons too poor to pay for it themselves, and in that where the expense and magnitude of the subject defied individual enterprise, as in the case of a University. By the act creating the University, an enlightened body of commissioners were called from all the senatorial districts of the State, to recommend the best site and the proper plan for a University.

In the summer of 1818, these commissioners met at Rockfish Gap, and in a report, which has done honor to the State, and been admired over the Union, recommended a plan for the University, embracing ten professorships, and the requisite buildings for the accommodation of the professors and the students.

At the session of 1818–19, the Legislature located the University at the Central College, and sanctioned the plan recommended by the University commissioners.

This measure of the State was hailed with enthusiasm in the States west and south of us, as well as from every part of our own State. Every account convinced the Visitors that the number of students would be great, if the institution could be promptly and completely carried into effect. Waiving other considerations, it was deemed wise policy, in a financial point of view, to hasten the accomplishment of the scheme. The more complete the institution, the greater the number of students, and the greater the number of students, the more considerable would be that important portion of the revenues of the institution dependent on free tuition. Consequently the less would the State be compelled to pay in the form of fixed salaries. The demand for professors of talents in the United States is greater than the supply. Virginia, in order to secure them, must offer all the advantages held out by other States. If she does not wish to pay high fixed salaries, she must make up the deficiency by fees of tuition, and this can only be effected by a completely equipped institution.

Again the Legislatures of neighboring States are making rapid advances in the organization and endowment of similar institutions, and it is important that Virginia should get her University into the literary market before them. From all parts of the State expressions of impatience have reached the Visitors. Under these circumstances the Visitors have pushed forward the buildings as fast as the funds would admit. It now is to be decided whether the Visitors shall be sustained in these views, by a further appropriation. That already made is inadequate, and no one could expect it to be adequate. The funds have thus far been economically applied, and a faithful account rendered of all disbursements. A partial appropriation to a University, is like a partial appropriation to a canal or turnpike road. The capital remains comparatively unproductive till the work is finished. Without a further appropriation, the institution will creep slowly along; will be stamped with an inferior character; it will be difficult to procure able men as professors; the State will have to pay high fixed salaries for them; the institutions of the neighboring States will tower over the University of Virginia, drawing away the crowd of students and the ablest professors."

The remainder of this history during the first decade from its origin, may be gathered from the following correspondence and the documents appended; especially from the reports of Mr. Jefferson as Rector. From them also will the attentive reader be enabled to judge of the part borne by Mr. Cabell, in this patriotic enterprise. Enough will appear, we doubt not, to corroborate the voluntary testimony offered by a fellow-senator, to the value of his services in the following:

Extract from Gen. Dade's speech in the Senate of Virginia, in support of the Convention bill, session 1827–8. See Constitutional Whig of March 12th, 1828.

"*Mr. Speaker*,—I fear from a remark which has fallen from my friend from Nelson, (Mr. Cabell,) I may have said something that wounded his sensibility. If I did so, I assure *him*, and the Senate, that I did not intend it. I would not wantonly assail any member; and surely the gentleman has given me no cause. In the course of the remarks of the member from Nelson, upon an amendment offered to this bill, he said he believed his constituents wished the passage of a bill submitting the question of a convention to the people; and although he was himself opposed, he felt bound to obey their will. I hail the declaration as one of the soundest republican principles; so long as it is cherished, our Commonwealth is safe. The gentleman has since said, 'that although he admits that his constituents wished the submission of the question, he was compelled to vote against this bill; having failed to introduce it in the guards provided in his amendments. In doing this he would rely upon his country on this occasion, for the correctness of his course, as he had done on many former occasions. It would do him justice.'

Sir, he deserves well of his country; his country will do him justice or be ungrateful. I have served with this gentleman seventeen years; nine of them in the Senate. I have witnessed his toils, his exertions in the cause of literature and internal improvement. If aught of good has come, or will come, of these two great objects of legislative patronage, as I am assured there will, his country must do him justice; his name is identified with them. If aught of good proceeds from the University, the pride and glory of Virginia, the member from Nelson cannot be forgotten; for he, in promoting that monument of wisdom and taste, was second only to the immortal Jefferson."

Mr. Cabell was a Visitor of the University from the beginning. He succeeded Mr. Madison as Rector in July, 1834, and held the post for two years, when he resigned, Mr. Johnson being appointed his successor. On Mr. Johnson's resignation in 1845, Mr. Cabell was re-appointed, and continued in office until his death, in February, 1856.*

It is proper to add, in conclusion, that though perhaps the most active, he was not the sole champion of this cause before the representatives of the people. In the following letters it will be

---

* After the close of this correspondence, Mr Cabell served out his term in the Senate, retiring in the spring of 1829. He re-entered the House of Delegates in 1831, with the view of pressing the claims of the James River Canal, and left in 1835. He was then elected the President of that Company, and after continuing in office nearly eleven years, retired to private life, retaining only his connexion with the University.

found, that he makes frequent, and honorable, and most grateful mention of the services of others. If, in this connexion, the thanks of posterity are principally due to Mr. Jefferson and Mr. Cabell, it should not be forgotten that they had most efficient co-adjutors; as Messrs. Watson, Broadnax, Samuel Taylor, R. Morris, (of Hanover,) Gordon, Stevenson, and many others from the East; and Johnson, Baldwin, Blackburn, and above all, a Breckenridge from the West.

☞ Occasional references to each edition of Mr. Jefferson's Works will be found in our notes; to that of Mr. T. J. Randolph as his "Writings;" to that of Professor Washington as his "Works."

CORRESPONDENCE

BETWEEN

THOMAS JEFFERSON AND JOSEPH C. CABELL,

RELATING, PRINCIPALLY, TO THE UNIVERSITY OF VIRGINIA.

I.

T. J. TO J. C. C.

MONTICELLO, June 27, 1810.

DEAR SIR,—I enclose you a letter from Judge Cooper, of Pennsylvania, a political refugee with Dr. Priestly from the fires and mobs of Birmingham. He is one of the ablest men in America, and that in several branches of science. The law opinion which he mentions, I have received, and a more luminous one has not been seen. It will produce a revolution of opinion on the question treated; not in the present day, because old lawyers, like old physicians, and other old men, never change opinions which it has cost them the whole labors of their youth to form; but when the young lawyers get on the bench, they will carry Cooper's doctrine with them.* The

* What the particular opinion or doctrine here referred to was, cannot be gathered from the context. On the receipt of Mr. Cabell's reply, Mr. J. responded to Judge Cooper, and from that letter, which appears in his collected "Works," V. 530, we learn that it was contained in a report of the case of "Dempsy *v.* The Insurers," which had probably been before Judge C. in his court in Pennsylvania.

best pieces on political economy which have been written in this country were by Cooper. He is a great chemist, and now proposes to resume his mineralogical studies; on this subject, you will perceive that he wishes a correspondent in our State. I know nobody to whom I can so advantageously commit him as to yourself. My information in mineralogy dates with Linnæus, and like other old men I have lost the ardor of science, and permitted egoism to qualify all its pursuits. I add another word to Cooper's question, "*mihi cui bono?*" but at your time of life I should have jumped at such a correspondent as Cooper; will you accept of him? You will be of mutual value to each other. Would you rather begin the correspondence by a reference to the enclosed letter and asking a more particular communication of his wishes? or shall I desire him to write to you first? My answer shall be shaped to your own, and therefore awaits it. Be so good as to return me the inclosed, and to accept the assurances of my friendship and respect.

TH: JEFFERSON.

Mr. Cabell.

II.

J. C. C. TO T. J.

EDGEWOOD,* 23d July, 1810.

DEAR SIR,—I have had the honor of receiving the friendly and obliging letter which you wrote me on the 27th of last month, together with the one enclosed from Judge Cooper, of Pennsylvania, to yourself, of 10th of May; and I feel some anxiety of mind least the tardiness of my reply to you may be the cause of procrastinating yours to Judge Cooper much longer than may be agreeable to you. But, as I did not reach this from below till it was entirely too late to consider the interesting proposition you have made me, and to write you

* Mr. C.'s residence, near the then village of Warminster in Nelson county.

the result by the last mail, you will do me the justice to regard this as the earliest reply which it has been in my power to send you.

The selection which you make of me, among the numerous persons to whom you no doubt have directed your looks on this occasion, is a circumstance that does me honor; but it is an honorable notice to which I am not entitled. And the friendship which you discover in the style of your letter makes the most agreeable impression on my feelings.

It would be very acceptable to me to enter into the correspondence proposed with Judge Cooper; and doubtless as advantageous as you suppose. But there is a *sine quâ non* wanting on my part. It is a sufficient knowledge of the science of mineralogy in general, and leisure to explore the country, and make the requisite collections. In the first I am deficient, and the second I could not promise myself with the least confidence.

When I went to Europe, my health was in too feeble a state to support even the effort of reading, and I found myself in a situation that called for a new source of mental recreation and improvement. There was also a chasm in the little circle of science which I had commenced in America that was yet to be filled up. France, moreover, presented to my view all the branches of Natural History, under the aspect of new and captivating splendor. These causes directed my attention to the natural sciences. I attended Mr. Delamèthrie's course. I traveled with Mr. Maclure over the mountains of Auvergne and the Alps, and assisted him to make collections. I bought a small cabinet in Paris, and a box of about one hundred specimens of volcanic substances thrown out by Mount Vesuvius. The book which I read (and that only in part) was Brochant's Werner. But my health was often so feeble, and my mind was so occupied by an infinite variety of objects, and, in short, my studies were so subordinate to my main object of traveling, that I found myself, on leaving France, only in possession of some elementary notions and a small cabinet of minerals, respectable enough for a private individual, all of which were valuable only as presenting the means of future improvement.

It was never my object to aim at extensive attainments in mineralogy, nor did I feel certain that my future pursuits in America would afford leisure to indulge the feelings of an amateur. However, I thought I would be provided for every event, and brought my cabinet along.

Since my return, I have become involved in the usual pursuits of Virginians, and my mind has been totally abstracted from Natural History. Instead of exploring the country and adding to my collection, I have actually lost a portion of the small stock of knowledge which I brought home with me. Foreseeing the situation in which I should stand for some years at least, and not wishing to act the part of the dog in the manger, I lent my cabinet of minerals to William and Mary College, and my herbarium to Mr. Girardin,* not long after I got back to Virginia. The time of the loan has expired, my situation is becoming rather more favorable for such pursuits, and I think of bringing home my little scientific treasures in the course of next spring. But judging from the past, and considering the nature of my pursuits, and the probable consequences to which they will lead, I shall have very little time for mineralogy. Ignorant as I am of the science at this time, and promising myself but little improvement in future, I should be unwilling to enter into an engagement with a man of science at a distance, which to be complied with would require considerable attention, and many and long journeys over the country. An additional reason is, that I am already under similar obligations to some friends, and my inability to comply with them has cost me severe feelings of regret. Under these circumstances, I have only to request

* At the time referred to, a Professor in William and Mary College, but afterwards removed to Milton, Albemarle, where he became the continuator of Burk's History of Virginia.

you to refer Judge Cooper to some suitable character, and to make you my acknowledgments for the compliment you have paid me.

I am, sir, with the highest respect and regard,

Your obliged friend,

JOSEPH C. CABELL.

Thomas Jefferson, Esq., Monticello.

III.

T. J. TO J. C. C.

MONTICELLO, January 5th, 1813.

DEAR SIR,—I learn by the newspapers that a petition has been presented to the Legislature by the Rivanna Company praying an enlargement of their powers. As these are to be executed wholly within my lands, and almost solely over my property, and have not hitherto been exercised with much forbearance as to the injury to which they expose me, it becomes necessary, while they ask for power, for me to ask protection from it. I have written a long letter on this subject to Mr. Philip Barbour, who was kind enough to ride over the ground of their operations, and to make himself acquainted with them. I have asked the favor of him to communicate that letter to you, and I have to request the favor of you to take the trouble of reading it, that when the bill comes before the Senate you may be acquainted with the facts to which it will have relation. The object is to extend the navigation of our river about four miles higher, to Moore's Ford near Charlottesville. Towards this I have given, and shall continue to give, every facility which does not go to a destruction of my mills, which have cost me $30,000. Your situation makes you the umpire between the Company and myself, and I ask no more than that the Legislature, acting on full information, may do what is just. Asking your friendly attention to the case, and your care that it shall be fully understood by the Senate, I shall be satisfied that what they think right is so. Accept the assurance of my great esteem and respect.

TH: JEFFERSON.

Joseph Cabell, Esq.,
of the Virginia Legislature, now in Richmond.

IV.

J. C. C. TO T. J.

RICHMOND, 12th January, 1813.

DEAR SIR,—I have received your favor of 5th inst., relative to the subject of the petition of the Rivanna Company. You may rest assured that I shall pay the most pointed attention to this business, and do every thing in my power to guard your rights from invasion. I immediately held a preliminary conversation with my friend Johnson,* after which I waited on Mr. Barbour, and obtained the use of your letter to him, as well as some explanations, which I have already communicated to the former. On the part of both Mr. Johnson and Mr. Barbour, I have discovered every possible disposition to unite with me in doing every thing that may be agreeable to you. This evening I shall wait on the delegation from Albemarle, to converse with them on this subject. From what Mr. Barbour tells me, I am happy to learn that no collision is likely to arise between yourself and the Company.

I am, dear sir, with great regard and respect,
Your friend and ob't serv't,

JOS. C. CABELL.

Mr. Jefferson.

---

* Chapman Johnson, Esq., then Senator from the Augusta District.

V.

J. C. C. TO T. J.

RICHMOND, 17th February, 1813.

DEAR SIR,—I have been prevented by business of late from writing you respecting the fate of the bill founded on the petition of the Rivanna River Company. The bill, as it came up to the Senate, contained merely a proviso saving private rights. Mr. Johnson drafted two amendments, one requiring that the tolls should be collected at the locks, and only on what should pass through them, so long as the Company should use your canal; the other requiring that the consent of the Company should be previously certified to the court of Albemarle before the law should take effect, and that in that event the charter should last till the year 1840. I exhibited your map of the river to the Senate, and made a full explanation of the subject. The amendments passed without opposition. I had previously ascertained that the delegates from Albemarle would be willing to exempt your own produce, but not that of your customers, from toll. Our amendments, conformably to your suggestions and what appeared to us to be just, from your statement of facts, went to the exemption of your customers, as well as of yourself. When the bill returned to the House of Delegates, one of your members from Albemarle moved to postpone it to the 31st March, which was done. Col. Bramham and Capt. Garth averred that the Company would never consent to the exemption of your customers, and that it was better to let the subject lie over till another session. Thus ended the bill. I can assure you, that I have paid the utmost attention in my power to this subject. Mr. Johnson and Mr. Barbour have been equally attentive. The delegates from Albemarle have expressed a willingness to enter upon any arrangement that might be mutually satisfactory to yourself and the Company; but they differ with you in regard to the extent of your claims. Provided I should be continued in the

Senate, I beg you to be assured of my anxiety to serve you on this or any other subject in which you may be interested.

I am, dear sir, with great respect and regard,

Your humble servant,

Jos. C. Cabell.

Mr. Jefferson.

VI.

T. J. TO J. C. C.

Monticello, November 7, 1813.

Dear Sir,—As the meeting of our Legislature approaches, and I shall be absent in Bedford from the 17th inst. to about the 8th of December, within which period you will possibly be passing, I have thought it best to inform you that the Rivanna Company and myself consent that the bill concerning us which was before the Legislature at their last session, should pass *verbatim* as amended by the Senate. This was stated to me three days ago, by Mr. Minor, their secretary, and had before been expressed to me by Mr. Divers,* and that Colonel Bramham's opposition at the last session was against their sense. I consider this matter then as so settled, so far as respects the parties: and I enclose you an abstract of the bill shewing what we understand it to be. I have suggested two verbal alterations in it, in red ink: the 1st, is to avoid making the act extend their power, by a side wind, over the whole river, which is neither agreeable to the title of the act, nor to the wishes of the company, or the consent of the people either above or below their portion of the river; the 2d, is to prevent the demand of toll for *vessels* either loaded or empty; which I mentioned to Mr. Minor, and he assured me they wished nothing to be taken for *vessels*, but only the *articles* they carried. I have not the least interest in either of these amendments, and only mention them on account of their general propriety.

---

* A well-known and opulent citizen of Albemarle, who took an interest in this improvement.

I make no opposition to the duration of the act, at the same time thinking it longer, by twenty years, than the Legislature ought to make it, and seven years longer than they have a power to make it. This last assertion depends on the question whether one generation has a power to bind a succeeding one?* a question which I think I have demonstrated in the negative, in a late correspondence with the chairman of the Committee of Ways and Means of Congress, on the subject of a financial plan for the war. This, should you have the curiosity to enter into it, I shall willingly communicate to you on any convenient occasion. Should you not be passing until my return from Bedford, I shall be very happy to see you here, and to take that occasion for the communication; and should you be done with Say, I should be glad to receive him then, as I wish to consult him on a part of the subject, and particularly on that of banks, a very important member of the discussion. Accept the assurance of my friendly attachment and respect.

TH: JEFFERSON.

Joseph C. Cabell, Esq., Williamsburg.

[The amended act referred to in the foregoing letter, with Mr. Jefferson's alterations, in red ink, which are noted by being underscored, is as follows:]

A bill to amend the act entitled an act incorporating a company to open the Rivanna River, from Milton to Moore's ford, &c.

§ 1. Be it enacted by the General Assembly, that instead of the tolls, &c. [this section goes on to fix the tolls].

§ 2. And be it further enacted, that it shall be lawful for the court of Albemarle, &c., [after reimbursement of the company, to appoint directors to take toll sufficient to rebuild the locks, &c.] and keep the same in repair as well as to keep open the navigation of THE SAID PORTION of the said river in other respects, &c.

Amendment of the Senate. } Be it further enacted, that so long as the company aforesaid shall continue to use the navigation of the canal leading to the Shadwell mills, no toll shall be demanded or received on their behalf,

* This question, which is referred to in the sequel, will be noticed hereafter

unless the same shall be demanded and received at the locks which now are, or hereafter may be erected by them on said canal, and shall be demanded and received ONLY ON ARTICLES [on vessels] passing the second locks.

All acts and parts of acts coming within the purview of this act are hereby repealed. Provided, nevertheless, that nothing in this act contained shall be construed to affect the private right of any person or persons whatsoever.

Amendment of the Senate.} This act shall be in force from [and after the time when the assent of the company aforesaid hereto shall have been given by the Directors thereof, and duly certified to the court of Albemarle county, and there recorded, and shall thereafter continue in force until the first day of February, in the year 1840, and no longer].

The following letter of Dabney Minor, relating to the same subject, is here inserted, viz:

ALBEMARLE, December 30, 1813.

DEAR SIR,—The Directors of the Rivanna Company, and Mr. Jefferson, are agreed that the law, as amended at the last session, in the Senate, be passed into a law. Will you, Dr. Everett, and Mr. Garth,* attend and have it made a law?

I am, dear sir,

Yours, respectfully,

D. MINOR.

Joseph C. Cabell, Richmond.

VII.

J. C. C. TO T. J.

WILLIAMSBURG, November 29, 1813.

DEAR SIR,—Your favor of the 7th inst., covering an abstract of the bill respecting yourself and the Rivanna Company, did not get to Warminster till nearly a fortnight after I had left home for the lower country; and it was not until the 26th inst. that I received it at this place. This will account for the delay of my answer; as well as for my not calling at

---

* Delegates from Albemarle this year.

Monticello, on my way down, agreeably to your obliging invitation.

I am happy to learn that the Bill of the last session, as amended in the Senate, is satisfactory to the parties concerned, and that it will pass through both houses, as a matter of course. To the verbal amendments suggested by yourself, in red ink, I presume, there will be no objection from any quarter, as they only remove defects in the wording of the bill, and cause it to express more accurately the real intentions of the parties.

On the subject of the duration of the charter, I can only say that it was made as short as was supposed compatible with the success of the amendments made in the Senate. Mr. Johnson advised me to attempt nothing further. I am extremely sorry that I cannot see your reasoning on the general question of the duration of charters, and the power of one generation to bind another. I should derive great satisfaction and advantage from such a communication; the more especially as it would throw light on the path of my official duties, in which I am desirous to move with all possible care and circumspection during the residue of the time that I have to act as the representative of the district. The ride from my house to Monticello would have been cheerfully taken for this object, had I not already left home. I beg the favor of you to communicate this production to me, whenever, in your opinion, a suitable opportunity may occur.

Though I shall not be able, personally, to deliver Say's work to you, I hope you will not be disappointed in receiving it, by the period mentioned in your letter, (7th December), as I shall take all possible care to cause it to be put into your hands by that time. I brought it as far as Richmond, where I left it; and from which I intended to send it to Monticello, at the close of the session. I feel ashamed of the length of time I have kept it from you. Soon after borrowing it, I determined on reading Smith's treatise first, which I did; and then, in order to understand him more clearly, I read him a second time;

afterwards, I read Say twice, with the exception of a small part. During these perusals, I took frequent occasion to refer to small tracts on branches of the science. These readings with my other studies and avocations, have filled up the long space of time that Say has been in my hands. I am much pleased with this author, and think he well deserves the praises you bestow on him. He is more concise, more methodical, more clear, and, in many passages, more correct than Smith. His work approximates perfection more nearly than Smith's; yet, I consider it only as an approximation. On the theory of money my mind is not yet satisfied, and I doubt whether new views of that branch of the science are not to rise upon the human mind. My studies on the subject of political economy, are, however, in an unfinished state; and things may appear to me obscure, because I do not understand them. This has been often the case in regard to commentators on Smith, and the remark, I think, at least in some degree applicable to Ganihl——, whose work I have partly read. I shall be happy to hear your opinion of this writer at a convenient opportunity.

I am, dear sir,

Very respectfully and truly yours,

JOSEPH C. CABELL.

Mr. Jefferson.

VIII.

J. C. C. TO T. J.

RICHMOND, December 8th, 1813.

DEAR SIR,—I expected when I wrote you from Williamsburg, that my servant would have come up with me from that place on the 5th inst.; but one of my horses being unavoidably detained, I was compelled to leave him behind, and was consequently disappointed, for the moment, in sending him on with your books. I was only waiting for his arrival, when to-day

I fell in with Gen. Moore,* who told me he should set out in the Charlottesville stage, in the morning, for the place of his residence, and politely consented to take charge of the packet and to deliver it to Doct. Carr,† on his way through that place. I hope it will reach you in a few days. I return you my grateful acknowledgments for the use of the books for so great a length of time.

We have just formed the two houses, and are proceeding to business. I think Governor Barbour will be re-elected without opposition, notwithstanding the great discontents which have prevailed in many parts of the State.

I shall seek the earliest opportunity of conferring with Doct. Everett and Mr. Garth relative to the petition of the Rivanna River Company. As yet we are scarcely placed in our respective lodgings. I expect to see them in the morning.

I am, dear sir, with high esteem and respect,

Your most obedient,

JOSEPH C. CABELL.

Mr. Jefferson.

IX.

T. J. TO J. C. C.

MONTICELLO, January 17, 1814.

DEAR SIR,—In your last letter to me you expressed a desire to look into the question whether, by the laws of nature, one generation of men can, by any act of theirs, bind those which are to follow them? ‡ I say, by the laws of nature, there being between generation and generation, as between nation and

---

* Of Rockbridge, sometime Senator of United States from Virginia.

† Dr. Frank Carr, a relative of Mr. J., and at a later day Secretary of the Board of Visitors of the University.

‡ This opinion with Mr. J. dates back at least as far as 1789. In a letter of that year, from Paris, to Mr. Madison, he states the principle, his reasons in defence, and submits them to Mr. M.'s judgment. The latter intimates his dissent in the modest form of doubts and queries. (Tucker's Life of J.,

nation, no other obligatory law; and you requested to see what I had said on the subject to Mr. Eppes.* I enclose, *for your own perusal*, therefore, three letters which I wrote to him on the course of our finances, which embrace the question before stated.† When I wrote the first, I had no thought of following it by a second. I was led to that by his subsequent request; and after the second, I was induced, in a third, to take up the subject of banks, by the communication of a proposition, to be laid before Congress, for the establishment of a new bank. I mention this to explain the total absence of order in these letters as a whole. I have said above that they are sent for *your own perusal*, not meaning to debar any use of the matter, but only that my name may in nowise be connected with it. I am too desirous of tranquillity to bring such a nest of hornets on me as the fraternities of banking companies; and this infatuation of banks is a torrent which it would be a folly for me to get in the way of. I see that it must take its course, until actual ruin shall awaken us from its delusions. Until the gigantic banking propositions of this winter had made their appearance in the different legislatures, I had hoped that the evil might still be checked; but I see now that it is desperate, and that we must fold our arms and go to the bottom with the ship.——I had been in hopes that good old Virginia, not yet so far embarked as her Northern sisters, would have set the example, this winter, of beginning the process of cure, by passing a law that after a certain time, suppose of six months, no

---

I. 291–8.) It appears, from the letters to Mr. Eppes and to Mr. Cabell, that Mr. J. still adhered to his view. Yet, perhaps, is there no opinion of his on political subjects which, at the present day, would be thought more open to criticism than this. The objections of Mr. M., and others which have been since suggested, would probably be regarded generally as conclusive. Most certainly, if not believed to be impracticable and unjust, it has been ignored by all our governments in practice.

* Hon. Jno. W. Eppes, son-in-law to Mr. J., and then a member of the House of Representatives of the United States.

† The letters referred to may be found in the first edition of Mr. J.'s Writings, IV. 196, 207.

bank bill of less than $10 should be permitted; that after some other reasonable term, there should be none less than $20, and so on, until those only should be left in circulation whose size would be above the common transactions of any but merchants. This would ensure to us an ordinary circulation of metallic money, and would reduce the quantum of paper within the bounds of moderate mischief; and it is the only way in which the reduction can be made without a shock to private fortunes. A sudden stoppage of this trash, either by law or its own worthlessness, would produce confusion and ruin. Yet this will happen by its own extinction, if left to itself; whereas, by a salutary interposition of the Legislature, it may be withdrawn insensibly and safely. Such a mode of doing it, too, would give less alarm to the bank holders, the discreet part of whom must wish to see themselves secured by some circumscription. It might be asked, what we should do for change? The banks must provide it; first, to pay off their $5 bills, next their $10 do., and so on; and they ought to provide it to lessen the evils of their institution; but I now give up all hope. After producing the same revolutions in private fortunes as the old Continental paper did, it will die like that, adding a total incapacity to raise resources for the war.*

Withdrawing myself within the shell of our own State, I have long contemplated the division of it into hundreds or wards,† as the most fundamental measure for securing good government, and for instilling the principles and exercise of

---

* We need not say that this prediction was not fulfilled; nor others of a similar strain in future letters. Mr. C., writing in 1851, says: "On re-perusing these letters, at this day, I am strongly impressed by the great mistake in regard to the total ruin of all the American banks in a very short time; also, as to the impracticability of carrying on the war without the substitution of treasury notes for bank paper; and the same errors in reference to banks and currency in this State, where those institutions furnished the means of carrying on the war in the State of Virginia, when every other resource had failed." The banking system of Virginia, under the limitations prescribed by experience, has, on the whole, proved eminently successful and useful to the community.

† See note on page 18.

self-government into every fibre of every member of our Commonwealth. But the details are too long for a letter, and must be the subject of conversation, whenever I shall have the pleasure of seeing you. It is for some of you young legislators to immortalize yourselves by laying this stone as the basis of our political edifice.

I must ask the favor of an early return of the enclosed papers, of which I have no copy.

Ever affectionately yours,

TH: JEFFERSON.

Jos. C. Cabell, Esq.

X.

J. C. C. TO T. J.

RICHMOND, 23d January, 1814.

DEAR SIR,—The last mail from Charlottesville brought me your letter of 17th inst., accompanied by your three letters to Mr. Eppes, on the subject of the ways and means of carrying on the war. Accept, I beseech you, my most sincere thanks for the communication of these papers, which, from the hasty perusal I have given them, already promise me a fund of valuable and highly interesting matter. I shall observe your injunctions in regard to the use of them, and the time during which they may remain in my possession. They have come too late to produce any effect on the principal proceedings of our session in regard to banks. The day the packet reached me, the Senate voted for the bill augmenting the capital and extending the charter of the Bank of Virginia. I was desirous to reduce the increased capital from one million to half a million of dollars, but could not prevail. I have, however, brought myself under the lash of your censure, by voting for this measure. I have thus voted from a wish, through the instrumentality of the Bank, to aid the State in the prosecution of the war. I have, of late years, come into the opinion of a limited, well regulated system of banking in Virginia, not so much from any fondness I have for the system in the abstract, as that I regard it as a sort of defensive system, imposed on us by the circumstance of our being a member of a confederacy, the other members of which have surrounded us with banks. In the language of the mountain hunters, "I am for firing against their fire." You have opened a vast horizon to my view. Indeed, sir, I most sincerely and heartily thank you for the high gratification you have given me in the perusal of these letters. A bill for the establishment of a small bank at Wheeling will probably come up to the Senate in a few days. On that occasion I shall avail myself of some of your ideas. I cannot now go into this subject, but will be extremely happy to resume it in conversation at a future day.

You would add greatly to the obligations already conferred on me, if you would inform me, by letter, what is your opinion in regard to the question, "whether the Legislature of a State has a right, under the Federal Constitution, to restrict the residence of a member of the House of Representatives to the district by which he is chosen?" And if your opinion should be in favor of the right, you would add greatly to the favor by stating the principal reasons on which your opinion is founded. This subject was agitated in the Assembly last winter; the Senate and the House of Delegates were opposed to each other on the question. I voted with the majority of the Senate against the right of the Legislature. A review of my opinion leaves me in some doubt as to its correctness. The subject is now before the House of Delegates, and probably it will be two weeks before the upper house will be called upon to vote on it. I should be much pleased to hear from you before the vote is taken; and should it be your desire that your letter should not be used, I will consider it a duty to hold it from the view of others.

The bill respecting the Rivanna River Company, is now progressing through the Lower House. It contains the verbal alterations you suggested. The assembly will rise about the middle or 20th of February.

I am, dear sir,
Very truly and sincerely yours,
JOSEPH C. CABELL.

Mr. Jefferson.

I shall be happy to learn your reasons for dividing the State into hundreds or wards. Mr. Coles mentioned this subject to me some years ago, but without stating the various considerations in favor of the measure.*

I sent your books to you by General Moore, at the commencement of the session, and hope they arrived safe and in a few days after they left this.

---

* The memory of the writer is here at fault. From a letter of Col. Coles, then Private Secretary of Mr. Jefferson as President, addressed to Mr. Cabell, and dated July 17th, 1807, we offer the following extract: "I have been lately thinking on a subject of some importance, and which I wish much to see treated by you in *an essay addressed to the Virginia Legislature.* It is the township division of the New England States to which I allude. Our division into counties is certainly much too large, and attended with a thousand inconveniences. The division into townships or hundreds might very easily be made in Virginia, if in forming them we would follow the bounds of the militia companies, which are already well known, and which exist in every county in the State. Each hundred should be a little republic within the republic of the county. Each hundred should regulate its own police, should have a magistrate to try warrants, &c., hold elections, at which the most aged and infirm might attend, should provide for its own poor, establish a public school, to which even the most indigent might send their children, should annually select a juryman who, with those selected by the different hundreds throughout the State, might be distributed by lot or otherwise among the superior and inferior courts, so as to provide a sufficient number for each. In this way the elective principle would be introduced into every department of the government, and an independent and impartial jury might always be had, which, under our present system, must depend entirely on the character of the marshal or sheriff. The people, too, of each hundred, becoming familiar with the transaction of business, when summoned together on an occasion of emergency, wou'd act with promptitude and force, which the *particular character* of a part of our population will render the more valuable. Each hundred—but it is for you to point out the advantages that would result from a system which I only suggest for your consideration." The case in its behalf is well put by both its advocates; but the argument is not wholly on one side,

XI.

T. J. TO J. C. C.

MONTICELLO, January 31, 1814.

DEAR SIR,—Your favor of the 23d is received. Say had come to hand safely, but I regretted having asked the return of him, for I did not find in him one new idea on the subject I had been contemplating; nothing more than a succinct, judicious digest of the tedious pages of Smith.

You ask my opinion on the question whether the States can add any qualifications to those which the Constitution has prescribed for their members of Congress? It is a question I had never before reflected on; yet had taken up an off-hand opinion, agreeing with your first, that they could not; that to add new qualifications to those of the Constitution, would be as much an alteration as to detract from them. And so I think the House of Representatives of Congress decided in some case; I believe that of a member from Baltimore. But your letter having induced me to look into the Constitution, and to consider the question a little, I am again in your predicament of doubting the correctness of my first opinion. Had the Constitution been silent, nobody can doubt but that the right to prescribe all the qualifications and disqualifications of those they would send to represent them would have belonged to the State. So also the Constitution might have prescribed the

---

as may be seen in Tucker's Life of Jefferson, II., 352-5. To which it may be added that the division into hundreds was tried in the infancy of Virginia as a colony, and afterwards laid aside. Experience had probably shown that it was less suited to that peculiar constitution of society, which grew out of the presence of the very population to which Col. Coles alludes. It may well be questioned also, whether the frequent attendance of the people at the ward meetings, would not materially interfere with the periodic and more general assemblage of citizens at their county courts—the manifold advantages of which have been so generally recognized, and which have contributed so much to the formation of the peculiar character of our State. Such has already been the effect of the division of the counties into districts, for electoral and other purposes, ordered by the new Constitution of Virginia.

whole, and excluded all others. It seems to have preferred the middle way. It has exercised the power in part, by declaring some disqualifications, to wit: those of not being 25 years of age, of not having been a citizen 7 years, and of not being an inhabitant of the State at the time of election; but it does not declare itself that the member shall not be a lunatic, pauper, a convict of treason, of murder, of felony, or other infamous crime, or a non-resident of his district; nor does it prohibit to the State the power of declaring these or any other disqualifications, which its particular circumstances may call for; and these may be different in different States. Of course then, by the 10th amendment, the power is reserved to the State. If, whenever the Constitution assumes a single power out of many which belong to the same subject, we should consider it as assuming the whole, it would vest the general government with a mass of powers never contemplated. On the contrary, the assumption of particular powers seems an exclusion of all not assumed. This reasoning seems to me to be sound; but on so recent a change of view, caution requires us not to be too confident; and that we admit this to be one of the doubtful questions on which honest men may differ with the purest motives; and the more readily as we find we have differed from ourselves on it.

I have always thought that where the line of demarkation between the powers of the General and State governments was doubtfully or indistinctly drawn, it would be prudent and praiseworthy, in both parties, never to approach it but under the most urgent necessity. Is the necessity now urgent to declare that no non-resident of his district shall be eligible as a member of Congress? It seems to me that, in practice, the partialities of the people are a sufficient security against such an election; and that if in any instance they should ever choose a non-resident, it must be in one of such eminent merit and qualifications, as would make it a good, rather than an evil; and that in any event the examples will be so rare, as never to amount to a serious evil. If the case then be neither clear nor urgent, would it not be better to let it lie undisturbed? Perhaps its decision may never be called for. But if it be indispensable to establish this disqualification now, would it not look better to declare such others, at the same time, as may be proper? I frankly confide to yourself these opinions, or rather no opinions, of mine; but would not wish them to go any further. I want to be quiet; and although some circumstances now and then excite me to notice them, I feel safe and happier in leaving every thing to those whose turn it is to take care of them; and in general to let it be understood that I meddle little, or not at all with public affairs. There are two subjects indeed which I shall claim a right to further as long as I breathe, the public education and the subdivision of the counties into wards. I consider the continuance of republican government as absolutely hanging on these two hooks. Of the first, you will, I am sure, be an advocate, as having already reflected on it; and of the last when you shall have reflected.

Ever affectionately yours,

TH: JEFFERSON.

Joseph C. Cabell, Esq.

XII.

J. C. C. TO T. J.

RICHMOND, February 5th, 1814.

DEAR SIR,—Your favor of 31st ult. has come to hand, and I am happy to learn from it that your books arrived in safety. The free communication of your opinion upon the subject of the alleged right of the General Assembly to annex additional qualifications to the members of the House of Representatives of Congress, places me under great obligations. Your letter did not get to hand before the subject was acted on in the Senate; yet it serves to satisfy my mind the more perfectly as to the course which I took on the occasion. I held the bill back as long as possible, in order to have time to get an answer from yourself, as well as to obtain some facts for which I had written to Washington. But the House growing every day thinner by the withdrawing of members, and the majority of the last year being urgent that the decision of the House should not be reversed by the accidental composition of the House at the moment of taking the question, I reported the bill, and informed the body that I should vote as I had voted the last year, because I still doubted the constitutional power of the General Assembly to pass the bill; but that these doubts had, in a considerable degree, been removed, and perhaps might have been entirely dissipated, if I could have continued my investigation a few days longer. At the same time I expressly reserved to myself the right of changing the vote I then gave, should the subject again be brought to the view of the Senate. It was admitted on both sides, that the subject was too important, and the period of the session too advanced to admit of its being then fairly and definitively disposed of, and it was agreed on both sides that the bill should be postponed, with a distinct understanding that it might be resumed with the consent of the House of Delegates, at a future session, as if no such postponement had taken place. On this safe ground the subject now stands. It will probably give rise to considerable discussion next winter. Should it not be disagreeable to you, I should be infinitely indebted to you for any further views you may take of the subject at any time during the year. Your repose shall not be disturbed by an improper communication of your name, in connection with this or any other subject, on which you may favor me with information. My object is to be useful to my country in the station which I occupy; and in availing myself, occasionally, of your valuable aid, it would be highly improper to disturb the tranquility of your retirement.

I have had the pleasure of seeing Col. Randolph,* from whom I learn that you are anxious to know the fate of the Rivanna Bill. I was about to write you on that subject when

* Col. Thomas Mann Randolph, son-in-law of Mr. Jefferson, and afterwards Governor of Virginia.

he came to town. The bill passed the two Houses a few days ago, in the shape agreed upon by yourself and Mr. Minor, including the two verbal alterations which were suggested by yourself, and not objected to by the delegates from Albemarle. The reason of the bill's not being sooner acted upon is this: Dr. Everett expected that communications from the parties concerned might be addressed directly to himself and Mr. Garth, and to give time for that expectation to be fulfilled, I agreed that the bill might be detained in the House of Delegates as long as possible. At length he consented to take the letters addressed by you and Mr. Minor to myself, as his authority, and then the bill passed into a law, as soon as the forms of the two Houses would permit. I congratulate you on being now exonerated from the trouble and vexation which this subject has given you.

It was my wish to send by Col. Randolph the papers on the subject of finance you were so kind as to lend me; but occupied as I am in the business of the Assembly, I cannot digest them as thoroughly as I could desire. I shall therefore take the liberty of keeping them in my possession, for about two weeks after the rising of the Assembly. I will send them to you by the 20th February, or at latest, by the 1st of March. If you should require them sooner, they shall be immediately forwarded. I avail myself of some of your facts and reasoning in a discussion in the Senate on the subject of a small bank at Wheeling, which excited considerable interest, as it was contended on one side and admitted on the other, that if this bill should pass, it would be the commencement of the system of covering our State with small banks. The bill fell by an equal division of the Senate.

On the subject of education, and the division of the State into wards, I shall be much pleased to communicate with you at some future period of leisure.

With highest regard,

Your friend and humble servant,

JOSEPH C. CABELL.

Mr. Jefferson.

XIII.

J. C. C. TO T. J.

CARYSBROOK,* 6th March, 1814.

DEAR SIR,—I have got thus far on my way home, and intrust to the neighboring post-office your letters on finance, which I hope will safely reach you. I must beg your pardon for having detained them longer than the period of my engagement. My private business in the lower country took up much more time than I had anticipated, and I was compelled to keep your letters thus long in order thoroughly to digest them. I have read them many times over, and most sincerely thank you for the perusal. The principal topics will form subjects of reflection for me during the residue of the year. I have suffered Mr. W. Rives, Mr. Tucker,† Mr. Thomas Ritchie, and Mr. Cocke,† to peruse them, on a promise from each not to communicate your name. I have also taken the liberty to transcribe a good many passages for *my private use.* You will, I hope, pardon these liberties. I write in great haste, in the midst of company. I hope to have the pleasure to see you between this and June.

I am, dear sir,

Most respectfully and truly yours,

JOSEPH C. CABELL.

Mr. Jefferson.

XIV.

J. C. C. TO T. J.

WARMINSTER, 17th September, 1814.

DEAR SIR,—The dangers of our country will be my apology for troubling you with this letter. I wish to draw your atten-

---

* In Fluvanna county and on the Rivanna River; then the seat of Wilson J. Cary, Esq.

† Judge St. George Tucker, the elder, and (probably) Dr. Charles Cocke, long after State Senator from the Albemarle district.

tion to the important subject of our financial difficulties, and particularly those which will present themselves to the General Assembly at its next session, and to solicit the favor of you to put me in possession of any hints or plans which you may think adapted to the crisis. I went to Richmond when the Governor issued his proclamation. When I called on him, he informed me that the enemy was expected every day; that a large militia army was assembling, which would, in a few days, be competent to repel any assault that would probably be made; but that this army must be disbanded for want of support, unless money could be procured; that there was no money in the Treasury, and none at Washington; that our only resource for the emergency was a loan from the banks, to the amount of fifty or one hundred thousand dollars, in anticipation of the revenue; but that the banks had declined lending, on the ground that they were already in advance to the State to the amount of $160,000, and that it was utterly out of their power to lend a further sum without imminent danger of inability to pay their notes; that he had exhorted them to hazard every consequence, sooner than suffer the country to be laid open to the incursions of the British army, but had found them deaf to his remonstrances; that it was yet possible that those institutions might be prevailed on to lend the State, provided the application should be seconded by members of the General Assembly; and that he wished me to undertake to renew the application on his behalf, supported by such arguments as it might be in my power to urge. I waited on some of the officers of the two banks, in compliance with the Governor's request. Among the arguments used, I stated, that though a stoppage of payment of specie was in itself a great evil, yet, I considered it less than that the enemy should march to Richmond and blow up our Capitol; and I had no hesitation in believing that the General Assembly would not be unmindful of the favor of co-operation by the banks at so critical a period. After some deliberation, the two banks agreed to advance the sum of $140,000, for the use of the State, which added to their previous advances, would make an aggregate of $300,000. The day after this loan, the Farmers' Bank stopped payment in specie, and the next day, the Virginia Bank also stopped; but under a promise to re-open their issues of specie, as soon as it could be got down from Lynchburg. Upon enquiry, I learned they expected $20,000, which would last but a few days, owing to the great drain of specie to supply change for the use of the army. The Virginia Bank, will, perhaps, go on; but I think it will not. The Farmers' Bank certainly will not. The alleged cause of this suspension is the late suspension in the Northern towns. The want of change was sensibly felt in consequence of this measure. It was believed, by some, that individuals had hoarded and were hoarding specie. It was feared that the supplies for the army, so much wanted, would be affected by fears of the solidity of the paper, and a meeting of the merchants was talked of, to support the character of the notes. Almost our whole revenue has been, or will have been anticipated by the 10th October. So many of the people are called out, or have left home, that the sheriffs will, probably, in many instances, find it difficult to collect the taxes. The General Government owed Virginia, last winter, upwards of $400,000, and passed a law to provide for paying the debt; but, from some cause or other, the account has not been settled and paid in conformity to the act; and now they have no money. An army of ten or twelve thousand men is now guarding Richmond, not to mention the force at Petersburg and in the Northern Neck. For the present, we are compelled to support this force; the expense of which is and will be vast, indeed; and one of the first duties of the Assembly will be to adopt measures for this purpose. We have a right to expect that Congress will take from our shoulders this heavy burthen; but that Government is without money, and we must defend ourselves, at every cost and hazard, trusting in ultimate remuneration. I came up on the 13th instant, to prepare my affairs for a long absence on the Assembly. I would wish to carry some useful ideas with me when I join the Senate, and I take the liberty once more to ask the kindness of you to furnish me with such suggestions as you may deem useful for the occasion. I will use them under such restrictions as you may think proper to impose. I should be happy to call on you, but I shall be so engaged in settling my necessary affairs I am not certain it will be in my power to pass through Albemarle. By the 5th October I count on leaving home. I wish to obtain Col. Nicholas's consent, that he may be put in nomination as our next Governor.

I am, dear sir,

With the most sincere respect and esteem,

Your friend and humble servant,

JOSEPH C. CABELL.

Thomas Jefferson, Esq., Monticello.

XV.

T. J. TO J. C. C.

MONTICELLO, September 23, 1814.

DEAR SIR,—Your favor of the 17th is just received. I shall answer it, as usual, frankly, adding my suggestions to those you may receive from others, or conceive yourself, that your own good judgment may examine all things, and hold fast that which is good. Having before imposed on you the corvèe of reading my general sentiments on the subject of our finances, I may be the shorter now. I then thought it so important for the nation to enter into its rights in the circulating medium that I proposed the legislative resumption of them, and the gradual abolition of the banks of paper discount and of their paper. It would have been a difficult task; but to get along with the war otherwise I thought more difficult. Providence has now done the work for us; the banks, from North to South, are all bankrupt, and have so declared themselves; covered, indeed, under the thin pretext of preventing our enemies from drawing off all our specie, and their assurance that they will re-assume business at a proper time. But I presume they will not invite the public authorities to inspect their books and vaults, to see if the latter contain one-third of what the former will prove they have in circulation. Their notes, already rejected by some, received, with hesitation, by others, may drag on a few weeks longer, for want of all other circulation, but they are essentially defunct; and it is incumbent on the public authorities to act on that ground. To Congress, it certainly should belong exclusively; and, I presume, they will immediately commence supplying the circulation with treasury notes. If bottomed on taxes, they will be received as willingly as gold and silver; if not so bottomed, they will soon, if not at the first, be on a footing with the bank notes and old Continental. They should, in the first place, issue as much as would repay all they have borrowed from the banks, requiring the banks to throw them into circulation, in exchange for their own notes: and they should issue so much more as will carry us through the ensuing year. If they were to buy up, with treasury notes, the certificates of all their former loans, they would scarcely furnish as much medium as is necessary to let us down easily from the present excess. Taxes, then, redeeming annually one-tenth of their issues, would gradually reduce them to a competent circulation; and whenever they should fall below that, the metals would come in and keep it up to its wholesome level.

But these measures may not, perhaps, be adopted by Congress, and would, besides, be too dilatory for the wants of our State, which you represent as urgent. The question, then, is whether we ought not to do ourselves what I have said it is the more peculiar duty of Congress to do? I acknowledge a difficulty arising from the words of the Constitution of the United States, and the construction which some may put on them, and that construction, too, which is safest for the general interest. The States are prohibited from "emitting bills of credit." It is impossible, however, but that these words must have some limitation to their meaning. They cannot mean, for instance, that a State may not give to those to whom it owes a debt which it cannot yet pay, an acknowledgment of what it owes. Our State, for example, has been in the constant practice of issuing, by its Auditor, certificates of what it owes to the bearer, whether the Treasurer can pay them immediately or not; and this has never been deemed a breach of the constitution. Continue this practice, then. You owe the banks $300,000; give them auditor's certificates of from fifty down to five dollars, declaring that the State owes them so many dollars, which shall be paid to them or bearer, out of the proceeds of such a tax, within such a term, or as much sooner as may be from other resources, and let the banks give out these certificates in exchange for so much of their own notes. You owe present sums also to your militia, contractors and furnishers, and will be incurring new debts through the ensuing year. Authorize the giving them due-bills, countersigned by the Auditor, to a corresponding effect. Suppose these, with the debt to the banks amount to $400,000—lay taxes of $40,000, annual amount, for ten years, appropriate them sacredly to the sole object of paying off that amount of these bills annually, and let them, moreover, be receivable in taxes. Were bank bills in credit, it might be necessary to make the Auditor's notes bear interest; but they will be taken now of necessity, and greedily, without interest, as the bank notes were. Their bearing an interest would produce two great evils: 1st. They would be hoarded, and the circulation starved. 2d. You would be twenty instead of ten years redeeming the debt, by the same tax, were you to allow the same interest which the United States give.

But the United States owe you $400,000. As soon, then, as this is paid, call in our own notes in exchange for those of the United States. Let the tax cease from that moment, and with it, the example of being in contact with the Constitution. That example continued, might lead to new deluges of paper circulation, and to new revolutions and convulsions in private fortunes. We shall now experience these in a higher degree than on the death of the old Continental money; but this evil is incurred, and cannot be cured; and it was long ago visible to experience and observation, that the bank mania had seized our citizens so universally as to admit no other remedy than ruin. That is now upon them, and will, I hope, convince the Legislatures that it is the interest of all that all should relinquish the right of establishing banks of paper discount; and that neither should that power be given to Congress; because it is an expedient which runs so certainly to abuse and the ruin of private fortunes, that no such power ought to be granted by the people to any of their public functionaries. The proceedings, I propose, in order to secure us permanently against the recurrence of this catastrophe, should declare that no bank note should be ever again transferable, or even again be evidence of a debt, or effect the discharge of a debt. But for this the Legislature will not be ripe until they are overwhelmed by the abyss of ruin, now only beginning.

Accept these suggestions, which have been invited by your own request; use them for your own consideration only, or that of confidential friends, and be assured of my great friendship and respect.

TH: JEFFERSON.

Joseph C. Cabell, Esq.

XVI.

T. J. TO J. C. C.

MONTICELLO, September 30, 1814.

DEAR SIR,—In my letter of the 23d, an important fact escaped me, which, lest it should not occur to you, I will mention. The moneys arising from the sales of the glebe lands in the several counties, have generally, I believe, and under the sanction of the Legislature, been deposited in some of the banks; so, also, the funds of the literary* society. These

* The editor is not aware of what society is here alluded to.

debts, although parcelled among the counties, yet the counties constitute the State, and their representatives the Legislature, united into one whole. It is right, then, that owing $300,000 to the banks, they should stay so much of that sum in their own hands, as will secure what the banks owe to their constituents as divided into counties. Perhaps the loss of these funds would be the most lasting of the evils proceeding from the insolvency of the banks.

Ever yours,

With great esteem and respect,

TH: JEFFERSON.

Joseph C. Cabell, Esq.

XVII.

[The letter enclosed in the following, having been published in the last edition of Mr. Jefferson's "Works," VI. 391, is not re-printed here.]

T. J. TO J. C. C.

MONTICELLO, October 16, 1814.

DEAR SIR,—Either inaccurate expression in myself, or the misapprehension of a friend, to whom I had communicated my former letters on our finances, having obliged me to write another in explanation, I enclose you a copy of it, because you had taken the trouble to read the others. I should wish this to be seen by those to whom you had communicated the former, lest they also should have misapprehended me, taking care only to keep it out of the public papers, and to return it when done with. I am aware of the nest of hornets it would raise upon me, and am too old to court controversy. Forty years ago I might have indulged the spirit of proselytism; but at present I seek not to disturb the opinions of others. Accept the assurance of my friendly and respectful attachment.

TH: JEFFERSON.

Joseph C. Cabell, Esq.

XVIII.

J. C. C. TO T. J.

RICHMOND, 19th October, 1814.

DEAR SIR,—Your favor of 23d September reached me before I left home; that of 30th since I came to this place. I have already given, and shall continue to give, to those letters the fullest consideration in my power. We have as yet settled upon no plan of finance or defence; and are waiting to hear the plans of Congress. Our difficulties are great and increasing. Your idea of issuing State certificates ought and, I trust, will be adopted, at least so far as to support the public credit of the State, when the treasury may happen to be empty. I was the only person in the Senate who voted against the bill which has this day passed, authorizing the two banks in this city to issue notes under five dollars. I should be extremely thankful for any further communication you may at any time be pleased to make me, feeling myself always highly gratified and instructed by any views which you take of any subject.

I am, dear sir,

Most respectfully and sincerely yours,

JOSEPH C. CABELL.

Mr. Jefferson.

XIX.

J. C. C. TO T. J.

RICHMOND, 27th December, 1814.

DEAR SIR,—The enclosed letter, which I received under cover of your favor of 16th October, having remained a sufficient length of time in my hands, I now return it, agreeably to your desire, and beg you to receive my sincere thanks for the communication. I have taken the liberty to keep a copy of it, for my own gratification and instruction, and for the occasional perusal of such friends as may be desirous to obtain information. It shall neither go into the papers nor be indiscreetly used. Should you continue your researches upon finance or any of the branches of political economy, you would gratify me extremely by affording me a perusal of your papers. Mr. Ritchie has shewn me your letter on the subject of Tracy's work on political economy. This was the first intelligence I have received of that work; and from the manner in which you speak of it, as well as from the high reputation of that illustrious senator, it must be a very interesting production. I therefore entreat the favor of you, in the event of Col. Duane's not publishing his translation, and of your recovering the French copy, to give me an opportunity of perusing the latter. I would take particular care of it, and return it safely into your hands in the course of a month or six weeks; so that none of your other friends, who might solicit a similar favor, should be disappointed from neglect or tardiness on my part.

The session will terminate about the end of this or the middle of next week. Our revenue will be swelled, by the new taxes we have imposed, to a million of dollars. The Farmers Bank has already advanced the sum of $200,000, and are now in treaty with us to advance the sum of $800,000, in anticipation of the revenue. In addition to this, a loan for a million of dollars will be probably attempted, on the terms stated in the report of the Committee of Finance of the House of Delegates, which you have seen in the papers. Constitutional difficulties deter many of the members from the idea of issuing treasury notes by the State, on the plan of the notes issued at Washington. Auditor's warrants, or certificates founded on real antecedent transactions between the State and its citizens, bearing 6 per cent. interest, will probably be authorized; and a further authority to fund these certificates at 8 per cent. will probably be given to the Treasurer. In the course of a few days, these measures will be decided on. From the commencement of the session, I have entertained doubts whether a million could be borrowed at 8 per cent.; and the money being clearly necessary to prepare the State for defence during the next campaign, I should have been willing, and indeed have been desirous, to ensure the loan, by making a contract with the Virginia Bank, on such a scheme of borrowing as would not have augmented the currency of bank paper, and yet would have procured for the State the amount wanted. But the officers of that institution, after first favoring the plan, suddenly tacked about, and put a stop to all ideas of the kind, by demanding such terms as no one can think of granting. We are thrown back on the scheme of a loan from individuals at 8 per cent., which I should greatly prefer, were such a loan practicable. In order to obtain the funds requisite for the use of the State, we have to wade with patience through the difficulties resulting from diversity of views and opinions in the Houses of Assembly, and conflicting anti-social interests in society. I still hope, however, that we shall provide the sums necessary for the defence of the State, whatever want of system or consistency may appear on the face of our measures. The defence bill, or bill for classing the militia, is still before the House of Delegates. It will probably be rejected.

Col. Yancey,* in the course of this session, has shewn me a petition signed by Col. Randolph, the object of which was to obtain the passage of a law authorizing him to open the mountain falls above Milton, and to receive a toll on vessels and produce passing the same. I observed to Col. Y. that the object of that petition appeared to me to conflict with the charter of the company with which you have had so much trouble, and advised him to procure from Col. R. an explanatory statement of the reasons that induced the petition; for without shewing that the company have forfeited their charter, I do not see how we could transfer the powers and rights of the company to an individual. Perhaps I do not understand Col. R.'s views on this subject. Col. Y. has determined to lay

---

† *Col.* Chas. Yancey was then a delegate from Albemarle, and is to be distinguished from his relative, *Maj.* Chas. Yancey, for many years a delegate from Buckingham. A letter to the former gentleman, treating principally on the same topics with this, appears in his Works, VI. 514.

over the petition till another session. A bill has passed authorizing Wm. Wood to open the river from Milton down to Columbia; but, in this case, it is understood that the company authorized by a former law has never been formed, and that the law is a dead letter. I need not observe that it would give me great pleasure to serve Col. Randolph, and that I remain,

Most faithfully and sincerely your friend,

JOSEPH C. CABELL.

Thomas Jefferson, Esq., Monticello.

XX.

[Mr. J. in the following letter, for the first time enters specially on that which is the principal subject of this correspondence. He refers to an institution to be called "The Central College," and which he had contemplated as the nucleus of a future University. This letter also shews the reliance he had placed on Mr. C.'s assistance in carrying out his future plans. Mr. C. before this had received offers of a diplomatic position abroad, or of some post under the General Government at home. Repeated overtures had also been made to him to offer his services as the representative of his district in Congress, and with every prospect of success; but he declined them all. His desire was to devote himself to the service of his native State; and in this he was confirmed by this letter and subsequent conferences with Mr. J. growing out of it.]

T. J. TO J. C. C.

MONTICELLO, January 5th, 1815.

DEAR SIR,—Your favor of December 27th, with the letter inclosed, has been received. Knowing well that the bank-mania still possesses the great body of our countrymen, it was not expected that any radical cure of that could be at once effected. We must go further wrong, probably to a *ne plus ultra*, before we shall be forced into what is right. Something will be obtained, however, if we can excite in those who think, doubt first, reflection next, and conviction at last. The Constitution, too, presents difficulties here with which the General Government is not embarrassed. If your Auditor's notes are made payable to bearer, and of sizes suitable for circulation, they will find their way into circulation, as well as into the hoards of the thrifty, especially in important payments for land, &c., which are to lie on hand some time waiting for employment. A bank note is now received only as a "Robin's alive."

On Mr. Ritchie's declining the publication of Tracy's work, I proposed it to a Mr. Millegan, of Georgetown, who undertakes it. I had, therefore, written to Gen. Duane to forward it to him; so that it will not be in my possession until it is published. Have you seen the Review of Montesquieu,* by an anonymous author? the ablest work of the age. It was translated and published by Duane about three years ago. In giving the most correct analysis of the principles of political association which has yet been offered, he states, in the branch of political economy particularly, although much in brief, some of the soundest and most profound views we have ever had on those subjects.

I have lately received a letter from Say. He has in contemplation to remove to this country, and to this neighborhood particularly; and asks of me answers to some enquiries he makes. Could the petition which the Albemarle Academy addressed to our Legislature have succeeded at the late session, a little aid additional to the objects of that would have enabled us to have here immediately the best seminary of the United States. I do not know to whom P. Carr (President of the Board of Trustees) committed the petition and papers; † but I have seen no trace of their having been offered. Thinking it possible you may not have seen them, I send for your perusal the copies I retained for my own use. They consist—1. Of a

---

* "The exalted opinion of this book, as also of the Political Economy—both by Tracy—expressed by Mr. J. here and elsewhere in this correspondence, has not been shared by many others in Virginia."—*Note by Mr. C.*

† These and other papers appeared in 1817, in a pamphlet printed by order of the Legislature, at the instance of Mr. C., and which was generally distributed over the State. Several of them will re-appear in the Appendix.

letter to him, sketching, at the request of the trustees, a plan for the institution. 2. One to Judge Cooper, in answer to some observations he had favored me with, on the plan. 3. A copy of the petition of the trustees. 4. A copy of the act we wished from the Legislature. They are long; but as we always counted on you as the main pillar of their support, and we shall probably return to the charge at the next session, the trouble of reading them will come upon you, and as well now as then. The lottery allowed by the former act, the proceeds of our two glebes, and our dividend of the Literary Fund, with the re-organization of the institution, are what was asked in that petition. In addition to this, if we could obtain a loan for four or five years only of seven or eight thousand dollars, I think I have it now in my power to obtain three of the ablest characters in the world to fill the higher professorships of what in the plan is called the second, or general grade of education; three such characters as are not in a single University of Europe; and for those of languages and mathematics, a part of the same grade, able professors doubtless could also be readily obtained. With these characters, I should not be afraid to say that the circle of the sciences composing that second, or general grade, would be more profoundly taught here than in any institution in the United States, and I might go farther. The first, or elementary grade of education is not developed in this plan; an authority only being asked to its Visitors for putting into motion a former proposition for that object. For an explanation of this, therefore, I am obliged to add to these papers a letter I wrote some time since to Mr. Adams,* in which I had occasion to give some account of what had been proposed here for culling from every condition of our people the natural aristocracy of talents and virtue, and of preparing it by education, at the public expense, for the care of the public concerns. This letter will present to you some measures still requisite to complete and secure our republican

---

* This letter may be found in the first edition of Mr. J.'s Writings, IV. 226.

edifice, and which remain in charge for our younger statesmen. On yourself, Mr. Rives and Mr. Gilmer,* when they shall enter the public councils, I rest my hopes for this great accomplishment, and doubtless you will have other able coadjutors not known to me.

Col. Randolph having gone to Richmond before the rising of the Legislature, you will have had an opportunity of explaining to him personally the part of your letter respecting his petition for opening the Milton falls, which his departure prevented my communicating to him. I had not heard him speak of it, and had been glad, as to myself, by the act recently passed, to have saved our own rights in the defensive war with the Rivanna Company, and should not have advised the renewing and carrying the war into the enemy's country.

Be so good as to return all the inclosed papers after perusal, and to accept assurances of my great esteem and respect.

TH: JEFFERSON.

Joseph C. Cabell, Esq.

XXI.

J. C. C. TO T. J.

WARMINSTER, 5th March, 1815.

DEAR SIR,—After a long detention on the road, by the deep snow that fell in the latter part of the month of January, I arrived here on 5th ult., since which I have had the pleasure to receive your favor of 5th January, together with the papers enclosed. You have imposed on me new obligations by this communication. The particular posture of my domestic affairs at the time I reached home, and the new arrangements in regard to my property demanded by the return of peace, have not permitted me to go over these interesting papers as often, nor to

---

* William C. Rives and Francis W. Gilmer.

consider their contents as fully and maturely as I could desire. I have read them several times, and bestowed a good deal of reflection on them; but I will beg the favor of another reading towards the end of the year, and immediately previous to the meeting of the Assembly. In the interval, I shall make a visit to Albemarle, when I should be happy to converse with you, and to express, more fully than I can at present, my views of this subject. Why the petition was not presented, I cannot inform you. The papers were never shewn to me; nor did I ever hear of them but incidentally, and I believe after it had been determined not to bring them to the view of the Assembly. Col. Yancey generally consulted with me on the business from Albemarle, and once observed that certain papers relative to an academy proposed to be established in Charlottesville, had been sent down; that they were drawn by yourself, and were so finished off and complete, that the delegates had only to determine on the expediency of presenting them. I collected from him that they were in the hands of some of the members of the House of Delegates, who would consider and exercise a discretion on the question of their presentment. Being a member of the upper house, I waited, of course, for the petition to make its appearance in the lower house before I could take up the subject; which at that time I supposed was one of a much more local and confined nature than I find it really is. Subsequently to this conversation with Col. Yancey, I was accidentally a witness to a small part of a conversation between Doct. Carr and Mr. Wirt upon the subject of these papers, when Doctor Carr remarked that they had been sent by Mr. Peter Carr to Mr. David Watson, of Louisa, who had determined, from some cause or other, that they should not be presented at the last session. I have the highest respect and friendship for Mr. Watson, and concluded that the reasons which had decided his mind, were solid and sufficient. This is the amount of the knowledge I then had on the subject. I assure you I had no hint from any quarter that I was expected to bestow particular care on this business, or I should have paid to it the greatest attention imaginable, and done anything in the compass of my feeble abilities to promote your views. I confess I see nothing at this time that ought to impede the passage of your bill through the Assembly; nor can I conceive from what quarter objections could arise, unless from some of the people of Albemarle who might not wish to appropriate the proceeds of the sales of the glebes to the establishment of an academy at Charlottesville, or from certain members of the Assembly who might have other views of the ultimate destination of the literary fund, or from certain delegates from the lower counties who might have fears for William and Mary, or from a certain class of members who might not wish to lend the amount prayed to be loaned. I hope there would be no other effect produced by the plan upon William and Mary than that necessarily resulting from another college in the State. Having had a considerable share in getting Mr. Smith to take the presidency, I should feel somewhat delicately situated in regard to that seminary. I should be much pleased if such men as Mr. Say could find it their interest to reside in Virginia. I have the commentary on Montesquieu, of which you speak, and have commenced its perusal. It is to be inferred from your letters, I think, that Mr. Tracy is the author. His Political Economy I will purchase on sight.

The honorable acquittal of my friend Coles gives me great pleasure. I leave this in a few days for the lower country, to make some new arrangements of my property in Lancaster. If Cockburn has not sent my negroes out of the United States,* I ought to have them again. But I presume they are now making sugar in the West Indies; and if they have not left the limits of the United States, I imagine the British will now, as formerly, disregard the treaty. The negroes from

* During the war of 1812–14, some forty slaves were taken from the Corrottoman estate by Admiral Cockburn. For these partial compensation was received in 1827, from the commissioners under the treaty of Ghent.

Corrottoman were carried to Tangier Island. From what I have heard, I am led to believe the enemy some time since broke up their establishment on that island.

I am, dear sir, with great respect, your friend,

JOSEPH C. CABELL.

Mr. Jefferson.

XXII.

T. J. TO J. C. C.

MONTICELLO, December 23, 1815.

DEAR SIR,—A petition has been presented to our present Legislature, by a Capt. Joseph Miller, praying a confirmation of the will of his half-brother, Thomas Read, who died not long since at Norfolk, possessed of lands and slaves, which he devised to his half-brothers and sisters, then living in England. This one bought up the shares of the whole, and came over to reside here as a citizen. He arrived after the declaration of war, and was instantly ordered up to Charlottesville. We, of course, became acquainted with him, and were soon attached to him by the honest simplicity of his character, so that he was soon at home in every house. We found him as zealous an American as any of ourselves, and I interceded with the Marshal to let him go to Norfolk to look to his property, making myself responsible for the fidelity of his conduct. He sat up a brewery there in partnership with a Mr. Hays, which he still carries on with great success, being, I verily believe, the most skillful brewer that has ever come to the country. But during his stay here, he has become attached to the neighbors and neighborhood, and is looking out for a farm to carry on the business of farming and brewing jointly, and on a moderate scale. He has now been with me two months, a very welcome guest to all the family, and this may explain the interest I take in his case. Considering him, too, as becoming one of your constituents, I have thought I might, without impropriety, solicit your patronage of his claim. His petition was put into the hands of Mr. Maury,* one of our representatives, and I now write to Mr. Baker,† to ask his aid in that house. The facts and principles of his claim are so fully stated in the petition that I need add nothing to them. I have been told the Commissioners of the literary fund habitually oppose these petitions. No one wishes more than I do, to see the literary fund increase, but not by the plunder of individuals. The testator in this case had a fair claim to the privilege of every citizen, of disposing of the property which he had made by his own industry, to those dearest to him. I believe I should be correct in saying, that England is the only country in Europe which seizes the property in such a case. I speak from a knowledge of the fact, as to several countries on the continent of Europe, and a full belief of it in others. France exhibits a remarkable instance. The Duke of Richmond is of French extraction, held, when I left that country in 1789, a great ducal estate there, and was one of the hereditary dukes and peers of France. This you will see in the Almanac Royal of that year, and in the Court Calendar of England of every year. His estate may have been confiscated in the mass of Seigneural property there during the revolution; but of this I am not informed. We have copied the barbarism from England in our general law, but the Legislature properly relaxes it in all reasonable cases, as I hope and believe they will in this, where the claimant desires to become a resident citizen as his brother was. I say nothing of the fact, that his parents were established in the United States at the time of the revolution, and himself born in them; because you will find the details of that specially stated in the petition. Pray obtain justice for him, and accept my respectful and affectionate salutations.

TH: JEFFERSON.

Joseph C. Cabell, Esq.

---

* Mr. Thomas W. Maury, grandson of Mr. Jefferson's old Preceptor, Rev. James Maury. A letter of Mr. Jefferson to him, touching on some of these subjects, may be found in his works, VI. 548.

† Probably Mr. Jerman Baker, then a delegate from Cumberland.

XXIII.

J. C. C. TO T. J.

RICHMOND, 16th January, 1816.

DEAR SIR,—I received in due time by the mail, your favor respecting Mr. Miller's petition; and I have deferred writing to you till the fate of that bill, and of the bill respecting the Central College, could be ascertained, so far as it depended on the House of Delegates. Both these bills arrived in the Senate this day; and I have had them committed, and shall take all the care of them in the compass of my feeble abilities. I should have preferred a delay of some days longer, before I should write to you; but the mail leaving town this evening, and being desirous to avoid the effect of too long a delay, I must not postpone my communication any longer. As to Mr. Miller's bill, I am not, as yet, aware of any opposition. In regard to the bill respecting the Central College, there is some little danger. The clause respecting the literary fund, was stricken out in the lower house. The actual destination which that fund will hereafter receive, is not decided. I think my letter to you from Warminster, apprised you that I apprehended sòme opposition to that part of the bill respecting that fund; and I advised Mr. Maury not to press that subject, if opposition should arise to such an appropriation at this time. Opposition was made to it, and that part of the bill was stricken out. The bill has passed quietly through the House of Delegates, with that single exception. After it had passed that house, and before it had reached the Senate, Col. Yancey came to me and requested me to oppose that part of the bill which gives to the trustees the power to fix the time for commencing on the plan of general instruction in the county of Albemarle. I endeavored to satisfy his mind. He appeared to be afraid of giving offence to the people of the county, by putting them on a different footing from the people of the other counties in the State. My resolution was formed, to endeavor to get the bill through the Senate without any change whatsoever; but I find some objection among some of the principal members of the Senate, to that part of the bill giving to the professors the power of imprisoning the students.* In this state of things, I have determined to write you, and request the favor of you, to inform me whether your letter to Mr. Carr contains all that you have written upon the subject of this seminary; and if it does not, to ask the kindness of you to transmit to me, by the return of the mail, any other communications which, in any shape, you may have made upon the subject. I beg also that you will enter into as full a statement, as your convenience will permit, of the reasons that induced you to give to the professors the power of imprisoning students. My object would be to show your letter to the leading members of the Senate. If there should be no particular objection, you would confer a favor by stating your reasons for taking from the Court of Albemarle, and giving to the Trustees, the power of fixing a period for the establishment of schools in Albemarle. The petition respecting the house in Charlottesville,† Mr. Maury and myself have determined not to press into view till the College bill gets well under way; because its fate should be made dependent on the latter. A Mr. Braidwood, teacher of the deaf and dumb, now established at some point on this river below the falls, would come to Charlottesville and establish himself there, provided he could get such a house as Mr. Estis's. How would it answer your purposes, to get an act passed for a lottery to purchase that house, for an establishment for the deaf and dumb, as a wing of the Central College. In your answer it would be well to separate any thing you may have to say of a private nature, from what it might be well to communicate to certain mem-

* This proposition, when first suggested, was somewhat startling to the friends as well as opponents of the institution. As afterwards explained by Mr. Jefferson, some of its repellent features were softened; but on consultation with judicious friends, it was finally dropped.

† See above in the introduction.

bers. Permit me to suggest the propriety of your requesting the co-operation of Mr. Johnson, Mr. Poindexter, Mr. Watts, and Gen. Green, of the Senate.* Their aid would be of infinite use at future stages of this enterprise; and a request from you to these valuable men, would have very great influence upon its ultimate destiny. I write in great haste, but beg you to rest assured of my constant attachment and great respect.

JOS. C. CABELL.

Mr. Jefferson.

XXIV.

J. C. C. TO T. J.

RICHMOND, 23d January, 1816.

DEAR SIR,—I wrote you, by the last mail, that the bills respecting the Central College and Capt. Miller's claim had just reached the Senate, and that the former was objected to in two points: 1. Because it gives to the trustees of the College the power of determining the time at which the act of 22d December, 1796, shall be carried into execution in Albemarle; and, 2. Because it confers on the Proctor of the College the powers and authorities of a justice of the peace, within the precincts of the institution. Since my letter was committed to the mail, I have conversed with the Governor, who considers the first objection of great weight, as it would probably place the people of the county in hostility to the College. Whilst I am awaiting your answer to my last letter, it becomes proper that I should address you on two other subjects before the Senate, in which you take an interest. I cannot find among the papers in Capt. Miller's case the evidences of the conveyance made to him, by the other devisees, of their portions of

* Mr. Poindexter was from the Goochland District; Gen. Edward Watts, then of Bedford, afterwards removed to the county of Botetourt; Gen. John W. Green, was afterwards Judge of the Court of Appeals.

Thomas Read's estate. I should infer from the manner in which they are referred to in the petition, that they would appear among the accompanying documents. Accordingly, I immediately enquired for them; but they are neither to be found, nor can either of the delegates from Albemarle give any account of them. Those papers are essential to the success of the bill in the Senate; and with their aid, I trust I can get it through the House. I beg the favor of you to request Capt. Miller to furnish me with these documents with as little delay as possible. Whilst I await their arrival, I will, by all means in my power, endeavor to smooth the way to the passage of the bill.

From a letter you recently wrote Col. Yancey, I perceive you consider the bill to prevent obstructions in the navigable water-courses of the Commonwealth, of importance to the people on the banks of the Rivanna. I enclose you a copy of the bill, and of some amendments hastily sketched by Col. Green, and would thank you to send me such corrections as you deem proper. These subjects may be suspended till I can get your answer, without injury to the parties concerned.

I regard the passage of the bill respecting the Central College as pretty certain, provided the modifications suggested in the points objected to shall be made; and perhaps, without those changes, its passage may be secured by your explanations. I believe the bill for internal improvement will pass; and that if the General Assembly should be disposed to give anything to education, it will be to the literary fund, for the establishment of free schools. It is barely possible that they may give something to the Central College, for teaching the deaf and dumb. I am endeavoring to prepare the more liberal part for an attempt at an endowment of a professorship of the deaf and dumb. Thus far it is well received; but I may be baffled. I have thought that such a plan might engage the affections of the coldest members. Any suggestions from you on this subject would be thankfully received. I beg you to pardon the trouble I give you, and to be assured it results from my wish to afford you satisfaction in the business entrusted to my care.

I am, dear sir,

Most sincerely yours,

JOSEPH C. CABELL.

P. S. Dr. Smith, President of William & Mary, has desired me to ask the favor of you to recommend a text-book on the principles of government, for the use of the students at that College. He is not satisfied with either Locke or Rousseau. Can you inform me whether Say on Political Economy has been translated into our language?

XXV.

T. J. TO J. C. C.

MONTICELLO, January 24, 1816.

DEAR SIR,—Your favor of the 16th experienced great delay on the road, and to avoid that of another mail, I must answer very briefly.

My letter to Peter Carr contains all I ever wrote on the subject of the College;* a plan for the institution being the only thing the trustees asked or expected from me. Were it to go into execution, I should certainly interest myself further and strongly in procuring proper professors.

The establishment of a Proctor is taken from the practice of Europe, where an equivalent officer is made a part, and is a very essential one, of every such institution; and as the nature of his functions requires that he should always be a man of discretion, understanding and integrity, above the common

---

* By this it is not to be presumed that he meant to exclude the references to it in private letters to one or more friends, and which have since been published.

level, it was thought that he would never be less worthy of being trusted with the powers of a justice, within the limits of the institution here, than the neighboring justices generally are; and the vesting him with the conservation of the peace within that limit was intended, while it should equally secure its object, to shield the young and unguarded student from the disgrace of the common prison, except where the case was an aggravated one. A confinement to his own room was meant as an act of tenderness to him, his parents and friends. In fine, it was to give them a complete police of their own, tempered by the paternal attentions of their tutors. And certainly, in no country is such a provision more called for than in this, as has been proved from times of old, from the regular annual riots and battles between the students of William & Mary with the town boys, before the Revolution, *quorum pars fui*, and the many and more serious affrays of later times. Observe, too, that our bill proposes no exclusion of the ordinary magistrate, if the one attached to the institution is thought to execute his power either partially or remissly.

The transfer of the power to give commencement to the ward or elementary schools from the court and aldermen to the visitors, was proposed because the experience of twenty years has proved that no court will ever begin it. The reason is obvious: The members of the court are the wealthy members of the counties; and as the expenses of the schools are to be defrayed by a contribution proportioned to the aggregate of other taxes which every one pays, they consider it as a plan to educate the poor at the expense of the rich. It proceeded, too, from a hope that the example and good effects being exhibited in one county, they would spread from county to county, and become general. The modification of the law, by authorizing the aldermen to require the expense of tutorage from such parents as are able, would render trifling, if not wholly prevent, any call on the county for pecuniary aid. You know that nothing better than a log house is required for these schools, and there is not a neighborhood which would not meet and build this themselves, for the sake of having a school near them.

I know of no peculiar advantage which Charlottesville offers for Mr. Braidwood's school of deaf and dumb. On the contrary, I should think the vicinity of the seat of government most favorable to it. I should not like to have it made a member of our College. The objects of the two institutions are fundamentally distinct. The one is science; the other, mere charity. It would be gratuitously taking a boat in tow, which may impede, but cannot aid the motion of the principal institution.

Ever and affectionately yours,

TH: JEFFERSON.

[Two postscripts, on separate slips of paper, enclosed in the foregoing letter.]

P. S. I detach the postscript of my letter for the reasons suggested in yours. You wish me to write to several gentlemen on the subject of our College. I could write to Mr. Johnson, with whom I am acquainted, and for whom I have a sincere esteem and respect; but I have no acquaintance with the others you name. And indeed, my friend, I am no longer equal to the labor. I pass from four to six hours of every day of my life at my writing table, in the drudgery of answering letters, in which I have no personal concern or pleasure. It is weighing and wearing down my life with an oppression of body and mind I am not able to bear up against. I must throw it off, and intrench myself within the limits of my friends and my own affairs. I want, too, to have some time for reading.

P. P. S. Shew the postscript to Mr. Johnson. It will apologize for my not writing to him; for, indeed, I consider the writing to you as to him also.

XXVI.

J. C. C. TO T. J.

RICHMOND, 24th January, 1816.

DEAR SIR,—Since writing the enclosed letter, I have conversed with Mr. Mercer,* of the House of Delegates, to whom I had lent your letter to Mr. Carr, upon being informed by him that he had it in contemplation to endeavor to get a considerable part of the debt due from the General Government to the State of Virginia, appropriated to the establishment of a grand scheme of education. He appears much pleased with your view of the subject, and as he proposes to make a report to the Lower House, concurs with me in the propriety of availing the country of the light you have shed upon this great interest of the community. Would you object to the publication of your letter to Mr. Carr? Indeed, sir, I may take the liberty to have your letter printed before I can get your answer. I do not believe the General Assembly will make so great an appropriation at this time as the one proposed by Mr.

---

* Charles Fenton Mercer, then a delegate from Loudoun, afterwards, and for many years, a representative in Congress from that district. This gentleman claims the paternity of the Literary Fund of Virginia, as appears in his Address on Popular Education, published in 1826. (Appendix, page XVII). It is proper to add, however, that on this point there is a conflict of pretension between him and Gov. Barbour, as may be seen in an address of the latter to a convention of agriculturists, in Richmond, in 1836. (Ruffin's Farmers' Register, III, 688). Without deciding on the question of origin, it may justly be said, that to Mr. Mercer, as Chairman of the Committee of Finance, in 1815–16, we owe a report recommending the increase of this Fund by appropriating to its use the residue of the debt due from the United States to Virginia; a resolution in pursuance of that report which passed, and at the following session a General Plan of Education for the State, embracing a University, Colleges, Academies and Primary Schools. This bill, which passed the House, but was dropped in the Senate, was one of the documents included in the pamphlet referred to above. But from this letter of Mr. Cabell, we learn, that Mr. J.'s letter to Peter Carr was shewn to Mr. M. before he had submitted either report or bill.

Mercer; but I will do anything in my power to promote it. And should the measure succeed, my object would be to make your plan the basis of our measures. The location of the principal Seminary would be a secondary condition; and it might happen that the people beyond the mountain would not come into the measure unless Staunton or Lexington should be made the principal site. This would be a disagreeable result to me, but I see a scheme already formed to carry the Seat of Government, sooner or later, to *Staunton*, and powerful *private interests* silently preparing and expecting that event. Should a great State Seminary be established at Charlottesville, it might touch the interests of this party. This suggestion I beg you to consider as confidential. My intention is, as soon as I hear from you, to secure the passage of the bill respecting the Central College, nearly, or entirely, in its present shape. Then, or previously, I will, if not prevented, publish your letter to Mr. Carr, so as to prevent this game from being easily taken out of the hands of those who are entitled to it.

In haste, I am, dear sir, most truly yours,

Jos. C. Cabell.

XXVII.

TH. J. TO. MR. CABELL.

Monticello, January 31, 1816.

Your letters of the 23rd and 24th came to hand just in the moment of the return of our mail. I have only, therefore, time to enclose the conveyances for which Mr. Miller's bill is hung up. I had no doubt but that he had deposited them with the other papers. Friendly salutations.

XXVIII.

T. J. TO J. C. C.

MONTICELLO, February 2, 1816.

DEAR SIR,—Your favors of the 23d and 24th ultimo were a week coming to us. I instantly enclosed to you the deeds of Capt. Miller; but I understand that the post-master having locked his mail before they got to the office, would not unlock it to give them a passage.

Having been prevented from retaining my collection of the acts and journals of our Legislature, by the lumping manner in which the Committee of Congress chose to take my library, it may be useful to our public bodies to know what acts and journals I had, and where they can now have access to them. I therefore enclose you a copy of my catalogue, which I pray you to deposit in the council office for public use. It is in the 18th and 24th chapters they will find what is interesting to them. The form of the catalogue has been much injured in the publication; for, although they have preserved my division into chapters, they have reduced the books in each chapter to alphabetical order, instead of the chronological or analytical arrangements I had given them. You will see sketches of what were my arrangements at the heads of some of the chapters.

The bill on the obstructions in our navigable waters appears to me proper; as do, also, the amendments proposed. I think the State should reserve a right to the use of the waters for navigation, and that where an individual landholder impedes that use, he should remove the impediment, and leave the subject in as good a state as nature formed it. This I hold to be the true principle, and to this Col. Green's amendments go. All that I ask in my own case is, that the Legislature will not take from me *my own works.* I am ready to cut my dam in any place, and at any moment requisite, so as to remove that impediment, if it be thought one, and to leave those interested to make the most of the natural circumstances of the place;

but I hope they will never take from me my canal, made through the body of my own lands, at an expense of twenty thousand dollars, and which is no impediment to the navigation of the river. I have permitted the riparian proprietors above (and they are not more than a dozen or twenty) to use it gratis, and shall not withdraw the permission, unless they so use it as to obstruct too much the operations of my mills, of which there is some likelihood.

Dr. Smith, you say, asks what is the best elementary book on the principles of government? None in the world equal to the Review of Montesquieu, printed at Philadelphia, a few years ago. It has the advantage, too, of being equally sound and corrective of the principles of Political Economy; and all within the compass of a thin 8 vo. Chipman's and Priestley's Principles of Government, and the Federalist, are excellent in many respects, but, for fundamental principles, not comparable to the Review.

I have no objections to the printing my letter to Mr. Carr, if it will promote the interests of science, although it was not written with a view to its publication.

My letter of the 24th ultimo conveyed to you the grounds of the two articles objected to in the college bill. Your last presents one of them in a new point of view, that of the commencement of the Ward Schools, as likely to render the law unpopular to the county. It must be a very inconsiderate and rough process of execution that would do this. My idea of the mode of carrying it into execution would be this. Declare the county *ipso facto* divided into wards for the present by the boundaries of the militia captaincies; somebody attend the ordinary muster of each company, having first desired the captain to call together a full one. There explain the object of the law to the people of the company; put to their vote whether they will have a school established, and the most central and convenient place for it; get them to meet and build a log school-house, have a roll taken of the children who would attend it, and of those of them able to pay; these would probably be sufficient to support a common teacher, instructing, gratis, the few unable to pay. If there should be a deficiency, it would require too trifling a contribution from the county to be complained of, and especially as the whole county would participate, where necessary, in the same resource. Should the company, by its vote, decide that it would have no school, let them remain without one. The advantages of this proceeding would be, that it would become the duty of the wardens elected by the county to take an active part in pressing the introduction of schools, and to look out for tutors. If, however, it is intended that the State Government shall take this business into its own hands, and provide schools for every county, then, by all means, strike out this provision of our bill. I should never wish that it should be placed on a worse footing than the rest of the State. But, if it is believed that these elementary schools will be better managed by the Governor and Council, the Commissioners of the Literary Fund, or any other general authority of the Government, than by the parents within each ward, it is a belief against all experience. Try the principle one step further, and amend the bill so as to commit to the Governor and Council the management of all our farms, our mills, and merchants' stores. No, my friend, the way to have good and safe government, is not to trust it all to one; but to divide it among the many, distributing to every one exactly the functions he is competent to. Let the National Government be entrusted with the defence of the nation, and its foreign and federal relations; the State Governments with the civil rights, laws, police and administration of what concerns the State generally; the counties with the local concerns of the counties, and each ward direct the interests within itself. It is by dividing and subdividing these republics from the great national one down through all its subordinations, until it ends in the administration of every man's farm and affairs by himself; by placing under every one what his own eye may superintend, that all will be done for the best. What has destroyed liberty and the rights of man in every Government which has ever existed under the sun? The generalizing and concentrating all cares and powers into one body, no matter whether of the autocrats of Russia or France, or of the aristocrats of a Venetian Senate. And I do believe, that if the Almighty has not decreed that man shall never be free, (and it is blasphemy to believe it,) that the secret will be found to be in the making himself the depository of the powers respecting himself, so far as he is competent to them, and delegating only what is beyond his competence by a synthetical process, to higher and higher orders of functionaries, so as to trust fewer and fewer powers, in proportion as the trustees become more and more oligarchical. The elementary republics of the wards, the county republics, the State republics, and the republic of the Union, would form a gradation of authorities, standing each on the basis of law, holding every one its delegated share of powers, and constituting truly a system of fundamental balances and checks for the government. Where every man is a sharer in the direction of his ward republic, or of some of the higher ones, and feels that he is a participator in the government of affairs, not merely at an election, one day in the year, but every day; when there shall not be a man in the State who will not be a member of some one of its councils, great or small, he will let the heart be torn out of his body, sooner than his power be wrested from him by a Cæsar or a Bonaparte. How powerfully did we feel the energy of this organization in the case of the Embargo? I felt the foundations of the Government shaken under my feet by the New England township. There was not an individual in these States whose body was not thrown, with all its momentum, into action; and, although the whole of the other States were known to be in favor of the measure, yet, the organization of this little selfish minority enabled it to overrule the Union. What could the unwieldy counties of the middle, the South and the West do? Call a county meeting, and the drunken loungers at and about the courthouses would have collected, the distances being too great for the good people and the industrious generally to attend. The character of those who really met would have been the measure of the weight they would have had in the scale of public opinion. As Cato then concluded every speech with the words "*Carthago delenda est*," so do I every opinion with the injunction "divide the counties into wards." Begin them only for a single purpose; they will soon show for what others they are the best instruments. God bless you, and all our rulers, and give them the wisdom, as I am sure they have the will, to fortify us against the degeneracy of our Government, and the concentration of all its powers in the hands of the one, the few, the well-born, or but the many.

TH: JEFFERSON.

XXIX.

J. C. C. TO T. J.

SENATE CHAMBER, February 14th, 1816.

DEAR SIR,—Mr. Miller's bill has passed. The bill respecting the Central College has also passed; but with modifications. The bill respecting the navigable waters of the Commonwealth, with Col. Green's amendments, has also passed. Your various letters of late have been gratefully received; and your copy of the books in the National Library has been deposited in the Council Chamber. I am compelled to write you in great haste; but will give you further particulars by the next mail.

With sentiments of the greatest regard,

I remain, dear sir, your obedient servant,

JOSEPH C. CABELL.

Mr. Jefferson.

XXX.

J. C. C. TO T. J.

RICHMOND, 21st February, 1816.

DEAR SIR,—I wrote you hastily, by a late mail, a short letter containing the substance of our proceedings respecting those bills in which you felt particular interest. A more particular statement may not be unacceptable to you. Captain Miller's bill passed, in the Senate, by a vote of 12 to about 5, after an elaborate discussion, in which not only the merits of the particular claim, but the general law of escheats, was brought into view. The style of the petition, and the support you gave Capt. Miller, were no doubt the cause of so large a majority in his favor. It was well that the title papers arrived when they did; otherwise the bill would have been lost, and Capt. Miller would have been driven to the sale of the real estate under the third section of the act of 8th February, 1813; on which Mr. Johnson thought he ought to be suffered to rely. The honest, but droll exultation of the worthy Captain, when he was informed of the passage of the bill, was a source of great satisfaction and merriment to Mr. Maury and myself. I am well persuaded he will always justify the statements you have made in his behalf, and that his gratitude to you will cease only with his life. His papers were returned to him, and were carried to Norfolk, to which place he hastened as soon as the bill passed.

I communicated to the Senate that part of your letter containing your motives for giving to the Proctor of the Central College the powers of a justice of the peace. Finding, notwithstanding, many members opposed to that part of the bill, and we deeming it not very important to carry it at this time, I consented to strike it out. I moved also to strike out those sections relative to schools in the county of Albemarle. This motion, however, was not made till I had fully consulted with Governor Nicholas, my brother William, and several other friends. It is unquestionably in the contemplation of the Assembly to establish a general system of education throughout the State; and for that purpose augmentations are made from time to time to the literary fund. A resolution has recently passed the House of Delegates, the object of which is to give to the literary fund the whole of the surplus of the debt due to this State from the United States over and above the sum of six hundred thousand dollars. Whether this resolution will finally grow into a law or not, the passage of it demonstrates the existence of a favorable temper, in regard to a speedy amelioration in the existing state of education in this State. As the revenue bill is now on the table of the Senate, and the estimated amount of the taxes embraces a sinking fund for paying gradually our debt of $750,000 to the banks, I presume the Assembly will give the surplus of the debt over $600,000 to the literary fund. As the people of Albemarle will be taxed to pay the debts of the State, or in other words, to form the literary fund, they probably would have very great objections to a power in the trustees of the Central College to impose additional taxes on them. Under these views of the subject, and supported by the unanimous advice of the above named friends, I made the motion to amend the bill in the part alluded to. Previous to its arrival in the Senate, the part respecting the literary fund was stricken out in the lower house. Mr. Poindexter had been very friendly in regard to this bill, and when he made a motion, at a late stage of the proceedings, to amend it, in such manner as to save to the counties of Louisa and Fluvanna their respective interests in the glebes of St. Anne and Fredericksville, I could but yield to it, the more especially as I am confident the Senate would have over-ruled me had I opposed him on that point. I was the more inclined to this conciliatory course, because Mr. Maury informed me that only a very small part of the two glebes could be claimed by Fluvanna and Louisa; and for this further reason, that the policy of the friends of the Central College must be to rely on funds to be hereafter obtained from the Legislature, rather than on the very limited means contemplated by the bill. With these modifications, the bill has passed into a law. The bill respecting Estis' lottery was rejected in the Senate. As it came to this house, it was a bill for a lottery, the proceeds of which was to be applied to the purchase of Mr. Estis' buildings, provided the trustees should consider them the best site for the Central College. I proposed, in the Senate, to amend the bill by directing the proceeds of the lottery to be applied to the use and benefit of the Central College, provided they should not wish to establish the College in Estis' houses, or provided they should not be able to purchase them on such terms as they should deem just and reasonable. It was suggested by a member of the Senate, that such a bill as this would be giving the petitioners "a stone when they asked for bread." I admitted the departure in the bill as it came from the House of Delegates, from the petition, and the still further departure contemplated by the amendments I proposed; but informed the House of the conflict that might arise between Mr. Estis' Academy and the Central College, if his petition should be granted, and urged such possible conflict as a sufficient reason for rejecting the application of the petitioners in the form in which it appeared before the House of Delegates. If, however, the views of the petitioners could be reconciled with the interests of the College, I could have no objections; and as an additional lottery for the benefit of the Central College might possibly succeed, I should vote for the bill, and proposed the amendments merely to clear up all doubts as to the destination of the proceeds of the lottery. The Senate rejected the bill; nor was I much grieved by the decision. You will have seen your letter to Mr. Carr in the Enquirer. It came out on the morning of the day* that the resolution passed the House of Delegates appropriating the surplus of our United

* "There are reasons to believe that the appearance of this letter, at that particular juncture, had a considerable share in the passage of that resolution." *Note by Mr. C.* See also the next letter.

States debt to the literary fund, and I have reasons to believe had a considerable effect in promoting the passage of that resolution. I fear, however, no measure will be founded on it. The manner in which it is generally spoken of induces me to believe that its publication will produce a very happy effect on the interests of science in this State. I should be pleased to see in print your remarks on the division of the counties into wards, as preparatory to the future introduction of that measure into the Assembly. The proper point of time for making the attempt, I presume, would be when the literary fund shall be applied to the establishment of schools.

The bill respecting the navigable waters of this Commonwealth, with Col. Green's amendments, has passed into a law. No retrospective provision is embraced in the law.

Having now given such information as I thought might be agreeable to you, I have to beg the kindness of you, at any leisure moment, to drop me a line, informing me whether Say's work on Political Economy has ever been translated. I have some idea of making the attempt, should it not already have been done by some other person. I feel myself infinitely obliged by the several letters you have had the goodness to write me during this session. I know the extent of your correspondence, and the drudgery it imposes on you; and all I ask is a line about Say.

Most respectfully and truly yours,

JOSEPH C. CABELL.

Mr. Jefferson.

XXXI.

J. C. C. TO T. J.

RICHMOND, 26th February, 1816.

DEAR SIR,—I have at length procured from the Editor of the Enquirer, and now return your original letter to Mr. Carr. Its publication, in my opinion, was well-timed, and has produced a happy effect on the measures of the Assembly. We have appropriated all our United States' debt, except $600,000, to the purposes of education, and have required the President and Directors of the Literary Fund to report to the next Assembly the best plan of an university, colleges, academies, and schools. The passage of both these measures is unquestionably to be ascribed, in a great degree, to your letter. But, it may be asked, why enquire of the President and Directors of the Literary Fund for plans, when one so satisfactory is already before the public? I will tell you. Appropriations abstracted from their location are most easily obtained. Should the next Assembly sanction the scheme of an university, you will see the Lexington and Staunton interests striving to draw it away from Albemarle, and the whole western delegation will threaten to divide the State, unless this institution should be placed beyond the Ridge. Staunton wants the seat of government, and considers the day near at hand, when she will be the metropolis of the State. Any brilliant establishment at the eastern foot of the Ridge, will shake those claims, and disturb speculations founded upon them. Mr. Mercer of the House of Delegates, will be an advocate for a western site. The *Washington* College at Lexington, will be the favorite of the Federalists. But I think the Central College will triumph over them all. I am pleased to think Governor Nicholas will be in office at the commencement of the next session of Assembly. In the interim, the friends of science will be able to form the necessary plans to promote the general weal. We have had some singular proceedings in the caucuses at this place, which were held for the purpose of making an electoral ticket. I had hoped * * * * *

I am, dear sir,

Yours most faithfully and truly,

JOSEPH C. CABELL.

Mr. Jefferson.

XXXII.

T. J. TO J. C. C.

MONTICELLO, February 28, 1816.

DEAR SIR,—You enquire whether Say has ever been translated into English? I am certain he never has in America, nor do I believe he has in England. I have never seen his work named in their catalogues or advertisements, nor do I believe it has been noticed by the Edinburgh Reviewers. Nor have they noticed the Review of Montesquieu, although Duane sent them a copy. You will render this country a great service in translating it; for there is no branch of science of which our countrymen seem so ignorant as Political Economy. The bulk and prolixity of Smith forbid venturing on him. I salute you always with affection.

TH: JEFFERSON.

Joseph C. Cabell, Esq.

XXXIII.

J. C. C. TO T. J.

WARMINSTER, July 4th, 1816.

DEAR SIR,—I saw Gen. Cocke on his way to Norfolk, early in June, and had a conversation with him on the subject of hedges; in the course of which he informed me that you were under the impression that Maine's method of preparing haws, so as to make them vegetate quickly, had died with him. It affords me pleasure to furnish you with it, in an extract of a letter written by Maine to Mr. James Henderson of Williamsburg, at the time that the latter purchased of him about 10,000 of his thorns. I was making enquiries in the month of May, with the view of collecting information as to the practicability and expediency of introducing live fences into Virginia, when I accidentally got sight of Maine's letter to Mr. Henderson. It differs from all other methods I have yet heard of; and is more expeditious, by one winter, than that of McMahon, who follows the English and Scotch methods; and is the quickest of all the processes that have come to my knowledge, unless it be that of immersing the haws in fermenting bran, as recommended by Sir Isaac Newton. I have no where read of a successful experiment on a large scale, of the latter method; and have seen it merely suggested as recommended by Sir Isaac Newton. Maine's method is simple, quick, and well suited to common practice. I should be glad to know why Maine selected the maple leaf thorn in preference to all others. It does not appear to me to be as vigorous in its growth, or as strong it its appearance, as the laurel leaf thorn; nor do I know whether it is to be found in this part of the country. In crossing Willis' river, on my way up the country, I found a thorn in great abundance, which, from the shape of the leaf, appeared to be the maple leaf thorn. There may, however, be other varieties with a leaf of the same shape. You planted some years ago, a hedge around your house, of Maine's thorn. I should be happy, before I commence experiments in this line, to know your impressions as to the practicability of making hedges of real use in this country where hogs are suffered to run at large; and as to the relative advantages of the holly, the cedar, and the thorn, for that purpose. I should also be much indebted to you, for a reference to such authors as treat best on the subject. I have consulted Dobson's Encyclopædia, Lord Kaimes, Maine's Pamphlet, and the articles in the ordinary books on agriculture. I have been informed by a young gentleman who attended the lectures of the Abbé Correa in Philadelphia, that the Abbé expressed the opinion, that hedges would not succeed in this country, because we have not the right kind of plant, and that the proper plant when imported, degenerates. The same person told me that the hedges about Wilmington, in Delaware, seemed to be declining. These are discouraging circumstances. Still I have a strong desire to go on. I had a cedar hedge of about two miles in length, planted on the Rappahannock low grounds, some years ago. It grew handsomely, and promised well. But during the war, it was neglected and beaten down by stock in many places. A part of it, about five hundred yards in length, is now entire and very beautiful. But whether it will be ultimately a secure fence, I am unable to say. As an object of ornament, I think it remunerates for the care and trouble it has cost; and it is of real use in breaking the force of the violent winds that often sweep those plains. I propose to renew it where it is defective, and to extend it to four miles in length. The holly is scarcely to be found in the woods of the upper country. Still I suppose it would succeed with the aid of cultivation, and I am about trying it as an enclosure for a yard and lots.

I mentioned to you, in a letter last winter, I had a thought of attempting a translation of Say's Political Economy. My health is now improving; but being still very much reduced by a severe disease of some months' continuance, I shall be unable to enter upon such an undertaking in the course of this summer or fall. I perceive, from the newspapers, that a catechism of Political Economy, by Say, has been translated into English; and this being a later work, I presume his former work must also have been translated. I have sent to England for it, and shall ascertain whether I am correct by the month of December.

I am appointed one of the members of a committee of three persons, to enquire and report to the court of this county, such information as we may be able to procure, to enable them to carry into successful execution the act of the last Assembly, directing an accurate chart of each county in the State to be taken. Could you do me the favor to recommend a man that ought to be employed on such an occasion? There is not one in this county. I have thought it would be well for several counties to join in the employment of the same man, so as to unite economy and uniformity in the execution of the maps. We are to make our report to the court of this county on the fourth Monday of August. If we cannot do better, I shall recommend it to the court to adopt the map of this county made in the year 1809, by the late Capt. Varnum,* son of the General, in order to ascertain the most convenient point for the establishment of the public buildings.

I am, dear sir,

With great respect and regard, yours,

JOSEPH C. CABELL.

Mr. Jefferson.

XXXIV.

T. J. TO J. C. C.

MONTICELLO, July 13, 1816.

DEAR SIR,—I thank you for Maine's recipe for preparing the haw, inclosed in your favor of the 4th. I really thought it lost with him, and that the publication of it would be a public benefit. I do not know that his hedge thorn is to be found wild but in the neighborhood of Washington. He chose it, I think, for its beauty. I have extensive hedges of it, which I have too much neglected. The parts well grown appear rather weak against cattle; yet, when full grown, will probably be sufficient. He proposed to keep out hogs by a couple of rails passed along the bottom, and, I think, it will be sufficient: and that, should the upper part prove too weak for very strong cattle, a pole run horizontally through will bind them together, and make them sufficient. Col. Randolph thinks the cockspur hawthorn (our common one) would be preferable as being stronger. My grandson, Jefferson Randolph, found one common, about Willis's mountains, which he thinks eminently preferable to all others. The Pyracanthus which I got from Maine is a beautiful plant, but not fit for a hedge. He tried the honey locust, meaning to keep it down by the shears; but I thought it too straggling. The holly certainly will not do

---

* Capt. Varnum had emigrated from New England to Amherst county, and had acted as county surveyor.

with us, because all but impossible to make live in our climate. I have one tree 44 years old, not yet taller than a hedge should be. Of the cedar I have no experience, but of the difficulty of either transplanting it or raising it from the berry. On the whole, I think nothing comparable with the thorn, and that they may be made to answer perfectly, with the aids I have mentioned.

I am sorry you hesitate about the translation of Say's Political Economy. I have not supposed his Catechism was a work of note, but rather an occasional criticism on the English practices; but I have not seen it, and I think you should not wait for it.

I think your idea a good one of employing a single person for half a dozen counties. I am sure the State does not furnish one for every county, qualified and willing. There is a son of Capt. W. D. Meriwether, in this county, who has had a collegiate education, and possesses geometry enough for this operation. He has expressed a willingness to undertake our county, and perhaps would yours, for a sufficient allowance; but what may be deemed a competent reward I know not, nor whether our court will employ Mr. Meriwether or the county surveyor. If the county surveyors are generally employed, the work will not be worth a copper, as few of them know any thing of geometry, but depend altogether on plotting. I salute you with great friendship and respect.

TH: JEFFERSON.

P. S. Col. Randolph tells me he has repeatedly heard Mr. Correa say that our cockspur hawthorn (crataegus crux galli) was the best for hedges he had ever met with.

XXXV.

T. J. TO J. C. C.

You have sometimes thought my political ramblings worth the time and trouble of reading. I enclose you a letter lately written on a subject now much agitated in our State.* I will ask the favor of its early return by mail, as I have no other copy. I salute you with friendship and respect.

JULY 14, 1816.

XXXVI.

J. C. C. TO T. J.

EDGEWOOD, 4th August, 1816.

DEAR SIR,—I beg you to accept my sincere thanks for your favor of the 13th inst., and for the communication of the accompanying letter, on the propriety of calling a convention to amend the Constitution of Virginia. The information you give me on the subject of hedges is very acceptable; it will exempt me from the mortification of failures in experiments that extend through so large a portion of human life. I have about half a bushel of holly seed now lying in my garden, undergoing the process of preparation for the seed-bed; but since the receipt of your letter, I have determined to throw them aside, or to make very small use of them. I shall direct my future attempts in this line towards the thorn, and to the variety you recommend, unless I should be able to procure that of which Mr. Jefferson Randolph speaks so highly,

---

* This was probably the letter to Samuel Kercheval, reviewing the then Constitution of Virginia, and suggesting the principles on which it should be revised. It may be found in his writings, IV. 285.

for which purpose I have sent him the enclosed letter of enquiry. I presume he alludes to a thorn in the old fields about Hendrick's tavern, the strength and density of which have frequently been mentioned to me by gentlemen who had been traveling that way. It is not certain, although it is probable, that Maine's recipe will succeed with all the different thorns.

I have written to Mr. Meriwether on the subject of surveying this county. The law authorizing a chart of the State passed hastily through both Houses of Assembly, at the close of the session, and is defective. I regret that the county courts have anything to do with the business. For though some may make judicious contracts, I am confident many of them will employ incompetent agents, and the map will be a half-formed, party-colored affair. In my opinion, it would be a commendable course if the executive would defer acting on any of the contracts till the meeting of the Assembly, when we might amend the law, by appointing a Surveyor General, who, with the aid of deputies chosen by himself, under proper checks, would make a map of which the State might justly be proud. If, as is to be apprehended, this well-intended scheme should be spoilt in the execution, the people, already dissatisfied with so large an appropriation for such an object, may, in a fit of disgust, insist on the repeal of the law for internal improvement. The difficulties which must by this time have been encountered, in every county of the State, in the attempt to procure suitable agents, have probably prepared the public mind for such an exercise of power on the part of the executive. I have written nothing on this subject, as any suggestions of mine would be entitled to but little attention on the part of the executive; but I wish some gentleman possessing the confidence of the executive would take the subject in hand.

I am extremely obliged to you for the perusal of your letter on the State Constitution. Many of the views are new; some in conflict with my previously formed opinions, and all, in the highest degree, interesting. I wish this letter could have fallen into my hands some years ago. Wishing to give to its various topics the fullest consideration,* I have taken the liberty to retain a copy, and unless you should forbid it, I will take the further liberty of shewing it to a few of my friends, who will not disregard the injunctions contained in a certain part of the letter.

* * * * *

I enclose, for the perusal of yourself and Col. Randolph, two interesting papers relative to the two Banks in Virginia, which were communicated to the last Assembly. I will thank you for the return of them by the 1st October.

Dr. Smith has adopted the Review of Montesquieu as the text-book on the Principles of Government, for the students of William & Mary. He will adopt either Say or Tracy on Political Economy, as the one or the other may appear best, when the latter comes out. We hear nothing of it. Owing to the weak state of my health, I shall be tardy about the translation of Say you recommend me to undertake. Perhaps I shall not be competent; but I will make the attempt as soon as my health will permit.

I am, dear sir,

Most respectfully and truly yours,

JOSEPH C. CABELL.

Mr. Jefferson.

---

* With the general tenor of that letter, Mr. Cabell, on full reflection, did not concur, but opposed the call of a convention. When this was determined on, in a speech addressed to the Senate, and which appeared in the Richmond Whig of March 6th, 1829, he urged the importance of adhering to the "Mixed Basis" of property and persons, in apportioning the districts from which the delegates to such convention were to be chosen. Several arguments, afterwards used in convention, appear to have been anticipated in this speech.

XXXVII.

T. J. TO J. C. C.

MONTICELLO, September 3, 1816.

DEAR SIR,—I am afraid I have kept your papers longer than you expected. Mr. Randolph's absence, till within these two days, has been the cause of it. They are valuable documents, and are now returned. With respect to the copy of my letter, I know it is safe in your hands, and I rely on your effectual care that it be kept out of the public papers.

Affectionately yours,

TH: JEFFERSON.

Joseph C. Cabell, Esq.

XXXVIII.

T. J. TO J. C. C.

MONTICELLO, January 1, 1817.

DEAR SIR,—A member of a family to which I have been much attached by long intimacies, solicits my asking the attention of some of my friends to his petition before the Legislature. He is the Viscount Barziza, youngest of two sons of Count Barziza, of Venice, by the only daughter and heiress of the late Mrs. Paradise, who was the daughter of Col. Philip Ludwell, proprietor of Greenspring, where she was born. Mr. Paradise,* her husband, was a naturalized citizen. Their grand-children petition for the maternal estate; and, as the rights of man do not depend on the geography of his birth, I hope they will obtain it. It is to this petition I solicit your attention; and that you will procure to be done in it what you think right.

---

* Something farther concerning this gentleman appears in a letter of Mr. Jefferson to Mr. Madison, written from Paris in 1786. Writings, II. 7.

There was a petition from Capt. Meriwether and others for the establishment of a turnpike from Rockfish Gap to Moore's Ford, designed to fix the passage of that road at Moore's Ford, to parry a process now in court to substitute a better ford and road. We counter-petitioned. Should this matter come up to your House, the counter-petition will inform you accurately of the circumstances of the case, in which I am sure you will do what is right, as well from a principle of justice as of regard for

Yours affectionately,

TH: JEFFERSON.

Mr. Cabell.

XXXIX.

J. C. C. TO T. J.

RICHMOND, 12th January, 1817.

DEAR SIR,—Your favor of 1st inst. is now before me. With the nature and object of the petition you allude to, I was already acquainted, from having received an explanatory letter from your grandson, covering a copy of the remonstrance. I had also conversed as well with him as with Mr. Maury. I advised Mr. Maury, without delay, to have an interview with his colleague, and to endeavor to obtain his co-operation. He took this course, and his colleague yielded a ready assent to the justice of the remonstrance. Very soon after this, Mr. Maury became ill, and for some time has not left his room. During this interval, his colleague has changed sides, and prepared the select committee for a report favorable to the petition. But at the date of my last enquiry, the subject was suspended till Mr. Maury's return to the House; when I expect he will be able to procure the rejection of the petition, or at least the modification you desire. Should it come to the Senate, you may be assured of my endeavors to have the bill altered in the manner you wish, which appears to me entirely conformable to reason and justice.

Should Count Barziza's petition succeed in the House of Delegates, I will not fail to pay every attention in my power to it, when it comes to the Senate.

Dr. Smith has received information that Say's Treatise on Political Economy has been translated into English. He shortly expects a copy from England. Under these circumstances, I consider myself absolved from my promise to you.

I imagine you would be pleased to see a copy of the bank bill which has recently passed the House of Delegates; and I accordingly enclose one. This bill is now under the consideration of a committee of the Senate, consisting of the four members from beyond the Ridge, and the senator from Loudoun. I think it will be much altered in the Senate, and perhaps it will fail entirely in the end. You will perceive that the part respecting the literary fund merely gives banking powers to the *present literary fund*, and in no other respect adds to the fund. The late Governor's original scheme of augmenting the fund to $2,000,000, by an addition of 6 per cent. stock, to be created by the Commonwealth, and of giving banking powers to the whole, has been defeated. This bill has engrossed nearly the whole attention of the Assembly since our meeting. It has not yet been accompanied in its progress by symptoms of great exasperation; but should it fail, as I think is probable, except as to a few Western banks, there will be much heat and violence. The petition from Port Royal is written by Col. Taylor.

I never received, until within the last few days, the late Governor's letter of 18th October, appointing me one of the visitors of the Central College. I shall, at all times, be ready to attend to any business to which the appointment may give rise. I fear it will be difficult, if not impracticable, to procure money for that institution. The prevailing opinion seems to be, to establish schools first, and colleges afterwards. Besides, when I was at Staunton, the very spot where the University was to be placed was pointed out to me. And should there be a bank at Staunton, you may expect to hear it called the *Central* Bank.

I am, dear sir, faithfully yours,

JOSEPH C. CABELL.

Mr. Jefferson.

XL.

J. C. C. TO T. J.

RICHMOND, 9th February, 1817.

DEAR SIR,—The petition of Count Barziza was rejected some time past in the House of Delegates.

I have kept a watchful eye on the turnpike bill to which you desired me to attend. Mr. Thweatt* has shown a very friendly anxiety on the occasion. I spoke to several of my friends in the House of Delegates, to co-operate with him. Mr. Maury has been ill nearly the whole of the session. But an agreement has been entered into by all the members of the House of Delegates who feel an interest in this subject, that when the bill shall have been read a second or third time, it shall be laid on the table in that house, and there remain. The object is to let the matter lie over till another session. This, I believe, will be agreeable to you.

I had some part in hewing down the mammoth bank bill sent us from the House of Delegates. In the share I bore in the discussion in the Senate, I took occasion to state the saving to the nation by the substitution of bank-paper for specie, and used your own calculation, referring to *anonymous* authority. It appeared to make a considerable impression.

Mr. Rives lately came on from Washington, and brings me the agreeable information, that Mr. Milligan will have Tracy's

---

* Mr. Archibald Thweatt, delegate from Chesterfield.

Political Economy ready for delivery in a month from this time.

I am, dear sir, most respectfully and truly yours,

JOSEPH C. CABELL.

Mr. Jefferson.

XLI.

J. C. C. TO T. J.

RICHMOND, 19th February, 1817.

DEAR SIR,—The bill respecting the turnpike from Rockfish Gap was this day postponed indefinitely in the House of Delegates. * * *, as I am informed by Mr. Thweatt, did every thing in his power to push the bill through the House, after having consented to lay it on the table for the balance of the session.

The bill for taking the sense of the people as to the expediency of calling a Convention, was rejected in the Senate. The bill for equalizing the Senatorial districts and the land tax has since passed. I was an advocate for this last bill, and used the first bill reported by yourself, Mr. Pendleton and Mr. Wythe, in the year 1779, to prove that we had the constitutional power to alter the classes.

The University bill is now under consideration in the Senate. I cannot predict its fate. It comes to us, however, at a most inauspicious period, when the members are impatient to break up and go home.

I am, dear sir, very truly yours,

JOSEPH C. CABELL.

Mr. Jefferson.

XLII.

J. C. C. TO T. J.

EDGEWOOD, 30th March, 1817.

DEAR SIR,—I have had a good hunt among my papers for Maine's recipe for the preparation of haws; and at length, after almost despairing, have found it in the midst of a small volume of extracts from Brown's Rural Affairs. I now send it to you, agreeably to your desire.

I am, dear sir, very respectfully and truly yours,

JOSEPH C. CABELL.

XLIII.

J. C. C. TO T. J.

BREMO, 23d April, 1817.

DEAR SIR,—I arrived at this place yesterday evening, on my return home from the election in Goochland. Gen. Cocke informs me that he met you at Enniscorthy as you were going to Bedford, and that he learned from you that the meeting which you proposed of the Visitors of the Central College was intended to be on the day fixed in the law for the general meeting in the spring, viz: on the first day of the Albemarle Superior Court, which will be on 13th of May. At the time of our last conversation on this subject, at Monticello, I understood that our meeting would take place on the day after the next Albemarle Inferior Court, which would be the 6th of May. I remember that Gen. Cocke observed, that the proposed meeting would occur on the very day fixed by the law for the first general meeting; and supposing he was accurate, I did not refer to the act. Having made arrangements to go to Williamsburg and Lancaster county immediately after the last election in the Senatorial district, which will be on the 28th inst., it was very inconvenient for me to postpone my departure till 6th of May, but as you seemed desirous for me to remain, I reluctantly consented. I then made my arrangements for going down the country on 6th May. It is with sincere regret that I inform you that it will be out of my power to attend on 13th. I will not trouble you with the various reasons which will prevent my attendance, but will content myself with observing, that Gen. Cocke considers me as entirely excusable; and, under these circumstances, I hope you will excuse my absence. The only case in which my presence could be of any importance would be to secure a meeting. But of the attendance of four members I hope there can be no doubt. Gen. Cocke will see Maj. Watson between this and the day of meeting, and correct the information I lately gave him as to the 6th May. And as Mr. Madison is now at home, and has promised to perform the duties of a Visitor, I presume there can be no doubt of his attendance. I beg you to be assured that no ordinary state of affairs should prevent my faithful attention to this business; and of this assurance I hope to furnish a proof in my future punctuality.

I remain, dear sir,

Most respectfully and faithfully yours,

JOSEPH C. CABELL.

Mr. Jefferson.

XLIV.

J. C. C. TO T. J.

EDGEWOOD, 18th August, 1817.

DEAR SIR,—I now do myself the pleasure to enclose you the list of English books sold by Barrois at Paris, agreeably to my promise to you at Mr. Madison's. Upon examination, I find there are but few works which you would probably wish to purchase. You would oblige me by the return of the catalogue at some future day, as I shall wish to make use of it from time to time. But I shall not want it for a good while.

I have sent subscription papers, enclosed in letters of explanation, to the following persons in the following counties and places: Campbell, Col. Wm. J. Lewis; Lynchburg, Dr. Geo. Cabell; Amherst, Roderick M'Cullock, Edm'd Winston, Rob't Walker, John Camm, Thos. Eubank, Sterling Claiborne, Hill Carter and David S. Garland; Nelson, Rob't Rives and Spottswood Garland; Powhatan, Wm. Pope; Winchester, Henry St. George Tucker; Stafford, William Brent; Lancaster, Ellyson Currie. It occurred to me, after we separated, that it was very doubtful whether the counties of the Northern Neck would contribute anything. It seemed to be the wish of yourself and Mr. Madison, and the general understanding, that except in the counties where a local interest would operate, the subscription papers should not be exhibited without a well grounded hope of success. The counties of the Northern Neck are not, in my view, locally connected with Albemarle in regard to the Central College, and having suffered excessively by the war, will probably have but little, if any, money to spare. Yet there are some liberal men in those counties, particularly towards Fredericksburg. I have, therefore, adopted a course somewhat different from the one I promised, and hope it will be satisfactory to you and the other gentlemen. I wrote to Mr. Currie, of Lancaster, enclosing him a subscription paper, and requesting him to shew it to some of the most liberal men in the counties of Lancaster, Northumberland, Westmoreland, and Richmond; to advise with them on the subject; and, if it should be their opinion that the measure would not meet with a decent support in that quarter, not to exhibit the paper publicly. In the opposite event, I desired him to give it currency and procure subscribers. To Mr. William Brent, of Stafford, I wrote to the same effect, in regard to the counties of Stafford, Fairfax, and King George. These are liberal, enlightened and active young men, with whom I am intimately acquainted, and are as suitable persons as any that could have been addressed on this occasion.

I fear the subscription in this county, Amherst and Campbell will be very small. I shall attend Nelson court on Monday, with the view of doing every thing in my power to promote it.

It appeared to be the opinion of so many of my friends that the publication of the catalogue of subscribers would be attended with no advantage, that I have declined, for the present, to trouble Mr. Ritchie with a request to that effect. Should it be the opinion of yourself and the other Visitors, when we meet in September, that such publication would be advantageous, I will then cause it to take place.

A genteel, sensible young man passed here yesterday, on his way from the upper part of the Northern Neck. He had called at the houses of many of the best informed people in the course of his journey; and heard every where the Central College spoken of in very high terms.

I am very happy to hear that the Albemarle subscription already amounts to nearly $30,000.

On my return from Mr. Madison's, I found my mother had relapsed. The fever continued for four weeks, at the end of which, all remedies proving unsuccessful, we had the affliction to lose her.

I remain, dear sir, very sincerely yours,

JOSEPH C. CABELL.

P. S. I have just copied your manuscript on meteorological* subjects, in which you have condensed a vast variety of most instructive and amusing information. It is astonishing how you could find time, in the midst of your other engagements, to make such a prodigious number of observations. I enclose the paper to Mr. Madson, by to-day's mail.

---

* Quere de hoc?

XLV.

T. J. TO J. C. C.

Poplar Forest,* September 9, 1817.

Dear Sir,—I promised you that I would put into the form of a bill my plan of establishing the elementary schools, without taking a cent from the literary fund. I have had leisure at this place to do this, and now send you the result. If twelve or fifteen hundred schools are to be placed under one general administration, an attention so divided will amount to a dereliction of them to themselves. It is surely better, then, to place each school at once under the care of those most interested in its conduct. In this way the literary fund is left untouched to complete at once the whole system of education, by establishing a college in every district of about eighty miles square, for the second grade cf education, to wit: languages, ancient and modern, and for the third grade a single university, in which the sciences shall be taught in their highest degree.

I should apologise, perhaps, for the style of this bill. I dislike the verbose and intricate style of the modern English statutes, and in our Revised Code I endeavored to restore it to the simple one of the ancient statutes, in such original bills as I drew in that work. I suppose the reformation has not been acceptable, as it has been little followed. You, however, can easily correct this bill to the taste of my brother lawyers, by making every other word a "said" or "aforesaid," and saying every thing two or three times over, so as that nobody but we of the craft can untwist the diction, and find out what it means; and that, too, not so plainly but that we may conscientiously divide, one-half on each side. Mend it, therefore, in form and substance to the orthodox taste, and make it what it should be;

* Mr. Jefferson's seat in Bedford county.

or, if you think it radically wrong, try something else, and let us make a beginning in some way, no matter how wrong; experience will amend it as we go along, and make it effectual in the end.

I shall see you, of course, at our stated visitation, and hope all the gentlemen will consider Monticello as the rendezvous of the preceding day or evening.

I salute you with friendship and respect.

TH: JEFFERSON.

Mr. Cabell.

[The bill referred to will be found in the Appendix.]

XLVI.

T. J. TO J. C. C.

POPLAR FOREST, September 10, 1817.

DEAR SIR,—I omitted, in my letter of yesterday, to return Barrois' catalogue, with thanks for the use of it. I omitted, also, to observe that it would be better that the bill for the elementary schools should not be known as coming from me. Not knowing the present pulse of the public, should there be any thing unpalatable in it, it may injure our college, as coming from one of its visitors. I wish it to be understood, also, that I do not intermeddle with public affairs. It is my duty, and equally my wish, to leave them to those who are to feel the benefits and burthens of measures. The interest I feel in the system of education and wards, has seduced me into the part I have taken as to them, and still attaches me to their success. I sent subscription papers, with a letter of explanation, to the counties allotted to me. I have given one to Charles Johnson, who is zealous, and I shall send one to Christopher Clarke on his return home; but I doubt their effect. The difficulty, I find, is to eradicate the idea that it is a local thing, a mere Albemarle academy. I endeavor to convince them it is a general Seminary of the Sciences meant for the use of the State. In this view all approve of the situation, and rally to the object. But time seems necessary to plant this idea firmly in their minds. Dr. Knox* has retired from business, and I have written to Cooper.

Affectionately, yours,

TH: JEFFERSON.

Mr. Cabell.

XLVII.

J. C. C. TO T. J.

CHARLOTTESVILLE, 7th October, 1817.

DEAR SIR,—Your note of this morning has this moment been received by General Cocke and myself. The association for an Agricultural Society† adjourned yesterday evening to 11 o'clock this day. Judge Stewart has been engaged to give an opportunity to the members of the bar to attend. If we let slip this occasion, perhaps it will be impossible to bring the gentlemen together a second time. Will you have the goodness, therefore, to excuse General Cocke and myself, if we do not come precisely at the hour you designate, but at 12 or 1? And we further ask the kindness of you to make this explanation to the President and Mr. Madison. No weather will stop us, the moment our existing appointment shall have been attended to. Mr. Watson went to Mr. Minor's last evening, and was to return here at 10 this morning; but it is probable he will not turn out in this weather.

I am, dear sir, most truly yours,

JOSEPH C. CABELL.

Mr. Jefferson.

---

* Of Baltimore, who had been invited to the Chair of Languages in the proposed Central College. See Appendix E.

† This was the Agricultural Society of Albemarle, so eminently useful in its day, for which Mr. Cabell had been required to prepare a Constitution. Mr. Madison was its first President. It was the first *district* association of the kind in Virginia, and though nominally local in its objects, the benefit of its example and instructions pervaded the State.

XLVIII.

J. C. C. TO T. J.

EDGEWOOD, 14th October, 1817.

DEAR SIR,—I thank you for the use of the enclosed papers, which I have copied and now commit to the first mail after my return to this place. I shall endeavor to make myself master as well of your plan for schools, as of that for colleges, before the period, at which those subjects will be taken up, in the House of Delegates. If you could conveniently spare the time, I think it would be of great benefit to the cause, were you to prepare bills for the College and University, or to enlarge the School bill and include them in it.* In laying the State off into Districts for Colleges, you seem to have had chief regard to territorial extent. There are powerful masses of interest accumulated *already* at particular points in the State—as, for example, at some of the Colleges and towns. Would it not be well to consult these in the arrangement of the collegiate districts, in order to obtain success?† I inadvertently left my copy of the members of the Cincinnati on the table where I made it at Monticello. Should you have found it, I will be thankful to you to keep it till I have the pleasure of seeing you again. I was at Buckingham court on yesterday. Mr. Eppes was there, endeavoring to procure subscribers for the Central College. But few persons seemed disposed to subscribe. Be so good as to mention to Colonel Randolph, that I fear the time allowed for us to prepare a report for the Agricultural Society is entirely too short, and that I regret exceedingly that I was instrumental in fixing the

---

* See Appendix, G.

† The suggestion here thrown out is that in the belief of whose expediency Mr. C. ultimately settled, though there were, for a long season, numerous obstacles to its fulfillment, and which have not yet been wholly overcome.

period. Having qualified as my mother's executor, and having in the course of the next fortnight to adjust my affairs, for an absence of four or five months from home, I shall be unable to prepare anything, and shall rely upon himself and General Cocke. I have borrowed of Mr. Patterson forty-five volumes of Young's Annals. There are valuable hints scattered up and down throughout this voluminous work. But it would take one or two months to search over these numerous pages, and condense the applicable and valuable thoughts into such method as would suit our purposes. I shall collect all the information from them that I possibly can, in the midst of many avocations that now press upon me; and attend at the time appointed. Perhaps it would be well to have a meeting of the committee at the November court, and of the Society at the December court, so as to give further time, with the advantages of an intermediate conference among the members of the committee. I suggest this merely for his consideration. Should he be ready to report at November court, that day would be more convenient, on account of the season and other circumstances. Two other courses might be adopted. Either to report in part, and ask time till the Spring meeting to conclude it, or to make no report at all, at the next meeting, and ask time to digest and mature one. I would vote for either of these three courses, as may be most agreeable to Colonel Randolph.

I remain, dear sir,

Most respectfully and faithfully yours,

JOS. C. CABELL.

Mr. Jefferson.

XLIX.

T. J. TO J. C. C.

MONTICELLO, October 24, 1817.

DEAR SIR,—Yours of the 14th came to hand two days ago. Soon after you left us, I received the pamphlet you were so kind as to have directed to me, containing several papers on the establishment of a system of education. A serious perusal of the bill* for that purpose, convinced me, that unless something less extravagant could be devised, the whole undertaking must fail. The primary schools alone on that plan would exhaust the whole funds, the colleges as much more, and an university would never come into question. However slow and painful the operation of writing is become from a stiffening wrist, and however deadly my aversion to the writing table, I determined to try whether I could not contrive a plan more within the compass of our funds. I send you the result brought into a single bill,† lest by bringing it on by detachment some of the parts might be lost. You ask if we should not associate with it the petty academies and colleges spread over the State, in order to engage their interest? Why should we? For their funds? They have none. Scarcely any of them have funds to keep their buildings in repair. They depend on what they get from their students. Aggregated to our regular system, they would make it like the image of brass and clay, substances which can never amalgamate. They would only embarrass, and render our colleges impracticable. I have always found it best never to permit a rational plan to be marred by botching. You would lose on the vote more honest friends than you would reconcile dishonest enemies, under which term I include those who would sacrifice the public good to a local interest. However, take it, and make of it what you can, if worth anything. Communicate it, also, to Mr. Rives, if you please. I meddle no more with it. There is a time to retire from labor, and that time is come with me. It is a duty, as well as the strongest of my desires to relinquish to younger hands the government of our bark, and resign myself, as I do willingly, to their care. Our Central College gives me more employment than I am equal to. The dilatoriness of the workmen gives me constant trouble.

* Mr. Mercer's. † See Appendix G.

It has already brought into doubt the completion this year of the building begun, which obliges me to be with them every other day. I follow it up from a sense of the impression which will be made on the Legislature by the prospect of its immediate operation. The walls should be done by our next court, but they will not, by a great deal. We hope to see you then. En attendant, I salute you with friendship and respect.

TH: JEFFERSON.

Joseph C. Cabell, Esq.

P. S. I drew a plan of a college in its dormitories, such as the bill calls for, to demonstrate that it will not cost more than the sum allotted.

L.

J. C. C. TO T. J.

RICHMOND, 3d December, 1817.

DEAR SIR,—The enclosed subscriptions to the funds of the college, by Mr. Tucker and Mr. Coalter,* are made by those gentlemen to demonstrate their favorable opinion of the institution, and friendly regard to those who have its management entrusted to their care.

Having been exposed five hours on the water, in going down the Rappahannock from Urbanna, and several in returning, an inflammation arose on one of my hips, which caused me to ride in great pain from that place to Richmond; and would have prevented me from arriving on the first day of the session, but for the politeness of two members of the House of Delegates, who alternately exchanged a seat in their carriages for my horse.

The Senate will adjourn in a few days, as usual, till the Christmas holidays are over; and during that interval I shall

---

* Judge Coalter of the Court of Appeals.

go down to Williamsburg in order to accompany my wife back to this place. But I shall not leave town till I have done every thing I possibly can towards the furtherance of the interests of the College. I am now, every day, engaged in deliberation and consultation upon that subject. I have examined your bill very carefully, and am shewing it to all such, both in and out of the Assembly, as I think ought to see it, before the subject is taken up in the House. I am of opinion, that your plan of the primary schools is much the best I have yet heard of; but I fear great difficulties will arise out of the sparseness of the population of the country.* Such appear to be the impressions of those who have seen it. But the bill is read with great admiration and pleasure by every one. These are first impressions. Rest assured, the subject will be turned over and over, and viewed on every side by the ablest men in Richmond, very many times, before the session closes. My wish is to produce, if possible, an agreement among the intelligent men, as to what ought to be attempted, and then to move in concert. But even this, I assure you, is very difficult; for there are almost as many opinions as there are members. If anything will unite us it will be your bill. The * * and the * * will probably exert all their influence to defeat the views of the Central College. Already I hear those interests are operating among the members of * * to our injury. The [Cincinnati] Society will meet on Monday. From what I learn from Judge Brooke and Major Quarles, a majority will be opposed to the plan of altering their former conditional resolution in favor of the Washington Academy. Added to these hostile interests, the friends of the Washington Academy are using great exertions to defeat the claims of the Central College. I hear of no diversion on the side of William & Mary. The friends of that institution appear to pursue a quiet, liberal course. If the general system should fail, I

* This has continued to be the chief obstacle to the success of primary education in Virginia.

trust, we shall be able to procure an appropriation for the Central College; were my abilities to convince and persuade proportionate to my zeal, success would not be wanting. A situation in the other House would be much better than the one I occupy; but I shall do every thing in the case, that lies within the compass of my limited means. Judge Brooke is very friendly to our cause. I am happy, also, to inform you that two members of standing, in the Senate, Col. Green, of Fredericksburg, and Mr. Hoomes, of King and Queen, who opposed the University bill of the last session, will advocate an appropriation to the Central College. It is very uncertain, at this time, what shape the subject will assume, or what will be the event of the proceedings, in the House of Delegates. I am informed a strong party in that body are in favor of the abolition of the Literary Fund.

I am, dear sir,

With great respect, very sincerely, yours,

JOSEPH C. CABELL.

Mr. Jefferson.

P. S. Mr. Watts has assured me, that he would advocate an appropriation to the Central College. Mr. Johnson has not arrived.

LI.

T. J. TO J. C. C.

POPLAR FOREST, December 18, 1817.

DEAR SIR,—I have been detained a month by my affairs here, but shall depart in three days, and eat my Christmas dinner at Monticello. I expect to find there the returns of our subscription papers, and I hope, the donation of the Cincinnati. These will enable me to make the report to the Governor which our Board determined on. It will have to go the rounds of their residences for their amendments and signatures; for this I will send an express, and not lose a day in sending it to you, open for your consideration and signature, then to be sealed and delivered to the Governor. I think you had better keep back the general plan till this report is made, as I am persuaded it will give a lift to that. I congratulate you on a letter I have just received from Dr. Cooper, engaging himself for our physiological and law schools. Pray drop me a line when any vote is passed which furnishes an indication of the success or failure of the general plan. I have only this single anxiety in this world. It is a bantling of forty years' birth and nursing, and if I can once see it on its legs, I will sing with sincerity and pleasure my *nunc dimittas*. My calculation is, that you will hear from me by the 10th of January.

Affectionately yours,

TH: JEFFERSON.

Mr. Cabell.

LII.

T. J. TO J. C. C.

POPLAR FOREST, December 19, 1817.

DEAR SIR,—I wrote to you yesterday morning, and put the letter myself into the post-office of Lynchburg, to which place I went to endeavor to engage bricklayers for our work the next season. I could not do it. They asked $15 a thousand for place brick and sand-stock brick work, and the double for the oil stock brick. They rose from $12 to $15 on the extraordinary price of corn a year or two past, and there is a struggle here at present to bring them down to 12 or $13. This is depending. I agreed, provisionally, with Brown (the most to be depended on of any) to give him what shall be given for similar work in Lynchburg the ensuing season, taking time to consult my colleagues. In the mean time, I think it possible we might get undertakers from Richmond for so large a job as three or four hundred thousand bricks. This I must get you to enquire into and give me the promptest answer you can. Are there in Richmond bricklayers of the first degree of skill? At what prices do they do the very best work? Will a responsible one engage to finish the half our work by mid-summer, the other half by the first of October? Our walls are generally one and a half brick thick—the whole to be grouted, not a single sammel brick, and but two bats to be used for every nine whole bricks. The front wall to be oil stock brick—the other outer walls sand stock—mortar one-third lime, two-thirds pure sand, without any mixture of mould. The work to be done as well as the very best in Richmond or Lynchburg. If you can make a provisional bargain with an undertaker to be depended on, taking only time for the approbation of the Visitors, this will give us choice between Brown and him. But this must be immediate, as I must answer Brown shortly. Pray make a business of it; turn out immediately, make such a bargain if you can, and inform me immediately, that I may fix the one or the other as shall be best.

Yours affectionately,

TH: JEFFERSON.

P. S. Sand is two miles off, and lime nine or ten. Its price at the quarry, 1s.

LIII.

J. C. C. TO T. J.

RICHMOND, 29th December, 1817.

DEAR SIR,—I arrived in town last evening, and received this morning at the post-office your two letters of 18th and 19th inst., which now lie before me. Before I reply to them, I will go back to circumstances that preceded their arrival. I presume you have reached Monticello, and have received my last letter from this place, touching our prospects with the Cincinnati and the General Assembly. Shortly after the date of that letter, the members of the Cincinnati, who appeared in Richmond, formed a meeting, and determined that they would not disturb the former conditional appropriation of their funds in favor of the Washington College. The meeting was but thinly attended; and I was informed that a pretty general impression among the members was that the funds ought not to be finally disposed of by so small a portion of the body, and that the question as to the ultimate appropriation ought to be deferred till a more full assemblage could be had; and that notice would be given to all the members to appear at a general meeting to be held in the course of the next year. A majority of the members present at the last meeting were opposed to the Central College and in favor of the Washington College; and from all I could hear, I am led to believe that a majority of the absentees would have voted in the same way had they been present. There are too many federalists in the Cincinnati for that body to look with favor on the Central College. Added to the federal interest, we had to contend with * * *, whose influence, I think, from all I could gather, had been all along opposed to the prosperity of that institution. The local friends of the Washington College co-operated of course; and were as much excited as if we had attempted to pull down their college. Should the Central College grow rapidly into distinction, and cast a shade on the surrounding institutions, it is possible, perhaps probable, that the Society of the Cincinnati may yet give us their funds. They would like to have them engrafted on a flourishing seminary, but they feel themselves in some sort committed to the Washington College, and the federal members are under strong political prejudices against yourself, whom they justly regard as the parent of the Central College. * * * * * * *

The plan which I determined to follow in regard to the Assembly was, first to endeavor to procure unity of opinion among the friends of learning, both in and out of the Assembly, and afterwards to aim at unity of action.

I was for some days engaged in conferring with some of the ablest men in Richmond on the subject of your bills; there was but one opinion in regard to the propriety of having an university; a pretty general concurrence as to the expediency of colleges, with some variance as to local situation and number; but a great contrariety as to the practicability and expediency of primary schools, and with respect to the mode of organizing them, if admitted to be practicable and expedient. The inherent and adventitious difficulties attending the subject of the primary schools, formed an insurmountable obstacle to the accomplishment of my object. During this period I determined to communicate only to a select few the bills with which you had entrusted me. I thought amendments might be required, and it would be better to settle upon those amendments before the subject should be taken up in the house. But it gradually became known that I was in possession of the bills, and the enemies of the Central College, who kept a constant watch on my movements, began to scatter about the imputation of intrigue. In this situation, I consulted my friends, who advised me to copy the bills off, with the omission of a few passages, and to enclose them to the Chairman of the Committee of Schools and Colleges in the House of Delegates, with a suitable letter to guard you from any illiberal imputations of interfering in the affairs of the Assembly. Governor Nicholas, Judge Coalter, my brother William, and others, approved the course I took on that occasion. I enclose you a copy of my letter accompanying the bills, as well as of the passages omitted in copying them. Judge Roane and others advised me to leave out the clauses respecting religion; if proper in themselves, they were supposed of a nature to excite prejudices, as coming from you; and they were not considered essential. The clause disqualifying persons unable to read, was deemed too rigorous. The alternative sections respecting the Central College were left out, because it appeared impossible to get a bill for an University through upon any other plan than that of separating the local question from the general question. This course might appear hazardous, and my friends in the upper country, judging of the feelings of the whole people by their own, might deem it an unnecessary concession.

But upon this point, there was not a dissenting voice among our friends here. Should the question of location be decided at this session, I confided in the Senate. Should it be deferred to another session, our claims would grow stronger every day of the interval. The Senate adjourned on the 6th till 29th. I did all I could in conjunction with Mr. Powell, to make the adjournment shorter, but in vain. This modern and improper usage in that body will, before long, I hope, attract public notice. I have never touched a cent of public money for the days of those long adjournments, and annually cause the clerk to make an entry to that effect on the minutes of our proceedings. In this, however, I am singular. I remained in town till the 15th, and then believing that my further stay would produce no benefit, whilst it might be ascribed to improper motives, I withdrew to Williamsburg, and remained there till the 29th. Mr. Scott,* Chairman of the Committee of Schools and Colleges, was in Williamsburg during the holidays, and informed me that at the next meeting of his Committee, after my departure, a member moved the production of the copied bills; whereupon they were exhibited along with my letter, and received favorably by those present. He was instructed to prepare some resolutions expressive of the propriety of appropriating the product of the literary fund towards the endowment of an university, academies, and primary schools, in order to ascertain the sense of the house. But on particular plans no opinions had been formed, and none were intended then to be expressed. Mr. Scott wished to examine the New York and South Carolina laws and sundry papers, which, together with his other duties in the house, would keep back his report for eight or ten days to come. Such was the state of things in regard to this subject on my return to town yesterday evening. You perceive there will be full time for your report to come down. You speak of addressing it to the Governor,

---

* Mr. Robert G. Scott of Richmond.

and not to the Assembly. I approve that course, because it will have the same effect, and look less like interference. The acceptance of Judge Cooper will have a happy effect here and over the country. I really fear, notwithstanding, that this Assembly will do nothing. I know of no one in the House of Delegates qualified, in every respect, to do justice to this subject. That house is greatly altered for the worse. Again, the discordant opinions about the primary schools seem irreconcilable. Nothing is agreed on: all unsettled and uncertain. The very efforts necessary to produce unity of design and action, meet on the threshold the imputation of management and intrigue. One favorable circumstance is, that there seems to be a pretty general impression that the fund should be devoted to literary purposes, and that something should now be done. Another is, that we have some strong men in the city, but out of the Assembly, in our favor. Judge Roane, Judge Brooke, Col. Nicholas and his brother, the editor of the Enquirer, and some others, are in favor of the Central College, and should the question of location come on, will be valuable friends. Most of the leading members of the Senate are on our side. Mr. Johnson has not yet arrived. Mr. Scott confirms Mr. Garrett's account of Mr. Johnson's favorable opinion; and yet Mr. George Tucker, now here, assures me that at the Chancery Court in Lynchburg, he (Mr. J.) was contending for Staunton, as the best site. I expect Johnson would prefer Charlottesville next to Staunton. Efforts have been, and doubtless will be made, to convert this subject into a question between the East and West side of the Blue Ridge. Some of my acquaintance from that country have assured me they will discountenance any such attempt; but my only sure reliance against the effects of such a scheme, is in the Senate.

I enclose a copy of the report of the President and Directors of the Literary Fund. It is supposed that the balance of our claim on the General Government will swell the fund to 12 or 1500,000 dollars.

Judge Roane, Col. Nicholas, and most of the persons with

whom I have conferred, disapprove of your plan of an assessment on the wards; they think neither the people nor their representatives would agree to that mode of taxation; they advise that the moneys should come out of the literary fund, but that your mode of administration should be kept up.

You may rest assured that I shall proceed with all possible dispatch, in procuring and transmiting to you the information you desire in regard to bricklayers in this town. The most of to-morrow I am compelled to be at the banks, as Chairman of the Committee of the Senate.

I will, from time to time, with great pleasure, give you an account of our prospects and proceedings.

Before I conclude, it may be proper to remark, that all liberal men duly appreciate the efforts you are making to advance the literary interests of your country; they speak of those efforts in the highest terms, and thank you for them.

I remain, dear sir,

Faithfully yours,

JOSEPH C. CABELL.

Mr. Jefferson.

Copy of the letter from Joseph C. Cabell to the Chairman of the Committee of Schools and Colleges.

RICHMOND, 13th December, 1817.

DEAR SIR,—You recollect, no doubt, that when you introduced at the last session of the General Assembly, the resolution for publishing the bill "providing for the establishment of primary schools, academies, colleges, and an university," I suggested to you the propriety of amending the resolution, so as to embrace in it other documents which are contained in the pamphlet, printed and distributed by the President and Directors of the Literary Fund.

I then expected that the destination of the literary fund would be decided at the present session of the Legislature; and I thought it would be useful to place in the public view, during the recess, the various schemes of public education which had been proposed, in order to attract attention to the subject, and to draw forth the views and suggestions of men of reflection throughout the State. These objects were stated and explained in the debate which took place in the Senate on the passage of the resolution.

In the course of the last summer I found, from a conversation I had with Mr. Jefferson, that he was of opinion that the primary schools might be provided for on a plan differing from any I had then heard of, and calling for no appropriation from the literary fund. Whereupon I earnestly requested him to commit his ideas to paper, and to throw them into the form of a bill, in order that I might readily avail the State of such of them as might be approved at the approaching session of the Legislature. He was kind enough to comply with my request, and shortly thereafter sent me a bill entitled, "an act for establishing elementary schools."

Subsequent to that period, I had another interview with him, in which I requested him to amplify the bill, and to extend its provisions to colleges and an university. With this request he also complied, and in a short time enclosed me a new and enlarged bill entitled, "a bill for establishing a system of public education." At the same time he sent the plan of a college which had been drawn by him for the purpose of shewing that the building would not cost more than the sum allotted for that purpose in the bill.

I was informed that in arranging the counties into collegiate districts, a leading object with the author was to place every parent in the State within a day's ride of the college of his respective district.

In his letter accompanying the "bill for establishing elementary schools," Mr. Jefferson observed, "I wish it to be understood that I do not intermeddle with public affairs. It is my duty, and equally my wish, to leave them to those who are to feel the benefits and burdens of measures. The interest I feel in the system of education and wards, has seduced me into the part I have taken as to them, and still attaches me to their success."

In a letter accompanying the "bill for establishing a system of public education," he says, "Take it and make of it what you can, if worth anything. I meddle no more with it. There is a time to retire from labor, and that time is come with me. It is a duty, as well as the strongest of my desires, to relinquish to younger hands the government of our bark, and resign myself, as I willingly do, to their care."

On subjects of such importance and difficulty as those embraced in these bills, there will be various opinions. But all that read them must agree that they are drawn with great ability, and throw great light on the subjects to which they relate.

I have brought these papers with me to the seat of government, with the intention of shewing them to the friends of literature and science, under the impression that in so doing I might render a service to the country. I have already exhibited them to several, and promised to shew them to others, in which number is yourself; but having to leave town, I shall be unable to call on the various persons who have asked a perusal of them.

I have, therefore, determined to desire the favor of you to take charge of the two enclosed papers, which are copied from the original bills in my possession, together with the accompanying plan of a college. You will be at liberty to make extracts and to avail yourself of the ideas they contain, in so far as you may think the public welfare might thereby be promoted. And I must also request the favor of you to exhibit them to any member, or to the Committee of Schools and Colleges, if they should be called for; and when you have done with them, to return them to me.

In addition to the preceding papers, I have procured some hints and sketches, on the same subjects, from some enlightened gentlemen of my acquaintance; they were hastily thrown on paper, in a form not intended for publication; but should you feel a desire to see them, they shall be at your service.

I am, dear sir, respectfully yours,

JOSEPH C. CABELL.

Mr. Scott, Chairman of the Committee of Schools and Colleges.

Passages omitted in the copies of the bills furnished Mr. Scott, Chairman of the Committee of Schools and Colleges, session 1817–'18, *by advice of Col. W. C. Nicholas and many others.*

BILL FOR ESTABLISHING ELEMENTARY SCHOOLS.

In the 6th and 7th lines of the first section, the following words, "and not being ministers of the gospel of any denomination."

The note on the same section in these words, "Ministers of the gospel are excluded to avoid jealousy from the other sects, were the public education committed to a particular one; and with the more reason than in the case of their exclusion from the legislative and executive functions."

§ 5, 17th line, after the word schooling, the following words, "and it is declared and enacted that no person unborn or under the age of twelve years, at the passing of this act, and who is *compos mentis*, shall, after the age of fifteen years, be a citizen of this Commonwealth, until he or she can read readily in some tongue, native or acquired."

In the note on § 5, the following words, "A question of some doubt might be raised on the latter part of this section, as to the rights and duties of society towards its members, infant and adult. Is it a right or a duty in society to take care of their infant members, in opposition to the will of their parents? How far does this right and duty extend? to guard the life of the infant, his property, his instruction, his morals? The Roman father was supreme in all these; we draw a line: but where? Public sentiment does not seem to have traced it precisely. Nor is it necessary in the present case. It is better to tolerate the rare instance of a parent refusing to let his child be educated, than to shock the common feelings and ideas by the public asportation and education of the infant against the will of the father. What is proposed here is to remove the objection of expense, by offering education gratis, and to strengthen parental excitement by disfranchisement* of his child while uneducated. Society has certainly a right to disavow him whom they offer, and are not permitted to qualify for the duties of a citizen. If we do not force instruction, let us at least strengthen the motives to receive it when offered."

§ 10, line 3d, after the word *Visitors*, the following words, "but no religious reading, instruction, or exercise, shall be prescribed or practiced inconsistent with the tenets of any religious sect or denomination."

BILL FOR ESTABLISHING A SYSTEM OF PUBLIC EDUCATION.

§ 1, 6th and 7th lines, the following words, "and not being ministers of the gospel."

---

* There are many who still think, that had such a provision been included in our several State Constitutions, it would have proved one of the surest safe-guards of our liberties.

§ 6, from the word *schooling*, in the 2d line, the following words, "And it is declared and enacted, that no person unborn, or under the age of twelve years at the passing of this act, and who is *compos mentis*, shall, after the age of fifteen years, be a citizen of this Commonwealth, until he or she can read readily printed characters in some tongue, native or acquired."

§ 11, from the word *Visitors* to the end of the section, the following words, "but no religious reading, instruction, or exercise, shall be prescribed or practiced inconsistent with the tenets of any religious sect or denomination."

The preamble to, and the 31st, 32d and 33d sections, respecting the Central College.

LIV.

T. J. TO J. C. C.

Monticello, December 31, 1817.

Dear Sir,—Our friend, Gen. Kosciusko, has warmly solicited my attention to the case of M. Poinsot des Essarts, stated in the enclosed papers. He wishes to be informed of the situation of the lands therein described, their quality and value, and whether any and what taxes are due on them. I suppose they must be in what is now Harrison county. Having no acquaintance in that part of the country, and supposing your situation may enable you to engage some member of the one or the other house to take the trouble of making these enquiries, I solicit your assistance to effect it. The motive which may induce us to this trouble must be the same with us all, a willingness to help a fellow-man to procure for him that information which our situation enables us to obtain, and his does not. If the gentleman whom you may engage will be so good as to enclose the information he may obtain to myself immediately, it will shorten delays, and lay me under personal obligations to him.

I have this morning sent to Mr. Madison a draught of the report* I promised you. When returned, I shall have to make out a fair copy, and send it the rounds for signature. You may, therefore, expect it about the last of next week.

Ever and affectionately yours,

TH: JEFFERSON.

Mr. Cabell.

LV.

J. C. C. TO T. J.

RICHMOND, 5th January, 1818.

DEAR SIR,—Your favors of the 18th and 19th ult. were both received at the same time, and had been lying in the post-office of this place some days before my return from Williamsburg. Since their receipt to this time, I have been unusually employed on a joint committee of the two houses of Assembly, and in the Senate. But I lost not a moment in attending to your request respecting the rates of bricklayers in this town. Col. Nicholas, General Preston, and others, to whom I shewed your letter of 19th, referred me to Major Christopher Tompkins, of this place, as an undertaker in the carpenter's line, who could give me correct information in regard to the bricklayers of Richmond. I waited on Major Tompkins, and on shewing him your letter, he assured me that he would, with the utmost pleasure, do anything in his power to promote the welfare of the Central College, having a son whose education he wished to be finished at that place. It was needless, he observed, for me to accompany him; he would go promptly around to all the principal undertakers of brick work in town, and bring me their terms. The enclosed letter presents the result of his enquiries; from which you will per-

---

* The first report of the Rector and Visitors of the Central College. See Appendix, E.

ceive that the rates here are very exorbitant, and that you can not do better than to close with Brown. I believe you may confidently rely on Maj. Tompkins' information. There are some six or eight skillful workmen in Richmond; most of them have families, and all of them prefer working in town; each of them contracts for one million or one million and a half of bricks every year, and has more work offered than he can well attend to. The price of oil stock brick is exactly double of the sand stock. The workman who is willing to come up and make bricks at $2 per M., he being found every thing, is named Night, and is the brother of Night who worked on the College walls in November. He is said to be a better workman. I regret that I am unable to send you a more agreeable answer.

The essays in the Enquirer, by * * *, are certainly from the pen of *****. They discover anything but a commendable spirit, and I am happy to hear they produce little or no effect.

It grieves me to tell you that I think our prospects are by no means flattering in the General Assembly. I shall not relax my small exertions in this noble cause. I hunt assiduously around me for every suggestion towards lessening the difficulties on the branch of the primary schools. The hostile interests, alluded to in my last, have been constantly at work, and I believe they have produced some effect on the House of Delegates. My belief is, that with such a House of Delegates nothing can be done. I begin to cast my eyes over the State in pursuit of suitable persons to come into the next. If I had the co-operation of some four or five men, such as I could describe, every thing could be effected. But I do not entirely despair.

Your letter of 31st, with the papers of Mr. Poinsot des Essarts, arrived this evening. They shall be faithfully attended to.

Mr. William Brent of Fairfax, to whom I wrote in the summer, in regard to the interests of the Central College in the upper counties of the Northern Neck, is now in Richmond; he was from home or would have answered the enquiries at an earlier day. He says nothing can be done in the way of subscription in that quarter. He will subscribe himself and send his sons to the college. His subscription is enclosed. Mr. Currie has sent me similar information as to the lower counties of the Northern Neck. Chancellor Taylor will also subscribe.

I remain, dear sir,

Faithfully yours,

JOSEPH C. CABELL.

Mr. Jefferson.

Letter of Major Tompkins to Joseph C. Cabell enclosed in the foregoing.

RICHMOND, January 4, 1818.

J. C. CABELL, ESQ.

Sir,—Agreeably to my promise, I have availed myself of every opportunity to get the best information respecting the price of brick work, such as your memorandum specified, and the probable chance of getting a suitable person to execute it.

I fear there is no chance to get a man, at least such an one as I would recommend. It appears their prices for such work vary from $17½ to $21. There is a brick maker who says he would go up and make the bricks for $2 per M., (every thing to be found the workmen.)

Although I have not been fortunate enough to serve you materially in the above, I hope that it may be in some way or other. If you think so, please call on me at any time you think proper.

I am respectfully yours,

C. TOMPKINS.

LVI.

JANUARY 6th, 1818.

[The originals of letters LVI. and LVII. have been lost or mislaid. The latter was printed in the Enquirer of February 10, 1818, and is here repeated.]

LVII.

T. J. TO J. C. C.

MONTICELLO, January 14, 1818.

DEAR SIR,—When, on the 6th inst., I was answering yours of December 29, I was so overwhelmed with *letters to be answered,* that I could not take time to notice the objection stated, that it was apprehended that neither the people nor their representatives would agree to the plan of assessment on the wards for the expenses of the ward schools. I suppose that by this is meant the "pecuniary expense of wages to the tutor;" for, as to what the people are to do, or to contribute in kind, every one who knows the situation of our people in the country, knows it will not be felt. The building of the log-houses will employ the laborers of the ward three or four days in every twenty years. The contributions for subsistence, if averaged on the families, would be eight or nine pounds of pork, and half a bushel of corn, for a family of middling circumstances; not more than two days' subsistence of the family and its stock; and less in proportion as it could spare less. There is not a family in the country so poor as to feel this contribution. It must then be the assessment of the pecuniary contribution which is thought so formidable an addition to the property tax we now pay to the State, that neither the people nor their representatives would agree to. Now let us look this objection in the face, and bring it to the unerring test of figures; premising that this pecuniary tax is to be of $150 on a ward.

Not possessing the documents which would give me the numbers to be quoted, correctly to an unit, I shall use round numbers, so near the truth, that, with the further advantage of facilitating our calculations as we go along, they will make no sensible error in the result. I will proceed therefore on the following postulates, and on the ground that there are in the whole State one hundred counties and cities.

	In the whole State.	In every co'ty on an average.
The free white inhabitants of all ages and sexes, at the last census were	600,000	6,000
The number of militia was somewhere about	80,000	800
The number of captain's companies, of 67 each, would be about	1,200	12
Free white inhabitants for every militia company, 600,000÷1,200	500	500
The tax on property paid to the State is nearly - - -	500,000	5,000

Let us then proceed, on these data, to compare the expense of the proposed, and of the existing system of primary schools. I have always supposed that the wards should be so laid off as to comprehend the number of inhabitants necessary to furnish a captain's company of militia. This is before stated at 500 persons of all ages and sexes. From the tables of mortality (Buffon's) we find that where there are 500 persons of all ages and sexes, there will always be 14 in their 10th year, 13 and a fraction in their 11th, and 13 in their 12th year; so that the children of these three years (which are those that ought to be devoted to the elementary schools,) will be a constant number of 40; about enough to occupy one teacher constantly. His wages of \$150, partitioned on these 40, make their teaching cost \$3¾ a piece, annually. If we reckon as many heads of families in a ward as there are militia (as I think we may, the unmarried militia men balancing in numbers, the married and unmarried exempts,) \$150 on 67 heads of families (if levied equally) would be \$2 24 on each. At the same time the property tax on the ward being \$5,000÷12, or \$416, and that again subdivided on 67 heads of families (if it were levied equally) would be \$6 20 on a family of middling circumstances, the tax which it now pays to the State. So that to \$6 20, the present State tax, the school tax would add \$2 24, which is about 36 cents to the dollar, or one-third to the present property tax; and to the whole State would be $150× 1,200 wards, equal to $180,000 of tax added to the present $500,000.

Now let us see what the present primary schools cost us, on the supposition that all the children of 10, 11, and 12 years old are, as they ought to be at school; and, if they are not, so much the worse is the system; for they will be untaught, and their ignorance and vices will, in future life, cost us much dearer in their consequences, than it would have done, in their correction, by a good education.

I am here at a loss to say what is now paid to our English elementary schools, generally through the State. In my own neighborhood, those who formerly received from 20s. to 30s. a scholar, now have from 20 to 30 dollars; and having no other information to go on, I must use my own numbers: the result of which, however, will be easily corrected, and accommodated to the average price through the State, when ascertained; and will yet, I am persuaded, leave abundance of difference between the two systems.

Taking a medium of $25, the 40 pupils in each ward, now cost $1,000 a year, instead of $150, or $15 on a family, instead of $2 24: and the 1,200 wards cost to the whole State $1,200,000 of tax, in addition to the present $500,000, instead of $180,000 only; producing a difference of $1,020,000 in favor of the ward system, more than doubling the present tax, instead of adding one-third only, and should the price of tuition, which I have adopted from that in my own neighborhood, be much above the average through the State, yet no probable correction will bring the two systems near a level.

But take into consideration, also, the important difference, that the $1,200,000 are now paid by the people, as a poll tax, the poor having as many children as the rich, and paying the whole tuition money themselves; whereas, on the proposed ward-levies the poor man would pay in proportion to his hut and peculium only, while the rich would pay on their palaces and principalities. It cannot, then, be that the "people" will not agree to have their tuition tax lightened by levies on the ward, rather than on themselves; and as I little believe that their "representatives" will disagree to it; for even the rich will pay less than they now do. The portion of the $180,000, which, on the ward system, they will pay for the education of the poor, as well as of their own children, will not be as much as they now pay for their own alone.

And will the wealthy individual have no retribution? and what will this be? 1. The peopling his neighborhood with honest, useful, and enlightened citizens, understanding their own rights, and firm in their perpetuation. 2. When his own descendants become poor, which they generally do within three generations, (no law of primogeniture now perpetuating wealth in the same families,) their children will be educated by the then rich; and the little advance he now makes to poverty, while rich himself, will be repaid by the then rich, to his descendants when become poor, and thus give them a chance of rising again. This is a solid consideration, and should go home to the bosom of every parent. This will be seed sown in fertile ground. It is a provision for his family looking to distant times, and far in duration beyond that he has now in hand for them. Let every man count backwards in his own family, and see how many generations he can go, before he comes to the ancestor who made the fortune he now holds. Most will be stopped at the first generation, many at the second, few will reach the third, and not one in the State go beyond the fifth.

I know that there is much prejudice, even among the body of the people, against the expense and even the practicability of a sufficient establishment of elementary schools, but I think it proceeds from vague ideas on a subject they have never brought to the test of facts and figures; but our representatives will fathom its depth, and the people could and would do the same, if the facts and considerations belonging to the subject were presented to their minds, and their subsequent as certainly as their previous approbation, would be secured.

But if the whole expense of the elementary schools, wages, subsistence, and buildings, are to come from the literary fund, and if we are to wait until that fund should be accumulated to the requisite amount, we may justly fear that some one unlucky Legislature will intervene within the time, change the whole appropriation to the lightening of taxes, and leave us where we now are.

There is, however, an intermediate measure which might bring the two plans together. If the literary fund be of one and a half million of dollars, take the half million for the colleges and university, it will establish them meagrely, and make a deposit of the remaining million. Its interest of $60,000 will $50 to each ward, towards the teacher's wages, and reduce that tax to 24 instead of 36 cents to the dollar; and as the literary fund continues to accumulate, give one-third of the increase to the colleges and university, and two-thirds to the ward-schools. The increasing interest of this last portion will be continually lessening the school tax, until it will extinguish it altogether; the subsistence and buildings remaining always to be furnished by the ward in kind.

A system of general instruction, which shall reach every description of our citizens, from the richest to the poorest, as it was the earliest, so will it be the latest, of all the public concerns in which I shall permit myself to take an interest. Nor am I tenacious of the form in which it shall be introduced. Be that what it may, our descendants will be as wise as we are, and will know how to amend and amend it until it shall suit their circumstances. Give it to us, then, in any shape, and receive for the inestimable boon the thanks of the young and the blessings of the old, who are past all other services but prayers for the prosperity of their country and blessings to those who promote it.

TH: JEFFERSON.

Joseph C. Cabell, Esq.

LVIII.

T. J. TO J. C. C.

MONTICELLO, January 15, 1818.

DEAR SIR,—The messenger who carried mine of yesterday, brought me in return yours of the 5th. I shall be anxious to hear from you after our report of the 8th shall have been laid before the Legislature, and to learn what impression it makes; because that shows how near we are to the accomplishment of a good college, one that cannot but be thought of some value to the State, and the urgency of their enabling us to complete it. $50,000 would give us the other two professorships, which would complete it; but unless we can get $25,000 at least, to give us a mathematical professor, we shall begin very inauspiciously. If even this is refused, perhaps the statement in our report developing the public (and not local) character of our institution, may give a spur to subscriptions in counties appearing as yet indifferent to it. The members of the Legislature might aid us in that way. Our subscriptions being annual only, and half the money at least being necessary the ensuing summer, we must get you to enquire which of the banks will advance us from ten to twenty thousand dollars through the course of the summer, and on what terms. This is absolutely necessary to be known, before we venture on contracts. I wrote my letter of yesterday in such haste, that I had not time to read it over before despatching it for the mail. On reading afterwards the polygraph copy retained, I observed in the antepenultimate line an error of one word for another, to wit: "blessings" of the young instead of "thanks" of the young, which be so good as to correct, and to accept assurances of my friendship and respect.

TH: JEFFERSON.

Mr. Cabell.

LIX.

J. C. C. TO T. J.

RICHMOND, 22d January, 1818.

DEAR SIR,—I hope you will not think me neglectful in not having sooner acknowledged the receipt of your letters of the 31st ultimo, and of 6th, 14th and 15th instants, to all of which I have paid all the attention compatible with my immediate and indispensable duties in the Senate. Your letter of 31st ultimo, not seeming to demand a speedy answer, I have taken the liberty to lay it by for some weeks, till I could conveniently institute the necessary search in the Register's office, and the proper enquiries from the members from the part of the State in which the land is supposed to be situated. It shall be attended to in the course of one or two weeks. All your letters relative to the Central College and the Literary Fund, are received with pleasure and gratitude, and immediately communicated to such gentlemen in the House of Delegates, as I think it important should see them. As soon as the report arrived, I read it with great satisfaction, waited upon the Governor and delivered it to him, and requested him to communicate it, without delay, to the Assembly. Two hundred and fifty copies were ordered to be printed by the House of Delegates, one of which I now have the pleasure to enclose you. I have been particular in my enquiries as to the impression made by it on the members of the House of Delegates. It seems to have been received as an able production with some great names attached to it; but does not appear to have had any material influence on the feelings or opinions of the majority of the House. Among an enlightened few it has been read with favor and admiration. It cannot but add weight to our claims on the Legislature. As soon as I opened your letter of 14th, defending your scheme of primary schools, I went in search of the Clerk of the Committee of Schools and Colleges, made him copy it, and handed the copy to Mr. Scott,

Chairman of the Committee, whilst I am myself communicating the original to other members of the House. The Committee, after long delays, have at length reported a bill containing the outlines of your bill, with some modifications. What these are I am unable now to inform you, but will enclose you a copy as soon as the printed copies come out, which will be to-morrow or next day. I am informed that the popular scheme is to give all the Literary Fund to primary schools. But nothing seems decided on. The bill will be taken up in the House of Delegates on 29th instant. A motion has been made in that House to remove the Seat of Government. It was brought forward by * * * * *, and I cannot but suspect that he has been stimulated to make it by some artful man beyond the Ridge, with the view of rekindling sectional feelings. * * * * * is indiscreet enough to appear among the advocates. I have endeavored, through * * * * * to keep him quiet; but he still goes on, and as far as his voice can be supposed to speak that of his enlightened constituents, his course is calculated to injure the cause of the College. He seems to be lukewarm in that cause, notwithstanding his professions to the contrary. The proposition to remove the Seat of Government has been voted reasonable by the Committee, but will be voted out in the House. * * * * * hang upon our flanks, and encumber every step of our progress. If that pitiful place were not in existence, we could get along, but, as it is, I fear they will mar our success. * * * * * has been drawn over to the opposite party. Should we fail here this winter, I beg leave to suggest the plan of your endeavoring to get men of talents and influence, in the middle country, to come into the next Assembly. I have already prevailed on Mr. William Brent, of Stafford, to become a candidate. Mr. John T. Brooke will probably join him. I applied to General Cocke a few days ago; he is very averse, but promised to think of it. Wm. G. Poindexter, of Goochland, would come in, but his health will not admit of it. You and Mr. Madison and Mr. Monroe might greatly aid in this business. Excuse the digression. I am now treating with the banks for the proposed loan. You shall hear from me again very soon. Before I conclude, I will barely observe, that if no University shall be created, I think of getting a bill introduced, praying for an annuity out of the Literary Fund, as the most acceptable shape in which we could approach the Assembly. Our $40,000 could be expended in the buildings, and the annuity might go to endow the professorships. Three thousand five hundred dollars would suffice, but ought we not to ask for $5000? I enclose you a note from Chancellor Taylor to shew the feelings excited in liberal men by your exertions in the cause of education.

I am, dear sir, faithfully yours,

JOS. C. CABELL.

Mr. Jefferson.

Note of Chancellor Taylor to Mr. Cabell.

MANCHESTER, 17th January, 1818.

Creed Taylor presents his affections to Mr. Cabell, of the Senate.

C. T. has read, with much interest, the bills and documents in relation to a system of public education; and he would be delighted to see such a system adopted. Amend it afterwards, if necessary, to remove those objections which may occur in the operations of the plan. He is pleased with the system, first, because he sees in it much public good; and secondly, because it comes from the pen of one who has done so much for his fellow-man; for C. T. would be among the last who should refuse to that distinguished sage anything that would enable him to sing with pleasure his "*nunc demittas.*" Should the plan, however, fail, Mr. Cabell may command freely the services of C. T., as one of the friends of the Central College, to which he means, if necessary, to make a liberal donation.

LX.

J. C. C. TO T. J.

RICHMOND, 23d January, 1818.

DEAR SIR,—As I came out of the Capitol to-day I received from one of the door-keepers the enclosed copy of the bill* reported by the Committee of Schools and Colleges, which I have hastily looked over, and in regard to which I confess myself greatly disappointed. Indeed, sir, the prospect before us is dreary. Perhaps the subject may be dressed up in the House, but when a committee begins so inauspiciously, the affair generally ends in smoke. I really think our only safe course is to look around, select suitable persons, and try to prevail on them to come into the next Assembly. It is a subject of infinite delicacy, and should be handled with great discretion; but a few weeks will shew it is our only dependence. I have not been as quick in getting an answer from the banks as you may desire. It will not be till Friday, 30th, that I shall be able to procure a written answer. But I have ascertained, to my satisfaction, that according to the rules of the institutions, the Visitors will be obliged to render themselves liable in their individual capacities, in order to procure the proposed loan. As I came from the Capitol, to-day, I heard the result of the ayes and noes in the Lower House, on the question to postpone the resolution for removing the Seat of Government. It was postponed by a large majority. It is just, that I should observe that *both* your representatives voted for the postponement. I hope you will excuse my writing you on such paper, as I did not know my deficiency till I sat down; and I believed you would like a speedy communication.

I am, dear sir, faithfully yours,

JOSEPH C. CABELL.

Mr. Jefferson.

---

* It appears, at length, in the Richmond Enquirer of the day.

LXI.

J. C. C. TO T. J.

RICHMOND, 1st February, 1818.

DEAR SIR,—Since I last wrote you, the enclosed substitutes for Mr. Scott's, or the Committee's bill, have been offered in the House of Delegates. Mr. Taylor, of Chesterfield, a member of good talents and standing in that House, has promised me to offer your bill as a substitute for the whole. I totally dispair of the success of any general plan whatsoever; but I think it important, in several points of view, that your bill should be printed, and get into the view of the public. Our only hope now is to get some small appropriation by a particular bill on the failure of the general plan. I have often observed a disposition in the Assembly to console the disappointed by granting them something on the failure of a favorite scheme. Miserable omen for science and literature that their friends should fly to such a sentiment, on such an occasion! Yet, it would be better to do this than to fail altogether. From my conversations with the members, I am induced to believe that an application for an annuity out of the produce of the Literary Fund would be most likely to succeed.* Our subscription money might be appropriated entirely to the buildings, whilst the annuity might be applied to the endowment of Professorships. I imagine it would be advisable to ask for a sum not exceeding $5000 per annum, and the smaller the more likely to succeed. Would you have the kindness to write a short bill upon the plan proposed, and to enclose it by the return of the mail, for every thing coming from your pen would have a peculiar weight with many persons here? I should

* As a sufficient appropriation for the completion of the buildings, and for other purposes, could not at once be obtained, it will hereafter appear that this was a most important step in their future progress, and that it continues to be a source of the prosperity and stability of the institution.

not trouble you with this request, after the vast trouble you have already had with this business, but I know that a very short bill will answer the intended purpose, and the last effort should be made as perfect as possible. Time is now precious, and I hope to hear from you without delay.

I am now in a course of enquiry relative to the land of Mr. Des Essarts. I have procured a duplicate patent from the Land Office, and find, at the Auditor's, that the land has never been listed on the Commissioner's books. I shall probably engage Mr. Davidson, the Senator from the North-west, in the requisite enquiries. You shall hear again from me on this subject.

I remain, dear sir, faithfully yours,

JOSEPH C. CABELL.

Mr. Jefferson.

LXII.

J. C. C. TO T. J.

RICHMOND, 1st February, 1818.

DEAR SIR,—Since the date of my last letter to you, I have had conferences with the Presidents of the three banks in this place, on the subject of the proposed loan, in the anticipation of the resources of the College. The enclosed letters between Dr. Brockenbrough and myself contain the best terms which it has been in my power to procure. From my conversation with Mr. Hatcher,* I am led to doubt whether the Farmers' Bank would give the same accommodation in point of time. And Colonel Nicholas assures me that the Visitors could not obtain better terms from any bank whatever. I had prepared the same letter *mutatis mutandis*, for Mr. Hatcher, but as my conference with him left me so little room to hope for an

* Mr. Benjamin Hatcher, President of the Farmers' Bank of Virginia.

amelioration of the terms, I thought it would be most agreeable to you not to send it to the bank. I endeavored to prevail on the Bank of Virginia, through the medium of the President, to consent to the loan, without making the Visitors liable in their individual characters; but such an idea was at once pronounced inadmissible as well by himself as by the Board of Directors. Col. Nicholas thinks no bank would or ought to accede to such a proposition. Mr. Watson is now in town. I met him on my way to the Bank of Virginia, read to him my letter to the President, and told him that I expected we should be required to sign the notes in our character as individuals. To this he seemed opposed; however, my opportunity of conversing with him was very unfavorable to satisfactory explanation. I expect to see him again before he leaves town. For myself, I can only say that I will be willing to follow your own example. My situation as to money matters would make it very inconvenient and hazardous for me to be called on to advance a large sum at any period within a few years from this time. But, in this case, I imagine,* there would be no danger. Though the bank is not pledged to wait for the fourth instalment, I am inclined to think they would continue our note for the amount of any deficiency in the payments of the second and third.

I am, dear sir, faithfully yours,

JOSEPH C. CABELL.

Mr. Jefferson.

P. S. *Since writing the above I have called again on Dr. Brockenbrough, and having shewn him this statement, I am authorized, by him, to inform you that he thinks my expectation would not be disappointed.

J. C. C.

Letter of Joseph C. Cabell to the President of the Bank of Virginia.

RICHMOND, 30th January, 1818.

DEAR SIR,—I am authorized and desired by the Visitors of the Central College to apply to the Banks of this city for the purpose of procuring a loan, in anticipation of a part of the money which has been subscribed to that institution.

I beg leave to enclose, for the consideration of yourself and the Board of Directors of the Bank, over which you preside, the accompanying report made by the Visitors of that College to the Governor, and by him communicated to the General Assembly. From this document, you will be enabled to judge of the character and prospects of the College, and to decide whether it does not merit the support and co-operation of every other patriotic institution in the Commonwealth.

From the fourth paragraph in the report, you will perceive that the moneys subscribed to the College amount to somewhat more than $40,000, and are payable in four annual installments. The first payment will take place on first April next. In the course of the ensuing summer, the Visitors will, probably, find it expedient to borrow ten or twenty thousand dollars, in anticipation of the second and third payments; and as a security for the re-payment of the loan would pledge the three last installments. I beg, sir, to be informed whether the Bank of Virginia would be willing to lend the money; and if willing, upon what terms as to the duration of the loan, and the nature of the security to be given.

Permit me, sir, to observe, that past experience induces me to hope and expect that on an occasion like the present, where the public welfare is deeply concerned in a valuable institution, the Bank of Virginia will shew every disposition to lend its funds, upon the most liberal and advantageous terms.

I am, sir, with sentiments of great respect and esteem,

Your obedient servant,

JOSEPH C. CABELL.

Answer of the President of the Bank of Virginia.

BANK OF VIRGINIA, 31st January, 1818.

DEAR SIR,—Your letter relating to a loan from this Bank for the use of the Central College, has been submitted to the consideration of the Board of Directors. It is contrary to the usage of the Bank to give any assurance of extending loans beyond the limit of time prescribed by the charter (sixty days); but for a purpose so beneficial to the community as the establishment of a college, the Directors are willing to renew notes, for the sums stated in your letter, from time to time, in anticipation of the periods at which the second and third payments of the moneys subscribed to the College will fall due. Notes in the usual form, made by the Visitors, or a part of them, will, on this occasion, be perfectly satisfactory, notwithstanding the general regulation that requires "either the payer or endorser of a discounted note to reside in the neighborhood of the Bank." Under this arrangement, any pledge of the subscriptions will be unnecessary as a security.

With great respect and esteem,

I am, sir, your most obedient,

JOHN BROCKENBROUGH.

Joseph C. Cabell, Esq.

LXIII.

J. C. C. TO T. J.

RICHMOND, 6th February, 1818.

DEAR SIR,—I now enclose you the duplicate patent of Mr. Des Essarts' land, which I procured from the land office, together with his letter to you, and the French copy of his patent. I have retained a copy of his letter to you, of yours to me on the same subject, and of the patent, which I shall put into the hands of Mr. Davidson, or some other member, for the purpose of procuring particular information about the quality and situation of the land. It is not an easy matter to find a suitable person to make these enquiries, but I will make the best selection in my power. I have paid $4 67 to the Register of the Land Office and to the Keeper of the Great Seal of the State; which I have done with pleasure, as it gave me a small opportunity of manifesting my gratitude for the many civilities I received from Mr. Des Essarts' countrymen. Situated as that gentleman is, and making his appeal through Gen. Kosciusko to the attention of Virginians, I should despise the man who would hesitate to lend his aid on such an occasion. I beg, therefore, that not a word may be said about returning the pittance I have contributed. I wish it were in my power to render more effectual services to him. You shall hear further from me on this subject.

Yesterday Mr. Taylor, of Chesterfield, offered your bill as a substitute for Mr. Scott's. I have already apprised you of the state of things upon this subject. A motion was made to print 500 copies, which failed. A motion to print 250 copies prevailed. But a part of the House opposed the printing at all. I have sought for information as to the cause of this opposition. I believe it proceeded chiefly from the back country members. For two months certain persons have been training those members to oppose all that could come from you. The back country spirit has been industriously excited. They are alarmed at the prospect of losing the future seat of government. * * * * * * * * * * * * You thought * * * would be with us. How much you were mistaken. * * * * * * He is for Staunton still. He tells me he thinks we have contrived to settle the question in favor of the Central College; and I think he considers the chances are against Staunton. But he will contend still for that place, and as long as a ray of hope remains, I believe he would be disposed to depress the Central College. In a contest between Lexington and Charlottesville, he would probably be neutral; but I believe he would not regret to see Charlottesville prevail. The friends of Staunton and Lexington wish to keep down the Central College. I believe they would oppose the appropriation of a dollar to it. Should it get even a little annuity, it would be *established;* and one year more would throw Staunton out of the chase altogether, and Lexington in the back-ground. For these reasons, I believe the back country will oppose a small appropriation to the Central College with nearly as much zeal as it would the establishment of the University at that place. Were it not for the clashing of local interests, it is probable something might be done. But there is no doubt of the failure of any general plan; and although, in that event, I should be disposed to try the experiment of a particular bill, I am informed there is but little prospect of success. But, in every point of view, it was right to have your bill brought in and printed. I remember, some years ago, your letter to Mr. Carr was handed about here, praised by a few and dropped. I got it printed, and enlightened men every where were pleased to see it. I cannot bear the idea to have put you to so much trouble for the apparent gratification of a few of our less enlightened members. Let the measure come out from private coteries, to the eye of the State; and men of intellect will again be pleased. Those who oppose your views, say that the bill is a finished production in *theory*. I will endeavor to send you some of the printed copies. There is but little prospect of doing anything in the way of subscription through the medium of members of Assembly. When every public prospect fails, I will consult with my friends on that subject. It would be very important to get liberal men to come into the next Assembly. The North-western part of Virginia begins to detach itself from the South-western. A leading man from that section would carry off a wing of the enemy's army. If such a man as General Jackson* would come here from that quarter, Wm. Burwell from the South, &c. &c., and would support your views, the game would be safe. This is a delicate subject. But perhaps the happiness of the present and future generations depend upon the execution of the plan. I write now, and shall continue to write to you, with freedom about men, because I know it to be impossible to lay open the secret springs of action without such freedom, and wherever confidence is proper, you will observe it.

I am, dear sir, faithfully yours,

JOS. C. CABELL.

Mr. Jefferson.

---

* Of Harrison county.

LXIV.

J. C. C. TO T. J.

RICHMOND, 10th February, 1818.

DEAR SIR,—I now do myself the pleasure to enclose you a printed copy of your bill, the printer having just sent the copies to the house. The subject will be agitated in the House of Delegates on to-morrow, or the next day. I have no reasons to change my anticipations as to the result of the measures respecting the literary fund, stated in my former letters to you. Yet I have thought it my duty still to persevere in efforts to secure a successful issue. In revolving the subject in my mind, I yesterday thought of a new expedient, which I have actually resorted to, and for which I wish to obtain your forgiveness and approbation. The measure alluded to, is the publication in the Enquirer, with some small modifications, of your letter to me of 14th January. It seemed to me that such a letter appearing in the Enquirer on the day on which the bill should be discussed in the House of Delegates, was calculated to give weight to the friends of science. I paused, however, at the idea of publishing a private letter from you, without your previous approbation. In this state of embarrassment, I consulted with Mr. Somers of the House of Delegates, with my brother William, and with Col. Nicholas. To those gentlemen I propounded these questions: First. Would the publication of the letter conflict with any thing in my letter to Mr. Scott, or injure the cause of public education, by furnishing a plausible ground for the imputation of interference on your part in the affairs of the Assembly. Secondly, ought I to take upon myself the responsibility of publishing your letter, without previously obtaining your consent. The second question was left entirely to myself. The first question was answered in favor of my wishes. It was agreed that if such explanatory sentence should appear, as will appear, prefixed to the letter, there would be no conflict with my letter to Mr.

Scott; and in regard to the effect of the letter, it was our united opinion that, whilst it ought, and probably would not do any harm, it would, and ought to produce much good. In that, we thought that such a production ought to be published for the public benefit, and in justice to yourself. Although the particular system of primary schools which it advocates, might not, in all its details, be approved, yet the united force of all its arguments and statements in favor of a general system of education, would have a most beneficial effect on every reflecting mind. Under these circumstances, I determined to publish the letter in the shape in which it will appear in to-morrow's Enquirer. Col. Nicholas advised me to leave out the statement in the latter part of the letter, of the amount which would be required for the establishment of schools altogether supported by the literary fund. The item for houses was deemed too high, and the amount of the whole was calculated, in our opinion, to deter the Assembly from continuing its support to the fund. There being great objections in the minds of many to a ward tax, and to any other system depending solely for endowment on the literary fund, so vast a sum appearing to be necessary on your authority, it is to be apprehended the enemies of the system would seize upon the estimate, and make use of it to throw the Assembly into a state of despair. A small alteration in a few words in that part of the letter became necessary in consequence of the omission of that statement. In the commencement of the letter, where you quote my letter, I think you make me speak more positively than the terms would warrant. But if I am mistaken in this point, I would wish to qualify my declarations. For this reason I have taken the liberty to interpolate the words "it is apprehended," before the words, "that neither the people nor their representatives," &c. With these small modifications, your letter will appear in the Enquirer of to-morrow. I beg, sir, that you will excuse the liberty I have in this instance taken with you, without previously consulting you. Time did not admit of consulting you, after the idea of publication occurred to me. And I cannot but hope, that after the communications that have passed between us, and the development of my motives, as now exhibited, you will not be offended at the unauthorized step which I have taken, and that you will have the goodness to sanction my conduct in this instance, as you did on a former occasion. Whatever the members of the General Assembly may be pleased to say on this occasion, I am satisfied every enlightened and liberal man in the State will thank you for the attention you have bestowed on the great subject of national education.

I remain, dear sir,

Your faithful friend,

JOSEPH C. CABELL.

Mr. Jefferson.

LXV.

J. C. C. TO T. J.

RICHMOND, 12th February, 1818.

DEAR SIR,—Mr. Louis Summers, of the county of Kanawha, and one of the members of the House of Delegates, proposes to leave town in the morning, on his return to his constituents. It is possible that he may have it in his power to call at Monticello, on his way through Albemarle. I have taken the liberty to offer him a letter of introduction to you. It would give him great pleasure to become personally acquainted with you; and I beg leave to present him to you as one of the most liberal, enlightened, and upright gentlemen in the circle of my acquaintance. He has shown every disposition to support your plans, both general and particular, for the advancement of science in this State; and if the General Assembly consisted of such men as he is, we should not be, as we are, the victims of local interests, factious views, and lamentable ignorance. I remain, dear sir, with unabated confidence and esteem,

Your faithful friend,

JOSEPH C. CABELL.

Mr. Jefferson.

LXV. (*a*)

J. C. C. TO T. J.

RICHMOND, 13th February, 1818.

DEAR SIR,—On the 11th instant the House of Delegates went into committee of the whole on the school bill, when your bill was offered as a substitute for the bill of the committee, and I regret to inform you that it received very few votes, whilst the substitute of Hill, of King William, containing a provision for the poor only, was adopted. The disposition of the present House of Delegates is now manifest, for a small appropriation for the education of the poor, and the application of the rest of the fund to the payment of the debts of the State. Col. Green of the Senate, suggested this idea at the last session; but since that period, he has so far changed his opinion, as to favor an appropriation for the higher seminaries at the same time. At least, as he informed me at the commencement of the session, he would advocate an appropriation to the Central College. From this circumstance, and from what I know of the sentiments of the members of the Senate, I am of opinion that the fund will not be misapplied at this session; but I utterly despair of any thing being done, either for the general system or for the Central College. Indeed, from the few votes your bill obtained, I now doubt the propriety of making any application whatever on behalf of the Central College, lest the result might not only be unfavorable, but depressing. If, therefore, you have not drafted the bill requested in my last, it is scarcely proper that I should now put you to that trouble. But, if you have done so, it may not be amiss to send it on ; because, if the present prospect should continue, it might be kept back till another session.

Mr. Garth spoke to me some time past in regard to an augmentation of the lottery of the College. I find that the President and Directors of the Literary Fund are authorized to sell lotteries for five per cent. of the profits ; and I presume from some conversation I have had with Mr. Nicholas, that they would be unable to accommodate us without demanding the five per cent. In the present posture of affairs, shall I get a bill brought in to augment the lottery or not? The session is hastening to a close, and we have no time to lose.

Indeed, sir, from the character of the present House of Delegates, as exhibited in their proceedings, I should fear the result of an application to them, even for a lottery. I cannot but think that certain local interests, as developed in former letters, together with another interest more widely diffused, have contributed largely to the overthrow of the interests of science and literature in the present General Assembly. A portion of the middle country delegation, however, by co-operating with these, have darkened our prospects on this occasion. These, it is thought, are opposed to the Central College, partly because of their hostility to some of the persons who support it, or from other motives but little more commendable. * * * * It is of infinite importance to the best interests of the State, to send some able and virtuous men to the next Assembly. I write you confidentially, and am with the highest esteem,

Your friend,

JOSEPH C. CABELL.

LXVI.

T. J. TO J. C. C.

MONTICELLO, February 16, 1818.

DEAR SIR,—A resolution which I saw in the papers for the adjournment of the Legislature, the day before yesterday, prevented my writing to you, in the belief that it would not find you in Richmond. Mr. Summers now tells me he thinks you will set into the next week. After acknowledging the receipt, since mine of January 14 and 15, of yours of the 22d and 23d, and of February 1, 6, 10, and 12, the object of this is merely to express my satisfaction with your publication of mine of January 14, and the corrections made in it, and the rather as the motives for my intermeddling at all, had better go forth with my own explanations, than under the misconstructions of those who differed from me in views. I suppose it probable that the next Legislature, after so much debating on the subject, will come with their minds made up for something, and that a provision of some sort will be made, which I think ought to be, whatever those who are to live under it think will be best. I believe I have erred in meddling with it at all, and that it has done more harm than good. A strong interest felt in the subject, and through my whole life, ought to excuse me with those who differ from me in opinion, and should protect me against unfriendly feelings. Nobody, more strongly than myself, advocates the right of every generation to legislate for itself, and the advantages which each succeeding generation has over the preceding one, from the constant progress of science and the arts.

We must turn to the affairs of the college, under our particular charge, and consider what we can do for it, on its own scanty funds. The impracticability of frequent meetings of the visitors, and the difficulty of consultations by interchange of letters, as well from the labor of that mode, as the delays and uncertainties of our cross posts, forces on me the necessity of assuming to act often without the authority or aid and counsel of my colleagues. The call for the return of the subscription papers has produced little effect, so that we are under considerable uncertainty as to the amount of our funds. Yet a serious view of that should now be taken that we may in nothing exceed our limits. What professors, and where and how to procure them, is a question of urgency. On that I have seen no cause for change of opinion; and I suppose I must now act on that formerly given, and which I had deferred until it could be seen whether the Legislature would give us any help. In the want of visitorial full meetings, I should be much relieved if the members would individually call here whenever they happen to pass this way. Even separate conferences with them would lighten my mind of some of its load. If you return to the upper country, I hope you will make a stage here, and give me the benefit of a consultation. Accept the assurance of my constant esteem and respect.

TH: JEFFERSON.

Joseph C. Cabell, Esq.

LXVII.

J. C. C. TO T. J.

RICHMOND, 20th February, 1818.

DEAR SIR,—Your favor of 16th is now before me. I thank you for your confirmation of what I did with your letter. Whatever may be the success of a few interested men in lessening the weight your advice ought to have with the Assembly, as soon as the present contest is over, your conduct will command the respect of all, as it now does of the enlightened and liberal. I hasten to apprise you, that our proceedings now seem likely to eventuate differently from what I have heretofore expected. The school bill came up to the Senate in the form of Mr. Hill's amendment. We engrafted upon it a provision for an University. In that shape, it passed here by a majority of *fourteen to three.* This important vote took place yesterday. The bill has gone back to the House of Delegates. An attempt has been made to postpone it, and lost by an immense majority. The bill, with the amendments of the Senate, is ordered to be printed. It is contemplated to amend it, so as to provide that the appropriation for the University shall not interfere with any further appropriation that may be necessary for the education of the poor. The bill now gives $45,000 per annum to the poor, and $15,000 to the University. It is believed that $15,000 more will be necessary for the poor; and $60,000 is all the product of the fund at this time. But the product will soon be swelled to $90,000, so that it will not materially affect the appropriation for the University. In this shape it is believed the bill will pass. It is provided in the bill, that the Governor and Council shall choose one commissioner from each Senatorial district in the State, as laid off by the act of the last Assembly; that these commissioners shall meet at Rockfish Gap on 1st August, and adjourn from place to place, and time to time; that they shall report to the next Assembly the best site, plan, &c., and the next Assembly will have the whole subject in their power. We have *fifteen* districts on this side the Ridge, and I think we are safe in the hands of the Executive. If this bill passes, perhaps, our policy will be to invest all our funds in buildings, and get them as far advanced by August as possible. But I will not speculate on uncertainties. I tremble with anxiety for the great result I anticipate.

Yours, faithfully,

JOS. C. CABELL.

Mr. Jefferson.

LXVIII.

J. C. C. TO T. J.

RICHMOND, 22d February, 1818.

DEAR SIR,—The University bill has passed in the form of the enclosed, with one small exception. The appointment of the commissioners is now a subject of infinite importance to us. The Executive, I think, will do us justice. But you will observe that vacancies are to be filled by the President and Directors of the Literary Fund. It was proposed, in the committee of the Senate, to give the appointment in the first instance to them. To this I objected, and then it was agreed to give it to the Executive. And the fact is, that the power left with the President and Directors of the Literary Fund, was kept in, contrary to my expectation and intention. I relied upon the understanding that the power was to be given to the Executive; and, in the hurry of the business, that part of the bill escaped amendment. * * * * *

I am discussing the question, among our friends here, whether it would be proper to name you as a commissioner. The duties of the Board will be various and important. It is of great consequence that I should be forthwith informed whether you would serve, if elected. In your answer, if possible, leave me a discretionary power. I see no objection to Mr. Madison's serving—and should he be appointed, I entreat that you will lay before him the high considerations that should induce him to accept the appointment. Be pleased to do this without delay. All I want in this business is fair play—to put this subject on a footing of just reciprocity between the two sides of the mountain. The suggestion in my last, relative to laying out all our funds in buildings, is now worthy of your attention. Nothing can be more important to us, than to hasten our operations. By the time your answer gets here, the Assembly will be up, but I shall still be in town.

Faithfully, yours,

JOSEPH C. CABELL.

Mr. Jefferson.

LXIX.

[It will have been seen, from the two preceding letters, that a provision was engrafted on the bill while passing through the Senate, for the appointment of Commissioners, one from each Senatorial district, who should meet, consult, and report to the Legislature their views as to the *proper location* of the University, as also on other fundamental matters. This measure was of Mr. Cabell's suggestion, who had anticipated much difficulty on that point. He was also desirous that Mr. Jefferson should serve on that commission. There are few letters of the entire series which exhibit more clearly the disinterested magnanimity of the writer than the following, and which, could it have been laid before the public at the time, would have tended more to disarm popular and political prejudice. Both Mr. Jefferson and Mr. Madison were finally nominated of the commission, and the former, as their Chairman, drew the report, which will appear in the Appendix, No. I.]

T. J. TO J. C. C.

MONTICELLO, February 26, 1818.

DEAR SIR,—Your two favors of the 20th and 22d came to hand last night. I congratulate you, sincerely, on having something begun on the subject of education. Whatever be its faults, they will lead to correction. You seem to doubt whether Mr. Madison would serve if named a commissioner for the location, &c. of the University? but there can be no doubt that he would, and it is most important that he should. As to myself, I should be ready to do anything in my power for the institution; but that is not the exact question. Would it promote the success of the institution most for me to be in or out of it? Out of it, I believe. It is still to depend ultimately on the will of the Legislature; and that has its uncertainties. There are fanatics both in religion and politics, who, without knowing me personally, have long been taught to consider me as a raw head and bloody bones, and as we can afford to lose no votes in that body, I do think it would be better that you should be named for our district. Do not consider this as mock-modesty; it is the cool and deliberate act of my judgment. I believe the institution would be more popular without me than with me; and this is the most important consideration—and I am confident you would be a more efficient member of that body than I should. Do, then, dear sir, act on this subject without any scruples as to me or yourself. Regard nothing but the good of the cause.

Affectionately, yours,

TH: JEFFERSON.

Jos. C. Cabell, Esq.

LXX.

J. C. C. TO T. J.

WILLS'S TAVERN, FLUVANNA, 11th March.

DEAR SIR,—I have just arrived here on my way home, having left my wife in the lower country till the roads get better. My plan is to stay at home about a week, and to call upon you either in going or coming. When I get to General Cocke's, this evening, I shall be informed whether there is any necessity for my calling on my way up; should there not be, as I have great occasion to see to my domestic concerns, I shall defer my visit to you, till I shall be coming down, a week or ten days hence. I should be tempted to come on to Monticello this evennig, but the roads are horrible, and I am glad to leave the stage, and beg the loan of a horse. I left Richmond yesterday morning. The Executive will appoint the commissioners on the 18th instant. Probably you will not be nominated in consequence of the considerations stated in your last. Upon that point, I consulted some four or five of your intelligent friends, and left the matter in their hands. As for myself, in the event of your not being appointed, I have taken so active a part, that I thought it would be injurious to the cause for me to be a member; and accordingly to a member of the Executive who spoke of me, I requested not to be put in nomination. I shall be able to say much more to you, on this subject, when I have the pleasure to see you. In the *interim*,

I remain, faithfully, yours,

JOSEPH C. CABELL.

Thomas Jefferson.

LXXI.

J. C. C. TO T. J.

WARMINSTER, 15th March, 1818.

DEAR SIR,—I wrote you a note from Wills's, in Fluvanna, on my way up, in which I mentioned my intention to call on you on my return to the lower country. From the state in which I find my affairs, I expect it will be the 26th of the month before I shall be at Monticello. In the interim, I think it may not be amiss for me to say a few words to you by letter. From the best information I can obtain as to the candidates in the surrounding counties, the most prominent characters are of that class of men in the middle country, who, though they may not be hostile, are not likely to be zealous advocates of the Central College. It was believed, in Richmond, during the last session, that if the location question had come on, that there would have been an extensive diversion in favor of the Rockbridge College, among the representatives all along the Eastern foot of the Blue Ridge. This evil is to be apprehended at the next session, even if the Board of Commissioners should recommend the Central College as the site. You will observe, that the law requires them to report any voluntary contributions, whether conditional or absolute, whether in land, money or other property, which may be offered through them, to the President and Directors of the Literary Fund, for the benefit of the University. I fear that the Washington Academy will be a dangerous rival, even although the Board should prefer our site. A man of the name of Robinson, now very old, and possessing an estate estimated to be worth $100,000, is said to be willing to give his estate, at his death, to the University, provided it should be located at Lexington. To this they will add $25,000 of private subscription, and the buildings and property of the Academy. So that their offer, at the period of Mr. Robinson's death, would amount to $150,000. A certain class of members would be disposed to put the institution up to the highest bidder. It is very important to have an intermixture of true friends and liberal spirits from the middle country. I turned my eye towards Randolph Harrison. He is precisely such a man as would have most effect on such an occasion. He would be a host on our side. I wrote to Gen. Cocke pressing him to come forward, and urging him to endeavor to prevail on Washington Trueheart, of Louisa, and Randolph Harrison, to offer for their respective counties. As I passed by Bremo, three days ago, I found General Cocke just returned from Mr. Harrison's, where he left him recovering from a dreadful wound in the abdomen he had received by a fall. Mr. H. sent me word that the people of his county had long been urging him to offer for the county, and, as he had refused to do so, he did not believe he could now be elected, were he to come forward. But Gen. Cocke thinks otherwise: the time is propitious, as only one of the old members would be a candidate, and there seems to be a difficulty to get men to serve. Gen. Cocke agrees with me entirely as to the importance of having Mr. H. in the House. I could not prevail on the General himself, nor on W. J. Carey. The latter could probably be elected at this time without difficulty. His grandfather's debts deter him from embarking in public life. But would one session seriously affect him? Surely not. I have had no communication with Mr. Trueheart, and shall not write to him, having been so unsuccessful heretofore. Mr. Harris will offer in Louisa, and he will do very well. Probably no one has as much influence with Mr. Carey and Mr. Harrison as you have. The crisis is great, and extraordinary means are necessary to accomplish the great object in view. I take the liberty to suggest to you the idea of your writing immediately to those gentlemen by special messenger. Mr. Eppes could awake his friends to the support of Mr. Harrison. Perhaps you may not approve this suggestion. If you should not, I hope you will ascribe it to an anxiety for the welfare of the Central College, and the cause of science, that rises above that which I feel for my domestic concerns. —— will favor the location of the Central College. I had this from his intimates in Richmond. He now says, the reason he did not subscribe was *because the subscription paper was never handed to him*. His new-born zeal promises to rise very high.

Faithfully, yours,

JOSEPH C. CABELL.

Mr. Jefferson.

LXXII.

J. C. C. TO T. J.

MRS. TINSLEY'S, 31st March, 1818.

DEAR SIR,—I forgot to leave with you, as I intended, a little book, called the Oxford and Cambridge Guide. It may be acceptable to you at the present crisis. I will thank you for the return of it, when I come up in May, as I shall wish to look over it in the summer.

I am, dear sir, very truly yours,

JOSEPH C. CABELL.

Mr. Jefferson.

LXXIII.

J. C. C. TO T. J.

WARMINSTER, 30th July, 1818.

DEAR SIR,—I send you, by my brother William, the signatures of the majority of the subscribers to the funds of the Central College in Nelson county, to the deed of conveyance of the property of the College to the Commonwealth, on the condition of the location of the University at the site of the College. I have met with the ready assent of every subscriber to whom I have yet presented the paper; and I am confident there will not be a single dissenting voice. Indeed, it is solely to be ascribed to my own forgetfulness that the paper has not yet been presented to all the subscribers. It did not occur to my recollection, till to-day, that the assent of the subscribers should be ready for the meeting of the commissioners; my notion had been, that it must be procured by the meeting of the Assembly. I will thank you to send the paper back by my brother, and I will not fail to procure the signature of every subscriber.

I remain, dear sir,

Most respectfully and truly yours,

JOSEPH C. CABELL.

Mr. Jefferson.

LXXIV.

J. C. C. TO T. J.

EDGEWOOD, 24th October, 1818.

DEAR SIR,—I am happily recovering from the severe fever which has of late confined me to my bed for twenty days, but am barely able to take a turn across the room. Col. Coles told me the substance of his conversation with you lately at Monticello; observing that you wished to go to Bedford, and had a thought of calling on me on your way, but your health being bad, it was doubtful whether you would be strong enough to perform the journey. It would give me very great pleasure to see you at my house. If you should come, you will find it necessary to make a circuit, by crossing at Warren, and taking the Warminster road at the church, or a little before you get to it. But I fear, sir, your state of health will not permit you to travel without danger of making it worse. Do not be apprehensive that you will not see me; as, if you do not come this way before I leave home, I will certainly come by Monticello. I think my health will admit of my traveling by the 10th of next month. I would wish to set out sooner, but weakness or the arrangement of my affairs for the winter, will probably detain me till then, if not longer. I shall be on the road a little before, or a little after, the 10th. The road between this and Warren is now impassable for a carriage; but I shall carry hands with me to help me over the gulleys.

I remain, dear sir, faithfully your friend,

JOSEPH C. CABELL.

Mr. Jefferson.

LXXV.

J. C. C. TO T. J.

ENNESCORTHY, 18th November, 1818.

DEAR SIR,—I arrived here on 11th instant, on my way to Monticello, and on 12th was visited by a most unexpected and mortifying relapse, which, though in part removed, still hangs lingering about me, has thrown me into a weak and delicate state of body, and threatens to deprive me altogether of the satisfaction and advantage of seeing you before the meeting of the Assembly. I yield the idea of a personal interview with great reluctance. I wished to peruse the report of the Commissioners, to converse with you fully on the subject of the University, and to state to you my present impressions relative to the proposition you think of making to me in the event of the passage of the bill. Situated as I am, I seem reduced to the necessity of adopting the more imperfect mode of communicating through a friend. If you could venture to trust the report out of your hands, before it goes into those of Messrs. Gordon and Carr, I think we could return it to you safely on Saturday or Sunday. In regard to the contemplated trip to Europe, our friend Col. Coles, who is intimately acquainted with my situation, will be able to give you the same information as I could myself, were I present. Probably such objections to me, as he will state, would be considered insurmountable by yourself; and if not by you, by the other Visitors. Suppose them, however, removed, the proposition is one of great importance, and I request a reasonable time to consider of it. It is my intention, in every event, to retire from the Senate at the close of the approaching session. The current of my inclination strongly inclines me to withdraw altogether, and endeavor by greater personal attention to derive a moderate revenue from my estate, and at the same time to cultivate science and literature. A part of the district are disposed to bring me forward as a candidate for Congress; conversations have passed amounting, perhaps, to something like a commitment on my side; but nothing having been finally decided on, and this cruel fever shaking my mind and body, and threatening to impair my already frail constitution, it is not improbable I may, in quitting the Senate, give up all pretensions to further popular preferment. The voyage you propose to me is, to my mind, truly interesting, and I cannot conceal the gratification I feel at the confidence the proposition discovers. Having said this, I must leave the rest to my friend Coles.

The Senate will doubtless adjourn in a week from the commencement of the session, and the first fifteen days will be employed by the House of Delegates in receiving petitions. The bill for locating the University might be introduced on 16th and decided on in that house by 20th. Should it succeed there, you may count on its success in the Senate. It would be beneficial, if you would write such a bill as you think the occasion will require, and commit it to the care of such person as you deem proper to be entrusted with it; as also, if you would write to Judge Roane, Judge Brooke, and a few select friends, and request them to speak to the active and influential members of the House of Delegates.

I am, dear sir, faithfully your friend,

JOSEPH C. CABELL.

Mr. Jefferson.

LXXVI.

T. J. TO J. C. C.

MONTICELLO, November 20, 1818.

DEAR SIR,—I very much lament the cause which has deprived us of the pleasure of seeing Mrs. Cabell and yourself at Monticello, on your way to Richmond. I now commit to your care a letter to be delivered to the Speaker of the Senate, which contains the report of the Commissioners who met at Rockfish Gap.* Having been written in great haste, and by several hands, dividing the work, in order to expedite their departure, it is very imperfectly legible; and as it is important that it should be printed correctly, I enclose you the original draught also, made literally conformable to the authenticated one, and which I would wish you to put into the hands of the printer. Being much more legible, he will be less liable to commit mistakes. It will serve for your own information in the mean time, which the Commissioners thought would be proper, while they deemed it disrespectful to the Legislature, and otherwise inexpedient, that its contents should be communicated but to particular persons before delivery. It was their opinion that it should be delivered to each Speaker, in the chair, on the second morning of the session.

Col. Coles will explain to you what has passed on the subject of the proposed voyage, which I consider as requiring indispensably a special agent, and in which Gen. Cocke concurred, without a doubt of the unanimous approbation of our colleagues.

With sincere wishes for the re-establishment of your health,

I salute you affectionately,

TH: JEFFERSON.

Joseph C. Cabell, Esq.

---

* See Appendix, I.

LXXVII.

J. C. C. TO T. J.

RICHMOND, 8th December, 1818.

DEAR SIR,—The Senate formed a house to-day; the House of Delegates yesterday. A conference between Messrs. Carr and Gordon and myself, held this morning, resulted in an agreement to get Mr. Taylor, of Chesterfield, to bring forward the subject of the University in the House of Delegates. Not to speak of those other circumstances, in his favor, which should induce me to prefer him, we thought his position in the State would give him less the appearance of local feelings and interests. I introduced those gentlemen to him, and Mr. Taylor undertook the task at our request. The report was read, and received with great attention in both the houses. A resolution to print a number of copies passed each house. The ability and value of the report, I am informed, are universally admitted. It was referred in the lower house to a select committee, and the Speaker is friendly to the measure. Present prospects are very favorable to a successful issue. Some votes about William & Mary may be lost; but nothing like a serious diversion in favor of a western site is, I believe, to be apprehended. Philip R. Thompson, of Kanawha, and the delegates from that quarter, will vote for Charlottesville. From the rest of the West, I have not had time to hear. A portion of the Assembly will be opposed to the whole subject; and how far a combination between this part and the Lexington interest may jeopardize the measure, I cannot now determine. All that I can now positively affirm is, that the clouds seem to be scattering, and the prospect to smile. I will do myself the pleasure to write you from time to time. My friends advised me to push on to Williamsburg, and to stay there till the entire recovery of my health; but feeling myself getting better, I resolved to stay and do what I could to promote this business.

At Bremo, my fevers returned, but since I left that place my recovery has been advancing uninterruptedly. I shall proceed to Williamsburg, and stay a week or two, as soon as the subject of the University shall be put on a footing satisfactory to my mind.

I am, dear sir, sincerely and faithfully yours,

JOSEPH C. CABELL.

Mr. Jefferson.

P. S. Mr. Hunter, of Essex, will support the report.

LXXVIII.

J. C. C. TO T. J.

RICHMOND, 14th December, 1818.

DEAR SIR,—Mr. Banks * has not appointed as good a select committee as I had expected. There is a decided majority of the committee in favor of the Central College; but the Eastern members are less attentive than the Western. I have urged the importance of having a full meeting before the final question is taken. Mr. Taylor is aware of the danger. The committee has had two meetings; at the first, it was decided to report by bill. Mr. Taylor has copied your bill, and at the second meeting offered it to the committee. The friends of Lexington wish to have the clause of location reported with a blank. I think it will ultimately be decided to fill the blank with the Central College. At the second meeting, this morning, the Valley members called for time to consider the provisions of the bill; the real object was to have time to manœuvre. The motion was resisted, but carried; some of the friends of Charlottesville voting with them. The members from Rockbridge

---

* Linn Banks, Esq., of Madison county, for many years Speaker of the House of Delegates of Virginia.

called for a calculation to prove the assertion in the report, that Charlottesville is nearer to the centre of population than Staunton or Lexington. The object seemed to be to draw out your calculations exhibited to the Commissioners. The answer given by an Eastern member was, that each member might satisfy himself, by reference to the census of 1810. The point was left unsettled. It will come on again at the next meeting, on a motion to strike out Charlottesville from the bill. The committee will meet again on Thursday morning. The Valley members will be strongly opposed to the Central College. The members from beyond the Alleghaney will divide. Those south of Kanawha will generally vote with us, as Mr. Thompson informs me. The prospect is still favorable; but the effect of intrigue and management is beyond the reach of calculation. There is a party in the House of Delegates opposed to the measure in every shape. I hope that party is not strong. The weight of character in the Board is working the effects I calculated on when I first suggested that measure. The wayward spirits on this side the Ridge are awed into acquiescence.

I am, dear sir, faithfully yours,

JOSEPH C. CABELL.

Mr. Jefferson.

P. S. * * * * * * * * *

LXXIX.

J. C. C. TO T. J.

RICHMOND, 17th December, 1818.

DEAR SIR,—The select committee of the House of Delegates, on the subject of the University, has just had a third meeting; thirteen members attended. On the question whether the bill should be reported with a blank as to the site, it was decided in the negative, by the casting vote of the chairman. The Central College was selected as the site, and the bill reported to the House. The Lexington party sought for further delays under the pretext of wanting time to consider the calculations as to the centre of population, and to bring forward their own claims. I am really fearful for the ultimate fate of the bill. Since the date of my last, I have discovered that the delegation from the West are forming a combination among themselves to vote against the bill on the passage. Finding themselves in a minority on the question of the site, they will endeavor to defeat the measure altogether for the present. There is a party in the East in favor of putting down the literary fund. Should these parties unite on the question on the passage of the bill, it will be lost; and this result is much to be apprehended. The fund cannot be put down, and I cannot but hope that many of its enemies will vote for the University as the best means of rectifying what they deem a bad appropriation. On consultation with Col. Nicholas and my brother William, I determined to publish your calculations as to the centre of population, in this morning's Enquirer. We deemed the publication essential to unite the Eastern delegation, and to put them under responsibility to their constituents. The anonymous shape was preferred; but the author is very well known. Knowing the course of argument which the Lexington party would take as to the progress of population since 1810, I have made some auxiliary statements, to shew that on the most liberal allowance to the West, we shall have, in 1820, a surplus of from eighty to one hundred thousand white persons. These will be used only in a defensive way.

I am, dear sir, faithfully yours,

JOSEPH C. CABELL.

Mr. Jefferson.

LXXX.

J. C. C. TO T. J.

SENATE CHAMBER, 2 P. M., 17th December, 1818.

DEAR SIR,—Since writing the within, I have conversed with Mr. Davidson, the Senator from Clarksburg. He arrived but two days ago. His friendship I was sure of: I feared the opposition had drawn him so far over as to silence him: but I did him injustice. He tells me he has conversed with twenty-two members from the northwest; and they all, except one, expressed themselves in favor of the Central College. Davidson's information again revives my hopes of a favorable issue. He will be very useful to us on this occasion, and his arrival is well-timed and very fortunate. Through him I can penetrate the designs of the opposition, and I trust be able to break their combination. Rest assured, sir, that nothing I can do on this occasion, shall be omitted to procure success. I will not stir from the seat of government till this business is settled; my friends have urged me to go to Williamsburg; but I have refused. Even if the dangers to my life existed, which they apprehended, I could not risk it in a better cause.

Faithfully yours,

JOSEPH C. CABELL.

Mr. Jefferson.

LXXXI.

J. C. C. TO T. J.

RICHMOND, 24th December, 1818.

DEAR SIR,—Conformably to your advice, I urged the friends of the University to hasten the proceedings of the House of Delegates upon that subject, and to get the bill up to the Senate before Christmas. Unfortunately, however, the bill is now lying on the table of the Lower House, after one reading and an order to print. As we met on 7th, and fifteen days are pretty fully employed in reading petitions, which this year are more numerous than usual, it would have been very difficult to avoid the delay which has taken place, especially as an artful opposition has been continually urging the necessity of time to consider, and to bring forward their claims. From thirty to forty members of the House of Delegates are now absent on a visit to their families, and it will be unsafe to take a vote on the bill till a week after Christmas. Two strenuous efforts have at different times been made to get an adjournment of the Senate. On the first, the vote was ten to five; on the second nine to five. But although the attempt failed in both cases, yet four or five of the Senators have gone off without leave, and broken up the House. There are now about ten of us in town. Some of our best friends are in the country; and we shall suffer by their absence. The delay upon the University bill is truly to be lamented. The hostile interests are daily acquiring new force by intrigue and management. The party opposed altogether to the University, is growing so rapidly, we have just grounds to fear a total failure of the measure. I this morning counted up twenty-six votes of this description, on this side the Ridge; and there are doubtless many others. Many of the western members will take the same course, particularly if they lose the site. If all the western votes could be united in opposition, we shall certainly be defeated. Some of the west will certainly be with us on the site, and I hope a respectable portion will be for the bill on the passage. Yet if this portion should be small, it will be insufficient to save the bill from eastern hostility. The friends of William & Mary demand $5,000 per annum, as the price of their concurrence; and in the event of a refusal, will carry off some votes. I have advised my friends not to enter into any compacts of the kind, and sooner will I lose the bill, than I will give my assent to it. The party hostile to the University, come chiefly from the lower country, and are within convenient distance of William & Mary. The better educated part of them, whilst they, their sons, connexions or friends have been educated at William & Mary, quote Smith, the Edinburgh Review, and Dugald Stewart, to prove that education should be left to individual enterprise. The more ignorant part pretend that the literary fund has been diverted from its original object, the education of the poor; and accuse the friends of the University of an intention to apply all the fund to the benefit of the wealthy. Mr. ******, very unintentionally, but very unfortunately, has given plausibility to this charge. Two days ago he offered a resolution to authorize the Committee of Schools and Colleges to consider of and report to the House, on the expediency of repealing that part of the law relative to the poor. The resolution was laid on the table. The exhibition of such a resolution from a friend to the University, at this time, has produced great, and, perhaps, irretrievable mischief. I have prevailed on him to consent not to call it up at all; or, if another course should be preferred, to suffer it to be withdrawn. It will probably lie on the table. In regard to Charlottesville, as a site for the University, many liberal and enlightened persons feel difficulties from the smallness of the town. They think a town of some size necessary, to attract professors, to furnish polished society for the students, to supply accommodations, to resist the physical force, and present the means of governing a large number of young men, &c. This last objection seems to make some impression. Mr. Johnson, of Staunton, arrived two days ago. He is very prudent, and very remarkable on all occasions for reserving till the last moment the disclosure of the opinion he means to advocate. On the day he arrived in the Senate chamber, he went to the map of Virginia, and in a tone half laughing and half earnest, observed to Gen. Preston and myself, that he always expected that those lines drawn across the State in the calculations published in the Enquirer, were not drawn in a proper manner; and proceeded to remark on the circumstance, that the eastern and western lines commencing at the middle of the mouth of the Chesapeake were nearer to the southern than northern side of the State. Should the bill get up to the Senate, it may be proper for me to be able to meet all possible objections on that subject. Perhaps Mr. * * * * may take the course you expect of him; but if he does, I shall be greatly disappointed. I should, therefore, be much obliged, if you will inform me whether due eastern and western, and due northern and southern lines, will materially change the position of the centre of population; or whether lines drawn in any other direction would materially vary the result; as also, whether the mode of ascertaining the centre, by the point of intersection of *only* two transverse lines, be liable to any well founded objection. I have Madison's map in my room, and shall make some calculations; but I ask you for information, because yours would be more accurate than my own, particularly as to the relative portions of counties bisected by the lines. I will, if you desire it, make no other use of your letter than to enable myself to meet any objections to the present mode of drawing the lines. My motive for asking for information on the preceding subject, is not that I myself doubt, but that I may meet and dissipate the doubts of others. You recollect, no doubt, the letter I wrote you last winter, stating my impressions that certain characters in the House of Delegates were hostile to the location of the University at Charlottesville. I have ascertained that upon that subject I was entirely correct. I was also correct in my anticipation that they would go with the Board of Commissioners. They will now give us their support. I lately wrote you that Mr. Hunter, of Essex, would unite with us. But in that I was mistaken. My first apprehensions were well founded. He will be opposed to the measure altogether.

I am, dear sir,

Most truly and faithfully yours,

JOSEPH C. CABELL.

Mr. Jefferson.

LXXXII.

T. J. TO J. C. C.

MONTICELLO, January 1, 1819.

DEAR SIR,—Although my revolt against letter writing has not permitted me to acknowledge, separately, your several favors of December 8, 14, 17, 24, as I received them, I am not the less thankful for their information. I take up my pen now on the subject of my estimate of the centre of white population. You say, it is objected, that the commencement at the mouth of the Chesapeake is nearer the southern than northern limit on the coast. That is true; but the greatest part of what is north is water. There is more land on the south than north. I do not think a fairer point of commencement can be taken, and being a remarkable one, I therefore took it. The point of commencement being determined, the direction of the line of equal division is not a matter of choice, it must from thence take whatever direction an equal division of the population commands; and the census proves this to pass near Charlottesville, the Rockfish Gap, and Staunton. The Blue Ridge again, in the cross division, is so natural a dividing line, as to have been universally so considered, and a parallel course with that should therefore be taken for the line of equal division that way. They talk of a division by an E. & W. line; but our northern boundary tending north of N. W., while the southern is E. & W., the fair direction is between the two, as that is which I took. Why should they divide by a parallel to our southern, more than to our northern boundary? What reason can be given for laying off the southern half in a parallelogram, and the northern in a triangle? Not a single one but to bring the course of that line nearer to Lexington. The State itself being triangular, each half should be so. An E. & W. line would take the line of equal division entirely from Staunton, but I do not believe it would from Charlottesville; and while a north and south line would take it entirely from

Lexington, I believe it would be still as near to Charlottesville; and, in my opinion, run your lines in what direction you please, they will pass close to Charlottesville, and for the very good reason that it is truly central to the white population. However, let those who wish to set up other lines in competition, make their own calculations. It is a very laborious business. Mine took me two or three days, and I know there can be no inaccuracy in it, except from a single source. Where a line divided a county into two parts, equal or unequal, I could only estimate by my eye the proportion between the two parts. No doubt there is error in some of these, but probably as much one way as another, and that contrary errors balance one another. I am certain there will not be found much error in the whole result. But I am saying to you things which would occur to yourself, and yielding to the *lex inertiæ* which, with respect to the use of the pen, is now become, uncontrolably, the law of nature with me, I will place here the assurances of my affectionate esteem and respect.

TH: JEFFERSON.

Joseph C. Cabell, Esq.

LXXXIII.

J. C. C. TO T. J.

RICHMOND, January 7, 1819.

DEAR SIR,—Your favor of 1st instant has been duly received, and I thank you for the information it contains. I also thank you for the copy of Tracy's work, which I received in a few days from the time it left you, but have heretofore omitted to mention.

In my last I gave you an account of our declining and gloomy prospects respecting the University. Just about Christmas, and from that period to the 1st instant, the success of the measure was despaired of. The Valley members first had united against us. Half the trans-Alleghaney members had followed them. The residue were neutral, and tending to the opposite party. Even my friend Thompson, of Kanawha, who had theretofore kept up my spirits, acknowledged that he believed the greater part of the members from beyond the Alleghaney had determined to oppose us, and the remainder were not to be depended on. I was also assured by acquaintances from that quarter, that the western delegates were prepared to vote against the measure, if a western site should not be preferred. In the lower parts of the State, the opposition to the measure was great and growing, whilst a line of votes at the foot of the Blue Ridge, to the north and south of my district, and a scattering vote in other parts of the eastern country were arrayed against us. In this state of affairs, with six or eight very active and dexterous opponents to contend with, and with but few to aid me, I advised our friends to preserve a cheerful countenance, and not to despair. Having lost, as I supposed, the western vote, I turned my views altogether to the east. The combination to the west justified an appeal to eastern feelings and interests. Our majority of votes, on the east of the Ridge, is sixty-two. Putting down twenty-two of these for absentees, our majority would be reduced to forty; of these if the opposition should obtain twenty-one, of course, we should be defeated. I knew we should get some few votes to the west, but these I thought ought to be placed to the account of absentees, inasmuch as twenty-two is but a small allowance. It was obvious, therefore, that it was necessary to reduce the opposition in the east to less than twenty. For this purpose, it was essential to ascertain who were the opponents, and to contend for them, with the enemy beyond the mountain. In this enquiry I have encountered very great difficulty, from the absence of the Senators, and the want of experienced friends in the House of Delegates. But I have at length succeeded with respect to all the counties, except a few low down on the south of James River. In the course of my search, I have had occasion to witness the vast and uncommon exertions of the opposite party. They have made great inroads into our ranks, whilst the greater part of our eastern members seemed to be asleep. My mind has sought far and wide for the means of awakening the eastern people to a just view of their rights, and of exciting the friends of learning to an exertion of their powers. I have passed the night in watchful reflection, and the day in ceaseless activity. Our ranks are filled with clever young men, who will, when the debate comes on, give us flowery speeches; but we want the practical wisdom and efficient concert of the year 1799. In this situation, I have sought to supply the defect, by conveying from person to person intelligence of our different views, and by endeavoring to reconcile differences of opinion, and to create harmony. I have written into the country for friends to come in, or to send letters to our aid. I have called on, and implored the aid of powerful friends out of the Legislature, such as Roane, the Nicholas's, Brockenbrough, Taylor, &c. I have actually destricted the country east of the Ridge, and obtained a promise from some gentleman of high standing and influence in each district, to use his best efforts to remove the prejudices of members, and to counteract the movements of the opposite party. I have procured most of the essays you have seen in the Enquirer, and furnished the probable topics of objection, to some of our friends in the House of Delegates, with reference to authorities for their refutation. Happily, sir, a counter current has been produced, and I am now confident of ultimate success. There are now thirty members on the east of the Ridge who have been prejudiced against the bill. But the number will be reduced. And whilst many of these will vote with us on the site, I hope their votes on the passage will be at least in part counteracted. Some valuable friends have lately arrived. Captain Slaughter, of Culpepper, Chancellor Taylor, Mr. Pannill, member of the Board of Public Works, Mr. Hoomes, of King & Queen, Mr. John Taliaferro, of the Northern Neck, and Chancellor Green. The latter and myself were up until three o'clock this morning, conversing on the means necessary to ensure success. I think he will be able to break down, in some degree, the influence of William & Mary, in the neck of land from this to Hampton. Our friends are at last roused, and as ardent as you could desire. The course of things here will surprise and distress you. But be assured, sir, I do not exaggerate, and we have been compelled to meet the opposition on their own ground. The liberal and enlightened views of great statesmen pass over our heads unheeded like the spheres above. When we assemble here, an eastern and western feeling supercedes all other considerations. Our policy now is to keep back the vote as long as possible. Thank heaven! my health has sustained me, and even improved in the anxious and trying situation in which I am placed. I hear you are still complaining. This intelligence comes through Col. Randolph, whom I sought this morning, but could not find at Mrs. Randolph's. God grant, sir, that you may soon be entirely restored to perfect health, and that you may in a few weeks be cheered by the intelligence of the final success of the bill for the University.*

I am, dear sir,

Most sincerely and faithfully your friend,

Jos. C. Cabell.

Mr. Jefferson.

LXXXIV.

J. C. C. TO T. J.

Richmond, 4 P. M., 18th January, 1819.

Dear Sir,—Grateful, truly grateful, is it to my heart, to be able to announce to you the result of this day's proceedings in the House of Delegates. In Committee of the Whole, the question was taken, after an elaborate discussion, on the motion to strike the Central College from the bill. The vote was as

---

* And the succeeding letter will inform the reader of the fate of the measure which, having so long trembled in the scales of chance, was yet environed with uncertainty.

follows: For striking out, 69; against, 114—majority against striking out, *forty-five*. This is a decisive victory. Immediately after this decision, Mr. Baldwin, of Augusta, rose and made a most eloquent appeal to the Western delegation, calling on them to dismiss local feelings, and to unite with the majority in the support of the measure.* The Bill passed to a third reading *mem: con.* Having left the House before the critical vote on the site, to avoid the shock of feeling, which I should have been compelled to sustain, I did not hear Mr. Baldwin. But I am told the scene was truly affecting. A great part of the House was in tears; and, on the rising of the House, the Eastern members hovered around Mr. Baldwin; some shook him by the hand; others solicited an introduction. Such magnanimity in a defeated adversary

---

* A sketch of this debate appears in the Enquirer of January 19, 1818. In the succeeding number, of January 21st, a correspondent (Mr. Gilmer) reports Mr. Baldwin's appeal more fully and accurately, having prefaced it with a tribute of high commendation. Those who feel an interest in the history of this institution will not object to find it here reproduced entire.

"Mr. B., with a magnanimity only equalled by his eloquence, then came forward to invoke the House to unite in support of the University. He said, he had attempted to discharge his duty to his constituents; he had supported the pretensions of Staunton as long as there was the slightest hope of success; but now he came forward to conjure the House to sacrifice all sectional feelings on the altar of their common country. In the name of Virginia, in the name of the dear land of his nativity, by that proud and dignified character which she had always borne, he conjured the members to unite in the vote for the University. Great in arms, great in character, she requires only to be great in science. Let us raise a pillar of fire to conduct her footsteps. If we make a retrograde movement now, if having accumulated a fund for education we refuse to appropriate it in this honorable way, we may, with the old Castilian, live to blush for our country. Let us, then, unite; let us do our duty. He shall have lived to little purpose who does not know that in political matters delay breeds danger. There is a tide in the affairs of nations as of men. Let us, then, all unite—let us erect a temple in which our youths may assemble in honor of science. Virginia! dear land of my birth! protectress of my rights! to thy glory let us consecrate the present hour."

It may not be known to all of the present generation of readers, that the author of this appeal was Judge Briscoe G. Baldwin, late of the Court of Appeals of Virginia.

excited universal applause. The discussion must have produced a considerable effect. This morning, Mr. Hunter, of Essex, an intelligent member, expressed great fears. The mode of drawing the lines was called in question, as favoring the Central College. I had prepared East and West, and North and South lines, which threw the point of intersection some where near the South end of Fluvanna. One of the Rockbridge delegates suggested another method of settling the pretensions of rival sites, with a view to discredit the mode pursued by yourself. His idea was this: draw a line from one of the places to the other—bisect this line by another line running across the State. And the place which should be found on the side of the line, where the greatest mass of population should fall, would be nearest the centre of population. This idea was suggested on Saturday; and I did not hear of it till last night. I rose early this morning, and with the assistance of Mr. Hoomes, of King and Queen, my room mate, applied this rule, and found, to the East of the line, 137,000 white inhabitants more than to the West. These tables were used in the debate. One of the Rockbridge delegates objected to the statement about the centre of population lately published in the Enquirer, that the free negroes and mulattoes were included—the fact was admitted and the colored people deducted, and the centre still fell East of Charlottesville. I imagine you fell into the error of including the colored population by deducting the slaves from the totals in the census of 1810. At a future day, I will give you further particulars, and inform you of the names of the genetlemen who have contributed to the happy results of this day. I have just received Chancellor Carr's letter. The hint was unnecessary—we shall take care of the bill in the Senate. I do not write to him, because I suppose he has left you. I awoke, two nights ago, about 3 o'clock, with an alarming spitting of blood, which continued till 10 o'clock. It was probably brought on by exposure to bad weather and loss of sleep. I have been twice bled, and have taken medicine; and feel myself on the recovery.

I feel happy in the idea that this note will give you great pleasure.

Faithfully, yours,

JOSEPH C. CABELL.

Mr. Jefferson.

LXXXV.

J. C. C. TO T. J.

SENATE CHAMBER, 21st January, 1819.

DEAR SIR,—On the 19th instant the University Bill passed the House of Delegates, only twenty-eight members voting against it. Yesterday I moved its commitment in the Senate. The committee are Messrs. Johnson, Alfred Powell, Taliaferro, Hoomes, of King and Queen, Mallory, Hay, and myself. We met to-day, at 10 o'clock, Mr. Mallory being absent. I had previously agreed with my friends to admit no admendments. Mr. Johnson proposed various amendments, beginning with such as were unimportant, and proceeding to one of vital importance, viz: to reduce the additional appropriation of $20,000 for the education of the poor to $5000. We voted him down, after full discussion in the Committee. The Committee has risen to meet again to-morrow, so as to give Mr. Johnson an opportunity to offer other amendments. I now think he will make efforts to change the site in the House. But I think you may be tranquil on this subject. The bill will probably be a law in three days from this time.

Faithfully, yours,

JOSEPH C. CABELL.

Mr. Jefferson.

P. S. My wife hearing of my late attack of hemorrhage has become very unhappy, and, in conjunction with my Williamsburg friends, urges me to withdraw to that place. Happily, I am getting over the attack, and my breast is much less sore than it was a few days past. I am strongly in hopes the rupture was confined to some of the vessels of the throat. As soon as the University bill passes I shall retire to Judge Coalters, and attend to my duties in the Senate, as my health will permit, from that place; and should it be necessary, I will go to Williamsburg. But the connection of the Eastern and Western waters is a subject of great importance in itself, and I have promised to render every service in my power to Mr. Thompson, of Kanawha.* Mrs. C. will come up on Sunday, with the Miss Coalters, from Williamsburg.

LXXXVI.

J. C. C. TO T. J.

RICHMOND, 25th January, 1819.

DEAR SIR,—The question on striking out the Central College, from the University bill, has just been taken in the Senate, and rejected by a vote of 16 to 7.

And I am happy to inform you, that immediately thereafter the question was taken on the passage of the bill, and that it passed by a vote of 22 to 1.

I began to take some part in the discussion which has taken up all Saturday and to-day; but, in my first effort, the blood vessel, which had broken within me, opened again, and I was compelled to abandon the attempt, by the discovery that I was spitting blood. I am now under serious apprehensions on the score of my health. I have retired to Judge Coalter's, where Mrs. Cabell met me on yesterday. Should I not get better, I must withdraw to Williamsburg.

Mr. Watts voted for striking out the Central College. Mr. Johnson made great exertions to get the bill amended, but we voted him down very easily.

Yours, faithfully,

JOSEPH C. CABELL.

Mr. Jefferson.

---

* Mr. Cabell here incidentally alludes to a measure of principal importance to the material interests of Virginia, and which was destined, in after years, to engage even a larger share of his attention than did the University while in progress towards its final establishment.

LXXXVII.

T. J. TO J. C. C.

MONTICELLO, January 28, 1819.

DEAR SIR,—I join with you in joy on the passage of the University bill, and it is necessary you should send me a copy of it without delay, that the visitors may have a meeting to see and to do what it permits them to do for the furtherance of the work, as the season for engagements is rapidly passing off. But we shall fall miserably short in the execution of the large plan displayed to the world, with the short funds proposed for its execution. On a careful review of our existing means, we shall be able, this present year, to add but two pavillions and their dormitories to the two already in a course of execution, so as to provide but for four professorships; and, hereafter, we can add but one a year; without any chance of getting a chemical apparatus, an astronomical apparatus, with its observatory, a building for a library, with its library, &c.; in fact it is vain to give us the name of an University without the means of making it so. Could not the Legislature be induced to give the University the derelict portions offered to the pauper schools, and not accepted by them? I mean so much, for example, of last year's $45,000 as has not been called for; and so much of this year's $60,000 as shall not be called for. These unclaimed dividends might enable us to complete our buildings, and procure our apparatuses, library, &c., which, once done, a moderate annual sum may maintain the institution in action. I shall be happy to hear of the improvement of your health, and salute you with affectionate respect.

TH: JEFFERSON.

Joseph C. Cabell, Esq.

LXXXVIII.

[A special interest attaches to the following letter; it being that in which the writer makes honorable mention of those gentlemen, both in and out of the two houses, who had been most active and efficient in promoting the success of the University bill.]

J. C. C. TO T. J.

RICHMOND, 4th December, 1819.

DEAR SIR,—Your favor of 28th ult. was received on Monday, time enough to be answered by the mail of that evening, but I declined doing so, in order to have an opportunity of conversing with some of my friends, before I should write. I am very sensible of the truth of all that you say on the inadequacy of the funds of the University; and most willingly would I co-operate in augmenting them; but knowing, as I do, the character and prejudices of the present Assembly, and what has occurred during the present session, I must say that I think that any such attempt would not only prove unsuccessful, but would be injurious to the interests of the institution. When Mr. ****** moved the house to enquire into the expediency of repealing that portion of the law which provides for the education of the poor, a murmur of dissatisfaction ran through the illiterate part of the house, that the friends of the University meant to apply the whole of the literary fund to the education of the rich. It required the most strenuous and persevering exertions of all the friends of the measure to counteract the effects of ******'s motion. Were we to move now for the derelict portion of the school fund, I am confident that the idea would be revived, that the friends of the University were grasping at the whole of the fund. It would be in vain to urge, that the proposition went only to the derelict portion; they would not believe us. *We have got possession of the ground, and it will never be taken from us.* True it is, the Western people will probably not now feel as desirous, as they were of late, to endow the University; but the enlightened part of the people are every where in favor of such an establishment. I consider it, therefore, our best policy to do nothing that is calculated to injure the character of its friends in the estimation of the Assembly, or of the great body of the people. Any proposition of the kind you suggest, though in itself highly proper and judicious, would, in my humble judgment, have this tendency, if brought forward *at the present session.* At another session, the attempt might be made, perhaps, with no injurious consequences, and with a probability of success. Such were the views that presented themselves to my mind, immediately on the perusal of your letter. Mr. John Taliaferro, Mr. Hay, Mr. Robertson, of the Senate, Chancellor Taylor, and Judge Coalter and Col. Carr, to whom I have mentioned the subject, entirely concur in my opinion. As I lodge two miles from town, and am not present, except from 11 to 3, I have not had an opportunity of seeing other persons on this subject. I shall endeavor to consult Col. Nicholas to-day, but I am sure of his concurrence. Col. Green left town a few days past. I told him, on parting, I thought it would be well to get a bill passed amendatory of the law respecting the education of the poor, so as to coerce the application of the money to the objects contemplated by the act. He assured me that, in his opinion, the best course would be to drop the whole subject of education; to say nothing more about it at the present session.

We are very much indebted to Mr. Taliaferro and Col. Green for the favorable change in the delegation north of James River and below tide water. At Christmas, every member from Richmond to Hampton, except one, was opposed to us. On the vote, all went with us, except one. This was very much owing to the correct views of the subject presented to them by Col. Green, who is very popular in that part of the State, as indeed he is every where. Capt. Slaughter, of Culpeper, made us a visit during the session, and co-operated with useful and commendable ardor. Judge Brooke, Judge Brockenbrough, Mr. Stanard, Mr. Ritchie, Mr. Hoomes, of King &

Queen, Dr. Nicholson, of Middlesex, Mr. Scott, of the Council, and Mr. Minor, of Spottsylvania, were active and valuable friends in the lower and northern sections of the State. Judge Roane was not much in the circle of the members, nor was Col. Nicholas; but these gentlemen lost no opportunity of lending their aid, in which course my brother William heartily co-operated. I advised with Col. Nicholas in every difficulty, and found him an invaluable friend. On the south side of James River, Chancellor Taylor, and Mr. Pannill, of the Board of Public Works, were useful auxiliaries. Mr. Gilmer wrote the essays signed a "Virginian" and "A friend of the State." *Mr. Rice, a Presbyterian clergyman of this place, wrote the essay signed "Crito." He discovered remarkable enthusiasm for the measure*, and although he did not advocate any particular site, *yet his liberal conduct*, as well as that of the delegates from the counties of Prince Edward and Charlotte, *satisfied me that the sect of Presbyterians did not (as I had expected) exert their influence against the Central College.**

* The italics are those of the Editor, and are employed for reasons which will hereafter appear. All the Essays here referred to were both able and well-timed—one of Mr. Gilmer, on *the site*, particularly so. From that of Dr. Rice we present a passage, which seems to have made a deep impression on the mind of Mr. Cabell, as I find it copied more than once among his papers, and was no doubt used by him with effect. Similar statements were made at the time by other writers, but this was perhaps more particular and authentic.

"This remark suggests the idea of the pecuniary losses which we have sustained by this most culpable negligence. This is no light matter. *Ten years ago* I made extensive enquiries on the subject, and ascertained to my conviction, that the amount of money annually carried from Virginia, for purposes of education alone, exceeded $250,000. Since that period it has been greater. Take a quarter of a million as the average of the last eight and twenty years, and the amount is the enormous sum of $7,000,000. But had our schools been such as the resources of Virginia would have well allowed, and her honor and interest demanded, it is by no means extravagant to suppose, that the five States which bind on ours would have sent as many students to us as under the present wretched system we have sent to them. This, then, makes another amount of seven millions! Let our economists look to that. Fourteen millions of good dollars lost to us by our parsimony!! Let our wise men calculate the annual interest of our losses, and add it to this principal! they will then see what are the fruits of this precious speculation. In the language of the craft, it may well be said "verily, it is a losing job.""

Judge Roane wrote the essay signed a "Farmer." But to no one are we more indebted than to Mr. Sam'l Taylor, of Chesterfield. That excellent and promising man deserves your highest commendation for the good temper, dignity, ability, perseverance and zeal with which he conducted the management of the subject in the House of Delegates. Mr. Gordon has since expressed to me, in the strongest terms, his approbation of the advice I had given himself and Mr. Carr in regard to Mr. Taylor. Mr. Broadnax, of Greensville, made an excellent argument on the site, and Mr. Thompson, of Kanawha, was a very valuable auxiliary in the West. To Mr. Daniel and Mr. Martin, of the Council, great thanks are due for their services, at the last session, in procuring the appointment of the distinguished characters who composed the Board of Commissioners. To that illustrious body we are infinitely indebted, and I shall ever derive great happiness from the thought of my having suggested the idea of that mode of settling the question of locality. It is a remarkable fact, that the report of the Commissioners has met with universal and loud applause, except as to the site recommended by it. Judge Coalter saved the bill last winter, by advising the separation of the local from the general question. Justice and feeling have prompted me to make this hasty sketch of the service rendered by our worthy friends in the cause of the University. It is right that you and Mr. Madison should know who are your most zealous co-operators in the great work you have undertaken for the good of your country and of mankind. In doing this, let me not be understood to disparage the exertions of persons not enumerated; and particularly of the local delegation, each of whom acquitted himself with unusual ability.

You requested me to send you a copy of the University bill, which I would do, but that it has already gone to you, in the Enquirer of the 28th ult.

You and Col. Randolph will receive a copy of the several reports on the subject of the navigation of James River, and of the connection of the eastern and western waters. I shall call on Mr. Peyton this morning to have Col. Randolph's copy hurried on. It would give me great pleasure to hear his views on this great subject, which I am now carefully investigating.

I am happy to inform you, that the alarming symptoms about my breast are now subsiding, and I am capable once more of attending to business.

I am, dear sir, faithfully yours,

JOSEPH C. CABELL.

Mr. Jefferson.

LXXXIX.

J. C. C. TO T. J.

RICHMOND, 8th February, 1819.

DEAR SIR,—Lest your Enquirer of the 28th January may have miscarried, I now have the pleasure to enclose you that paper.

The President and Directors of the Literary Fund have placed us in an awkward dilemma, by an egregious mis-statement of the amount and proceeds of the fund. Relying, as usual, on the statements of that Board, we have appropriated $80,000, as part of the revenue of the fund, when in fact that revenue will not amount to more than $60,000. There can be no doubt of the propriety of the repeal of that part of the law which adds $20,000 to the fund for educating the poor; and I hope that this will be done. Yet I am assured, by several leading men of the lower house, that, in that house, the majority would sooner repeal the appropriation for the University. Probably they are mistaken; but you must not be surprised, if such should be the result. The Senate may be entirely depended on. The Executive intended on this day to appoint the Visitors, but have not done so, because the bill was not signed by the Speakers of the two houses. This was not a sufficient cause of delay; yet some one or more of the Councillors feeling difficulties, the business was deferred; and will probably not be resumed till Monday next.

I am, dear sir, faithfully yours,

JOS. C. CABELL.

Mr. Jefferson.

[The following correspondence between Governor Preston and Mr. Cabell, being something more than formal, is deemed worthy of insertion in this place.]

COUNCIL CHAMBER, February 27, 1819.

SIR,—I have the honor to enclose you your appointment of Visitor of the University of Virginia, together with the advice of Council fixing on the day of your first meeting.

I have a peculiar gratification in the discharge of this duty, as I am persuaded that the foundation is now laid of an institution that will form a new and important era in the science and literature of our native State. My gratification is much increased by the recollection that this institution will commence under auspices that will insure its success, and cannot fail to answer the most sanguine expectations of every friend to knowledge and to the improvement of the human mind.

With great respect, I have the honor to be,

Your obedient servant,

JAMES P. PRESTON.

Joseph C. Cabell, Esq.

RICHMOND, 17th March, 1819.

SIR,—I have had the honor to receive your favor of 27th ult., enclosing my commission as Visitor of the University of Virginia, and the advice of Council fixing on the day for the first meeting of the Board.

In notifying yourself and the members of the Council of my acceptance of the appointment, I beg leave to make you my acknowledgments for the polite and obliging terms in which it was conferred.

I am very sensible, I assure you, sir, of my unworthiness of this honorable appointment. Yet, having been called to the station by the unsolicited voice of the proper authority, my humble services shall not be withheld. And I am happy in the reflection, that my own insufficiency will be compensated by the great abilities of my distinguished associates.

I remain, sir, very respectfully,

Your obedient servant,

JOSEPH C. CABELL.

Governor Preston.

XC.

J. C. C. TO T. J.

RICHMOND, 15th February, 1819.

DEAR SIR,—On Saturday, the Visitors of the University were appointed. They are, Thomas Jefferson, James Madison, Chapman Johnson, James Breckenridge, Robert B. Taylor, John H. Cocke and Joseph C. Cabell. I communicated to the Governor a message from Gen. Cocke, purporting that a report was in circulation that the Visitors of the Central College were about to be appointed Visitors of the University; that he did not wish to be appointed, as he was well persuaded there were many characters in the State who would be better qualified than himself to vote on the many important and difficult questions that would arise in the progress of the institution; and his only desire was to see the University flourish, and answer the expectations of the country. I availed myself of the acquaintance I have with the Governor, and with a member of the Council, who spoke to me on the subject, to express my deep conviction of the application of such observations to myself; and to assure them that any little zeal and activity which I may have heretofore discovered, sprang from no interested motive, and must not weigh a feather in the scale of appointment. I besought them to look abroad, and select men calculated to give you efficient co-operation, and to have weight with future legislatures. They have thought proper, notwithstanding, to put General Cocke and myself on the list. I recommended, very earnestly, the appointment of Mr. Johnson.

Indeed, situated as I was, it was a subject in which I did not wish to interfere; but as I was consulted, *in regard to the Valley*, I urged the appointment of Mr. Johnson as a point of importance. He has treated your name with great respect and deference throughout our contests for the site; and that question being determined, he will go with you in future. No man on the other side of the Ridge could have as much influence in breaking down future opposition from that quarter of the State. I was consulted as to the quarter of Winchester, and recommended Tucker, Carr, Hoomes, &c. &c. They were all inadmissible; every distinguished character in that part of the State was objected to, either as holding the office of judge, or as being a member of Congress, or upon some other ground. The policy of the Executive differed in some degree from that which I was told you preferred; which was, to select the Visitors from the neighboring counties. They preferred to take a majority from the vicinity, and the rest from a distance. Gen. Taylor will scarcely accept the appointment. * * * * * * * * * * * * The last Monday in March is fixed on for the first meeting of the Visitors. I hope it will not be necessary for me to come to any intermediate meeting of the Visitors of the Central College, as I should fear the effects of the keen air of the mountains at an earlier period than the latter part of March. My health is greatly improved, and the only thing now necessary to my entire re-establishment, is to avoid the exposure of my lungs to keen air or unusual exertion. I regret exceedingly that a report has prevailed in the circle of the members that I was to go to Europe in pursuit of professors; inasmuch as it will enable my opponents to ascribe to me personal views, and to injure me with illiterate men, who are as ignorant of my real motives on this occasion as they are of the nature and responsibility of the agency in question. To one or two of my friends, I shall state the substance of the communications that passed between you and myself in regard to this subject. I deem it unnecessary to consider this proposition again, inasmuch as the deficiency of the appropriation will necessarily defer any such measure for the present. Viewing the whole ground, I consider it good policy to employ all the funds for some time in building, and not to put the institution into operation till sufficient arrangements shall have been made for a brilliant commencement. Suffice it to say, for the present, that the appointment I now hold, I regard as the highest honor ever conferred on me, and that I shall look far around for the means of duly fulfilling the duties it imposes. But in this pursuit, I shall look up to you as my principal guide and support. My fervent wishes for the entire restoration and long continuance of your health continue invariable.

Faithfully yours,

JOSEPH C. CABELL.

Mr. Jefferson.

P. S. Since writing the preceding letter, I have conversed with another friend, and from the representations made by him, I am induced to doubt whether the wicked construction stated above to have been placed upon my conduct extends to many persons. *In the heat of the conflict, aspersions were thrown out on both sides. Time dissipates these mists of prejudice; and upon this subject** I now feel relieved.

Mr. Taylor, of Chesterfield, thinks the House of Delegates will not consent to repeal the additional $20,000 appropriated for the education of the poor. Even should this temper continue, the appropriation for the University will not be endangered, as it may be drawn at any time of the year.

It is of the utmost importance for the friends of the University to procure the election of able and liberal men to the next Assembly. Gen. Tucker will be a valuable accession to the Senate.

---

* The italics are again the Editor's.

XCI.

T. J. TO J. C. C.

Monticello, February 19, 1819.

Dear Sir,—Your favor of the 15th was received yesterday. The appointment of Visitors of the University is entirely unexceptionable to me; the only fear is, that the distance of Gen. Breckenridge and Mr. Taylor will render their attendance uncertain. I should have been sorry indeed, if either yourself or Gen. Cocke had been left out. The lateness of the day (March 29) appointed for their first meeting renders that of the present set immediately necessary, as we should otherwise lose the chance of employing workmen, and consequently lose a year in our preparation. I think, with you, that we must apply all our funds to building, for the present year, and not open the institution until we can do it with that degree of splendor necessary to give it a prominent character; consequently, that we must defer the mission for professors to another year. I never mentioned that subject but to General Cocke, and that with a view only of his mentioning it to you. I have requested a meeting of the Visitors, at Mr. Madison's, on Friday next, where I wish it were possible for you to meet us, although not if it will jeopardise your health. It is necessary to determine at once what buildings we can undertake this season, and to engage undertakers. I believe the extent to which our funds will permit us to go will be to two pavilions, in addition to the two we have, one boarding-house, and twenty or thirty more dormitories. Our engagements with Dr. Cooper* oblige us to receive him, and I shall propose to let an usher of our nomination, and under our patronage, open a grammar school for the Junior classes in Charlottesville, on his own account altogether, receiving nothing from the college.

---

* Something will be said of this appointment in a future note.

In that case, Cooper may take the highest or the higher classes only, and may open his law school. So far, I think we can begin in May.

Ever and affectionately yours,

TH: JEFFERSON.

Mr. Cabell.

XCII.

J. C. C. TO T. J.

RICHMOND, 22d February, 1819.

DEAR SIR,—Your favor of 19th has this moment arrived. I am sorry that it is out of my power to attend the meeting at Mr. Madison's, on Friday. In the present state of the roads, and with such symptoms as I have lately experienced, it would be improper in me to undertake the journey. I hope you will be able to secure the attendance of Mr. Watson and General Cocke; and even if you should not, I am pretty confident that what the members present may agree upon will receive the sanction of future meetings. You speak of our engagements with Doctor Cooper. I did not know that any engagements existed. The last information I received on this subject was either from Gen. Cocke or Col. Coles, during my illness last fall. I was then told that *you* had been under the impression that Doctor Cooper had laid himself under an obligation to come to the Central College; but that *he* had written you a letter from Fredericksburg, apprising you that he did not consider himself bound in any way whatsoever. I confess I was not mortified at the occurrence; for whilst Dr. Cooper's talents and acquirements are unquestioned, I find the impression very general, that either in point of manners, habits, or character, he is defective. He certainly is rather unpopular in the enlightened part of society. This may be because he is not as well known to the world as he is to you and Mr. Madison. The fact, however, is worthy of notice. A motion was made a few days ago, by Mr. Taylor, in the House of Delegates, for leave to bring in a bill to repeal the additional appropriation of $20,000 for the education of the poor, and leave was refused by a majority of ten. I mention this to shew you what difficulties lie in the way of getting adequate funds. I cannot think that the next General Assembly, prepared as it may be by the press, will refuse to correct this false step in our proceedings. But rest assured that this House of Delegates would sooner repeal the provision for the University than any part of that made for the poor. And there will probably be some struggle on this subject next winter. This furnishes with me a strong reason not only to lay out all the money at present in building, but convinces me of the importance of rather keeping the houses empty till a sufficient number can be got into a state of readiness to receive some half dozen eminent professors, than to fill them successively as they are finished, with perhaps here and there a man obnoxious to public prejudice. If Doctor Cooper comes, let him come unaccompanied by other professors. But if he is to come alone, permit me to recommend that no final decision to that effect shall be taken till the meeting of the Visitors of the University, when Generals Taylor and Breckenridge may be fully informed of the reasons for and against the appointment, and *their* acquiescence *previously* secured. I have spoken with Mr. Johnson on this point. He, like myself, has the highest opinion of the abilities of Doctor Cooper; but he considers the appointment one of great delicacy and importance, and thinks it would be advisable to pause, in the manner, and for the reasons, I have stated. I have devoted two winters and one summer of my life to the most sincere co-operation with you in getting this measure through the Assembly. I think I am well apprised of the state of the public mind; and, believe me, the contest is not over. The very same interests and prejudices which arrayed themselves against the location at Charlottesville, will continue to assail that establishment. They will seize upon every occasion, and avail themselves of every pretext, to keep it down.

On the motion for leave to bring in a bill to repeal the $20,000, these interests were visible in the opposition. I write you in haste, as the mail is about to leave town. Perhaps I may have taken up erroneous views; but I thought it my duty to state them. I beg the favor of you to present my respectful compliments to Mr. Madison and other gentlemen present at the meeting, and to assign the causes for my absence.

Faithfully yours,

JOSEPH C. CABELL.

Mr. Jefferson.

XCIII.

T. J. TO J. C. C.

MONTICELLO, March 1, 1819.

DEAR SIR,—On my return yesterday from our visitorial call, I found here your favor of February 22, and I now enclose you a copy of our proceedings, with the request of our colleagues to lay them before the Governor and Council; for although their assent is not by the law necessary to give them validity, yet they have a right to negative, which makes it a duty to communicate them, that they may have an opportunity to exercise it if they disapproved any of the proceedings. I am sorry to learn that the continuance of the patronage of the Legislature is doubtful; but we should go on in our duty, and hope the same from them, or leave on them the blame of failure. Accordingly you will see that we have adopted your idea of applying our funds to preparing buildings, except so far as current services and actual engagements require. On the subject of engagements, I must quote a passage in your letter to me, to wit: "you speak of our engagements with Dr. Cooper. I did not know that any engagements existed." In answer to this, I have made transcripts from our journals, which I now enclose, and which you will recollect the more satisfactorily, as the original is in your own hand writing. To this I must add some facts.

After the resolutions of the 7th and 8th of October, 1817, which had the approbation unanimously of the whole of the six visitors, on learning that Cooper had a prospect of the Chemical chair in Philadelphia, worth $7,000 a year, we voluntarily wrote to let him know he might suspend his acceptance of our appointment until a decision of the Philadelphia election; and if he failed to be elected, we should hope his acceptance here. He failed in that, but they proposed to establish a new chair, to keep him there. In this state of things, we came to the resolution of May 11 of the last year 1818; by which it appears we considered an appointment of him as still obligatory on us. At the same time, New York was offering him a salary of $2,500 a year, besides tuition fees, to accept a professorship there. I saw the letter from Governor Clinton, making this offer. But his inclinations being for this place, next to Philadelphia, he came on in October to see the place, the country, &c., and then stated to me in writing what he should expect. By this time the expectation that the Legislature would adopt the College for the University, had induced us to enlarge our scale, to purchase more lands, make our buildings larger, &c., so that if that hope failed, it was doubtful whether the state in which our funds would be left, would not make it desirable to be off with Dr. Cooper. In answering his paper, therefore, I availed myself of the opportunity to premise to the articles agreed to, that they were to be considered by him as founded on the hypothesis of the Legislature's adopting our institution, and entitling us consequently to the additional funds of $15,000 a year. I considered his not replying to this paper as evidence of a tacit acceptance, and so spoke of it to Mr. Correa, although assuredly he had not, by word or writing, signified an acceptance. Learning this on the journey from Correa, he immediately wrote back to correct me, and said he had supposed he was to hold the thing under advisement until the legislative decision should be known, and in the mean time to weigh our propositions with others; for, besides that of New York, he had a most liberal offer from New Orleans. As soon as I heard of the first vote of our Legislature on the site of the University, carried by so large a majority, I informed Cooper of it, and that as soon after the passage of the law as a meeting of the visitors could be procured, I would write to him finally, and request his decision, and expect him, if he accepted, to come on in early spring. From all this it appears to me that we are bound, not only in consistency and reputation, but in law, if Dr. Cooper accepts our propositions. And why should we wish otherwise? Cooper is acknowledged by every enlightened man who knows him, to be the greatest man in America, in the powers of mind, and in acquired information; and that, without a single exception. I understand, indeed, that a rumor unfavorable to his habits, has been afloat, in some places, but never heard of a single man who undertook to charge him with either present or late intemperance; and I think rumor is fairly outweighed by the counter-evidence of the great desire shown at William & Mary to get him, that shown by the enlightened men of Philadelphia to retain him * * * * * * * *, the anxiety of New York to get him, that of Correa to place him here, who is in constant intercourse with him, the evidence I received in his visit here, that the state of his health permitted him to eat nothing but vegetables, and drink nothing but water, his declarations to me at table, that he dared not to drink ale or cider, or a single glass of wine, and this in the presence of Correa, who, if there had been hypocrisy in it, would not have failed to tell me so.

The College is in distress for $1,500. The visitors have authorized Mr. Garrett to receive that sum from the treasury, but we must ask the favor of you to pave the way for it, and to learn when we may draw on that fund for moneys, on whom, and by whom, the drafts must be made.

Ever and affectionately yours,

TH: JEFFERSON.

Mr. Cabell.

XCIV.

T. J. TO J. C. C.

Will you be so good as to have the enclosed inserted immediately in the Enquirer, and to place the expense to account of your next instalment?

Affectionate salutations.

MONTICELLO, March 6, 1819.

XCV.

J. C. C. TO T. J.

RICHMOND, 8th March, 1819.

DEAR SIR,—I am happy to inform you that since I last wrote you, the Legislature has repealed the additional appropriation of $20,000 to the education of the poor. The question came up again by an amendment in the Senate to the revised bill respecting the literary fund; it passed the Senate unanimously, and the House of Delegates by a majority of eighteen. We are thus happily extricated from an awkward dilemma; and an obstacle to further improvement in future is removed. This retrograde movement on the part of the Legislature, tends to show the probability of a mistake on my part as to the future patronage of the State; and I would wish the statement in my last letter as to the continuance of the hostility of rival interests to be understood with an exception of Mr. Johnson. The whole income of the literary fund being now appropriated, it is questionable how any good disposition of the people towards the University may hereafter be made available. New funds will scarcely be created. In revolving the subject in my mind, I have thought of an expedient for the next session. If the whole of the balance due from the general government should not be discharged in the course of this year, perhaps it might be practicable to obtain a donation out of that balance, for the purpose of fitting up the institution.

I have received your favor of 1st instant, and hastened to fulfill your instructions. The proceedings of the meeting at Mr. Madison's have been laid before the Governor and Council, and have been approved by them. I have conversed with the Governor and Treasurer in regard to the state of the literary fund, and the persons on whom and by whom drafts are to be made. The fund is overflowing; and were it desired, the whole annuity of the University might be called for at this time. I am authorized to say, that a copy of the proceedings at Mr. Madison's being in possession of the Executive, a draft from the Treasurer, Mr. Garrett, for $1500, would be honored by the President and Directors of the Literary Fund. The regular course would be for the Visitors to draw on the President and Directors; and for these to draw on the Treasurer. If the Visitors think proper, they may continue to delegate their power in this respect to their Treasurer.

My last letter to you was written under considerable pain, (arising from an eruption on my side,) and I wrote more concisely, and perhaps abruptly, than I should have written in a different situation. I had, by no means, forgotten the proceedings of the Visitors of the Central College, as stated in the copy of the record which you have had the kindness to send me. You will recollect, that I was prevented by a severe spell of sickness from attending the meeting of the Visitors last fall, and I can assure you I was entirely ignorant, till the receipt of your favor of 1st instant, of the nature of the communications between yourself and Dr. Cooper, about that time. I not only did not know of any new engagements with that gentleman, but had been led to believe that the obligations under which he had had it in his power to place us by the acceptance of our proposals of former dates, had been dissolved by a course of conduct on his part, with which you were by no means satisfied. My information was derived from Col.

Coles or Gen. Cocke, but to the best of my recollection from the former, during my illness last fall. I was told that Dr. Cooper's letter, from Fredericksburg, was not satisfactory to you; that you were so disgusted you would not answer it, and that your engagements with him were at an end. Hence, I observed, "I did not know that any engagements existed." As you must have been misunderstood by that one of these two friends who gave me this information; or, if not misunderstood, as you must have been subsequently satisfied by other communications from Dr. Cooper, the statement of these circumstances is not made with any other view than to account to you for what must appear to you a strange inconsistency or want of recollection on my part.

I am sure it is unnecessary for me to request you to consider every thing I say upon this or any other matter touching the University, as proceeding from a friend anxiously disposed to serve you personally, and to promote the welfare of the institution.

May it not be questioned whether the Visitors of the Central College possessed the power to enter into engagements with Dr. Cooper, which would be obligatory on the Visitors of the University. If they possessed the power, would not the policy of exercising it be somewhat doubtful? In common with the other friends of the Central College, I censured very freely that part of the proposed donation from Lexington, which subjected us to the necessity of providing for their professors.

As I shall probably have an opportunity of conversing with you before the meeting of the Visitors, I will not now trouble you with unnecessary remarks on this subject. A course may be taken, which will preserve essentially your engagements with Dr. Cooper, and guard against the injurious consequences of the prejudices existing against him.

I am, dear sir, faithfully yours,

JOSEPH C. CABELL.

Mr. Jefferson.

XCVI.

J. C. C. TO T. J.

SENATE CHAMBER, March 12th, 1819.

DEAR SIR,—Your note of the 6th instant, by Mr. Garrett, covering the advertisement for workmen for the University, has been received. I walked immediately to the office of the Enquirer, and had the advertisement inserted in that paper, where I shall cause it to be continued for some successive papers. I have introduced Mr. Garrett to the Governor, who will have a meeting of the President and Directors of the Literary Fund to-morrow; at which I have no doubt his draft for the $1,500 will be honored. The Auditor has promised me that he will have no objection to the execution of the indemnifying bond, in the case of the certificate in the county of Albemarle, so as save the necessity of a visit to this place by the Proctor of the College. I have seen Colonel Nicholas respecting Mr. Brockenbrough's being employed as Proctor; and he and Mr. Garrett are now communicating on that part of the business. From every thing I can learn in regard to Mr. Brockenbrough, it would be important to engage him, and as any salary we could give a Proctor would not secure his services, neither Mr. Johnson nor myself, as at present advised, see any impropriety in combining for that object, the appointment of Proctor with that of undertaker of the wooden part of the buildings. I have had an application from a Mr. Montcarrel, of this place, for some station in the University as a teacher of the French language. I have informed him that the institution will not go into operation for at least a year to come; and, in the meantime, I shall have it in my power to procure information for him. We rise this evening or in the morning. I shall go on a visit, with Mrs. Cabell, to some of her relations in Alexandria, and shall certainly be with you on 29th. One slight attack of blood-spitting, after a long speech, excepted, the symptoms in my breast have not reurned, since I last mentioned the subject of my health; and I am relieved from serious apprehensions, and the symptoms that produced them. It gratifies myself and all your friends exceedingly to hear of your recovery.

I am, dear sir, faithfully yours,

JOSEPH C. CABELL.

Mr. Jefferson.

XCVII.

[The plan of the University has often been subjected to criticism, both by the Virginia public and traveling visitors. The following letter will shew, that in the view of some of the colleagues of Mr. J., it lay open to objection in certain particulars. For some of these acknowledged defects, however, Mr. J. was not wholly responsible; as a more eligible site which he had once hoped to procure, and which would have admitted a better aspect and more economical construction, was lost to the public through the political prejudice of the owner against himself. Mr. Cabell was wont to relate several pleasant anecdotes—better suited to a social circle than to a permanent record here—relative to the dissent of the other Visitors, not only from the plan of the buildings, but other novel and cherished ideas of the author; to the respectful manner in which their counter-opinions were conveyed to the venerable rector, and to the adroitness with which they were met. Their motives for general acquiescence are well stated by his biographer, Mr. Tucker. Though every essential part of the establishment required the sanction of the Board of Visitors, yet, on almost all occasions, they yielded to his views, partly from the unaffected deference which most of the Board had for his judgment and experience, and partly for the reason often urged by Mr. Madison, *that as the scheme was originally Mr. Jefferson's, and the chief responsibility for its success or failure would fall on him, it was but fair to let him execute it in his own way.*" They doubted, also, concerning one or more features of its organization, and certain principles on which it was proposed to conduct its government. These they knew would be tested by time and trial, and errors, when manifested, could be corrected by their successors.]

J. C. C. TO T. J.

RICHMOND, 17th April, 1819.

DEAR SIR,—Mr. Brockenbrough left this for Gen. Cocke's yesterday morning. It seems he cannot establish at the University until 1st August; yet, I hope you may be disposed to engage him, as I think he will be a source of great comfort and relief to you. I have reflected a good deal on subjects connected with the University since we separated—some thoughts have occurred to me which I beg leave to communicate to you with the freedom of a friend. The plan of pavilions and dormitories along the area of the University will be beautiful and magnificent, and unlike anything which I have seen in Europe or America. The continuation of the same style of architecture till the two sides of the area shall have been filled up, will follow, as a matter of course. But permit me to suggest a doubt whether the plan of pavilions and dormitories should not be confined to the area, and some other styles adopted for the hotels and back ranges. The dormitories, though extremely beautiful, are liable to some objections in point of convenience. With an Eastern and Western aspect, with a single window in each, and with flat roofs, I am inclined to think they will be very warm in summer ; and with a contiguous public passage, it is to be apprehended that the students will be less retired from noise and other interruptions than might be desired. For these reasons, I should be disposed to depart from that mode of building, with respect to the hotels and back ranges. In regard to flat roofs, on the plan now pursued, it seems to be much doubted, whether they will not leak, and require renewal in the course of six years. This seems to be the prevailing opinion of the best workmen in the country. With respect to the lecturing rooms in the pavilions, permit me to ask whether a more spacious plan would not be advisable in the further prosecution of the buildings? Some of the Professors will probably not have crowded classes, and these might have the use of the halls now finished, or in state of preparation. But many of the Professors will, in all probability, have very numerous attendants; and the idea of repeating the same lecture, to the residue of a large class, would be very disagreeable to a man who would ascribe the necessity of doing so to a supposed defect in the structure of the pavilions. It occurred to me, at one time, that the lecturing halls in the pavilions should be constructed on the model of the Greek and Roman theatres and amphi-theatres, which has been adopted since the revolution in France; but as this would deprive the Professors and their families of the use of them at other hours than those of lecturing, and as it might produce too considerable a departure from the plan now adopted, I presume it would be most advisable merely to enlarge the halls. In the lapse of years, it may be proper to resign the pavilions entirely to the accommodation of the Professors, and to provide lecturing rooms in separate buildings.* I was extremly happy to be informed, by Gen. Cocke, that you had annexed the gardens to the back-yards of the pavilions. In the suggestions I have now ventured to make, I am mainly governed by the wish to remove every possible ground of objection to the further patronage of the Assembly. Whilst I think the Visitors should be guarded in communicating to the public any little differences of opinion which now and then may occur among them, so as to prevent unfounded inferences from being deduced, I am of opinion that each individual should think and speak freely his impressions upon every point; and I am well persuaded that a contrary course ought and would be regarded by you as uncandid and unfriendly.

I have heard, with great concern, of the accidental fire which lately occurred at Monticello, and of the injury which you are said to have sustained. That your health may be soon entirely restored, and that you may long enjoy every earthly good is the continued and unceasing prayer of

Your faithful friend,

JOSEPH C. CABELL.

Mr. Jefferson.

---

* This suggestion was carried out either on the opening of the institution, or soon after.

XCVIII.

J. C. C. TO T. J.

BREMO, 2d November, 1819.

DDAR SIR,—Being now at this place, on my way to the lower country, I avail myself of the opportunity by Mr. Neilson to return the plan of your house in Bedford, for the use of which I beg you to accept my sincere thanks. I admire it very much. But the want of suitable instruments, and continued indisposition almost ever since I left Monticello, have prevented me from taking a copy. It is not, however, important at this time, that I should have the plan in my possession to study or to imitate. The wish which I felt so ardently to move into your neighborhood, and that of the University, cannot now be indulged. I do not believe that there is, at this time, any opening for me to get into that neighborhood, with the advantages of soil and position which I should desire.* Nor could I sell either of my estates in the present state of the country, but at a sacrifice which even prodigality would condemn. And the stock of money in hand, on which I counted when I left Monticello, as a fund to begin upon, I now find must be loaned to a friend to prevent the sacrifice of his property. I must, therefore, postpone any change of my situation at this time, and make such additions to my establishment at Warminster as will not materially affect its sale in future, and are demanded by present convenience.

I am extremely sorry to hear of the severe attack of illness you have had since the meeting of the Visitors; and I earnestly hope it may wear off without any injury to your constitution.

I am, dear sir, faithfully yours,

JOSEPH C. CABELL.

Mr. Jefferson.

---

* Mr. C. had once contemplated a change of residence and removal to Albemarle, that he might be in the neighborhood of his friend Col. Coles, as also of Mr. J., a scheme in which both of those gentlemen had manifested a friendly interest. The several negotiations, however, conducted by others on Mr. C.'s behalf, had failed with the proprietors of more than one estate, much to his regret.

XCIX.

T. J. TO J. C. C.

MONTICELLO, January 22, 1820.

DEAR SIR,—I send you the enclosed as an exhibit to our enemies, as well as friends. Kentucky, our daughter, planted since Virginia was a distinguished State, has an University, with fourteen professors and upwards of 200 students; while we, with a fund of a million and a half of dollars, ready raised and appropriated, are higgling without the heart to let it go to its use. If our Legislature does not heartily push our University, we must send our children for education to Kentucky or Cambridge. If, however, we are to go a begging anywhere for our education, I would rather it should be to Kentucky than any other State, because she has more of the flavor of the old cask than any other. All the States but our own are sensible that knowledge is power. The Missouri question is for power. The efforts now generally making through the States to advance their science, is for power; while we are sinking into the barbarism of our Indian aborigines, and expect, like them, to oppose by ignorance the overwhelming mass of light and science by which we shall be surrounded. It is a comfort that I am not to live to see this.

Our exertions in building this last year have amounted to the whole of the public annuity of this year, for which, therefore, we have been obliged to draw to relieve the actual distresses of our workmen; and the subscriptions come in slow and grudgingly. You know that we are to pay Doct. Cooper $1,500 in May, and his family will depend on it for subsistence in his absence. We have been obliged, therefore, to set apart, as our only sure dependence, six particular subscriptions, on the punctuality of which we can depend, to wit: yours, Mr. Madison's, Gen. Cocke's, Mr. Divers', John Harris' and mine, which exactly make up the money.

Affectionately yours,

TH: JEFFERSON.

Mr. Cabell.

Estimate of the money necessary to finish the buildings at the University.

Amount necessary to finish the buildings already commenced, as per Proctor's estimate, page 23 of the report and documents respecting the University,	$38,898 25
Amount necessary to erect the buildings not yet commenced, but which are requisite to complete the establishment, as per the aforesaid page 23 of the report,	58,200 00
Total,	$97,098 25

Funds estimated by the Proctor as available for the purpose of carrying on the buildings, after meeting sundry engagements specified in the report; the public annuity of the year 1820 having been included in the estimate,	$39,020 03
Deduct amount of subscriptions to the Central College, included in the Proctor's estimate of funds, the whole or the greater part of which will not be collected in the course of the year 1820,	30,220 01
Balance of available funds,	$8,800 02

Balance of money required, after deducting the aforesaid amount of available funds,	$88,298 23
Deduct this amount on account of supposed collections from the subscribers to the Central College in the course of the year 1820,	8,298 23
Amount necessary for the completion of the buildings at the University,	$80,000 00

Statement of the amount of subscriptions to the College, included in the Proctor's estimate, of 1st *October*, 1819, *of funds available in time to meet the expenses of carrying on the buildings.*

Balance of 1st installment,	$2,001 08
Balance of 2d installment,	6,186 27
Amount of 3d installment, due April 1st, 1820,	11,016 33
Amount of " " due April 1st, 1821,	11,016 33
Total,	$30,220 01

Being requested to state my impressions as to the probable amount of receipts, in the course of the year 1820, on account of subscriptions to the Central College, I declare it to be my opinion, founded as well on my knowledge of the manner in which the subscription moneys have heretofore come in, as on what is generally known of the pressure of the times, that not more than $8,800 02 will be obtained from that quarter, in aid of the funds of the University, previous to the 1st of January, 1821.

ALEX'R GARRETT,
Bursar of the University of Virginia.

7th February, 1820.

C.

J. C. C. TO T. J.

RICHMOND, 3d February, 1820.

DEAR SIR,—I arrived here the day before yesterday, and found your favor of 20th ult. in the post-office. The unfortunate and long-continued illness of my wife, kept me in Williamsburg till the 1st inst. The session is now far advanced; but I hope it is not too late to procure a further endowment of the University. The lamentable occurrence in the treasury, increases the difficulties we had already to encounter. Some enlightened men tell me there is no prospect of success; and I candidly think it doubtful. But I am now urging the subject in every quarter where I think I can be useful. Your letter and the important paper it contained, I took the liberty to shew to most of the members at the Eagle, this morning; and I found a good disposition on the subject. I am sorry there has been so little yet done in regard to this great subject. A detailed report from the President and Directors of the Literary Fund will appear in a few days, whereupon propositions will be submitted to the House of Delegates. In the mean time, I shall see the friends of the measure. You may expect to hear more fully from me hereafter. I write now merely to inform you that misfortunes have kept me in Williamsburg till the 1st instant; but that I am now in place, and engaged on this subject, which is so interesting to your feelings. I am rejoiced to hear of your good health. I have thought it unnecessary to trouble you with letters heretofore, because our mutual friend, Col. Randolph, would write you fully on every subject.

In haste, I remain, dear sir,

Faithfully yours,

JOSEPH C. CABELL.

Mr. Jefferson.

CI.

J. C. C. TO T. J.

RICHMOND, 17th February, 1820.

DEAR SIR,—The result of all my enquiries convinced me that the only course left us was to aim to get the present and future surpluses of the literary fund, and to amend the bill lying on the table of the Senate, and giving the counties the right of drawing out their arrears. Mr. Johnson and myself concerted measures; and, with the aid of Mr. Hay in the debate, carried the amendment unanimously through the Senate, save one vote (Davidson's). The amendment went down yesterday morning, and was laid on the table, with the concurrence of our friends. It was understood the Committee of Schools and Colleges were about to act on the same subject, and would give us their support. They met yesterday, when Mr. Bassett made a motion to give William & Mary $5,000 per annum; which being rejected, he rose, in apparent excitement, and abruptly left the room. Whilst this was going on, I was sent for by the late Treasurer, and confidentially told the deficiency in the treasury would fall on the literary fund. I consulted with Mr. Johnson, and Mr. Morris, of the House of Delegates, who agreed with me that Preston would, to avoid the penalty, be compelled soon to pay up the money, and that we must persevere in our views to the present and future surpluses, till we could raise $80,000. *By the documents*, it would seem, there ought now to be a disposable surplus of $40,000; and from a power to pledge the future surpluses of some three or five thousand dollars per annum, we proposed to raise the balance. This morning the Committee of Schools and Colleges met, and Col. Bassett contrived to amend our proposition, so as to give us the surplus, now supposed to be on hand, of $40,000, and to give William & Mary an annuity of $5,000 annually. And thus the business stands. Gen. B. was on the committee, and remained silent, lest his opposition might defeat the James River and Kanawha bill, which passed an hour after. They have got the vantage ground of us, by this unfortunate management of the committee. To-morrow our friends will make a great effort in the House, but really I cannot flatter you. Nothing shall be left undone within the compass of my power. I beg you to excuse my not writing you more fully and more frequently, as I am much engaged. I took the liberty to insert extracts from your letter in the Enquirer.

I am, dear sir, faithfully yours,

JOSEPH C. CABELL.

Mr. Jefferson.

CII.

J. C. C. TO T. J.

SENATE CHAMBER, 24th February, 1820.

DEAR SIR,—The enclosed bill has this day passed into a law. The House of Delegates having first rejected the amendment of the Senate for $80,000; and then that for $40,000, and having postponed the whole bill on 22d; Gen. Breckenridge, Mr. Johnson and myself had a consultation, and agreed that the interests of the institution would be promoted by the bill now enclosed. Our friend Mr. Gordon had already moved for leave to bring in a bill, and was in the midst of an animated discussion, when Mr. Johnson and myself got to the House. We prevailed on him to withdraw his motion, to make way for the introduction of the subject by Gen. Breckenridge, who, we supposed, not being from the local district, would have more influence with the House. The bill went through this morning, with but little opposition. We hope we have taken the course which yourself and the other Visitors will approve, considering the circumstances in which we were placed. The University is popular in the Senate, and unpopular in the House of Delegates. I hope the President and Directors of the Literary Fund, or the Board of Public Works, will be able to lend us the money; but upon this point I cannot speak positively. An immediate meeting of the Visitors is necessary. On 29th new Visitors are to be appointed. I shall ask the Governor to bring on the appointments speedily, and if the old Visitors should be re-appointed, I shall propose to Gen. B. and Mr. Johnson to proceed directly to Monticello; and I would take Gen. Cocke along with me from Bremo.

I am, dear sir, faithfully yours,

JOSEPH C. CABELL.

Mr. Jefferson.

CIII.

J. C. C. TO T. J.

CHARLOTTESVILLE, 3d October, 1820.

DEAR SIR,—I neglected to bring with me Mr. Garrett's account, which I am instructed to examine and verify; and beg the favor of you to send it by the bearer. I wish to compare it with the account in the Bursar's books, from which it was copied; and at the same time that I check the latter by the vouchers. Perhaps I shall be induced to take the account home, in order to examine the additions at my leisure.

I am, dear sir, faithfully yours,

JOS. C. CABELL.

Mr. Jefferson.

CIV.

T. J. TO J. C. C.

POPLAR FOREST, November 28, 1820.

DEAR SIR,—I sent in due time the report of the Visitors to the Governor,* with a request that he would endeavor to convene the Literary Board in time to lay it before the Legislature on the second day of their session. It was enclosed in a letter, which will explain itself to you. If delivered before the crowd of other business presses on them, they may act on it immediately, and before there will have been time for unfriendly combinations and manœuvres by the enemies of the institution.

I enclose you now a paper presenting some views which may be useful to you in conversations, to rebut exaggerated estimates of what our institution is to cost, and reproaches of deceptive estimates. $162,364 will be about the cost of the whole establishment when completed. Not an office at Washington has cost less. The single building of the courthouse of Henrico, has cost nearly that; and the massive walls of the millions of bricks of William & Mary, could not be now built for a greater† sum.

---

* See Appendix M., No. 2.

† I find among Mr. Cabell's papers the following, in which he states in tabular form the cost of several buildings designed for public use. The facts here collected were used to confirm the assertion of the text, and to repel the popular charge of extravagance.

Cost of the new courthouse in the city of Richmond, exclusive of the ground,	$105,000
Cost of the houses and lots of Farmer's Bank of Virginia,	170,080
" " Bank of Virginia,	165,115
recent expenditures on Public Square and Capitol,	99,614
Eagle Hotel and offices, exclusive of ground,	94,000
Union Hotel and stable, " "	70,000
Twenty pillars in House of Representatives at Washington, at $5,000 each,	100,000
Two last offices of department at do.	95,908
Gross sum given by South Carolina to her University in twenty years,	200,000
Annuity given by South Carolina to the same,	12,000

Surely Governor Clinton's display of the gigantic efforts of New York towards the education of their citizens will stimulate the pride as well as the patriotism of our Legislature, to look to the reputation and safety of their own country, to rescue it from the degradation of becoming the Barbary of the Union, and of falling into the ranks of our own negroes. To that condition it is fast sinking. We shall be in the hands of the other States, what our indigenous predecessors were, when invaded by the science and arts of Europe. The mass of education in Virginia, before the revolution, placed her with the foremost of her sister colonies.* What is her education now? Where is it? The little we have, we import, like beggars, from other States; or import their beggars to bestow on us their miserable crumbs. And what is wanting to restore us to our station among our confederates? Not more money from the people. Enough has been raised by them, and appropriated to this very object. It is that it should be employed understandingly, and for their greatest good. That good requires that, while they are instructed in general, competently to the common businesses of life, others should apply their genius with necessary information, to the useful arts, to inventions for saving labor, and increasing our comforts, to nourishing our health, to civil government, military science, &c.

Would it not have a good effect for the friends of the University, to take the lead in proposing and effectuating a practicable scheme of elementary schools? To assume the character of the friends, rather than the opponents, of that object? The present plan has appropriated to the primary schools $45,000 for three years, making $135,000. I should be glad to know if this sum has educated one hundred and thirty-five poor children? I doubt it much. And if it has, they have cost us $1,000 a piece, for what might have been done with $30. Supposing the literary revenue $60,000, I think it

---

* See Introduction.

demonstrable that this sum equally divided between the two objects, would amply suffice for both. One hundred counties divided into about twelve wards each, on an average, and a school in each ward, of perhaps ten children, would be 1,200 schools, distributed proportionably over the surface of the State. The inhabitants of each ward, meeting together, (as when they work on the roads,) building good log-houses for their school and teacher, and contributing for his provisions, rations of pork, beef, and corn in the proportion, each of his other taxes, would thus lodge and feed him without feeling it, and those of them who are able, paying for the tuition of their own children, would leave no call on the public fund, but for the tuition fee of here and there an incidental pauper who would still be fed and lodged with his parents. Suppose this fee $10, and $300 apportioned to a county on an average, (more or less duly proportioned,) would there be thirty such paupers for every county? I think not. The truth is, that the want of common education with us is not from our poverty, but from the want of an orderly system. More money is now paid for the education of a part, than would be paid for that of the whole if systematically arranged. Six thousand common schools in New York, fifty pupils in each, 300,000 in all; $160,000 annually paid to the masters; forty established academies, with 2,218 pupils, and five colleges with 718 students; to which last classes of institutions $720,000 have been given; and the whole appropriations for education estimated at two and a half millions of dollars! What a pigmy to this is Virginia become! With a population all but equal to that of New York! And whence this difference? From the difference their rulers set on the value of knowledge and the prosperity it produces. But still if a pigmy, let her do what a pigmy may do. If among fifty children in each of the six thousand schools of New York, there are only paupers enough to employ $25 of public money to each school, surely among the ten children of each of our 1,200 schools, the same sum of

$25 to each school will teach its paupers, (five times as much as to the same numbers in New York,) and will amount for the whole to $30,000 a year, the one-half only of our literary revenue.

Do then, dear sir, think of this, and engage our friends to take in hand the whole subject. It will reconcile the friends of the elementary schools, (and none is more warmly so than myself,) lighten the difficulties of the University, and promote in every order of men the degree of instruction proportioned to their condition, and to their views in life. It will combine with the mass of our force, a wise direction of it, which will ensure to our country its future prosperity and safety. I had formerly thought that visitors for the schools might be chosen by the county, and charged to provide teachers for every ward, and to superintend them. I now think it would be better for every ward to choose its own resident visitor, whose business it would be to keep a teacher in the ward, to superintend the school, and to call meetings of the ward for all purposes relating to it; their accounts to be settled and wards laid off by the courts. I think ward elections better for many reasons, one of which is sufficient, that it will keep elementary education out of the hands of fanaticising preachers, who in county elections would be universally chosen, and the predominant sect of the county would possess itself of all its schools.

A wrist stiffened by an ancient accident, now more so by the effect of age, renders writing a slow and irksome operation with me. I cannot, therefore, present these views by separate letters, to each of our colleagues in the Legislature; but must pray you to communicate them to Mr. Johnson and General Breckenridge, and to request them to consider this as equally meant for them. Mr. Gordon being the local representative of the University, and among its most zealous friends, would be a more useful second to General Breckenridge in the House of Delegates, by a free communication of what concerns the University, with which he has had little opportunity of becoming acquainted. So also would it be as to Mr. Rives, who would be a friendly advocate.

Accept the assurance of my constant
And affectionate esteem and respect,

TH: JEFFERSON.

Mr. Cabell.

Estimates in Mr. Jefferson's hand-writing enclosed in the foregoing.

A general view of what the lands, buildings, and all other expenditures for the University will have cost when completed, estimated from the moneys actually received, and what the Proctor states as further necessary.

Received of the subscriptions about -	$19,000
Loan from the Literary Fund, -	60,000
Annuities of 1819, '20, - -	30,000
To be received, the annuity of 1821, included in Proctor's estimate, - - . - -	15,000
Further necessary to complete the Pavilions, Hotels and Dormitories by do. - - - -	38,364
Probable actual cost of whole establishment, (exclusive of Library,)	$162,364

ESTIMATES HERETOFORE MADE.

10 Pavilions for accommodation of Professors at $6,000 each, - - - - - -	$60,000
6 Hotels for dieting the students, at $3,500 each, -	21,000
104 Dormitories, at $350 each, - - - -	36,400
200 acres of land, and buildings purchased, may be stated as worth - - - - - -	10,000
Covering with tin instead of shingles, levelling grounds and streets, bringing water in pipes, and numerous other contingencies, say - - -	10,000
Excess of actual cost above the estimates (about 18 per cent.) - - - - - - -	24,964
	$162,364

To liberate the funds of the University, and to open it in 1821, with only six professors, will require—

1. A remission of the loan of $60,000.
2. A supplementary sum to liberate the annuities of 1821, 2, 3, - - - - - - $45,000
3. To make good the deficit estimated by the Proctor, 8,364
4. An additional sum for the building of the Library, 40,000
5. And to establish and maintain ten Professorships an equal partition of the Literary Fund between the University and elementary schools will be necessary, say $30,000 a year to each.

A building for an Observatory not having been mentioned in the Rockfish report, is not brought into view here. It will cost about ten or twelve thousand dollars, and may be accomplished by the balance of subscription money not taken into account in the report of 1820, and by the rents for the hotels and dormitories.

CV.

J. C. C. TO T. J.

SENATE CHAMBER, 20th December, 1820.

DEAR SIR,—I thank you sincerely for your favor of November 28, which I received on my arrival here on 5th inst.

* * * * * * *

I have shown your letter to General Breckenridge and some other friends. Mr. Johnson will not be here till Christmas. We have agreed, for reasons I will more fully detail hereafter, to let the subject of the University lie over till after Christmas. I am going to spend the holidays with Mrs. Cabell in Williamsburg, from which I will write you at leisure. For the present I will only say that we shall probably have to fall down in our petition for a sum sufficient to finish the buildings, and let the rest lie till another session. We shall have the academies to contend with this year. Our difficulties are great, but every effort will be used to carry the bill. Some objections are made to the mode in which our accounts are presented. Some ask why the items are not more detailed; others why Mr. Garrett's accounts do not go back farther than April. I would advise the fullest and freest rendition of accounts. *There* lies our hold on the public affections. * * *

Yours faithfully,

JOSEPH C. CABELL.

Mr. Jefferson.

CVI.

J. C. C. TO T. J.

WILLIAMSBURG, 22d December, 1820.

DEAR SIR,—On consultation with General Breckenridge and others, it was decided that we should bring forward nothing in regard to the University till after Christmas. I got leave of absence till 29th, and left town on 20th. The evening before my departure, I was informed that Mr. Griffin of York had brought in a set of resolutions, the evident effect of which would be to embarrass the disposable part of the literary fund, so as to defeat the claims of the University; and these resolutions were warmly supported by the friends of Hampden Sidney, but particularly by Mr. Miller of Powhatan. They give the right to the counties to draw out the direlict part of the fund, provide against the recurrence of a similar state of things, and make an appropriation to William & Mary, Hampden Sidney, Washington College, New London, the University, &c. I went immediately to see General Breckenridge, and spent the evening in conversing with him on this subject. He was glad the opposite party had come forward so early in the session. Instead of getting an advantageous start of us, he thought they would only defeat themselves, by disclosing their plans and conflicting with each other; and our friends, he thought, should attend the Committee and let them run on for a time. Mr. Bowyer and Mr. Gordon seemed to be fearful of the consequences of this course. I got leave of absence, with the intention of carrying Mrs. Cabell up on 29th; but owing to this movement of the opposition, I have determined to leave her in Williamsburg, and to return in the steamboat on the 26th. I left your letter with General Breckenridge, and had shown it to many of our friends. There was a general concurrence in the opinion, that we should not succeed in an attempt at a general system of schools, and that we should aim at only so much money as would finish the buildings, leaving the mortgage for the present on our funds. It will be a hard struggle to get even this. The hostile interests are strong, and well conducted this session.

I have looked over the accounts since I last wrote you. I am now satisfied that Mr. *** was only seeking for materials of opposition; and I think it unnecessary for Mr. Garrett to send down the detailed account before 1st April. The summary statement covers the whole ground. Should it be necessary, I will hereafter call for explanations as to any part of the accounts. Gen. Breckenridge thinks Gen. Blackburn will run with us. Mr. Doddridge comes down in a good humor; has candidly acknowledged that I was in the right as to the great litter of banks, and avowed himself a friend to the University. He is anxious for an endowment of the Randolph Academy. But I hope he will ultimately unite with us. Bowyer, of Rockbridge, is my intimate friend, and heartily with us. Otey, of Bedford, advocates an appropriation to New London Academy; but I believe will, in the end, go right. Mr. Watson, of Louisa, is our zealous friend. I fear Mr. Crump, of Goochland, will be induced to insist on an appropriation to Hampden Sidney; yet I hope he will ultimately co-operate with us. His local position is unfortunate. ****** will be violently opposed to the University; but I hope that influence is now but small. I am advised by Gen. Breckenridge not to stir the question relative to the old charters but as a dernier resort. Some have thought it a dangerous weapon, inasmuch as it would divide the friends of science, and throw the majority against us. Morris, Breckenridge, Bowyer, Gen. Taylor, Coalter—all—think the principle sound, and that it can not ultimately be resisted. Our object is now, to finish the buildings. If this could be done without resort to this doctrine, I would willingly put it aside for the present; but I do not see how we can avoid calling it in, unless they should defeat themselves, and leave the field open to us. I will keep you fully informed, from time to time. Let me urge you to write to Judge Roane and one or two other friends; but at least to Judge Roane. * * * * * * * *

I am, dear sir, faithfully yours,

JOSEPH C. CABELL.

Mr. Jefferson.

CVII.

T. J. TO J. C. C.

MONTICELLO, December 25, 1820.

DEAR SIR,—Your letter of the 20th was the first intimation that I had omitted to enclose, with the documents of our report, the first half year's account of the Bursar, which had been duly rendered in April, and filed away. I now correct that error, by enclosing it to the Governor, with a letter of explanation, to be communicated to the Legislature.

You may have observed an apparent difference of $38,364, between the Proctor's estimate of what is wanting to complete the buildings, and our estimate embodied in the report. With the report and letter enclosing it, I wrote an additional one to the Governor, shewing that this difference was merely apparent. As the evidence of this, on the face of the two estimates, if closely observed, redered its communication to the Legislature not absolutely necessary, I observe it has not been sent to them with the other papers. I enclose you, however, a copy of it, in the hand-writing of one of my grand-daughters; for my dislocated wrist is failing so fast, that I apprehend the loss of the power of writing altogether. This explanation may be necessary in both houses; but may be given verbally, as well as by the formal letter.

I lately saw in a newspaper an estimate in square miles of the area of each of the States, of which the following is an extract: Virginia 70,000 square miles, Massachusetts 7,250, Connecticut 4,764, Delaware 2,120, Rhode Island 1,580." By this it appears that there are but three States smaller than Massachusetts; that she is the twenty-first only in the scale of size, and but one-tenth of that of Virginia; yet it is unquestionable that she has more influence in our confederacy than any other State in it. Whence this ascendancy? From her attention to education, unquestionably. There can be no stronger proof that knowledge is power, and that ignorance is weakness. *Quousque tandem* will our Legislature be dead to this truth?

Ever and affectionately yours,

TH: JEFFERSON.

Mr. Cabell.

Letter enclosed in foregoing.

MONTICELLO, November 9, 1820.

SIR,—The Rector and Visitors of the University of Virginia, at their last semi-annual meeting of October 2, having agreed to a report of the condition of that institution, its disbursements and funds, as required by law, I now enclose it, with the accounts of the Bursar and Proctor. Some difference will be found between the Proctor's account and the general view presented in the report of the Board, which it is my duty to explain.

After the separation of the Board, it occurred to the Proctor that the account he had last rendered, and on view of which their report was formed, might, in some of its articles, be made more specific and correct. It was given to him, therefore, and that now enclosed was returned in its stead. By the last article of this, it might be understood that the buildings whose completion was contemplated in this report, would require an additional sum of $38,364 to complete them. But this apparent excess proceeds chiefly from the circumstance that the annuities of 1822 and '23 are not entered in this account, as they are in the general statement made in the report. This lessens the apparent difference by $30,000, leaving a real one of $8,364 only; and this the Proctor properly accounts for by observing, that the former estimates comprehended buildings only, omitting the cost of 200 acres of land, and several other contingent expenses not then foreseen. We are now so near the end of our work as to leave little room for future errors of estimate. The building requisite for a library, however, is not included in this estimate.

It will readily occur that these observations cannot have had the sanction of the Visitors, because the circumstance producing them arose after their separation. I have the honor to be, with the highest consideration, sir,

Your most obedient and most humble servant,

TH: J.

Governor Randolph.

CVIII.

J. C. C. TO T. J.

RICHMOND, 4th January, 1821.

DEAR SIR,—I thank you sincerely for your letter of December 25th, which I found here on my arrival on 30th. Indisposition confined me in Williamsburg rather longer than I expected when I last wrote you. Since my arrival I have been incessantly engaged on the subject of the University. We have a powerful combination to oppose, and the result is extremely doubtful. If you will examine the enclosed resolutions of Mr. Griffin, you will find them drawn with great art; and on full consultation, I have boldly put forth the doctrine relative to the old charters, which I announced to you and Mr. Madison at the spring meeting, and to the Board in the autumn.* It seems to be spreading rapidly among our friends,

---

* The doctrine relative to the old charters, here referred to, was, that an appropriation of public money to the uses of either of the old colleges ought not to be granted by the Legislature, except upon the express condition that such college should, like the University of Virginia, be at all times and in all things subject to the control of the Legislature.—*Note by Mr. C.*

and doubtless disconcerts our enemies. My time is spent entirely in endeavoring to rekindle the flagging zeal of our friends, to drill them on the subject, and to prepare them well for the struggle. I fear Johnson may be averse to go with us, in the attempt to annex terms of admission to the colleges. He is expected to-day. But all the rest are for it, and I hope he will join. My health is not good, owing to a bad cold; and I beg you to excuse the manner in which I write. Rest assured that my best exertions will be used to carry the appropriation; and if we fail, the opposition shall feel our strength. Could you point my attention to any tract on the policy of the new charters in preference to the old? I am now endeavoring to shake the William & Mary party by offering the lower country an equal participation in the academical fund (hereafter to be distributed), leaving William & Mary out of the system. The leaders of that party were not prepared for this, and will try to divert the funds to the college. But I think we will disconcert their combination by this proposition. Mr. Watkins, of Prince Edward, has resigned, and Mr. Rich'd Venable, a man of talents and influence, offers in his place. Doddridge is with the opposition. Blackburn has gone home, for a season. It is reported he is against us, but I hope not. Bassett, Griffin, Smith, Garland, Miller, Doddridge, are leaders on the other side. You may rest assured that every exertion will be made to keep down the University, and you must be prepared for a failure this session. We hope to get $50,000; but that is extremely doubtful. I find my collection of documents and my knowledge of facts of great use to me at this time. I have shewn your last letter to Mr. Miller, and he is satisfied *as to that point*. Should I be silent, ascribe it to my engagements here.

Faithfully, yours,

JOSEPH C. CABELL.

Mr. Jefferson.

CIX.

J. C. C. TO T. J.

RICHMOND, 18th January, 1821.

DEAR SIR,—I am sorry to inform you that it seems to be the general impression here that we shall be able to effect nothing for the University during the present session. It is with the most heartfelt grief that I acknowledge this to be my own impression. The reports relative to the literary fund are not yet before us, and this delay operates against us. The Governor has done all in his power, but the delay seems to be unavoidable. This seems as an excuse for the inactivity of our friends. I must confess that it seems to me that there is not the desirable zeal, activity, or concert on the occasion. I foresaw this result two weeks ago, but was told I was over-anxious, and unnecessarily alarmed. Yesterday Mr. Morris came to me in the lobby, and with much concern told me all seemed to be going against us in the House of Delegates, and urged the necessity of a meeting among the leading friends of the University. This measure I earnestly pressed a fortnight ago. A time was fixed, but bad weather intervened, and the want of a report being stated as an impediment, I suffered the measure to lie. We shall get the report next week; but now gentlemen are alarmed, and to-morrow evening some half dozen of our leading friends are to meet at my lodgings. In the mean time, the state of the fund is understood to be very unfavorable. The annual revenue falls short of the appropriation; the school fund cannot be touched; and the small surplus of uninvested revenue and capital will be a bone of contention. Mr. Johnson told me to-day he saw no prospect of success, from the state of the fund. But I do not despair, and all that I can do shall be done. I am turning my attention to a future and better Assembly. I shall endeavor to get back Taylor, of Chesterfield, (to whom I spoke yesterday,) Broadnax, of Brunswick, General Taylor, &c. &c. We have many local or secret powerful influences to oppose; of which I will say more to you in future. Whilst we do every thing in our power to stem the torrent, it would be well if you and Mr. Madison would aid in getting some efficient friends into the next Assembly. In haste,

I remain, dear sir, faithfully yours,

JOSEPH C. CABELL.

Mr. Jefferson.

CX.

[The writer having here intimated the desire and intention of retiring from public life, was met by a remonstrance and appeal from his correspondent, so urgent and earnest, that he was induced to renounce his purpose, at whatever hazard to his health or private fortune. The latter had suffered much from his absence and other causes; the former was put in extreme peril more than once by his exertions in the cause to which he stood pledged. The spirit of self-sacrifice and patriotic devotion here exhibited by each, and in a manner which can leave no doubt of the sincerity of either, cannot fail to command the respect of the reader.]

J. C. C. TO T. J.

RICHMOND, 25th January, 1821.

DEAR SIR,—Since the date of my letter of 18th inst. the meeting therein alluded to has taken place. I find Mr. Johnson averse to any expression of opinion on the subject of the ancient charters. Our meeting broke up without any valuable result. The want of a report on the state of the literary fund, retards our movements. There is a current constantly setting against us on Richmond Hill. It scatters discord in our ranks, and undermines the zeal of our friends. Preston's last deficiency falls on the literary fund, and augments our difficulties. The counties that neglected to draw, insist pertinaciously on their "equal rights." That claim, I suspect, will nearly exhaust the surplus on hand. Even some of our friends, Johnson, Breckenridge, &c., think we should not touch the principal of the fund; and the balance still due from the General Government forms a part of the principal. The annual revenue falls short of the annual appropriation. There is no prospect that we shall be able to get into the poor school fund. In this situation, hemmed in by difficulties and obstacles on all sides, one only prospect opens itself to my view. I presume that it is in every case proper to finish the buildings. To get the necessary funds for this object must be our polar star. For this purpose, we must get our credit for the existing loan of $60,000 put on one of the two bases which I proposed last spring; and obtain a power to make another loan of $50,000 on similar terms. This would give us the buildings, and a clear income of about $7,000. Future Assemblies must be looked to for the balance. I spoke of this plan to General Breckenridge and Mr. Johnson yesterday, and spoke of it as a dernier resort. They seemed to approve it. We shall first, however, ask for further funds in some shape or other. Gov. Randolph told me, some time since, we should have to content ourselves with this. He has gone into the country, and I presume will see you before his return.

I will now touch upon a subject that has engaged my thoughts for a long time past, and been often mentioned to some of my intimate friends: it is that of my withdrawing altogether from public life, at the end of my present term of service. Gen. Cocke will be with you shortly, and will explain to you the grounds on which I think, with some of my friends, that this measure becomes proper. I pause to give my friends an opportunity to cast about for a safe depository for the great interests of our district. A Mr. ********, of Nelson, has notified me of his intention to offer. At first I thought it might be improper to retire under the imputations that might be made, and so expressed myself to ****, Governor Randolph. But on further reflection, and on consultation with my brother and Gen. Cocke, I do not think *that* circumstance should have the least weight with me. *All other reasons* apart, I do not suppose that a canvass could be dispensed with, and such is the weakness of my breast, that to ride from Court-house to Court-house, making speeches to large crowds, exposed to the rigors of the season, might carry me to the grave, or bring on me further and more distressing symptoms of pulmonary affection. Do not suppose, I beseech you, that my feelings and opinions have undergone any change. On the contrary, in retiring, I will do all in my power to bring in such persons as may be calculated to effectuate in future your great views of literary improvement. In the course which I contemplate, I have no view or wish to go to Congress, or into any other public station. I have been here thirteen winters. My object now is domestic, rural and literary leisure. I thank my friends in Albemarle, and the district, but, above all, yourself, for the confidence so long bestowed on me. The little share which I have had in promoting the establishment of the University, and in seconding your views on that subject, will always constitute one of the most agreeable reflections of my life. May you succeed to the utmost of your wishes, will ever be my constant and fervent prayer. But that great and valuable institution, I hope, is now on a safe and permanent footing; and although its endowment is, for the present, too small, yet it must and will ultimately triumph over all its enemies.

I presume it is unnecessary to announce my final determination till the close of the session.

I remain, dear sir, faithfully your friend,

JOSEPH C. CABELL.

Mr. Jefferson.

CXI.

T. J. TO J. C. C.

MONTICELLO, January 30, 1821.

DEAR SIR,—You will recollect that at the meeting of the Visitors of the University on the 4th of December last, Mr. Johnson being disabled, by sickness, to attend, and having been prevented at the April meeting by bad weather, we were apprehensive his commission might be vacated, *by a failure to act for the space of one year*, and I was requested to apply to the Governor for a renewal of the commission. I accordingly communicated the request to the Governor by letter. He observed to me, that Mr. Johnson could not have failed to act for the space of a year, because he had not been one year in office under the present commission, which commenced only on the 29th of February last; and he suggested that a meeting, or any other act *as a visitor* before the 28th of February ensuing, might yet save the lapse. I know of but one act which the law authorizes to the visitors individually and out of meeting, to wit: the concurrence in the call of a special meeting. This is undoubtedly a *visitorial act;* and I propose, therefore, that the visitors shall, individually, sign such a call, annexing the date of their respective signatures, which will prove it done within the year. I accordingly sign such a paper myself, and forward it to Mr. Madison for his signature, with a request to forward it on to you to obtain yours, Mr. Johnson's, General Breckenridge's, and General Taylor's. On your returning it to me, I will obtain General Cocke's. I have fixed on the 1st of April, because we meet of course at Monticello, on or before that day, for the preparation of business. It will not be necessary to repair actually to the University, the *signature* of the call being the essential act, and the actual meeting at the University not necessary to its validity. A re-appointment by the Governor and Council might have saved us this ceremony, but for the use of the unlucky word "successor" in the law; and although I suggested to the Governor that that might be got over by a first appointment and resignation of John Doe, he thought some might raise scruples on it, as an evasion, and that we had better prevent it by an act of our own; and I think myself that, as this accident will frequently happen, we had better keep the remedy within our own power, by setting this precedent at once. Affectionate salutations to yourself and our colleagues.

TH: JEFFERSON.

Joseph C. Cabell, Esq.

CXII.

T. J. TO J. C. C.

MONTICELLO, January 31, 1821.

DEAR SIR,—Your favors of the 18th and 25th came together, three days ago. They fill me with gloom as to the dispositions of our Legislature towards the University. I perceive that I am not to live to see it opened. As to what had better be done within the limits of their will, I trust with entire confidence to what yourself, General Breckenridge, and Mr. Johnson shall think best. You will see what is practicable, and give it such shape as you think best. If a loan is to be resorted to, I think $60,000 will be necessary, including the library. Its instalments cannot begin until those of the former loan are accomplished; and they should not begin later, nor be less than $13,000 a year. (I think it safe to retain $2,000 a year for the care of the buildings, improvement of the grounds, and unavoidable contingencies.) To extinguish this second loan, will require between five and six instalments, which will carry us to the end of 1833, or thirteen years from this time. My individual opinion is, that we had better not open the institution, until the buildings, library and all, are finished, and our funds cleared of incumbrance. These buildings, once erected, will secure the full object infallibly at the end of thirteen years, and as much earlier as an enlightened Legislature shall happen to come into place. And if we were to begin sooner, with half funds only, it would satisfy the common mind, prevent their aid beyond that point, and our institution remaining at that forever, would be no more than the paltry academies we now have. Even with the whole funds, we shall be reduced to six professors, while Harvard will still prime it over us, with her twenty professors. How many of our youths she now has, learning the lessons of Anti-Missourianism, I know not; but a gentleman lately from Princeton, told me he saw there the list of the students at that place, and that more than half were Virginians. These will return home, no doubt, deeply impressed with the sacred principles of our holy alliance of Restrictionists.

But the gloomiest of all prospects is in the desertion of the best friends of the institution; for desertion I must call it. I know not the necessities which may force this on you. General Cocke, you say, will explain them to me; but I cannot conceive them, nor persuade myself they are uncontrolable. I have ever hoped that yourself, General Breckenridge, and Mr. Johnson, would stand at your posts in the Legislature until every thing was effected, and the institution opened. If it is so difficult to get along with all the energy and influence of our present colleagues in the Legislature, how can we expect to proceed at all, reducing our moving power? I know well your devotion to your country, and your foresight of the awful scenes coming on her, sooner or later. With this foresight, what service can we ever render her equal to this? What object of our lives can we propose, so important? What interest of our own, which ought not to be postponed to this? Health, time, labor, on what in the single life which nature has given us, can these be better bestowed than on this immortal boon to our country? The exertions and the mortifications are temporary; the benefit eternal. If any member of our college of visitors could justifiably withdraw from this sacred duty, it would be myself, who, "*quadragenis stipendiis jamdudum peractis*," have neither vigor of body nor mind left to keep the field. But I will die in the last ditch. And so, I hope, you will, my friend, as well as our firm-breasted brothers and colleagues, Mr. Johnson and General Breckenridge. Nature will not give you a second life wherein to atone for the omissions of this. Pray then, dear and very dear sir, do not think of deserting us; but view the sacrifices which seem to stand in your way, as the lesser duties, and such as ought to be postponed to this, the greatest of all. Continue with us in these holy labors, until having seen their accomplishment, we may say with old Simeon, "*nunc dimittis, Domine.*"

Under all circumstances, however, of praise or blame, I shall be affectionately yours.

TH: JEFFERSON.

Mr. Cabell.

CXIII.

J. C. C. TO T. J.

RICHMOND, February 8, 1821.

DEAR SIR,—I have received your letter of 31st ult., and return you many thanks for the kind and friendly expressions it contains. It is not in my nature to resist such an appeal. I this day handed into the office of the Enquirer, a notification that I should again be a candidate. We will pass on to matters of more importance. I have shown your letter to Gen. Breckenridge and Mr. Johnson, who seemed (and particularly the former) to be as much affected by it as myself. We are all in confusion here about the accounts of the literary fund. The statements of our public officers differ, and there seems to be no surplus on hand, although the Auditor says there should be $101,000. The opposite party secretly exult at this state of things, although they pretend to be much disappointed. Our plan of a second loan may yet succeed, if the House should not get disgusted by the confusion of the public accounts, and reject every thing. Your letter has kindled great zeal in Gen. Breckenridge. Yesterday Gen. Blackburn, in discussing Selden's resolutions, spoke of the University as "*a grand institution highly deserving our patronage.*" We have great difficulties to contend with. Your name and handwriting have great effect here. Let me entreat you, with the freedom of a friend, immediately to write to Gen. Breckenridge a letter on the subject of the University, such as may be shown generally, showing no preference and making no imputations. He wishes it, and will make powerful use of it.

You may rely on our discretion. I write you with his privity, and at his instance.

Ever and faithfully yours,

JOSEPH C. CABELL.

Mr. Jefferson.

CXIV.

T. J. TO J. C. C.

MONTICELLO, February 15, 1821.

DEAR SIR,—I address this day to Gen. Breckenridge a letter* as you desired; to be shown if it is thought expedient, within the circle of discretion. I doubt much, myself, whether its exhibition to members independent in their purposes, and jealous of that independence, may not do more harm than good. On this I put myself into the hands of my friends. I am sure you will see the propriety of letting no copy be taken, or possibility occur, of its getting beyond the limits of our own State; and even within these limits, some of its expressions should not go forth.

Ever and affectionately yours,

TH: JEFFERSON.

Mr. Cabell.

CXV.

J. C. C. TO T. J.

RICHMOND, February 20, 1821.

DEAR SIR,—I return you the enclosed paper, calling a meeting of the Visitors of the University, having procured the signatures of Mr. Johnson and Gen. Taylor, and annexed my

---

* For this letter see "Writings of Thomas Jefferson," IV. 341.

own, as requested in your favor of the 30th ult. I have also shown the paper to Governor Randolph, and the course pursued is satisfactory to him and the executive.

A bill in favor of the University has been reported by the Committee of schools and colleges. It proposes to authorize a loan by the President and Directors of $60,00, to be paid out of the balance due from the General Government, or any other part of the uninvested principal of the fund. It puts the principal on the footing on which my first proposition to the President and Directors of last spring would have placed the loan then proposed, with a small variation. The bill was drawn by Mr. Johnson, on consultation with Gen. Breckenridge and myself. Its fate will be decided in a few days. It will be powerfully opposed; but I hope it will get through, and if it does, I trust the money will finish the buildings; and if it should not, that the people of Albemarle will make up the deficiency. * * * * has at last thrown off the mask, and avowed his hostility to the bill. Like many others, he calls himself a friend to the institution. Our worst enemies are pretended friends.

I have written a very urgent letter to Gen. Taylor, begging him to come into the Assembly. He declines the proposition. So does Broadnax of Greensville. I enclose you their letters. I have written again to the latter, enclosing for his perusal your letter to me on the subject of my continuance, and proposing to him to come for one session. I showed your letter to Mr. Taylor of Chesterfield. He had before declined, but when he saw your letter, he promised me to think of it. I shall endeavor to get Chancellor Taylor to use his influence with him. Mr. William Archer, of Powhatan, has promised me to offer, and we shall get rid of * * *, who declines. Mr. Mallory, of Orange, has become a very active friend. I have written to Mr. Currie, of Lancaster, inviting him to join us. This is the only effectual way to break down the opposition. William & Mary, Hampden Sidney, and Washington Colleges are, in my opinion, decidedly hostile. * * * * * will oppose our bill; but thinks himself a warm friend. I am almost worn out with anxiety, and wish the matter settled. We have gotten our James River bill through the House of Delegates. It is of vast importance, and the whole country will soon be alive from Richmond to the mouth of the Kanawha.

Faithfully yours,

JOS. C. CABELL.

Mr. Jefferson.

CXVI.

J. C. C. TO T. J.

RICHMOND, 22d February, 1821.

DEAR SIR,—The University bill passed to a second reading in the House of Delegates, by a majority of one vote only. It is now on its third reading, and will be read to-morrow. Our friends, I think, are increasing. General Blackburn will support it. Mr. Garland came over and voted for it. If we lose the bill in the Lower House, we shall hang on upon the Poor-school Bill. I hope we shall work it through, in one way or the other. The enemies, seeing its decisive character, have done their best to destroy it. Heaven grant that I may be able to send you good news in my next. Your letters to myself and General Breckenridge have arrived and are thankfully received. Mr. —— has withdrawn; and, as I suppose no one else will come forward, I need not come up till the elections.

Yours, faithfully,

JOSEPH C. CABELL.

Mr. Jefferson.

CXVII.

T. J. TO J. C. C.

MONTICELLO, February 22, 1821.

DEAR SIR,—I some time ago put in your hands a pamphlet proving indirectly that the College of William & Mary was intended to be a seminary for the Church of England. It had been so long since I had read their printed statutes that I had forgotten them. Looking lately into them, I find they declare that the three fundamental objects of the institution are, 1. Learning and morals. 2. To prepare ministers for the Church of England. 3. To instruct Indians. And they require that the Visitors be all of the Church of England, that its professors sign its thirty-nine articles, and that the scholars be all taught the Catechism of that Church, first in English, then in Latin. Wishing to get my copy bound, I have enclosed it to a book-binder, but open, and under cover to you, that you may turn to pages 121, 125, 131, 247, for the above. When I was a Visitor, in 1779, I got the two professorships of Divinity and grammar school put down, and others of law and police, of medicine, anatomy and chemistry, and of modern languages substituted; but we did not then change the above statutes, nor do I know they have been since changed—on the contrary, the pamphlet I put into your hand proves, that if they have relaxed in this fundamental object, they mean to return to it. When you have read the passages, will you be so good as to re-enclose the book, stick a wafer, and have it handed to Mayo?

Ever and affectionately yours,

TH: JEFFERSON.

Mr. Cabell.

P. S. February, 23. I have this movement received your favor of the 20th, and finding that things are not in a state to require enclosing the college statutes, I withdraw them; and return the two letters you sent me.

CXVIII.

[Gives intelligence of further success. "We must not come here again for money to erect buildings." In the letter next succeeding he desires the co-operation of certain efficient friends in the next Assembly.]

J. C. C. TO T. J.

RICHMOND, 25th February, 1821.

DEAR SIR,—I have the pleasing satisfaction to inform you that the University Bill passed yesterday, not exactly in the shape its friends preferred, yet in one not very exceptionable. The first intelligence of its passage in the Lower House, was conveyed to us in the Senate Chamber by a tumultuous noise below, like that which is usual on the adjournment of the House. This was the tumult of rejoicing friends coming to bring us the glad tidings. Gen. Blackburn took the floor most zealously in favor of the measure, and is now fairly enlisted. I wish you could see him on his way through Charlottesville, accompany him to the University, and invite him to return to the Assembly. I am satisfied he is now very much disposed to support your literary views; but from the course of his past life,* and the pride of his character, he will be shy, and the first advances must come from yourself. Doddridge also came over and heartily supported the bill. Our great friend in that House is Gen. Breckenridge. He is, in truth, a powerful friend, and you must insist on his remaining in the Assembly. We are also much indebted to Mr. Johnson, of the Senate. In the House of Delegates, Mr. Gordon has shewn himself an able, valuable and efficient friend. Mr. Watson, of Louisa, Mr. Crump, of Cumberland, Mr. Loyall, of Norfolk, Mr. Bowyer, of Rockbridge, Mr. Chamberlayne, of Henrico, were zealous and valuable friends. Mr. Morris, of Hanover, and Mr. Stevenson, of the city of Richmond, deserve the most

* He had been of the Federal party.—Ed.

honorable mention. Stevenson will leave us, but I hope Morris will remain. I wish you could see Morris. He is a man of decided talents, and distinguished himself by his zeal in support of the University. I hope Mr. Gordon will return. The cordiality and generosity of his nature make him the favorite of a large circle of friends. Mr. Hunter, of Essex, would have united with us, but he was called home by the illness of one of his family. He talks of not returning; but I will endeavor to prevail on him by letter. I have failed in regard to Currie, whose letter I enclose you. It is the anxious wish of our best friends, and of no one more than myself, that the money now granted may be sufficient to finish the buildings. We must not come here again on that subject. These successive applications for money to finish the buildings, give grounds of reproach to our enemies, and draw our friends into difficulties with their constituents. The people of Albemarle would consult their own interests by making up any little deficiency. I hope the buildings may be ready by the next winter. Then I hope we shall be able to disencumber the funds. Rest assured, however, that the opposition will not cease. The enemies of the institution will send up their friends to oppose us. In the Southern parts of the State, in the quarter of Brunswick, Greensville, &c. I am informed, it is now the fashion to electioneer by crying down the University. We must cultivate the West, and unite with it as much of the East as possible.

My competitor having withdrawn, I propose to accompany Mrs. Cabell to Williamsburg, and to come up to the elections. Should any new opponent arise, I hope my friends will give me the earliest notice.

Faithfully, yours,

JOSEPH C. CABELL.

Mr. Jefferson.

CXIX.

J. C. C. TO T. J.

RICHMOND, 10th March, 1821.

DEAR SIR,—I have not deemed it necessary to write you in reply to your letter relative to the charter of William & Mary College, because the passage of the University bill rendered it unnecessary. But, although I shall see you on the first Monday in next month, yet it becomes necessary that I should say a few words to you at this time. The bill concerning the appropriation of the literary fund, by which the counties were to be authorised to draw the derelict quotas, failed between the two Houses. The Senate insisted on reasonable amendments to prevent waste and misapplication, and the House of Delegates indignantly rejected them. The enemies of the University contrived to create a general impression in that House, that this was a breach of faith in the Senate. I need not tell you this was false. Whatever may have been promised in the other House, none of the Senators, as far as my knowledge extends, had made an unconditional promise. Gen. Breckenridge approves our course. But I am assured, that many men of respectability, who heretofore have voted with us, went away, solemnly declaring that they would never again vote one cent to the institution. I am greatly fearful that the elections will be regulated by this question, and our enemies will increase. All our friends, about Richmond, entreat me to write to you, to commence no building which cannot be finished, and, above all, not to come here again for money to erect buildings. The general impression seems to be, that the Legislature will do nothing more for some years; and many think it would be wise policy to abstain from encumbering the annuity to the amount allowed by law, and to reserve as much of it as possible for the annual support of the professors. It is thought, too, it would have a favorable effect on the Legislature, if we were to keep a balance unexpended at the end of the year. The popular cry is, that there is too much finery and too much extravagance. You will be better informed on these points when the board meets. I see no prospect of our being able to get rid of the encumbrance on the annuity, but by some source of revenue other than the literary fund; and this will be very difficult. My principal object, in writing you at this time, is to apprise you that we are likely to lose our friend Gen. Breckenridge, and to ask you to use your influence to prevent it. He told me he could not consent to come again; but at last said he would not commit himself till the meeting of the Board of Visitors. I am told, however, that when he left town he said he should not offer, and would not serve again. He is the only man that can keep the Western delegation correct; *and is worth more than all the rest of us put together.** If he quits us, I shall be in utter despair for years to come. Therefore, I beseech you and Mr. Madison both, to write him earnestly and without delay. Botetourt court is on Monday, and I fear a candidate will be brought forward in his place on that day. I have reasons, however, to believe that it will be our late speaker, Watts, his son-in-law, who has moved into Botetourt; and if he should be declared on Monday, he may, without discredit, give way to his father-in-law. Broadnax persists in not offering. I saw Mr. Taylor, of Chesterfield, yesterday, and found he had not consented to offer, as I had supposed. But I hope what I then said to him will induce him to come out. Himself and Gen. Breckenridge are the men, above all others, I should be pleased to see in the House of Delegates. Mr. Tazewell, of Norfolk, would be a powerful auxiliary. I have no influence with him. If you were to invite him, probably he would offer. I submit to your better judgment, whether you should write him on this subject. He is thought, by some, to be favorably

* This well-merited tribute excites our regret, that the surviving friends of this gentleman have not given to the public some fuller and more adequate memorial of his private worth and public services.

disposed to such an application, and there is now a vacancy in the borough of Norfolk, Mr. Loyall having determined to withdraw. Tazewell has always been friendly to the University. He is versatile on some subjects, but I believe steady on this; and he is, without exception, the most powerful advocate I ever heard.

I am, dear sir, faithfully yours,

JOSEPH C. CABELL.

Mr. Jefferson.

CXX.

J. C. C. TO T. J.

EDGEWOOD, 1st April, 1821.

DEAR SIR,—I am much concerned not to be able to attend the meeting of the Visitors or the Albemarle election, in consequence of an indisposition contracted in traveling through the late severe weather. I hope my friends will make known the cause of my absence from the election, and make my apology to the people. I shall endeavor to call on you, on my way down the country. I profit of the opportunity by Mr. Southall to convey you this note. My respectful compliments and friendly salutations attend all the gentlemen of the Board.

I am, dear sir, faithfully your friend,

JOS. C. CABELL.

Mr. Jefferson.

CXXI.

J. C. C. TO T. J.

JUDGE COALTER'S, Henrico, 28th April, 1821.

DEAR SIR,—It was not until the 25th inst. that I found my health sufficiently restored to enable me to set out for the lower country. By traveling slowly, and lying down some hours in the day, I was enabled to get down from my brother's in three days, but not without being compelled to go to bed with a high fever at Powhatan Court-house, which continued half a day and one night. I arrived here much indisposed yesterday, but am better to-day, and hope that my journey to the Northern Neck, whither I am now going, will entirely restore my strength. The cold which I took in traveling up the country greatly affected my muscular and nervous system. The consequence is, I am thrown into so weak and delicate a state, that I could not move out of the house without taking fresh cold that would bring back in an aggravated form all my complaints. The extraordinary prevalence of winds, and the sudden and frequent changes in March and April, prolonged my confinement. Knowing how little would overset me, I determined to rely on the liberality of the people, and confine myself to the house. Mrs. Cabell had come up to this place, and was very uneasy about me. I was not in a situation to visit you with the tranquility and strength that were requisite for the objects of my call. The heats of summer were advancing apace, and a full month is necessary to make my journey to Corrottoman, where the state of my affairs demands my immediate presence. I therefore determined to postpone my visit to the University till my return in June, when I hope to be entirely well, and will come down at leisure, to converse with you fully on the affairs of the University. Since I last wrote you by Mr. Southall, I have learnt from General Cocke that he was also prevented by ill-health from attending the last meeting. I am entirely ignorant of what passed at the meeting, and feel very anxious for information. I regret to find that Gen. Breckenridge will not be in the next Assembly; as also to discover in Gen. Blackburn's speech on the University some remarks which I did not know it contained, till I saw it in the Enquirer, not having been present at its delivery. I regret that Mr. Maury was not returned from Buckingham. Both the delegates from that county will probably be in the opposition. Amherst and Nelson will go with ****. My friend Col. Shelton was shut out by his own son-in-law. * * * * * * * * * The elections, as far as I have heard from them, are as favorable as I could expect. It is reported that the University has lost ground considerably of late among the mass of the people. Some efforts ought to be made, in the course of the season, to regain and strengthen the public confidence. We have every thing to hope from the importance and singleness of the object, and the progress of information. But I fear the results will be too slow. I did not like the manner in which the business was conducted last winter. The whole of the literary fund being now disposed of, we are driven upon a difficult and thorny path.* We must look for a sinking fund to pay the interest and principal of the debt, or strive to get it remitted. Rest assured, my dear sir, that a call must be made upon all the friends of literature and science to unite their influence on this great occasion—a call such as made by myself and others on the question of location. But the minds of leading men over the State should be drawn early to this subject. Much may be done by yourself and Mr. Madison. I have not time to go more fully into the subject, at this time; but will come to see you as soon as I return. In the *interim*,

I remain, dear sir, very sincerely yours,

JOSEPH C. CABELL.

Mr. Jefferson.

---

* His anticipations were verified. Various financial expedients—some of which had been suggested before, (see Letters 87, 95, 101)—in the next three years, were presented, discussed, modified, withdrawn or rejected. Those which met with partial or entire success are detailed in future letters. See in particular Nos. 125, 131, 132, 135, 136, 141, 142, 144, 154, 166.

CXXII.

J. C. C. TO T. J.

EDGEWOOD, 5th August, 1821.

DEAR SIR,—My servant comes down to Mr. Minor's on business relative to my farm, and I profit of the opportunity to drop you a line, and to assure you that I should have been at Monticello a month ago, but for a return of bad health. I arrived here on 2d June; was employed four or five weeks in necessary attention to my affairs, when I had an attack of the prevailing epidemic, from the effects of which I have not yet entirely recovered. I anxiously wished to come down about this time, but could not ride so far at this season, without excessive pain, and imminent danger of a bilious fever. Mrs. Cabell is also in bad health. If we do not get better, we shall spend the first fortnight in September at some of the Springs. I count confidently on being at the next meeting of the Board. I shall husband my health, so as to meet our friends in the next Assembly, and do anything in my power to promote the interests of the University. In the mean time, permit me to recommend a complete liquidation and lucid statement of all accounts; and, should it be requisite, the employment of a skillful accountant, to state all the accounts in a regular set of books; and to have the books ready to be sent to the Assembly. [You, doubtless, observe the movements of the Presbyterians at Hampden Sidney, and the Episcopalians at William & Mary.* I learn that the former sect, or rather the clergy of that sect, in their synods and presbyteries, talk much of the University. They believe, as I am informed, that the Socinians are to be installed at the University for the purpose of overthrowing the prevailing religious opinions of the country. They are therefore drawing off, and endeavoring to set up

* This subject will be touched in a future note.

establishments of their own, subject to their own control. Hence the great efforts now making at Hampden Sidney, and the call on all the counties on the south side of James River to unite in support of that college. They calculate on Robinson's estate at Washington College, and are opposed to any substantial change in the old charters.

I hope your health continues good. Should you write to Mr. Madison, be pleased to remember me with great respect and regard to him.

I remain, dear sir, faithfully your friend,

JOSEPH C. CABELL.

Mr. Jefferson.

CXXIII.

(CIRCULAR.) T. J. TO J. C. C.

MONTICELLO, August 15, 1821.

DEAR SIR,—In obedience to the resolution of the Visitors of the University, at their last session, the Proctor has been constantly employed in "ascertaining the state of accounts under contracts already made, and the expense of completing the buildings begun and contemplated;" and we have consequently suspended, according to instructions, "the entering into any contracts for the library until we see that it may be done without interfering with the finishing of all the pavilions, hotels and dormitories begun and to be begun." The Proctor will require yet a considerable time to complete his settlements; insomuch that it is very doubtful whether there will be any thing ready for us to act on at our stated meeting in October, should that take place. But by deferring our meeting to the approach of that of the General Assembly, it is believed we shall be able to report to them that nearly the whole of the buildings of accommodation are finished, and the sum they will have cost; that the few remaining will be finished by the spring, and what their probable cost will be, as ascertained by experience, and further to shew the balance of the funds still at our command, and how far they will be competent to the erection of the library. On this view of the unreadiness of matter for our next stated meeting, and the prospect that a deferred one will enable us to make a clear and satisfactory report, I venture to propose the omission of our October meeting, and the special call of an occasional one on the Thursday preceding the meeting of the Legislature. That day is fixed on for the convenience of the gentlemen who are members of the Legislature; as it brings them so far on their way to Richmond, with time to get to the first day of the session. Not having an opportunity of personal consultation with my colleague of the committee of advice, I pass the letters through his hands. If he approves the proposition, he will subjoin his approbation and forward them to their several addresses; otherwise, not. If approved, it will be proper you should subscribe the enclosed notice and return it to me, to be placed among our records.

I have just received an order of the Literary Board for $29,100, in part of the loan of $60,000 lately authorized; and, following the practice of the Legislature, I have thought it just and safest to have the deposit made by moieties in the Virginia and Farmers Banks.

I salute you with great friendship and respect.

TH: JEFFERSON.

Joseph C. Cabell, Esq.

Approved.

JOHN H. COCKE.

CXXIV.

J. C. C. TO T. J.

EDGEWOOD, 31st August, 1821.

DEAR SIR,—By the last mail I received the Circular of Gen. Cocke and yourself, proposing to the Visitors to omit the regular autumnal meeting, and in lieu thereof to hold a special meeting on the Thursday preceding the meeting of the Assembly. The reasons stated in the Circular in support of this proposition are entirely satisfactory to my mind. I shall accordingly decline carrying Mrs. Cabell with me to Corrottoman, as I wished and intended, in order that I may return on horse back, travel quickly, and be certain to attend. I shall shift my overseer here on 1st November, depart immediately, leave my wife with her parents in Williamsburg, hasten on horse back across the lower ferries, spend a fortnight on my estate below, and return by Tappahannock and the upper ferries. Nothing but death or illness shall prevent my coming. The time is extremely inconvenient to me, and mars some favorite and long projected arrangements for the autumn. But what of that? If I can but retain the little stock of health, it has been my good fortune to re-acquire, I will come to Monticello with a heart warm with zeal in the holy cause. I have devoted myself to some favorite improvements on my farm this summer; have kept out of the sun; and walked from four to five miles each day; and though I have had a severe attack of illness in the summer, I am pretty well again, and feel nothing of the affection of my side, except in cloudy weather. Had I kept up my practice of walking in the winter mornings, I should probably have avoided the severe illness I suffered in the spring. It gives me great pleasure to hear that your good health continues uninterrupted. I am going to next Albemarle court, and shall commit this to the post-office at Charlottesville.

I remain, dear sir, faithfully yours,

JOSEPH C. CABELL.

Mr. Jefferson.

CXXV.

T. J. TO J. C. C.

MONTICELLO, September 30, 1821.

DEAR SIR,—Mr. Brockenbrough has been closely engaged since our last meeting in settling the cost of the buildings finished at the University, that we might obtain a more correct view of the state of our funds, and see whether a competency will remain for the library. He has settled for six pavilions, one hotel, and thirty-five dormitories, and will proceed with the rest; so that I hope, by our next meeting, the whole of the four rows will be nearly settled. From what is done, he has formed an estimate of the cost of what is yet to be done; and guided in it by actual experience, it is probably nearly correct. The result is, that our actual receipts heretofore, with what is still to be received of the loan of this year, after paying for the lands and all incidental and current expenses, will exactly complete the four rows of buildings for the accommodation of the professors and students, amounting in the whole to $195,000, and leave us without either debt or contract.

In the conjectural estimate laid before the visitors at their last meeting, it was supposed that the three annuities of 1822, '23 and '24, would suffice for the library and current charges, without the aid of the *unpaid subscriptions* which were reserved therefore as a contingent fund. By this more accurate estimate, it appears that the unpaid subscriptions, valued at $18,000, will be *necessary* to complete that building. So that the conjectural estimate fell short by $18,000 of the real cost of the four rows; which in a total of $195,000, is perhaps not over-considerable. I call it the *real* cost, because that of the unfinished buildings is reckoned by the real cost of those finished. The season being now too far advanced to begin the library, and the afflicting sickness in Gen. Cocke's family having deprived me of the benefit of consultation with him, I think it a duty to leave that undertaking entirely open and undecided, for the opinion of the Visitors at their meeting in November, when it is believed the actual settlements will have reached every thing, except one pavilion and three hotels, which alone will be unfinished until the spring.

The considerations which urge the building the hull, at least, of the library, seemed to impress the Board strongly at their last meeting; and it is put in our power to undertake it with perfect safety, by the indefinite suspension by the Legislature, of the commencement of our instalments. This leaves us free to take another year's annuity, to wit: that of 25 before we begin instalments, should the funds fall short which are here counted on for that building. The undertakers are disposed to accept and collect themselves the outstanding subscriptions in part of payment. You will distinguish, in this statement, by their enormous cost, the pavilions No. 3 and 7, and 16 dormitories contracted for in 1817 and '18, at the inflated prices prevailing then, while we acted as a Central College only. In 1819, and the following years, prices were reduced from 25 to 50 per cent. The enlarged cost of the latter dormitories has been occasioned by the unevenness of the ground, which requires cellars under many of them.

I shall hope to have the pleasure of receiving you at Monticello a day, at least, before that of our meeting, as we can prepare our business here, so much more at leisure than at the University. I salute you with great friendship and respect.

TH: JEFFERSON.

Mr. Cabell.

ESTIMATES ENCLOSED IN THE FOREGOING.

A view of the whole expenses of the Funds of the University.

	Actual Cost.	*Estimated Cost.*	*Averages.*
Pavilions No. 3 and 7 undertaken in 1817 and 1818, - - -	$19,149 81		$9,574 90
Pavilions No. 4, 5, 9, - - -	33,563 15		8,390 78
17 marble capitals from Italy for No. 2, 3, 5, 8, - - - - -	1,784 00		
Pavilions No. 1, 6, 8, 10, not finished,		33,563 15	
Hotel BB. - - - - - -	4,609 58		
Five-sixth other hotels not finished,		20,000 00	4,000 00
Dormitories, 16 undertaken in 1817,	13,898 34		868 64
19 - - - - -	11,083 63		583 34
74 not finished, -		38,462 60	519 76
109			
Lands, wages, and contingencies (suppose for round numbers,)		18,885 74	
	$84,088 51	$110,911 49	
	$195,000		

Funds:		
Glebe Lands, - -	$3,104 09	
Annuities of 1819, '20, '21,	45,000 00	
Loan of 1820, - -	60,000 00	
Loan of 1821, - -	60,000 00	
Subscriptions received to Sept., 1821, about	25,000 00	
Bal. to be carried forward,	$1,895 91	195,000

Expenses to be still incurred:	
Walls of back yards, gardens, &c., about 100,000 bricks,- - -	1,500 00
Wages and contingencies for 1823, '24,	6,000 00
Library: hull 30,200, & interior 13,475,	43,675 00
Interest for 1821, '22, '23, -	13,700 00
	$64,875 00

Funds:		
Balance brought forward,	$1,895 91	
Subscriptions $19,133 33, of which are separate	18,000 00	
Annuities of 1822, '23, '24,	45,000 00	
		64,895 91

A more summary view of the cost of the four rows of buildings and library.

Ten Pavilions, - - - -	$88,060 11
Six Hotels, - - - - - -	24,609 58
One hundred and nine Dormitories, - -	63,445 57
Library, - - - - -	43,675 00
	$219,790 26

CXXVI.

J. C. C. TO T. J.

WILLIAMSBURG, 21st November, 1821.

DEAR SIR,—I most heartily regret to be under the necessity of again apologising for my absence from the meeting of the Visitors. The cause of my disappointment is fresh indisposition, the character and tendency of which Gen. Cocke will more particularly explain to you. I am pursuing a course recommended by two physicians in Richmond, and thus far approved by Dr. Smith of this place. They have all advised me to decline my visit to Corrottoman, and my attendance at the meeting on Wednesday next; but I think I may attend to my duties in the Senate. Mr. Johnson will enable me to understand the views and wishes of the Board, which I regret very much not to be able to learn from them personally. If I had a vote on the question of finishing the buildings, I should vote for it, as a measure correct in itself, and prudent with reference to the present state of the public mind. If there be not money enough to finish them, I would go on as near to the object as possible. But I am at this time inclined to think I would ask nothing of the present Assembly. I would go on and complete the buildings, and at another session make the great effort to emancipate the funds. Last spring I rather inclined to the opinion expressed by many friends in Richmond, that we should commence no building, which we could not finish. But I now think otherwise. I see no essential good to result from stopping short of our object, merely to have the credit of having a little money in hand, which the enemies of the institution would aver that we wished to spend, but had not the courage to part with. They would exaggerate the sum eventually necessary to complete the establishment, and laugh at our policy. Such are my views. But you and the enlightened gentlemen of the Board know better how to steer the ship than I do. I will heartily co-operate in such measures as your better judgments will propose. Be pleased to remember me most respectfully and kindly to all the gentlemen of the Board, and believe me to remain faithfully and unchangeably your friend.

JOSEPH C. CABELL.

Mr. Jefferson.

CXXVII.

[Policy to be pursued during the present session. New movement of the opposition. Mode in which it was met. "*Timeo Danaos.*"]

J. C. C. TO T. J.

RICHMOND, January 3, 1822.

DEAR SIR,—I arrived here on the 30th ult., and took my seat in the Senate on the 31st. My general health is good, and the disease in my ear considerably diminished. I feel myself in a situation to return zealously and vigorously to the duties of my station, and for that purpose have taken my lodgings at the Eagle Hotel. I trust there will be no relapse in the local affection; and as to my general health, my morning walks will preserve it, unless the exertion of my mind and anxious watching of nights should greatly impair it, as they have done heretofore. But I will trust myself to Providence, and hope for the best. I have been so long cut off from my accustomed communications with you, that I almost fear you doubt my fidelity and constancy. I intend to write you as I did formerly, and shall endeavor to keep you fully and regularly informed of our proceedings in regard to the University. For, as you will have seen in the papers, the subject has been brought forward to the surprise of us all, by Mr. Griffin of York. Mr. Minor of Spottsylvania, had written to me to hasten up; but I did not receive his letter, nor hear of the motion till my arrival here on Sunday. At first, Mr. Griffin's motion gave great satisfaction to the friends of the University.

Coming from a quarter deemed so hostile, we thought it a harbinger of a favorable change in the public feeling and opinion. I confess I had my doubts from the beginning, and now those doubts are confirmed. I knew from information received from Mr. Saunders in Williamsburg, that Mr. Griffin had been apprized that his course last winter was thought by the friends of the University, to have had for its principal object the destruction of that institution, and I thought it not improbable that he sought to redeem himself from the charge of insincerity in the estimation of the more enlightened part of the community. Some supposed he wished to prevent the literary board from completing the loan. Others, that he wished to force the friends of the University to a premature movement at an inauspicious time. All of us, however, thought that so remarkable a movement from an opponent, whatever the motive might be, was calculated to do good. How far it may influence our movements, will depend on circumstances. Yesterday Mr. Griffin sought a conversation with me, which satisfied me that his support would not be given to his own motion. He called on me to know if the Legislature would consent to cancel the bonds of the University, on condition that we should never apply for any further appropriation, whether we would consent to give the pledge. I replied to him, that I could not speak for others, but for myself, I would not hesitate to avow that I would give no such pledge, and I was very confident that the other friends of the University would give a similar answer. Indeed, I told him, that I would sooner see the measure which he had offered rejected, than to accept it on any such condition. All the obvious objections to such a pledge were urged, and I need not repeat them to you. He contended that unless such a pledge was given, he was sure the motion to cancel the bonds would be rejected by an immense majority; and I understood him to say that in such case he would himself vote against it. He furthermore observed, that even that pledge would not carry the measure; and finally remarked that he should urge the measure no further. Among other things, he assured me that he began to feel apprehensions for the safety of the literary fund. The University, he said, was evidently more and more unpopular, and his motion was opposed by all the leading members of the House. I told him that his measure would of itself enable the University to get into operation in a short time, and to flourish greatly, but individually, I was of opinion that future Legislatures should go further. I remonstrated with him on the impropriety of his withdrawing himself from the support of his own proposition, because we would not agree with him on ulterior measures not necessarily connected with it; and invited him to aid us in removing the popular prejudices. But all would not do, and we separated without coming to any agreement of opinion. In parting, I requested him to converse with Mr. Johnson, inasmuch as I did not wish to be singly consulted on the occasion. He declined doing so, as unnecessary after what had passed. This conversation has been a subject of much merriment among our friends; and we are amused at the effort thus gravely made to bind us to our good behaviour in all time to come. Mr. Ritchie will come out with an encomium on Mr. Griffin's liberality. We are not yet decided whether we shall profit of the opening made by Mr. Griffin, or let the subject lie over till another session. I am endeavoring to ascertain our best policy, by consultation with our friends. The laborious task again falls to my share to go the rounds, and to endeavor to rekindle the enthusiasm of our friends. In the course of the last three days, I have seen enough to convince me that the Senate is well disposed, and the House of Delegates, perhaps, more than usually hostile. The temper and disposition of that House is distressing and alarming. To-day a motion was made and supported by Morris and Blackburn, to authorize the Committee of Schools and Colleges to *enquire* into the expediency of making an appropriation to Washington and Hampden Sidney Colleges, and it was rejected by a large majority. These colleges have both three or four respectable agents here, soliciting aid from the Legislature. It is true that there is no

15

money to dispose of; but to refuse enquiry to the colleges, indicates great hostility to the literary interests of the State, as they are more popular than the University. Indeed, it is doubted whether there is not a strong party in the House for the total abolition of the literary fund. Our prospects are certainly gloomy in a high degree. I have recommended to our friends to keep back the subject as long as possible, and in the interim to endeavor to make friends. We all agree thus far, that Griffin's proposition is the proper one, if we make any; and that we should ask for nothing more. I still have hopes that explanation may pave the way to final success; but in all our struggles, never have I seen a more gloomy prospect. Blackburn is said by some, to take to heart the removal of the seat of government to Staunton. I am not sure of this, but I suspect he seeks it with deep anxiety. Is it not possible that calculations may be made on our anxiety to endow the University? May they not say—these men would not oppose us, least we may retaliate? I feel the dilemma—I regret it—but I cannot vote to carry the seat of government to Staunton. We are committed against Charlottesville; because of the University being there. And I presume our best course is to keep it here. I shall not be busy or noisy, but my purpose is settled, be the consequences what they may.

4th January: I hear to-day a general concurrence of opinion as to the hostile character of the House of Delegates, and the probability that we ought not to apply for any thing. Yesterday in the debate on the motion to refer the consideration of the college question to the Committee of Schools and Colleges, I understood Gen. Blackburn strongly committed himself against any and every proposition to touch the *capital* of the literary fund. Mr. Ritchie's remarks of this morning, will probably carry Mr. G. to the point of voting for his own motion. Mr. Watkins of Prince Edward, one of the Commissioners at Rockfish Gap, is here on a visit. He is a friend to the University, and to Hampden Sidney. He strongly advises that we shall make no such application this session; he says we should ask for no more money, and let the debt stand for the present; that by the remission of the debt, we shall not get money, &c. But I think otherwise. We should get our annuity, and after that the momentum of the institution would carry it along. There is an almost unanimous opinion, that if we should move at all, we should present and support Griffin's proposition. And we generally think that we ought to keep back the proposition, and then be governed by circumstances. Col. Archer of Powhatan, has just given his support to this course, and he moves much among the members. He thinks at this time we should meet with a decided repulse. I should be happy to receive any advice from yourself or Mr. Madison; but will certainly write you from time to time.

I am inclined to think it would be good policy to show a friendly disposition towards the colleges. The friends of Hampden Sidney are anxious for aid, and are not so lofty in their tone as they were last winter. I came here disposed, if there should be money to spare, to vote something to them, on conditions not very rigorous; to meet them in friendly consultation; in short, to conciliate them. As far as I have had an opportunity to observe, they are disposed to meet us in the same temper.

4 *P. M.* Since writing the above, I have seen the Speaker of the House of Delegates, who is warmly our friend. He thinks much may be done to change the minds of members. And so do I. I am going around and soliciting the aid of all the *speakers*, and the more liberal members. I have moved Ritchie, and I will bring the press to bear on the House. I will also get the aid of the Senators. In short, if any exertions of my mind can put a lever under the weight that bears us down, it shall be raised this session. I shall also endeavor to promote the completion of the loan. In four days, I am again fairly out at sea, struggling with the tempest.

I am, dear sir, faithfully yours,

JOSEPH C. CABELL.

Mr. Jefferson.

CXXVIII.

J. C. C. TO T. J.

MONTICELLO, January 3, 1822.

DEAR SIR,—I have received a letter from *******, a member of the Legislature, on the subject of the University, to which I have this day given an answer. Not knowing to what purpose it may be used, I enclose the letter and a copy of the answer, for the information of Mr. Johnson and yourself, to enable you to meet any quotation which might be made, otherwise than in the genuine terms and spirit of the answer. I will ask your return of these papers, when the term of their use shall be past. Affectionate and respectful salutations.

TH: JEFFERSON.

Mr. Cabell.

CXXIX.

T. J. TO J. C. C.

The enclosed was omitted in my letter of yesterday. Friendly salutations.

January 5, 1822.

Perhaps some other paper was inadvertently put in its place. If so, be so good as to return it by mail.

[*Memorandum.*]

To liberate the funds on 1st January, 1822:

1. A remission of the debt, - - - - -	$60,000	
2. To liberate the annuities of 1822 and 1823, -	30,000	
		90,000
Wanted to finish the buildings, - - - - -		55,564
Total sum necessary to complete the buildings and to liberate the funds of the University, - - - - -		$145,564

In addition to the aforesaid sum of $145,564, the Rector and Visitors recommend an augmentation of the annuity of $15,000, but leave the amount to the discretion of the General Assembly.

CXXX.

J. C. C. TO T. J.

RICHMOND, 7th January, 1822.

DEAR SIR,—I have just received your favor of 3rd instant, and have shewn it to Mr. Johnson. Should the case occur, for which it was intended to provide, it shall be used. For the present, Mr. Johnson and myself think it best not to exhibit it generally, as it might be the means of throwing still farther from us the gentleman to whom it was addressed. What course he will ultimately pursue no one seems to know. We deem it prudent not to enquire whether the "*insurance*" was necessary to carry him along with us, or whether it was called for merely to promote the success of the resolution. The former is the obvious inference; but we leave him to account for the singularity of his course. The general impression among the friends of the University, is, that the movement of this gentleman was dictated by some unfriendly design.

Things have remained nearly *in statu quo* since I last wrote you. In the Senate there would be no difficulty in getting a large vote to cancel the bonds. I am inclined to think the measure is gaining some friends in the Lower House; but, from all I can learn, there is now in that body a large majority against it. Postponement is the advice which I have given to all our friends. We cannot lose, and may gain by it. I find most difficulty to arise from an imprudent commitment of our friends in that House at the last session, not to encroach on the capital of the literary fund. I differed with them then, and warned them of the consequences. The occasion on which this took place was the discussion of our Loan Bill. They were driven, by the force of circumstances, into these declarations, by the allegation of our opponents, that our loan would ultimately be taken from the capital of the fund. ****** is of this number. I have been laboring to prevail on him to make a public recantation of his error: and nothing is yet decided on. I hope the force of enlightened opinion will come to my aid in this respect. What I most fear is that ******* will adhere to that ground. The style of his opposition, added to the inconsistency of our friends *in that House*, would very certainly defeat us. He is not to be approached, unless when he has an evident and strong desire. In general, he affects to be Jupiter in a cloud. In the present case, I apprehend that his views on another subject, in which I differ with him, would make me not a very welcome guest; and I stand aloof. By the bye, I see a whole group of gentlemen here from Staunton; *apparently* on ordinary business. In reflecting on the causes of the opposition to the University, I cannot but ascribe a great deal of it to the clergy. William & Mary has conciliated them. It is represented that they are to be *excluded* from the University. There has been no decision to this effect; and, on full reflection, I should suppose that religious opinions should form no test whatever. I should think it improper to exclude religious men, and open the door to such as Doctor Cooper. Mr. Johnson concurs with me in this view. And I have publicly expressed the opinion. The clergy have succeeded in spreading the belief of their intended exclusion, and, in my opinion, it is the source of much of our trouble. I am cautious not to commit yourself, or Mr. Madison, or the board. I have also made overtures of free communication with Mr. Rice, and shall take occasion to call on Bishop Moore. I do not know that I shall touch on this delicate point with either of them. But I wish to consult these heads of the church, and ask their opinions. I have suggested also to ******* and ******* ***** plans of finance to aid them in the accomplishment of their objects. Nevertheless, I suspect the Colleges will not succeed, as they are sure to interfere with one another; and the most that could be done for any of them would be to lend them a little money out of the capital on the credit of the future surplus, which is generally appropriated to the colleges. William and Mary seems to withdraw her claims.

* * * * * * * * * * *

The county arrears must be given out, for we are now apparently at war with the democracy. Such are my present views. I will write you weekly; but fear I shall not send you any good tidings this session.

In great haste,

I remain, dear sir, faithfully yours,

JOS. C. CABELL.

Mr. Jefferson.

CXXXI.

J. C. C. TO T. J.

RICHMOND, 14th January, 1822.

DEAR SIR,—I wrote you on this day week relative to our views and movements as to the University up to that date. On the 11th instant I directed the public printer to send you a copy of the Accountant's report on the literary fund, on the last page of which you will see that the revenue of the fund barely satisfies existing appropriations. This fact was announced to me on the 8th instant, by Mr. Watson. On the discovery, we were compelled to abandon the ground of Mr. Griffin's proposition. The aversion to encroach on the capital of the fund furnished a popular theme to our adversaries, which was strengthened by the commitment of our friends in the Lower House at the last session. The hostile character of the House of Delegates, and the opposition of a part of the local delegation from some of the neighboring counties, rendered these circumstances more weighty. On consultation with some of my friends, I determined to enter on some other plan. At first, I thought of Preston's debt. But, on this subject, there is a peculiar feeling. Mr. Johnson thought that two dollars would be given out of any other fund, sooner than one dollar out of that. He informed me that you had advised him to turn our attention to the amount claimed of the General Government, on account of interest paid on sums borrowed and expended by the State in our defence during the late war. At length this was agreed upon, and this is the plan that now occupies our attention. It is something like working for a dead horse, it is true. But it seems to be the only plan likely to go down with the Assembly; and should we fail at Washington, the passage of the bill will give us an equitable hold on future Assemblies. I called on the Auditor on 9th for the necessary information as to the amount of this interest debt, and received from him an account of interest paid to the amount of $430,000, which had been made out for the Executive last winter. The Auditor informed me that the accountant at Washington had given him to understand that the claim had been, or would be rejected by the United States Government. Presuming that that amount was due, I entered into conferences with some of the friends of the colleges, and proposed that we should all unite in supporting a bill giving half the amount to the University, and the other half to the colleges. I found great readiness in the friends of the two upper colleges, but one of the gentlemen from near William & Mary was in favor of giving a fourth to the primary schools, and a fourth to the colleges in the form of a specific appropriation. Thus it is, that even those gentlemen from that quarter who profess to be our friends are as difficult to please as our open enemies. There seemed, however, to be less objection to this scheme than any other; and Mr. Watson thought it would go down. Since the 10th I have discovered that the Auditor's statement embraced as well interest paid since the reimbursement of the principal by the General Government, as interest paid anterior to that time. This will cause a heavy deduction. How much I do not know. It may reduce it by half; and if so, I must endeavor to obtain the consent of the college party to let it all go to the University. This may affect the extent and cordiality of their support, and possibly divide us. But I hope not, as Hampden Sidney and Washington Colleges have a particular bill under way, proposing to lend them a small portion of the principal of the literary fund. The exclusive primary school party will oppose us in every case. A call has been made on the Executive for information as to the state of our claim, preparatory to the bringing in of a bill. This is the present posture of affairs.

I have had a very long interview with Mr. Rice. He and myself differed on some points; but agreed in the propriety of a firm union between the friends of the University and the Colleges, as to measures of common interest, and of postponing for future discussion and settlement points on which we differ. I think this safe ground. We shall be first endowed; and have the vantage ground in this respect. Accordingly I assented to the propriety of waiving all discussions about charters at this time. * * * * * * * They have heard that you have said they may well be afraid of the progress of the Unitarians to the South. This remark was carried from Bedford to the Synod, beyond the Ridge, last fall. The Bible Societies are in constant correspondence all over the continent, and a fact is wafted across it in a few weeks.* Through these societies the discovery of the religious

* In those who are conversant with the objects and operations of these societies, the surmise suggested in the text cannot but excite a smile, and a feeling somewhat akin to sadness, that statesmen who are so familiar with matters coming within their own sphere, should, at times, entirely mistake the motives and purposes of those who in other departments are laboring for the public good. Mr. Cabell himself, in after years, and on better knowledge, became the patron of these associations, as Mr. Jefferson had been before. (See his letter to Samuel Greenhow, of January, 1814. Works VI, 308. The present is also the most suitable occasion for adverting more particularly to another error into which both himself and his distinguished correspondent had fallen, and of which some traces have appeared in former letters. This arose from an act of the Visitors, which was much canvassed at the time, and caused no little excitement; which, however, had well nigh subsided, when it was revived, with increased fervor, by the first publication of Mr. Jefferson's writings. The editor of these papers, in the performance of a task assigned him by others, and which he did not feel at liberty to decline, has yet not thought it incumbent on him to intrude himself unnecessarily between the

opinions of Ticknor and Bowditch was made. Mr. Rice assured me that he was a warm friend of the University; and

---

public and two such men as the authors of this correspondence. But, as this affair may be thought to require some farther explanation than is afforded by the text, he supposes that he shall not exceed his privilege in stating, with that view, certain facts, as coming either within his own knowledge, or as received from undoubted authority.

Dr. Thomas Cooper, an Englishman of great and versatile talents, learned in many sciences, and a liberal in politics, fled with his father-in-law, the celebrated Dr. Priestley, from persecution, in his native country, to the United States. Pennsylvania at first afforded them both an asylum. Here Dr. C. engaged in the practice of the law, and in no long time rose to the bench. In a few years he retired from this post, became a Professor successively in Dickinson College and the University of Pennsylvania; edited a periodical devoted to science and the useful arts; and, at length, was invited to the College of South Carolina, with which he was connected during the remainder of his active life. In the interval between his sojourn in Pennsylvania and his transfer to South Carolina, he had been offered a chair in the proposed Central College of Virginia, and when that institution was merged in the University, the same was again proffered to his acceptance.

This appointment, which, as now appears, was thought impolitic by some of Mr. Jefferson's colleagues, as soon as generally known proved distasteful to very many citizens of Virginia, including all classes of what are called the "religious community." Nor was it long ere that dissatisfaction found expression through the public prints. The reason alleged was, that Dr. Cooper held, on many subjects, extreme opinions, which he was at no pains to conceal; and some of which, they honestly believed, struck at the very foundations of social order, of morals and religion. Dr. John Rice, a distinguished Presbyterian clergyman, then pastor of a church, and editor of a literary and religious periodical in Richmond, became the organ through whom their dissent was declared. His opposition was based, not on common rumor or vulgar misapprehension, but was justified by the express declarations of Dr. C. himself, as set forth in his edition of the works of Priestley, and the passages containing them were cited by Dr. R. for the judgment of his readers. Of the fairness of this mode of procedure there can be no doubt, provided the reviewer refrained from low appeals to prejudice or fanaticism; and on a re-perusal of the article, at this day, we do not find that he is obnoxious to the charge. It soon appeared that he was sustained, not by his own sect alone, but by the general sentiment of the Virginia public—and the appointment was quietly rescinded after making an equitable pecuniary compensation to Dr. C. for his losses consequent on the new arrangement. Here the affair might have terminated and passed into oblivion without sequel. But the having been thus traversed in a favorite measure, seems to have somewhat disturbed the usual philosophic serenity of the venerable rector. In subsequent letters to Dr. Cooper and others of his correspondents, not the

that, as a matter of policy, he hoped the Visitors would, in the early stages of its existence, remove the fears of the religious

---

author of the offensive article alone, but the entire sect of Presbyterians were reflected on, and in no very measured terms. Their religious opinions were severely criticised; a belief was intimated, that they desired to have them established by law; as also to monopolize the education of the country; in a word, that they cherished a factious, ambitious spirit, against which the friends of freedom and progress should be on their guard. These were serious charges; and yet, so long as they were confined to private letters (some of them confidential,) the parties assailed would have been content to leave the correction to time and the progress of events. But when those letters were published, they had a right to reclaim against their injustice.

And surely there was a cause. The University was the property of the whole State. It was to be erected, endowed and sustained at the public expense. Of the Virginia public, the Presbyterians, although a minority, constitued a large and respectable part. We do not learn that they questioned the ability or scientific attainments of Dr. Cooper; that they objected to his having been employed by the proper authorities in Pennsylvania; or by those of the Central College, so long as it continued a private corporation—nor yet by those of South Carolina at a later day. That was the affair of others, to whom it was left in every case. So far as appears from any overt act, they desired to participate in, not to monopolize the advantages of the institution to the establishment of which they had contributed their due quota, and it was both natural and proper that they should enquire and judge of the characters and sentiments of those who were to be the future instructors of their sons.

For the rest, they had fought manfully for independence during the revolution—they had, from whatever motive, been among the first in this State to proclaim the principles of religious liberty, and to urge their legal establishment. Many of them had been active members of the republican party—so called—and, distinguishing between Mr. J.'s accredited opinions on religion, and his political system, had given their cordial support to his administration of the General Government. If their faith was repulsive to him, his, which has now been made public, was as little acceptable to them; and each could enjoy his own under the broad shield of that Constitution which was raised for the protection of all. It should be added, that this class of our citizens, who had theretofore shewn a commendable zeal in the cause of education, were among the earliest advocates of the University, as they have, since its establishment, been its steadfast friends and patrons.

Of Dr. Rice, in particular, it may be said, that there are many now living who remember him as the learned and exemplary Divine, decided in his own opinion, but liberal towards others, and courteous in general society; devoted to the regular duties of his calling, and so studiously observant of clerical propriety as to refrain from the least appearance of mingling in party politics. Rarely, if ever, did he even use the common privilege of citizens—that

orders. He avowed that the Presbyterians sought no peculiar advantage, and that they and the other sects would be well satisfied by the appointment of an Episcopalian. I stated to him that I knew not what would be the determination of the board; but I was sure no desire existed any where to give any preference to the Unitarians; and, for my own part, I should

---

of recording his vote at the polls. And yet it is believed, that Virginia did not contain, within her broad limits, and among her most enlightened sons, one who was more truly attached to her soil and people, or who more ardently desired both the diffusion of knowledge among the masses and the improvement of education in its higher grades. His influence had been exerted, by tongue and pen, in behalf of the University, while its fortunes were yet doubtful, and when it most needed friends; and those who knew him will not doubt the sincerity of his declarations to Mr. Cabell, as recorded in this and other letters.

But the misapprehension had been not wholly on one side. A notion had got abroad among some of the less informed, that Mr. J. was not merely hostile to a particular sect, but that he would endeavor to exclude all religious instruction and influence from the precincts of the University. This idea will appear chimerical to all who recollect that this institution was the creature of the Legislature, and wholly subject to its control. To remove an impression as injurious as it was absurd, Mr. J., in his next annual report, was prompt to disclaim any such purpose, and actually suggested a plan by which aspirants to the clerical profession, in the different sects, could each be taught his own peculiar theology in the immediate vicinity of the University, and yet enjoy the proper benefits of the latter by attending its course of lectures at other hours.

The friends of *Hampden Sidney College* may also learn, from this correspondence, that there was no particular desire on the part of the Visitors of the University to depress that institution. They did not deny its former usefulness or capacity for future service. Believing that a general system of education for the whole State should embrace primary schools, colleges, and a single university; and thinking it but just that all of the second class which received aid from the State, should, like the University, come under State control; when the condition was rejected, they acquiesced in an arrangement which appears to be better suited to our peculiar circumstances, and which has certainly succeeded beyond all prior expectations—that of leaving each sect to establish its own college and academies, and using the funds of the State principally for the maintenance of a University which could only be sustained by the united strength of all, and for the tuition of the poor whose parents were unable to bear the expense.

not vote against any one on account of his being a professor of religion or free-thinker.

Faithfully, yours,

JOSEPH C. CABELL.

Mr. Jefferson.

CXXXII.

T. J. TO J. C. C.

MONTICELLO, January 14, 1822.

DEAR SIR,—I have duly received your two favors of the 3d and 7th, and in them the proof of your continued zeal for the object of our joint labors.

Of the course most prudently to be pursued, Mr. Johnson and yourself are best judges. You alone are in a situation to know the state of the pulse of the body on which our institution depends for life or death; and to you I leave it entirely. Silence and resignation have sometimes greater effect than importunity. The obtaining a relinquishment of the debt at this time is not material; for we could not open the institution while our funds would be employed in building the library. With time, perhaps the public opinion may become more and more reconciled to it. The only thing of real importance, at present, is a suspension of the *payment* of interest for four or five years. We could then be going on with the library, and the cancelment of the whole within that term would be in good enough time. But, in all this, do what yourself and your colleague shall think most practicable and desirable.

Affectionately, yours,

TH: JEFFERSON.

Joseph C. Cabell, Esq.

CXXXIII.

J. C. C. TO T. J.

RICHMOND, 21st January, 1822.

DEAR SIR,—I thank you for your favor of 14th instant, which arrived to-day, and has been shewn to Mr. Johnson. The plan of suspending the interest would be practicable, if the increase of the fund were not too low even to satisfy existing appropriations. The accountant's estimate makes the revenue more than $62,000; but the stocks are ascertained to be so unproductive, as to bring the income for this year below $60,000. Since the date of my last, individual conferences have taken place, and from these I should judge there would be no difficulty in getting the arrears of interest due from the General Government. The members seem liberal in giving lands in the moon. From this, I judge that the dread of the people is at the bottom of most of the objections made to the appropriations; * * * * * * * * * Some of our friends are very much dissatisfied with what is called the intended Dead Horse Bill; but all estimate it as better than nothing; and the greater part of the leading friends of the institution think that nothing better would go down. Whilst the executive is preparing the account, we shall hold conferences, and if anything better can be done, you may rest assured I will not hesitate to ask. I think it important to make no application that will be rejected; and if they will give us the arrears of interest only, we shall seem to be under the patronage of the Legislature, and in the event of our failure at Washington, we can return here on equitable grounds. Mr. Fenton Mercer has written to Mr. Bowyer, who brought in the resolution respecting the arrears of interest. From this I judge he thinks still there is some plausibility in the scheme. I shall soon see the letter, and will say a word about it in a postscript.

Faithfully yours,

JOSEPH C. CABELL.

Mr. Jefferson.

P. S. I have seen Mr. Mercer's letter. He encourages Mr. Bowyer to prosecute the subject, and says he has always thought the claim might be sustained at Washington. He believes it to amount to $250,000. He blames a former Governor for inattention to this business.

CXXXIV.

[It turned out the hope of the writer, as expressed in the following letter, was much too sanguine. The prosperous condition of the institution now, and for some years past, has brought it nearer to fulfillment. Its previous patronage fluctuated with the state of the times and other circumstances.]

T. J. TO J. C. C.

MONTICELLO, January 25, 1822.

DEAR SIR,—In a conversation with Mr. Garrett, after his return from Richmond a few days ago, he mentioned to me that the general opinion in the circles there in which he was, seemed to be, that we could not expect, within any moderate time, more than 100 students at our University. This wonderful error proceeds from a want of information, even as to our own State. My position with respect to that institution occasions me to be the centre of the enquiries and information on that subject, and those from our own State prove that that alone will immediately furnish far beyond that number. And the letters I have received from almost every State south of the Potomac, Ohio and Missouri, prove that all of these are looking anxiously to the opening of our University as an epoch which is to relieve them from sending to the Northern universities. And when we see that the colleges of those States, considered as preparatory only for ours, have one, two, and three hundred students each, we cannot doubt that ours will receive the double and treble of their numbers. I have not a doubt our accommodations for 218 will be filled within six months after opening, and for every fifty coming afterwards, we shall have to build a boarding-house and twenty-five dormitories. Immediately after my conversation with Mr. Garrett, I happened to receive the enclosed from Maryland, and I thought it not amiss to send it to you, to be used as you please, except not to be published. I could send you a volume of such.

I hope some means will be devised of suspending the actual payment of interest by the University for four or five years. It would be a real misfortune to let our workmen be dispersed before the whole buildings are accomplished. I have duly received your favors of the 3d, 7th, 14th and 21st.

Ever and affectionately yours,

TH: JEFFERSON.

Joseph C. Cabell, Esq.

CXXXV.

J. C. C. TO T. J.

RICHMOND, 3d February, 1822.

DEAR SIR,—I did not write you this day week, because the posture of affairs had undergone no change, and I had nothing to communicate worthy of your attention. I thank you for your two favors of 14th and 25th ult.; both of which I have shewn to many friends. Since the date of my last, Mr. Johnson has suggested to me an expedient, perhaps freer from objection than any heretofore thought of since the beginning of the session. It is to leave the debt of the University as it now stands, and to ask for an additional appropriation out of the surplus revenue of the literary fund, over and above the $60,000 already appropriated. I am inclined to think this a better scheme that the preceding; because it is free from the objection of touching or giving up any of the capital of the fund; from that of taxing the people; and from that of trenching on existing appropriations. It is not more inconvenient to the college interest than the plan of cancelling the bonds, which Mr. Griffin proposed; and it is equally as beneficial to the University, except that, perhaps, if the bonds should be cancelled, and the fund in its revenue fall short of $60,000, we might hereafter claim arrearages. It is better than an appropriation *pro tanto* out of the interest claim, because it gives us the benefit of every addition to the fund. I should prefer the cancelling of the bonds, because I think a fair construction of the University act would give us the arrears as soon as the fund should be able. But Mr. Morris told me to-day he was so committed he could not support that measure; and probably Blackburn and many others would object, and the wavering would avail themselves of the pretext. Something will be attempted in a few days; and our election seems to be confined to these two measures. Your plan of suspending the interest seems to be regarded as equivalent to cancelling the bonds. I think we should get rid of the debt, if possible. We could then go into operation without the library, or get it from the annuity or other sources. I consider the cancelling the bonds, and the appropriation of $7,200 per annum out of the surplus as substantially the same thing. The latter measure has the advantage only of relieving our friends from embarrassment. I fear nothing will be done; and that we shall be voted down promptly. I shall endeavor to enlist the speakers on our side, and there is my only hope.

The subject of the Kentucky mission* is now before us, and likely to take up some time. That of State Rights is also on the carpet. I think it would have been better postponed till the next session.

Faithfully yours,

JOSEPH C. CABELL.

Mr. Jefferson.

---

* The mission here referred to was that in which Messrs. Henry Clay and George M. Bibb, both natives of Virginia, appeared before the bar of the House of Delegates, in vindication of the laws giving to occupying claimants a right to certain lands in Kentucky, by which many citizens of the parent State thought themselves aggrieved.

CXXXVI.

J. C. C. TO T. J.

RICHMOND, 11th February, 1822.

DEAR SIR,—In my last I informed you that we then contemplated the plan of asking the Legislature to give the University the surplus revenue of the literary fund, to the amount of $7,200, which would be equivalent to the release of the debt. Mr. Johnson and myself had thought, by this expedient, we should get clear of the commitment of our friends in the House of Delegates against any scheme which would go to the diminution of the capital of the literary fund. To my great regret, however, I discovered that our friend Mr. Morris, of Hanover, Chairman of the Committee of Schools and Colleges, would not support this measure. He assured Mr. Johnson and myself that himself and Gen. Breckenridge had been compelled, by an express call from Mr. Miller of Powhatan, to get up on the floor of the House of Delegates, at the last session, and pledge themselves to support the appropriation to the colleges of the surplus of $20,000; and this pledge ought, in his opinion, to debar him from voting for any measure which would go to the withdrawal of the surplus from that destination. It was vain for me to deplore the imprudence of such pledges. It was the price, he said, of the loan bill of the last winter. It being most clear that we could carry no measure in which the friends of the University should be divided, and it being every way important to have the support of Mr. Morris, I was compelled to abandon that measure. My patience was nearly exhausted, and I felt an inclination, almost irresistible, to return to my family. I, however, remembered the great interests at stake, and chided my own despondency. Some how or other we had taken up the impression that your proposition to suspend the payment of the interest of the debt was equivalent, in point of principle, to cancelling the bonds. On a sudden it struck me, like a flash of light, that your suggestion might be viewed otherwise; and that it would at least serve as an entering wedge, and give time to rally the resources of the State. I hastened to Mr. Morris' room, and invited him to unite with us in the support of the plan contained in your last letter. In stating it to him verbally, I mistook a suspension of payment for a remission of interest. Mr. Morris objected to a remission of interest, as conflicting with his pledge of last winter. I handed him your letter, saying, "that is my last hope; that being rejected, my heart fails me, and my hands fall." He read the letter again; and marked the distinction between a suspension and remission of interest, which I had overlooked. He expressed himself entirely willing to support your proposition. We discussed it at large in the presence and with the aid of Doctor Cocke, and finally agreed to make your letter our rallying point. Mr. Morris was to see Mr. Johnson to procure his co-operation, which I expected as a matter of course, and was to prepare and bring forward the bill without delay. But, unluckily, the business of the Kentucky commissioners just then was pressed before the Legislature, and has diverted the attention of the leading members from all other subjects. I am aware of the imminent danger of the delay which has taken place. But I have urged the subject by all the means in my power, and I assure you I have not been able to get it forward at an earlier day. Should the measure fail, I shall be blamed by certain persons for the failure, by the late period of bringing it forward; but I have been unable to procure co-operation and action at an earlier period. To-day I got Mr. Morris and Mr. Johnson together; when I found Mr. Johnson very difficult to persuade to support your plan, on the ground that he did not wish to put the institution so much in the power of the Assembly, or House of Delegates. However, at length I prevailed on him to unite, and at his instance agreed that the bill should contain another provision, viz: a power to the President and Directors to apply any moneys which they may receive from the government of the United States, on account of interest, to the re-imbursement of the principal and interest of the debt. Thus, then, the bill is at length agreed upon, and about the 13th, or 14th, or 15th inst., it will come before the House of Delegates. Whether it will pass or not, I cannot tell; but I hope it will. I shall immediately go around to enlist about a half dozen speakers from different parts of the State. I am inclined to believe the institution is gaining ground. *Would it be believed in future times, that such efforts are necessary to carry such a bill, for such an object!!** In haste and truth,

Faithfully yours,

JOSEPH C. CABELL.

Mr. Jefferson.

CXXXVII.

J. C. C. TO T. J.

RICHMOND, 25th February, 1822.

DEAR SIR,—I am very sorry to inform you, that the resolution of the Committee of Schools and Colleges in favor of a suspension of the interest of the University debt was this day called up and postponed in the House of Delegates, by a vote of 86 to 66. The poor school or arrearage bill is on the table of the Senate, and we shall send them down an amendment. I fear we shall be compelled to vote for a modification going to put off the library for the present. I am very much opposed to Mr. Johnson on this point; but I fear I must give way. I wish I could have your advice on this point; but it would come too late. Never have we had so untoward a House as that of

* This exclamation might be repeated with greater emphasis at the present day, when we can look back to the liberal appropriations which, in the interval, have been made by the Legislature of Virginia to the cause of education—military and medical; to various public charities, and, above all, to the great cause of internal improvement. The revival of the spirit which has given favor to the last, was in no small degree owing to the early and persevering efforts of Mr. Cabell.

this year. Mr. Watson and Mr. Bowyer are gone. It has been utterly out of my power to hasten Mr. Morris and others. Mr. Watson retires. But you would do well to get his friends in Louisa to open a poll for him. He would be a great loss indeed. He cannot now come unless the people choose to send him, as he is committed. Could you not get Mr. Taylor, of Chesterfield to come? I have tried in vain. Six clever men, in addition to our present friends, would turn the tide. Morris retires also.

Faithfully yours,

JOSEPH C. CABELL.

Mr. Jefferson.

CXXXVIII.

[Explantory of the causes of failure—Repelling the popular charges of extravagance—Acknowledging the assistance of friends—And taking courage for the future.]

J. C. C. TO T. J.

WARMINSTER, 6th March, 1822.

DEAR SIR,—I returned on 3d instant to my family at this place, after having experienced the mortification of losing all our propositions in favor of the University. Shortly after the date of my last letter to you, I determined to give my assent to the restriction, in regard to the rotunda, insisted on by Mr. Johnson, Gen. Blackburn and others. I yielded this point most reluctantly; but, on full reflection, I thought it better to do so. In the first place, I thought they would be able to carry it against us. Next, I thought it important that the friends of the institution should not waste their strength against each other. Lastly, I was the less opposed to the measure, inasmuch as the application of the proceeds of the bill to the houses of accommodation would enable the Board to keep back the arrears of subscription and the glebe money as a contingent fund for miscellaneous purposes. At one time I had hopes that I could raise a party strong enough to defeat the attempt at restrictions. I found no difficulty in satisfying intelligent men, who had not committed themselves. But the idea of extravagance in the erection of the buildings, had spread far and wide among the mass; and even among a part of the intelligent circle of society. The admissions of our own friends, and *the known opinion of a part of the Board of Visitors*, have mainly contributed to give currency and weight to the prejudice prevailing on this subject. Believing, as I did, that instead of extravagance, there had been great economy, and feeling the deepest conviction that the erection of the rotunda was essential to the best interest of the institution, it was, I assure you, a source of bitter mortification to me, to be compelled to yield my assent to an amendment to the Senate's amendment respecting the suspension of interest, which prohibited the erection of the rotunda. And I do not believe I could have been induced to yield my own impressions on this subject, had I not seen Mr. Brockenbrough, the proctor of the University, and heard him express the opinion that in the existing state of the institution, it would be advisable for its friends to take the bill with the limitation, rather than lose it altogether.

It is not improbable that our measure suffered by being offered so late in the session. A certain degree of delay, I thought not disadvantageous; but the extreme delay which took place, I foresaw would jeopardize our interests, and by every means in my power, I endeavored, though vainly, to lessen it. From the 31st December when I arrived, till the day preceding that on which Mr. Clay addressed the General Assembly, I was employed, as I believe I have already informed you, in ascertaining what proposition would meet with the concurrent support of our own friends. On the latter date, Mr. Morris, Chairman of the Committee of Schools and Colleges, consented to support the measure you had recommended, of suspending the payment of the interest of the University debt. In a day or two after, at the instance of Mr. Johnson, the plan was enlarged so as to embrace an appropriation of the claim of the State on the government of the United States of interest paid on our advances to that government during the late war, to an amount sufficient to pay the principal and interest of the debt of the University. The bill was drawn by Mr. Johnson, with the consent of Mr. Morris, and on consultation with us three, Mr. Morris was engaged to bring it forward on the first favorable opportunity. But Mr. Morris was then engrossed by the business of the Kentucky mission, and unfortunately he continued so, till the last days of the session, when Hanover court, in which he is much employed as a lawyer, called him from the seat of government, and deprived us entirely of his aid. If I could have foreseen the effect of the Kentucky mission, on Mr. Morris's mind, I would have prevailed on Mr. Watson to take the lead in this business. But to take it out of Mr. Morris's hands, without a manifest necessity, would have been every way ungracious and imprudent.

Pending the latter part of the delay on this subject, Mr. Bowyer, of Rockbridge, Mr. Watson, of Louisa, and Mr. Morris, of Hanover, left us. I called on each of them, and conjured them not to leave us. But it was all in vain. Their minds were made up to return home, and I could not shake them. Morris promised me to return, if possible; but he did not return, on account of the pressure of his causes in Hanover court. All the exertions of which I was master, were put forth to accelerate the march of our measures, and to keep our friends together in the latter part of the session. But they were fruitless.

After the Committee of Schools and Colleges had reported a resolution in favor of suspending the interest, and on the day before the resolution was postponed in the House of Delegates, we determined to let the resolution lie on the table, and to move in the Senate suitable amendments to the bill which had been sent up on the subject of the arrearages due the counties. The resolution was called up and postponed, contrary to the wishes of our friends, in the absence of the Chairman of the Committee.

When the arrearage bill was amended in the Senate, Mr. Johnson advised that we should ask for $200,000, out of our claim on the General Government for interest, instead of asking only for a sum sufficient to pay the principal and interest of the debt. His advice was acceded to.

When the amendments of the Senate were taken up in the House of Delegates, Blackburn moved his restrictive clause, and it was rejected by a large majority. There was an union of enemies and friends in that vote. Those who wished to reject the Senate's amendments did, many of them, vote against the prohibition to build the rotunda, because they thought it would make the bill more popular, if the prohibition should prevail. And some of the warm friends of the institution, particularly those with whom I had conferred on this point, voted against it on correct principles. The House of Delegates then disagreed to our amendments, and the subject came back to us.

At that stage, I called on Gen. Blackburn. He was in bed. I stood by his bed-side, and addressed him for near an hour, with the view of prevailing on him not to renew his motion to restrict the Board of Visitors when the bill should return from the Senate. I went into a general view of the causes of hostility to the University, and endeavored to prove that the sources of opposition were deeper than they appeared to be; and that the expenditure in building was only a popular topic seized on by the hostile interests with which we were contending. My efforts were vain. He had taken up different views, and moreover had pledged himself to the House. I should then have endeavored to get his restriction rejected in the House of Delegates, but for the conversation with Mr. Brockenbrough, to which I have already referred. The Senate insisted. The House of Delegates adhered. The Senate asked a free conference, which was agreed to. It took place in the chamber of the House of Delegates, in the presence of most of the members of both Houses. Gen. Blackburn's amendment relative to the suspension of further buildings than the houses of accommodation, was offered by Mr. Johnson as an amendment to the suspending clause, and he proposed to strike out the $200,000. The Committee of the Senate was unanimous, and a majority of the other Committee concurred. The House of Delegates refused to accede to the advice of the committee of conference. And the question now occurred, shall the Senate adhere to their amendments, and thereby defeat the passage of the original bill respecting the arrearages, or recede, and let it pass. On consultation with my friends, I determined to recede. The bill contained some valuable provisions respecting the primary school fund. This in particular—that a county should account for a former quota, before it should draw a new quota, and should account according to a form to be prescribed. I have ever thought that the true interest of the University would be promoted by a correct and judicious administration of the primary school fund. The law was very defective, and great abuses prevailed. An attack on the whole literary fund was made during the past session, and bottomed in part on the waste of the primary school fund. The whole fund was jeopardized by the abuses connected with the administration of the popular branch. A party was forming itself in the bosom of the Legislature, and apparently gaining strength, whose object was to break up the literary fund, and put the money in the treasury. They seized upon the waste of the funds sent out for the education of the poor, and wielded it against the whole establishment. The best interests of science and literature seemed to me to enjoin it on us to rescue the system, as far as practicable, from disgrace, by prudent amendatory provisions. I had also made up my mind, that it was expedient to let the arrears go out. You remember, no doubt, the excitement at the close of the preceding session. A number of the counties had suffered their quotas to accumulate in the treasury, under the impression that they would be authorized to draw them at discretion.

This was particularly the case with the small counties in the eastern parts of the State, where they draw least relatively to their rate of contribution. The President and Directors of the Literary Fund did, in my opinion, construe the law correctly. But as the law was not very clearly expressed, there was room for misconstruction among honest minds. The idea of inequality is odious to the people; and the inhabitants of the counties claiming the arrears, considered themselves unequally dealt by. The enemies of the University had made powerful use of this weapon; and doubtless hoped and expected we would preserve it to them. These considerations induced us to recede, and suffer the original bill to pass. I am well pleased on reflection, that we did so. Before I left Richmond, I understood that although all our measures had failed, there seemed to be prevailing a general sentiment of regret that nothing had been done for the University. I ascribe this sentiment in no small degree to our moderation in suffering the arrearage bill to pass. After the failure of our amendments from the Senate, an effort was made by original bill in the House of Delegates, to procure the $200,000, separate and distinct from the suspension of interest, which failed.

Mr. Johnson made a long and able speech in the Committee of Conference, in support of the suspension of interest. In the course of this speech, he took occasion to express it as his opinion, that the plan of the buildings was not the best which might have been adopted. But on this point, he said, he was opposed to such high authority, he confessed he was induced to doubt the correctness of his own judgment.

On this occasion, * * * * * * of * * * * took an active part against us, on the ground that the suspension of the interest would impair the principal of the literary fund. He voted the next day in favor of the bill giving $200,000 to the University, having in the debate on the suspension committed himself to that effect.

Such, sir, are the results of a session of two months, during which I may have erred in the course of measures which was adopted, but in which I never for one moment lost sight of the great object of our pursuit. I am not, however, disheartened; and look forward to the future with better prospects of success. So far from despairing, I rely on the virtue and intelligence of our countrymen, and so expressed myself in the closing debates of the Senate. I shall, if life and health permit, attend the meeting of the Visitors, on the first Monday in next month. I expect to leave this place on the 19th, spend a few days in Richmond, pass up by Bremo, to my house, and return by the way of Monticello. As the House of Delegates did reject Gen. Blackburn's restrictive amendment on a question propounded on that subject, and disconnected from any other, and afterwards rejected the proposition connected with the suspension of interest, we are left fairly where we were as to the rotunda. I shall endeavor to see some of my leading friends on this subject as I come through Richmond. It would be well to move cautiously on this part of the buildings, more because of the part that some of our friends have acted, than from respect to our adversaries.

I write in haste, and as the mail is about to close, have no time to correct mistakes, which I hope you will excuse.

Faithfully yours,

JOSEPH C. CABELL.

Mr. Jefferson.

CXXXIX.

J. C. C. TO T. J.

WILLIAMSBURG, 10th March, 1822.

DEAR SIR,—When I last wrote you, I forgot to enclose you the letters which passed between yourself and Mr. ——, relative to the University. I now enclose them to you by mail, lest some unforeseen accident may prevent me from getting to the meeting on the first of next month. Information but recently received from my farm in Lancaster, renders it highly important that I should go there without delay. But I shall not suffer this, nor any other cause within my own control, to prevent me from attending at the meetings of the Board of Visitors, as long as I continue to hold the appointment. I may be prevented hereafter, as I have been heretofore, by ill-health. I have determined to remain here a week longer than I intended when I last wrote you, and now propose to leave this on 25th inst., to arrive at Gen. Cocke's on the Saturday before the meeting, and to ride with him to Monticello on the next day. I should be glad to see you before the meeting, but as it is impossible for me to do so (as I shall travel in the stage) without setting out a week sooner than I wish to leave this place, and as I have written you very fully, I must be deprived of that satisfaction for this time. My object would be to consult yourself and Mr. Madison as to the policy which, under existing circumstances, ought to be adopted in regard to the central building. In my last letter, I unfolded to you the difference of opinion between Mr. Johnson and myself in regard to this subject, and the reasons which induced me to yield up the opposition which I contemplated to the restrictive amendment proposed by himself and Gen. Blackburn. On this last point, I was, perhaps, not as circumstantial as I might have been. When matters were rapidly hurrying on to a crisis, I was informed by Mr. Cary, of Fluvanna, that Mr. Brockenbrough (whom I had not then seen) had stated to him, that if you were in Richmond, you would yourself support the bill with the restrictive clause, sooner than lose it. There was not a moment to lose, and immediately on receiving this communication, I advised Mr. Cary, and through him my other friends in the House of Delegates, to yield to the amendment. Under such circumstances, I had not the courage or the rashness to array one part of the friends of the institution against another, when you yourself would not do it, were you present. Afterwards, I saw Mr. Brockenbrough, and was informed by him, that Mr. Cary had misunderstood him. He doubted whether you would approve the course, but expressed it to be his opinion, that we had better pursue it.

I never in my life felt more deeply convinced on any subject, than I am as to the soundness of the policy of going on with the buildings, in preference to the plan of putting the institution into operation, with half the buildings finished. The President of the College and Judge Semple, in conversation with me, a few days ago, candidly acknowledged the policy of our course in this respect. They observed, that Virginians would never be pleased with anything on a small scale. Judge Semple adduced a fact, by way of illustration, which I was pleased to hear. Mr. John Tyler, of Charles City, late member of Congress, was formerly opposed to the institution. In a trip which he made last year to the Springs, he called and inspected the buildings; and the Judge assured me that Mr. Tyler was so much impressed by the extent and splendor of the establishment, that he has become an advocate for the University, and would have voted last winter, had he been in the Legislature, for cancelling the bonds. Mr. Tyler is a candidate for the Assembly, and will doubtless be elected. From what the Judge told me, I suspect the opposition will attempt to fetter Mr. Tyler by instructions. Dr. Crump, of Cumberland, was as much influenced by the sight of the buildings as Mr. Tyler. He abandoned us last winter, on other, and, as I think, insufficient grounds. The opinion which I had previously entertained on this subject, has been confirmed by many facts of this description.

With every sentiment of respect for the judgment and services of our colleagues, and particularly Mr. Johnson, I can not but deeply regret the views he has formed in regard to the library. But for the weight of his own opinion, I think the opposition on that subject might have been disregarded. It is important to carry him along with us. How far this consideration, and the state of the funds, may induce us to put by the library for the present, I really feel very great doubts. About *Richmond*, and *Staunton*, and with the *Federal* party, I observe the opposition to the library to be strongest. I shall be mainly governed by the opinion of yourself and Mr. Madison on this subject.

Faithfully yours,

JOSEPH C. CABELL.

Mr. Jefferson.

CXL.

J. C. C. TO T. J.

EDGEWOOD, 3d October, 1822.

DEAR SIR,—Gen. Cocke will inform you that the cause of my failure to attend at the University on yesterday was that I had not sufficiently recovered from the severe and tedious illness, by which I have been unhappily visited. My convalescence is much slower than I expected, and is further prolonged by successive relapses. Some days past I was taken with the ague and fever, which often follows in the rear of the bilious fever. For two days I have been taking bark, and its salutary effects induce me to hope I shall miss my ague to-day. If I should be so fortunate as to escape a return, and the weather should be favorable, I think of setting out in a carriage on Saturday, so as to get to Monticello on Sunday or Monday to dinner. If I should not come, you may conclude that my state of health forbids the journey; for I am never absent from your meetings but with the greatest reluctance; and, on this occasion, feel a particular desire to be present. I ardently hope that Mr. Dawson has reached the end of his labors, and found all things to come out clear and satisfactory.* General Cocke seemed reluctant to commence the

---

* So it proved; and their clear exposé was of essential aid in future operations. The associate examiner was Mr. MARTIN DAWSON, a native of Nelson county, but then a worthy citizen of Albemarle. It is pertinent to our general subject, and should be mentioned in his honor, that at his death in 1835, *he bequeathed* $39,500, *the bulk of a fortune accumulated during a life of diligence and thrift, in aid of primary education of the poor in these two counties,* between whom its annual interest is divided.

inspection of the books without an associate. I should think, however, that with Mr. Dawson's assistance it would be an easy task. He is now, probably, in Albemarle, on his way to fulfill this duty. Should I not attend, be pleased to remember me kindly to all the gentlemen of the Board.

I remain, dear sir, faithfully your friend,

JOSEPH C. CABELL.

Mr. Jefferson.

CXLI.

J. C. C. TO T. J.

RICHMOND, 19th December, 1822.

DEAR SIR,—I reached this place on the 17th instant, and write now merely to apprise you of my arrival. I returned to Williamsburg from the Northern Neck on the 6th instant, and immediately wrote to a friend in this place to ascertain whether the usual recess of the Senate would take place. I counted on a recess as a matter of course, and was willing to avail myself of it, in order that I might enjoy some rest after much fatigue and trouble. By some accident, I did not hear of the determination of the Senate not to adjourn till the 16th, when a letter from my brother, and Judge Tucker on his return from the Federal Court, informed me of the fact. On the 17th I came up in the stage. Yesterday and to-day, I have been engaged in fixing myself in my lodgings at the Eagle. I have had short interviews with Mr. Gordon, Mr. Rives, Mr. Cary, and others. All that I can now tell you is, that the House of Delegates has greatly improved in ability, and I am informed that the leading members generally seem well disposed towards the University. The accompanying report, respecting the literary fund, will shew you that the state of the finances is very unfavorable. From what source we are to procure the necessary funds, is a subject on which I have not as yet formed any opinion. And I am equally undecided how much we ought to ask in our bill; whether the funds necessary to build the library, and the relinquishment of the debt—or the former singly, leaving the debt to be hereafter disposed of—or the relinquishment of the debt without conditions. This, I presume, is the order of preference. It is the order in which I should myself arrange the propositions. I greatly doubt the practicability of carrying the first or second. The third would be apt to succeed, if we should hit judiciously on the proper funds. A certain party will attempt to impose conditions to the third proposition. Some of our friends will concur in this view. I hear that Mr. *** professes himself friendly; but requires that we should state what the cost of the necessary apparatus and library will be, and that we should go into *immediate operation.* He complains that he has not heretofore been consulted. He will be conferred with by some of our friends. But there is some danger in such consultations; for, unless you accede to their views, such friends often fly off altogether. We shall endeavor to get ready to bring some thing forward about the 1st January; about which time I hear the report will be down, together with the estimate of the cost of the centre building. Some delay is necessary to ascertain what is best to be done. After that, a straight forward, open and bold course is what I shall recommend to our friends. Mr. Johnson is not yet arrived; and I hear he is sick. I fear we shall differ again about *conditions;* but I wish to have the advantage of his talents and influence. Thank God, my health is now uncommonly good. But it requires that I should often reflect on the great object in view, to prevent my spirits from sinking under the combined influence of a painful separation from my family, an increasing debt, and the reflection that such great exertions are necessary to do the least service to science in this State. I hope I shall have the pleasure to see Col. Randolph before he leaves town. If I have not heretofore mentioned the subject of your late unfortunate wound, it is not because I was not deeply concerned for your sufferings. I hear, with great pleasure, that you are recovering.

I am, dear sir, faithfully yours,

JOSEPH C. CABELL.

Mr. Jefferson.

CXLII.

[Suggesting a plan of operations during the present session.]

J. C. C. TO T. J.

RICHMOND, 23d December, 1822.

DEAR SIR,—Mr. Gordon and Mr. Rives left this for Albemarle on yesterday, and will not probably return for eight or ten days. The latter went for his family, and the former to visit Mrs. Gordon in her distress for the loss of a child. I am very sorry that they were obliged to leave town, as we want the aid of all our friends at this time.

Mr. Gordon shewed me, on Saturday, a letter which he had just received from Mr. Dinsmore, stating that the undertakers had ascertained that they could not afford to build the library for less than $70,000. At my instance, Mr. Gordon threw the letter in the fire. My object was to prevent it from being made an improper use of, in the event of its being seen by our enemies. I have spoken with one or two friends confidentially on this subject, and we all agree that if the price of the undertakers should rise above $50,000, and more especially if it should reach $70,000, it would be better to abandon the project of a conditional contract on their parts, and leave us at large. In our opinion, we should not ask for more than $50,000 for the library; suggesting, that if the job should be put up to the lowest bidder among the workmen of first rate ability in the United States, that sum would probably suffice, and if it should fall short, the deficiency could be made up from the annuity, or from some other source. At all events, we could hope not to trouble the Legislature again on that subject. *If matters have not gone too far*, we would prefer that no such document as one calling for $70,000 for the library should be sent here. It would probably blow up all our plans. Perhaps a conditional contract for $60,000 might not do harm, as it would bar the door to all doubt about the price of the house. But if $70,000 should be asked for, I fear we shall be totally overthrown. Could you not reject the offer of the undertakers, on *the ground that we may be able to get better terms*, and authorize me by letter to ask for $50,000 for the library? I suggest these ideas with deference to your better judgment. I should observe to you, that even now there is great hesitancy in the ranks of our friends as to the propriety of building the library at this time; this, too, whilst the belief is that it would cost at most about $50,000. One or two of my best friends in the Assembly tell me, they think that many who would vote for cancelling the debt, would oppose any further appropriation for building. I am endeavoring to remove the objections, but am uncertain how far I shall be able to succeed.

What I think of at present is to ask for the first proposition in my last letter: that is, to cancel and appropriate both. The ways and means which I now contemplate are, to ask for a loan of $50,000 out of *the surplus capital on hand*, to build the library; and to put the whole debt of the University, thus augmented to $170,000, along with the other debts of the State, under the operation of the sinking fund. I have latterly struck on this plan, on consultation with your grandson, who suggested the idea of resorting to the sinking fund. I have mentioned it to Mr. Loyall, Mr. Bowyer and Mr. Hunter, who all, on first view, highly approved it. On the best reflection I can give the subject, it is the best plan we can adopt. We had better let the literary fund stand as it is—not intermeddle with the provisions for the schools, or the surplus appropriated to the colleges. Let us have nothing to do with the old balances, or dead horses, or escheated lands, but ask boldly to be exonerated from our debts by the powerful sinking fund of the State. This is manly and dignified legislation;

and if we fail, the blame will not be ours. Such are my present views. Some there are who think we had better ask for the loan only, at this time, and leave the debt for another session. There are arguments for and against this course. It would lessen the present demand. But it would leave the door open for future applications, and postpone the time of our commencement. The public mind seems impatient for a commencement of the operations of the institution. My present impressions are in favor of asking for the whole. I think it would be important to show that if we could finish the buildings, and get rid of the debt, we could go on without troubling the Assembly again. There are some who say, "you will want a library and apparatus, and you will be obliged to come here for more money, and is it not better to expend the $50,000 in that way, than in buildings?" I am taking *this* ground—that occasional gifts from the Legislature for the purchase of books and apparatus would be of service—nay, of great importance; but that we could get along without them, by appropriating half the fees of tuition to that object, and that we have already adopted a resolution, whereby half the fees will go into the coffers of the institution; and that we had rather have $50,000 to finish the buildings, than to purchase books and apparatus. I should wish to be corrected, if I err on any of these important points.

I have very great confidence in Mr. Hunter. Last night he pressed me to write for the report. He says members will take time to consider the subject, and there is no time to lose. Unfortunately, the question about the seat of government is fixed for the 10th January. It is to be regretted that they could not be separated by a greater interval. I think we should bring our business forward early in January. The prints will be kept back till the report is made. I am very happy to hear from Mr. Garrett, that the Proctor's accounts are satisfactorily settled.

I am, dear sir, ever faithfully yours,

JOSEPH C. CABELL.

Mr. Jefferson.

CXLIII.

T. J. TO J. C. C.

MONTICELLO, December 28, 1822.

DEAR SIR,—Yours of the 19th was received some days ago; those of the 23d, the day before yesterday. At the same time with the former, I received one of the same date from Mr. Rives, proposing a question to me, which, as he is absent, I will answer to you. It was—if the remission of the principal debt, and an accommodation of the cost of the library cannot both be obtained, which would be most desirable? Without any question, the latter. Of all things the most important, is the completion of the buildings. The remission of the debt will come of itself. It is already remitted in the mind of every man, even of the enemies of the institution. And there is nothing pressing very immediately for its expression. The great object of our aim from the beginning, has been to make the establishment the most eminent in the United States, in order to draw to it the youth of every State, but especially of the south and west. We have proposed, therefore, to call to it characters of the first order of science from Europe, as well as our own country; and, not only by the salaries and the comforts of their situation, but by the distinguished scale of its structure and preparation, and the promise of future eminence which these would hold up, to induce them to commit their reputation to its future fortunes. Had we built a barn for a college, and log huts for accommodations, should we ever have had the assurance to propose to an European professor of that character to come to it? Why give up this important idea, when so near its accomplishment that a single lift more effects it? It is not a half project which is to fill up the enticement of character from abroad. To stop where we are, is to abandon our high hopes, and become suitors to Yale and Harvard for their secondary characters to become our first. Have we been laboring then merely to get up another Hampden Sidney or Lexington? Yet to this it sinks, if we abandon foreign aid. The report of Rockfish Gap, sanctioned by the Legislature, authorized us to aim at much higher things;* and the abandonment of the enterprise where we are, would be a relinquishment of the great idea of the Legislature of 1818, and shrinking it into a country academy. The opening of the institution in a half-state of readiness, would be the most fatal step which could be adopted. It would be an impatience defeating its own object, by putting on a subordinate character in the outset, which never would be shaken off, instead of opening largely and in full system. Taking our stand on commanding ground at once, will beckon every thing to it, and a reputation once established, will maintain itself for ages. To secure this, a single sum of fifty or sixty thousands of dollars is wanting. If we cannot get it now, we will at another or another trial. Courage and patience is the watchword. Delay is an evil, which will pass; despair loses all. Let us never give back. The thing will carry itself, and with firmness and perseverance we shall place our country on its high station, and we shall receive for it the blessings of posterity. I think your idea of a loan, and placing it on the sinking fund, an excellent one.

Dinsmore's $70,000 evidence only the greediness of an undertaker. He declined communicating the details of his estimate, lest their exaggeration should be visible. From the undertakers we have the following offers:

The brick work complete, including columns, -	$11,300—Perry.
Stone work, - - - - - -	3,940—Gorman.
Carpentry and joinery of the lower rooms, -	12,000—Oldham.
	$27,240

There remain the inside work of the upper room, the roof, and

* This consideration alone, if there were no other, should suffice to vindicate Mr. Jefferson and his colleagues in their adherence to a plan projected on a liberal scale. Yet how often and generally was it lost sight of by the people and their representatives in opposition during this protracted struggle.

the two appendages or covered ways in the flanks to connect with the other buildings, of which we have no estimate; but they cannot cost as much as all the rest of the building. I asked at what they had estimated the stone work? The answer was $6,000. I knew at the same time that Gorman must do it for them, and would do it for $3,940; so that fifty per cent. was laid on this article for their gains, and probably like advances on the other articles. Mr. Brockenbrough's original estimate was carefully and minutely made, and allowing for the two covered ways, we are safe in saying that another loan of $60,000 will place us beyond the risk of our needing to ask another dollar on that account.

You propose to me to write to half a dozen gentlemen on this subject. You do not know, my dear sir, how great is my physical inability to write. The joints of my right wrist and fingers, in consequence of an ancient dislocation, are become so stiffened that I can write but at the pace of a snail. The copying our report, and my letter lately sent to the Governor, being seven pages only, employed me laboriously a whole week. The letter I am now writing you has taken me two days. I have been obliged, therefore, to withdraw from letter writing, but in cases of the most indispensable urgency. A letter of a page or two costs me a day of labor, and a painful labor. I have few now to live; should I consign them all to pain? I ought, if I could, to write to yourself, to Mr. Johnson, Mr. Rives, Mr. Gordon, and to Mr. Loyall too, now one of our fraternity. But what I say to one, you must all be so indulgent as to consider meant for the whole. Be so good as to express to Mr. Loyall my gratification at his being added to our Board, and my hope that he will make Monticello his head-quarters whenever he comes up. Our meetings, you know, are always on Mondays, and the stage passes us the previous Saturday evening. This gives an intermediate day for rest, enquiry and consideration.

Ever and affectionately yours,

TH: JEFFERSON.

Mr. Cabell.

CXLIV.

J. C. C. TO T. J.

RICHMOND, December 30, 1822.

DEAR SIR,—I am happy to inform you that Mr. Gordon and Mr. Rives arrived in town last evening, and have attended the House to-day. Mr. Gordon called on me this morning, when I disclosed to him what I had done in his absence, and my present views and prospects. I have conferred with Mr. Hunter, Mr. Cary, Mr. Bowyer, Mr. Taylor, of Botetourt, Mr. Baldwin, &c., and the almost unanimous opinion of us all is, that we should ask for another loan to finish the buildings, and to leave the debt untouched for the present. We propose to move for one object at a time, in order not to unite the enemies of both measures against one bill. Should we succeed in getting the loan, we may afterwards try to get rid of the debt. But the general impression is, that we cannot carry both measures at this session. I presume I am clearly right in the assurance which I give to our particular friends, nay to every body, that if both measures cannot pass, the Board of Visitors would prefer the loan to the cancelling of the bonds. It gives me heartfelt pleasure to inform you that the intelligent members generally express the opinion that the institution should be finished. This confirms the propriety of the course we have taken. Of the propriety of that course, you know, I have never doubted. And I may be allowed to feel the gratification natural on such an occasion. Last winter I had to encounter a mingled host of friends and enemies, on this point, and yielded it from a mistake existing between Mr. Brockenbrough and Mr. Cary. Now the leading members generally say, the institution should be finished. Mr. Baldwin has assured me of his hearty co-operation to this effect. From himself, and from Mr. Taylor, of Botetourt, I hear that Mr. Sheffey will go with us. Mr. Doddridge, I expect, will do the same. Mr. * * * * * has twice announced to Mr. Cary, on being consulted by him, that he would oppose any further building; yet Mr. Gordon thinks he may be brought over. * * * * * * * The President of Hampden Sidney is here, making interest for that institution. I am on good terms with him. He is very friendly to the University. To-day he advised me to aim only for a loan, and said he was confident from what he had heard among the members, that the debt should be left untouched for the present. I advised him to take care that * * * * will not kindle a flame against his college, by throwing himself athwart the course of the friends of the University. He observed that * * * * had not made up his mind finally how he would vote on a bill authorizing us to finish the buildings of the University; but he believed that unless the bill for Hampden Sidney should be supported, he would oppose us. I advised him to remonstrate with him as to the propriety and policy of that mode of legislation, and cautioned him not lightly to depart from the system of voting for every measure on the foundation of its own merits. I hope * * * * * may be prevailed on to relinquish his opposition. I am now more in dread of Mr. Johnson's coming to town, and advocating the doctrine of curtailing the building, than I am of any other danger. But as the popular prejudice on that subject has abated, I hope he would go with us. The report was in town on Friday. Mr. Daniel told me he was waiting for Governor Pleasants to communicate it. The Governor will probably be in town this evening. The report will probably be made to-morrow. As soon as it is printed, I will get Capt. Peyton to exhibit the prints of the plan of the University. In a few days thereafter our bill will be brought in. I have a loan bill ready drawn. The subject of interest is somewhat embarrassing. We shall be obliged to lose the interest. I conclude it is better to do so, than stand in our present situation. We must limit the time of our election on the subject of the loan to some short period, to avoid the loss of interest to the fund. Such a proviso will help to carry our bill. There shall be no difficulty on that score about a Board. If the bill passes, I will come up immediately in the stage, and I make no doubt Gen. Cocke and Mr. Loyall will also attend. I still think a conditional contract on the part of the undertakers for $70,000 would do more harm than good. But if they will engage for $60,000 to finish the building out and out, I would rather have the contract than not. If they will not, I will ask for fifty—perhaps, sixty thousand dollars. The year before last, we estimated the library at $40,000. Last year at $45,000, as well as I recollect. Should I now rise to $60,000, some reason will be asked for the difference in the estimates. I have heretofore grounded myself on Mr. Brockenbrough's estimates. If no other document can be furnished, I would suggest the propriety of your writing a short letter to some one here, asking for such sum as you may think proper for the object. The sooner it comes, the better. The affair of the Proctor's accounts seems to be unknown here. I am happy to hear from Gen. Cocke, that that business has been satisfactorily adjusted. I write in great haste,

And remain, dear sir,

Ever faithfully yours,

JOSEPH C. CABELL.

Mr. Jefferson.

CXLV.

J. C. C. TO T. J.

RICHMOND, January 9, 1823.

DEAR SIR,—I thank you very sincerely for your letter of 28th December, and am mortified with the circumstance of my having been the cause of so much trouble to you. I am happy to inform you that our prospects are now very favorable. Every thing is understood; every thing is arranged. Our bill will be introduced in the Committee of Schools and Colleges, in a day or two. We ought to have had a select committee, to get rid of enemies and to expedite; but the report was committed to the Committee of Schools and Colleges by a member who knew not our views, and there would be *certain* difficulties in getting it away from that committee. We hope we are strong enough to meet our adversaries at every stage. The report, I am told, will have a very happy effect. I heard a thing last evening, which is very pleasing. In Mecklenburg, Lunenburg, Brunswick, Greensville, Norfolk, and Essex counties, the University was made a test in the election last spring. The members who voted against us last year, were turned out, or compelled to promise to vote with us. I have the facts as to the four first counties, from Col. Powell of Brunswick, as to Norfolk from Col. Lee, and as to Essex from Mr. Hunter. The institution is gaining greatly to the south and to the east, and indeed every where. Clopton will be elected from the Williamsburg district. The University was made a test on the Henrico Hustings yesterday, and Clopton almost universally voted for. I got * * * * to withdraw. If he had offered, he would greatly have jeopardized Mr. Clopton's election. The prints of the University will be bought up rapidly.

Ever faithfully yours,

JOSEPH C. CABELL.

Mr. Jefferson.

CXLVI.

T. J. TO J. C. C.

MONTICELLO, January 13, 1823.

DEAR SIR,—Yours of the 9th is quite reviving. You say that as soon as the bill has passed, yourself and colleagues will come up to a special meeting. This will be indispensable, because our workmen will be obliged to be looking out for other work for the ensuing season, if their employment here is not soon decided on. But observe that, to make a special call legal, reasonable notice must be given to all the Visitors. As soon, therefore, as the bill has passed the Lower House, (as I suppose we may rely on the Senate,) yourself, Mr. Johnson and Mr. Loyall, may sign a special call, and send a copy by mail to Mr. Madison, Gen. Breckenridge, Gen. Cocke, and myself, each fixing a day of meeting within such term as the proceeding of the Senate may require, and not less than a fortnight. The object of the meeting will be to authorize the commencement of the building, and to talk over some ulterior measures which, however, cannot be finally concluded till April.

Mr. Dawson tells me we must not commit ourselves too strongly as to the amount of our debts, as stated in my letter to the Literary Board. Further investigations incline him to apprehend they will be sensibly more than the Proctor authorized me to say, there being yet some large accounts to settle. It would be well if you would always send me a copy of the printed report for the more convenient use of the Board. With respect to the claims of the local academies, I will make no compromise. The second grade must not be confounded with the first, nor treated of in the same chapter. The present funds are not sufficient for all the three grades. The first and third are most important to be first brought into action. When they are properly provided for, and the funds sufficiently enlarged, the middle establishment should be taken up systematically. In the mean time, it may more conveniently than either of the others be left to private enterprise; 1, because there is a good number of classical schools now existing; and 2, because their students are universally sons of parents who can afford to pay for their education. I am glad to see that Mr. Rives has taken up the subject of primary schools; the present plan being evidently inefficient, we should take the lead in a new one, and become equally their patrons as of the University. The hostile attitude into which we have been brought apparently is equally impolitic and unuseful. Were it necessary to give up either the Primaries or the University, I would rather abandon the last, because it is safer to have a whole people respectably enlightened, than a few in a high state of science, and the many in ignorance. This last is the most dangerous state in which a nation can be. The nations and governments of Europe are so many proofs of it.

Affectionately yours,

TH: JEFFERSON.

Mr. Cabell.

CXLVII.

J. C. C. TO T. J.

RICHMOND, 23d January, 1823.

DEAR SIR,—Your favor of 13th instant came safely to hand by the mail. I have shewn it to Mr. Gordon and Mr. Rives. My own impression is, that in touching the subject of the unliquidated debt, we should merely guard against future unfavorable imputations, by stating that it might and probably would exceed the conjectural amount mentioned in your letter, and that when you wrote, the settlement was in a progressive state. The county delegates seem disposed to say nothing about it. I have referred the matter to their discretion. When the bill gets to the Senate, I shall say something on the subject.

In regard to the academies and primary schools, I think our most prudent course, at this time, is neither to enter into an alliance with them, nor to make war upon them. It would be difficult to imagine a state of things in regard to these other branches of the system more favorable to us than that which now exists. The funds are limited, and we wish to avoid a competitor. The colleges cannot all be gratified, and they will defeat one another. The primary schools are in a state of discredit, and the public mind is not now disposed to increase the appropriation to them. If we amend the system at this time, and give it credit and honor, this ally will become our worst enemy. The popular branch of the system would swallow up all the funds. Even now an effort will be made to divide with us in every appropriation; but the discredit into which the popular branch has fallen, will defeat the measure.

Besides, there are great intrinsic difficulties in the subject. When your bill was brought in some years ago by Mr. Taylor, of Chesterfield, I consulted all the best heads of my acquaintance* then about the Seat of Government, and every effort was made to smooth away the difficulties of the subject; and though many plans were suggested, none met with general approbation. At some future time, I would cheerfully enter again on this difficult and thorny question. I think we would do well to decline it at this time, and take advantage of the favorable breeze that now wafts us along.

I have imparted these views to Mr. Rives, and left him to pursue his own course. Mr. Gordon concurs with me. Mr. Rives did not propose to move the subject of the primary schools till the Loan Bill should be acted on. But the bonds will remain to be cancelled, and the objections would continue till the University should get into operation. I have thought, and still think, that we should act with good faith to the primary schools; but *that* would dictate merely that we should not attempt to take from them any of the $45,000, till experience and public opinion demand the measure. I have attempted, in the county where I reside, to exhibit proofs of my real desire to give that system a fair trial. Our proceedings were printed and distributed over the State.† But, last year, I saw more clearly than ever the inherent defects of that system. It will require great alteration and amendment. But for us to move in it, I think, the time has not arrived.

As to the colleges and academies, I differ from some of our friends. I would vote for an appropriation to Hampden Sid-

---

* Among Mr. C.'s papers are several from his distinguished friends, containing hints on this subject, written at the time specified, and which he appears to have selected out of many others for preservation and future use.

† Many of the suggestions and forms contained in this pamphlet having been enacted into law, were adopted, and are pursued at this day in the disbursement of this fund throughout the State.

ney, and not wait till the funds shall be sufficient for the whole corps of colleges. I think some aid to that college would now be useful and well-timed. However, on this subject, as on that of the question of removing the Seat of Government, I think we should not discover the zeal of partizans. Politeness to all, interference with none, and devotion to our object, constitute the policy that ought, in my opinion, to govern the course of the friends of the University at this time.

You must be surprised at the slow progress of our bill. The tardiness of its movement is to be regretted. But I do not know how it could be avoided. If it had been called up out of its regular turn, perhaps the irregularity of the course might give rise to animadversions. It will be read, in its turn, for the first time, to-day or to-morrow. It went through the committee without opposition. It will doubtless be opposed in the House, but from every thing I can learn I think there cannot be much doubt of its success. Should it pass late in the session, I should hope that a meeting on the 1st Monday in April might answer the purposes of the institution. There could be no doubt of the confirmation of the loan by the board, and the delay would probably throw the loss of interest on the literary fund, and save so much to the University.

I am, dear sir,

Ever faithfully, your friend,

JOSEPH C. CABELL.

Mr. Jefferson.

CXLVIII.

T. J. TO J. C. C.

MONTICELLO, January 28, 1823.

DEAR SIR,—I have received your favor of the 23d, and it has entirely converted me to your opinion that we should let the primary schools lie for the present, avail ourselves of their temporary descredit, and of the breeze in our favor, until the University is entirely secured in the completion of its buildings and remission of its debt; and then to come forward heartily, as the patrons of the primaries, on some plan which will allow us a fairer share of the common fund. Our present portion would enable us to have but six professors, whereas the law contemplates ten, which number is really necessary, and would require at least $10,000 additional to our present annuity. I have accordingly written to Mr. Rives to retract the opinion I had expressed to him in favor of immediately taking up the subject of remodelling those schools. But I still differ from you as to giving a dollar to Hampden Sidney. Let this, with all the other intermediate academies, be taken up in their turn and provided for systematically and proportionally. To give to that singly, will be a departure from principle, will make the others our enemies, and is not necessary. The University is advanced to that point, from which it must and will carry itself through; and it will strengthen daily. In the mean time we need take no part for or against either the academies or schools. If, after the passage of the bill for the loan, the remission of the whole debt can be obtained without difficulty at the present session, it would have the effect of enabling us at once to take measures for engaging professors, and for opening the institution at the end of the year, which a postponement to the next session would delay another year.

You supposed that our April meeting will be early enough for acting on the law to be passed. The only thing pressing will be the engaging our workmen. If Mr. Johnson, Mr. Loyall, and yourself should advise me, by letter, that you approve of the acceptance of the loan, I will take measures to get the same opinion from the other three gentlemen, and shall not scruple to engage the workmen, and to have preparations for bricks commenced. We can do without the money till the April meeting. If this opinion be given as soon as the bill passes the Lower House, I presume we may act immediately, without fearing a veto from the Senate. I salute you with cordial affection and respect.

TH: JEFFERSON.

Mr. Cabell.

CXLIX.

[This letter expresses a hope of obtaining a liberal appropriation to the University, which was confirmed in that which followed—and in the next succeeding he makes mention of those who favored the measure, and of its more active friends.]

J. C. C. TO T. J.

RICHMOND, February 3d, 1823.

DEAR SIR,—I thank you for your favor of 28th ultimo, and feel much gratified that you approve the view which I took of the subject of the primary schools. I am very much pleased at your suggestion of a method by which a meeting of our board may be deferred till the regular period in the month of April. It would be very inconvenient for me to attend an intermediate meeting, and the method you suggest will be readily assented to by all the Visitors here. I take this for granted without the formality of a consultation. It gives me the most heartfelt pleasure to inform you that there is now no doubt of the success of our Loan Bill. I enclose you a copy of the bill, and of the amendments which were proposed last week. Our friends came to an understanding, that in order to detach the primary school party from the college party, they would vote for Doddridge's amendments, with some alterations. The bill was taken up to-day in the House of Delegates, when Griffin's amendments were rejected, and the bill, with Doddridge's amendments amended, was ordered to be engrossed by a large majority. The sense of the House is considered to be definitively ascertained. It will come to the Senate in a day or two, where it will pass without amendment. On Friday I hope to send you intelligence of its passage.

We would most cheerfully amend the bill in the Senate, so as to provide for the extinction of the debt; and Mr. Johnson wished to do so. But I have persuaded him to let the bill pass. We had better run no risks. Let us make sure of the $60,000, and then we will survey the ground. It is doubtful whether we can, with prudence, attempt the extinction this winter. If, on consultation, it should be deemed practicable, you may rely on our will to make the effort. We are within two weeks of the end of the session. I see clearly that we may save a year by extinguishing now. But I fear another year's delay is the price of eventual success. I earnestly hope that this loan will finish the buildings. *We must never come here again for money to erect buildings.** It would be good policy to expend $60,000 on the library should it require so much, and not divert any part of it to the payment of existing debts. Should the funds fall short, I would rather ask for money hereafter to pay off old debts, than to finish the Library.

The settlement of Mr. Brockenbrough's accounts, in the mode in which they were settled has produced capital effects here. The result has even transcended my expectations. The members of the Legislature will take to themselves the satisfaction of finding fault with this and that, but they are all pleased to see the public money so accurately accounted for, and so faithfully applied. I was, from the first, confident that no weapon could be wielded by us with more efficacy than this annual rendition of accounts which seemed to be a rod in pickle for us. I think also that your suggestion respecting the religious sects has had great influence. It is the Franklin that has drawn the lightning from the cloud of opposition. I write you, dear sir, with a heart springing up with joy, and a cheek bedewed with tears of delight. Accept, I beseech you, my cordial congratulations at this evidence of the returning good sense of the country, and of its just appreciation of your labors. Long may you live to enjoy new and ever recurring proofs of your country's confidence and favor, is the unceasing prayer of your faithful and affectionate friend,

JOSEPH C. CABELL.

Mr. Jefferson.

---

* The frequent reiteration of this caution shews the extreme sensitiveness of the Legislature on this head.

CL.

J. C. C. TO T. J.

RICHMOND, February 5, 1823.

DEAR SIR,—I have now the satisfaction to enclose you a copy of the act concerning the University, which has this moment passed the Senate, and is now the law of the land.

The vote on the passage of the bill in the House of Delegates was 121 to 66.

The vote in the Senate was 19 to 3.

I hereby give my assent to the loan authorised by this act. I shall get Mr. Johnson and Mr. Loyall to write you to the same effect. Mr. Johnson is now out of office, but I shall get the Executive to re-apppoint him. Of course, he and Mr. Loyall will assent, because they have advocated the loan.

I am now casting about to see if we can cancel the bonds. On that subject you shall hear from me in due time. In the interim, accept, I beseech you, my congratulations, and believe me, ever faithfully yours,

JOS. C. CABELL.

Mr. Jefferson.

P. S. Mr. Gordon distinguished himself in the discussion in the House of Delegates; and the county was well represented by both the members.

CLI.

J. C. C. TO T. J.

RICHMOND, 11th February, 1823.

DEAR SIR,—Your favor by Mr. Brockenbrough has been duly received. I have shewn it to some members for the purpose of evincing the willingness of the Board to meet all charges. But the letter of Oldham made no impression here; and I believe it was met so promptly, there has been no attempt to use it for mischievous purposes. It deserves, in my opinion, no serious notice from any one. Mr. Brockenbrough's feelings may prompt him to ask a further scrutiny of his conduct, but I believe no candid man would request it.

Mr. Johnson informs me, that by his failure to attend two successive meetings, he is no longer a Visitor. I called to-day to notify the Governor of the fact, and to request his re-appointment. The Governor said he would have him re-appointed, as soon as he should be regularly notified. Not having time to examine into the subject of the form prescribed by law, I promised to see Mr. Johnson again, and to return to the Executive. I mention this circumstance merely to account for your not hearing from Mr. Johnson in regard to the loan.

Yesterday, Mr. Gordon moved, in the House of Delegates, the adoption of a resolution authorizing the Committee of Finance to enquire and to report to the House, the best means of paying the debts of the University. It was rejected by an overwhelming majority. To-day, a similar resolution was moved by Mr. Loyall, and supported by Mr. Baldwin. The vote was seventy-odd to ninety-odd. The subject is at rest for this session. Some of the friends of the University were opposed to bringing forward the motion at this session. However, Mr. Johnson, Mr. Loyall, Mr. Baldwin, Mr. Taylor (of Botetourt), Mr. Bowyer, Mr. Gordon, Mr. Watkins (of Goochland), Gen. Tucker, &c. &c., being of opinion that the character of the present Legislature having shewn itself to be very favorable, we should not lose the opportunity it might afford for getting the debt remitted; and the measure being right in itself, and important to the State, I entirely concurred in the movement of the question, and wish to share with my friend Gordon in the responsibility arising out of the proceeding. I know our indulgent friends would forgive us, if we had done wrong. But the failure of the proposition does not demonstrate that we were wrong. We have broken the ice, and prepared the public mind for a future application. Besides, if such men as I have named above agreed with us, the movement must have been justified by appearances. We could not dive into the hearts of members.

I have now a strong wish to return to my family, and as soon as I can dispose of some small local bills for my district, I shall go to Williamsburg and remain there, engaged in reading, till our regular meeting in April; when, if life and health should permit, you may expect to see me at Monticello. We have done much; but much, very much remains to be done.* In the course of the ensuing year, we must avail ourselves of the press. This Assembly has gone as far as the public mind will now bear. It is necessary to bring up the people to the level of the age. Their representatives will readily go along with us. I think the best interests of the institution require that we should come here for no more money for buildings. Doddridge and others have told me their patience is thread-bare on this subject. It is of the utmost importance that the buildings should be finished with this third loan. Fortunately, no one thought of limiting the time within which we should avail ourselves of the power to borrow. Till April the loss of interest will fall on the literary fund, and not on the University.

I have received a letter from Doctor Jones, of Williamsborough, North Carolina, formerly Professor of Chemistry in the College of William & Mary, desiring to know of me if I thought he could obtain the chemical chair in the University of Virginia. I have, in reply, advised him to look elsewhere for promotion. You have already heard from him.

I have found nothing like hostility, this session, from the delegation about Staunton. Mr. Johnson has made no sort of opposition to the plan of finishing the buildings. On the contrary, he has encouraged the loan for that purpose. Mr. Sheffey and Mr. Baldwin have shewn a friendly disposition. The latter has been very friendly. Mr. Taylor, of Botetourt, has ably supported us. At one time we feared Doddridge;

---

* Another proof that the course of the friends of the University was a "progression by antagonism."

but, I believe, on the whole, his primary school amendment was of service to us. We have shaken hands and interchanged cordial congratulations. Mr. Loyall, Mr. Hunter, and many other gentlemen, have greatly aided us. The Hampden Sidney interest was opposed to us. The influence of William & Mary, as usual, was adverse; but it is sensibly diminishing. Mr. Garland, of Amherst, gives us now a pretty uniform support. I heard of hostile remarks from him early in the session, but his future course, I think, will be friendly.

I am, dear sir, ever faithfully yours.

JOSEPH C. CABELL.

Mr. Jefferson.

CLII.

J. C. C. TO T. J.

WILLIAMSBURG, 26th February, 1823.

DEAR SIR,—The Legislature being on the eve of adjournment, and all the business of my district, and indeed of the State in general, being completed, or so nearly so as to admit of my departure, I left town on the 23d inst. and arrived here on the evening of the same day.

During the latter part of the session, we provided by law that Visitors of the University should not lose their seats by the mere fact of being absent from two successive meetings, but only after a notification of that fact to the Executive by the Board of Visitors. I do not recollect whether the provision had a retrospective bearing, so as to embrace Mr. Johnson's case. Perhaps it did not. I think Mr. Johnson seemed to wait for you to state to the Governor whether you would wish him re-appointed. I would take the liberty to recommend that you should do so. Then you would certainly hear from him in approbation of the loan.

Gen. Cocke, in a letter lately received from him, expresses the strongest wish that in contracting for the building of the library, the undertakers should be bound down to complete it for a definite amount. This wish is general among our friends. Nothing, in my opinion, would be more advantageous or grateful to them. Great fears are entertained that the workmen will be left too much at large. A strong and general wish prevails that we should finish the buildings with the third loan. If we do this, I think all will ultimately succeed. The opposition in this quarter is broken. I think the enemy is ready to strike his colors. My friend Doct. Smith confesses that the public sentiment is decidedly with us; and if *he* admits it, it must be so. Through the Senators and Delegates, I have, in conjunction with the delegates from Albemarle, dispersed the circulars respecting the Professorship of Agriculture over the whole State.*

I remain, dear sir, faithfully yours,

JOSEPH C. CABELL.

Mr. Jefferson.

CLIII.

T. J. TO J. C. C.

MONTICELLO, March 12, 1823.

DEAR SIR,—Having received from all our brethren approbations of the loan, I authorized Mr. Brockenbrough to engage

---

* Mr. Jefferson's sense of the importance of having Agriculture regularly taught as a branch of education is expressed in a letter to David Williams, in 1803. (Writings IV. 9.) The Rockfish report contemplates a chair for that purpose among those to be established in the University, when its endowments would permit. In the mean time, it was expected that the Theory of Agriculture would be expounded by the Professor of Chemistry. Whether this was incompatible with his other duties, or from whatever cause, it has, we believe, been very inadequately done, or not at all. In 1822, Gen. Cocke offered to the Agricultural Society of Albemarle a series of resolutions, presenting a plan of raising a fund for the endowment of a chair of Agriculture in the University, by joint contribution of other Agricultural Societies in Virginia, and of such farmers in the State as approved the measure. The President of the Society, Mr. Madison, prepared a letter in recommendation of

the work of the rotunda, and have it commenced immediately. We had only two bricklayers and two carpenters capable of executing it with solidity and correctness; these had not capital sufficient for so great an undertaking, nor would they have risked their little all but for a great advance on the estimated cost, probably 50 per cent. For this reason, and others very decisive, Mr. Brockenbrough declined that mode of engagement, and, on consideration of his reasons, I approved of them. He has engaged Thorn & Chamberlain for the brick work, and Dinsmore & Nelson for the roof and carpenter's work, on terms which I think will make our money go the farthest possible, for good work; and his engagement is only for the hull complete. That done, we can pay for it, see the state of our funds, and engage a portion of the inside work, so as to stop where our funds may fail, should they fail before its entire completion. There it may rest ever so long, be used, and not delay the opening of the institution. The work will occupy three years. All this will be more fully explained at our meeting, and will, I hope, receive your approbation. I shall hope to see you at Monticello the day before, at least. Accept the assurance of my friendly esteem and respect.

TH: JEFFERSON.

Mr. Cabell.

---

the object, and both letter and resolutions were embodied in a Circular by Mr. Peter Minor, their Secretary, and dispersed through the State in the mode mentioned by Mr. Cabell. For the resolutions and Mr. Madison's letter, see Skinner's American Farmer, IV. 273.

Some three or four thousand dollars were raised in this way; but the person to whom it was loaned omitting to give security for its return, and his circumstances having changed, the money was lost. Repeated efforts were afterwards made by different individuals to procure a special endowment for such a chair from the Legislature—as by Gov. Barbour, Mr. Edmund Ruffin, and others—but hitherto without effect. See Am. Far. VII. 289, Far. Reg. II. 703, III. 274, 625, 687, VI. 707. A proposition is now before the Agricultural Society of Virginia for the maintenance of such a Professorship with a part of their funds, and is favored by many. Its fate will probably be decided at their next annual meeting in the coming autumn.

CLIV.

J. C. C. TO T. J.

WILLIAMSBURG, March 24, 1823.

DEAR SIR,—I have had the pleasure of receiving your favor of the 12th instant. I am at all times disposed favorably to every thing which you think best for the University, and make no doubt but that on this occasion you have pursued the course best calculated to promote its interests. I certainly intend to leave this on Thursday, the 27th instant, and after making a visit to my farm in Nelson, to come to Monticello on the day before the next meeting. But something now unforeseen may occur to prevent my coming. I will, therefore, remark to you by letter, that it is highly probable that our friend General Cocke may propose at the meeting to adopt a course of proceeding somewhat different from the one you seem to have adopted in regard to the library. He has written to me that he should propose, first, to pay off all existing debts, and then to adapt the plan of the library to the residue of the funds. Perhaps contracts which you have authorized may divert him from this course. Possibly Mr. Johnson may concur with Gen. Cocke in this opinion; but of this I have no evidence. I shall be at Bremo on the 29th, when I will endeavor to divert the General from the course he lately contemplated. I fear, from the indications furnished by your late letters, that the money will fall short. Be that as it may, I would venture to recommend to you, to conduct affairs in such a way as to avoid another application to the Legislature for building funds. It appears to me that the plan you have adopted of engaging for the hull of the library is a prudent one, in reference to this object. I earnestly hope that the house may be got into a condition to be used, with the proceeds of the last loan; and that we may be able to make this assurance to the next Assembly, when we apply for the remission. I am persuaded that this is a point of great importance. Mr. Doddridge requested me to state to you that he had supported the third loan, but that his patience was worn out, and that another application would not and could not be received. Such, he said, was the sentiment of all his friends. It would probably be in itself useful, and very satisfactory to the Board of Visitors, and the public, if some unusual degree of care should be given to the subject of the materials of the library, so as to ensure their being furnished at prices the most reasonable, and worked up without waste or imposition. Precautionary measures, such as resolutions of instruction to the Proctor, and requisitions of particular and detailed reports, would probably allay the anxiety of some of the members.

We have a difficult course to steer in the Assembly. Among the most dangerous of our opponents, are a certain class of politicians, who are friendly to the University, but very fastidious about the manner in which you conduct it. These persons seem desirous to exhibit themselves in the ranks of its friends, as leaders whose support is a *sine qua non* of its existence, but nothing which they do must imply an approbation of its management. Perhaps I may be uncharitable; but it does appear to me that there is a powerful party in this State, with whom it is almost a passport to reputation to condemn the *plan and management* of the University. They have extended their influence over some honest and intelligent men, who do not concur in their political prejudices. Perhaps this may be the natural result of old political conflicts. Yet I sometimes think I can see something more.

Another difficulty which embarrasses our course, is that of not asking too much on the one hand, and not committing ourselves improperly as to the future on the other. I was often enquired of last winter, as to what we should do about a library and apparatus. My reply was, that it would certainly be good policy in the Legislature to grant occasional aids towards those objects; but that the institution could go into operation and flourish without them. I stated that a portion of the fees of tuition, by a resolution of the Board of Visitors already adopted, was to pass into the coffers of the institution, and would probably be appropriated to the purchase of books and apparatus. I think it would be politic and proper, at a suitable time, to ask the Legislature to anticipate this fund, by a loan of some 50 or $60,000 for the purchase of books and apparatus, charging the loan on that portion of the fees as a sinking fund, and pledging the State merely eventually, by way of ensuring the success of the loan. Not a man of sense in the State would deny the great importance of furnishing to the professors of physical science the means of bringing out with them from Europe the necessary apparatus collected by themselves. It would be well not to give currency to this scheme (should it be approved) till about the time of bringing it forward. It is the only plan on which I could venture to approach the Legislature on that branch of our affairs after the ground we have taken; but I am strongly in hopes it would be admissible and successful. I shall be gratified if you and Mr. Madison would take it under your consideration.

I am, dear sir,

Ever faithfully yours,

JOSEPH C. CABELL.

Mr. Jefferson.

CLV.

J. C. C. TO T. J.

EDGEWOOD, 27th October, 1823.

DEAR SIR,—I herewith return you Mr. Coffey's work on the State Prison of New York, with my best thanks for the use of it. I will take the liberty to retain Roscoe's work a little longer, as I have been so much engaged in my brother's affairs of late, as to have been unable to read it. I am sorry to inform you that I am unable to find the Oxford and Cambridge Guide any where about my house, and that I know not what has become of it. It is probably in the hands of some one to whom it has been lent, but I fear it will not be recovered. I will send it to you without delay, if I ever get hold of it.

Looking to a better eventual arrangement of my property, I became, at my brother's sale, the purchaser of one of his valuable tracts of land, formerly a part of my father's estate. This purchase will greatly augment, for a few years, my pecuniary difficulties, and will probably render it necessary for me to withdraw for a time altogether from public business. I shall attend at the next session of the Legislature, and if I should sell my farm here or in Lancaster, I might still persevere in my present course. But as neither of these events is probable, I have thought it proper to apprise you of the purchase, and of its probable consequences, that you might not be unprepared with a fit person to execute your views in Europe.*

I am, dear sir,

Ever faithfully yours,

JOSEPH C. CABELL.

Mr. Jefferson.

CLVI.

T. J. TO J. C. C.

I received with real regret yours of October 27. The necessity of looking out for a substitute, obliged me to act immediately. I consulted Mr. Madison, but it is of great importance to see you. Pray, therefore, call on me as you go down.

Affectionate salutations.

November 13, 1823.

---

* Mr. Cabell had, on the urgent instance of Mr. Jefferson and his colleagues, consented to go to Europe for the purpose of employing suitable Professors for certain of the chairs in the University; but, for the considerations mentioned in this letter, was induced to forego his purpose. Mr. Francis W. Gilmer was selected as his substitute, and discharged his mission to the satisfaction of all concerned.

CLVII.

J. C. C. TO T. J.

RICHMOND, 22d November, 1823.

DEAR SIR,—I arrived at this place on yesterday, and to-day shall proceed on my journey to the county of Lancaster; but from my detention in Nelson, in consequence of my late purchase, it will probably be out of my power to get back to the meeting of the Assembly. Indeed, I fear I shall be compelled to be absent nearly all the month of December, as I shall probably have to return to Nelson. As Gen. Breckenridge is in the House, I presume it would be advisable to take time to get our measure through. Col. Randolph and himself and others will be able to chalk out the course most likely to conduct us to a successful issue. I hope I may be able so to arrange my affairs as to retain my seat in the Senate till the end of my term. I shall endeavor to do so, by the employment of the best managers at high wages. Nothing on earth would give me more pleasure than to comply with any wish of yours, particularly in regard to the University, but candor requires me to state that such is now the posture of my affairs, I shall be unable to leave the country. I will continue my best endeavors to co-operate with you in the State, and for that purpose I hope I shall be able to remain in the Legislature. I enclose you Roscoe's work, which, from my multiplied engagements of late, I have been unable to read; but I am unwilling to keep it from you any longer, and hope you will pardon the delay which has already taken place.

I am, dear sir,

Faithfully yours,

JOS. C. CABELL.

Mr. Jefferson.

CLVIII.

J. C. C. TO T. J.

RICHMOND, 3d December, 1823.

DEAR SIR,—By the aid of my valuable friend, Col. Boyd, of the county of King & Queen, I have been enabled to finish my business in the Northern Neck, and to return to this place on the second of this month. I took my seat in the Senate to-day. Finding that my private affairs could be so speedily adjusted, I returned hastily over stormy rivers, and frozen roads, to re-join the band of steadfast patriots engaged in the holy cause of the University. I am now fixing myself in my old apartment at the Eagle, where there is a crowd of members, and many of them men of influence. I have had but little opportunity to catch the popular sentiment. The Governor, who is a man of great prudence and discretion, and answers all our expectations, has put our claims before the Legislature in his happiest manner. As far as I can learn, the public sentiment is decidedly in favor of removing our debt. I shall go around and endeavor to excite the enthusiasm of our friends, and to rouse them to action, and to prepare the public mind before the Senate adjourns. Gordon is in the Eagle with me. Col. Randolph* is at Mrs. Higginbotham's; and I have seen him but for a moment. I shall consult with them in every thing. Rest assured of my unceasing and unchangeable devotion.

Your faithful friend,

JOSEPH C. CABELL.

Mr. Jefferson.

---

* Col. Randolph having filled the Gubernatorial chair from 1819 to 1822, had now re-entered the Legislature as a delegate from Albemarle.

CLIX.

J. C. C. TO T. J.

RICHMOND, 29th December, 1823.

DEAR SIR,—I reached this on 26th instant, and have got into lodgings, and am entering into communications with our friends on the subject of the University. Col. Randolph has probably shown you the enclosed documents, but lest he may have forgotten them, I send you the enclosed copies. I fear this bill is all we can get. Hearing that the surplus was ample, I did, till to-day, eulogize our friends on the ability with which they had taken their position. But on inspection of the state of the fund, I find there would be a deficiency of revenue to meet all the appropriations, and our annuity would fall short. This has filled me with inquietude. Nevertheless, we hear from Washington that our old claim for interest has been allowed.* If so, we must at least have it added to the capital of the fund, and then the surplus would suffice.

6 *P. M.* I had written thus far when I had a conversation with Mr. Loyall. He tells me our friends were aware of the deficiency of the surplus income of the fund. But the average amount of undrawn quotas of the counties were considered amply sufficient to supply the defect. I again think our position is well chosen. Col. Randolph has doubtless explained all these things to you much better than I can. I trust we shall be able to get rid of the debt. And there I fear we shall halt.

I am, dear sir, ever faithfully yours,

JOSEPH C. CABELL.

P. S. The college party will be incensed at our taking hold of the surplus, notwithstanding the pledge of $20,000 of surplus revenue to the colleges some years ago, on the motion of Mr. Miller, of Powhatan.

Mr. Jefferson.

---

* We shall hear more of this fund—of the farther efforts necessary to secure it, and of the timely and important aid it afforded.

CLX.

T. J. TO J. C. C.

January 19, 1824.

CLXI.

T. J. TO J. C. C.

January 22, 1824.

CLXII.

T. J. TO J. C. C.

January 23, 1824.

[The Editor has been unable as yet to procure copies of these letters. He hopes to supply the omission hereafter.]

CLXIII.

[Anticipating farther success—which is related in the next.]

J. C. C. TO T. J.

RICHMOND, January 26, 1824.

DEAR SIR,—I thank you sincerely for your three letters of 19th, 23d and 24th instant, all of which I have shewn to our friends in the Senate. The University bill is now before the Senate, and will be acted on in a day or two. I confess I differ with you as to its importance and character. We do not here care in the least for the proviso giving to the General Assembly the power of revocation. You know the University is at all times, and in all things, subject to the control of the General Assembly. The annuity cannot be revoked but by the concurrent vote of both houses, and the Senate will never concur in any such measure. The provisoes are mere surplusage, consented to by our friends to furnish an excuse to wavering men to come over to us. We would gladly take in the back interest if we could. It is doubtful whether the bill does not now do it. But I believe we shall be compelled in the Senate to take away all doubt and give it up. We have gained a great victory. The bill is worth $10,800 per annum to the University. The word "*income*" is more extensive than "*revenue.*" We shall have the income from fines, &c. to aid the surplus revenue in satisfying our appropriation. Am I right in supposing that $50,000, payable in ten annual installments, for the purchase of books and apparatus, with a power to the Visitors to anticipate the money, for those purposes, and *for those purposes only*, would be a good measure next to be adopted? I am thinking of it. We can get no more money for building this year.* I write in haste. I have been confined to my bed a week, and to my room a fortnight, by an excruciating rheumatic affection of my head, contracted by sleeping near a damp wall. This is the reason that I have left altogether to Col. Randolph to inform you of our proceedings. As soon as the bill passes, I will send you a copy.

Faithfully, yours,

JOSEPH C. CABELL.

Mr. Jefferson.

CLXIV.

J. C. C. TO T. J.

RICHMOND, 29th January, 1824.

DEAR SIR,—I have now the gratification to enclose you, by our friend Mr. Garrett, a copy of the University act of the present session. It passed the Senate unanimously. Attempts were made to amend it; but we were determined to pass the bill as it came to us; because our friends in the other house warned us of the imminent danger of its return. I was ill

---

* Ecce iterum.

in bed when the proviso to which you so much object was added to the bill. It was deemed perfectly harmless by our friends, and useful as furnishing an excuse to some who wanted an excuse to join us. We are all concerned to find you so much opposed to it, and still hope you will be reconciled. After it was proposed, it would have been difficult to resist it; and when engrafted on the bill, an attempt to strike it from the bill would have endangered our success. We had always plumed ourselves on our democratic character. We had fought the college party with that clause in our charter which says, "the University shall be at all times, and in all things, subject to the control of the General Assembly." We were seizing on all occasions to engraft a similar provision on new charters. If on this we had shewn a distrust incompatible with former professions, our good faith would have been impeached, and we should have alienated our most powerful friend, the General Assembly of the State. The annuity cannot be withdrawn but by a concurrent vote of the two houses, and I think the time will never come when such a vote will be obtained. Such is the opinion of all the four Visitors in town. We shall want further aids in future, and it would be unfortunate to lose any portion of the favor we now possess. Col. Randolph concurs in these views. So does Mr. Gordon. I suggested in my last the idea of trying to obtain $50,000, in ten annual installments, for the library and apparatus. Perhaps $40,000 would be more apt to succeed; and I wish to know your views as to the adequacy and expediency of either provision. I incline to think nothing of the kind can succeed this session. But I have a scheme in contemplation,* of which I will say more in future. * * * * * * * * * * * Gen. Cocke and myself have long been thinking of Chancellor Carr as the Law Professor; and we would be happy if there could be no commitment on that question. Mr.

* For an account of this, and of the tempest evoked by its enunciation, see below, letter 166.

Carr's happy temper and manners, and dignified character, to say nothing of his talents and acquirements, induced us to think of him, as the head of the institution.

I am, dear sir, faithfully yours,

JOSEPH C. CABELL.

Mr. Jefferson.

CLXV.

T. J. TO J. C. C.

MONTICELLO, February 23, 1824.

DEAR SIR,—I am favored with your two letters of January 26 and 29, and am glad that yourself and the friends of the University are so well satisfied that the provisoes amendatory of the University act are mere nullities. I had not been able to put out of my head the Algebraical equation, which was among the first of my college lessons, that a—a=0. Yet I cheerfully arrange myself to your opinions. I did not suppose, nor do I now suppose, it possible that both houses of the Legislature should ever consent, for an additional fifteen thousand dollars of revenue, to set all the professors and students of the University adrift; and if foreigners will have the same confidence which we have in our Legislature, no harm will have been done by the provisoes.

You recollect that we had agreed that the Visitors who are of the Legislature should fix on a certain day of meeting after the rising of the Assembly, to put into immediate motion the measures which this act was expected to call for. You will of course remind the Governor that a re-appointment of Visitors is to be made on the day following Sunday, the 29th of this month; and as he is to appoint the day of their first meeting, it would be well to recommend to him that which our brethren there shall fix on. It may be designated by the Governor as the 3d, 4th, &c. day after the rising of the Legislature, which will give it certainty enough.

You ask what sum would be desirable for the purchase of books and apparatus? Certainly the largest you can obtain. Forty or fifty thousand dollars would enable us to purchase the most essential books of text and reference for the schools, and such an apparatus for Mathematics, Astronomy and Chemistry as may enable us to set out with tolerable competence, if we can, through the banks or otherwise, anticipate the whole sum at once.

I remark what you say on the subject of committing ourselves to any one for the Law appointment. Your caution is perfectly just. I hope, and am certain, that this will be the standing law of discretion and duty with every member of our Board in this and all cases. You know that we have all, from the beginning, considered the high qualifications of our professors as the only means by which we could give to our institution splendor and pre-eminence over all its sister seminaries. The only question, therefore, we can ever ask ourselves, as to any candidate, will be, is he the most highly qualified? The College of ****** has lost its character of primacy by indulging motives of favoritism and nepotism, and by conferring appointments as if the professorships were entrusted to them as provisions for their friends. And even that of Edinburgh, you know, is also much lowered from the same cause. We are next to observe, that a man is not qualified for a professor, knowing nothing but merely his own profession. He should be otherwise well educated as to the sciences generally; able to converse understandingly with the scientific men with whom he is associated, and to assist in the councils of the Faculty on any subject of science on which they may have occasion to deliberate. Without this, he will incur their contempt and bring disreputation on the institution. With respect to the professorship you mention, I scarcely know any of our judges personally; but I will name, for example, the late Judge *****, who, I believe, was generally admitted to be among the ablest of them. His knowledge was confined to the common law merely, which does not constitute one-half the qualification of a really learned lawyer, much less that of a Professor of Law for an University. And as to any other branches of science, he must have stood mute in the presence of his literary associates, or of any learned strangers or others visiting the University. Would this constitute the splendid stand we propose to take?

The individual named in your letter is one of the best, and to me the dearest of living men. From the death of his father, my most cherished friend, leaving him an infant in the arms of my sister, I have ever looked on him as a son. Yet these are considerations which can never enter into the question of his qualifications as a Professor of the University. Suppose all the chairs filled in similar degree, would that present the object which we have proposed to ourselves, and promised to the liberalities and expectations of our country? In the course of the trusts which I have exercised through life, with powers of appointment, I can say with truth, and unspeakable comfort, that I never did appoint a relation to office, and that merely because I never saw the case in which some one did not offer or occur, better qualified; and I have the most unlimited confidence that in the appointment of Professors to our nursling institution, every individual of my associates will look with a single eye to the sublimation of its character, and adopt as our sacred motto, "*detur digniori.*" In this way it will honor us, and bless our country.

I perceive that I have permitted my reflections to run into generalities beyond the scope of the particular intimation in your letter. I will let them go, however, as a general confession of faith, not belonging merely to the present case. Name me affectionately to our brethren with you, and be assured yourself of my constant friendship and respect.

TH: JEFFERSON.

Mr. Cabell.

CLXVI.

J. C. C. TO T. J.

RICHMOND, February 19, 1824.

DEAR SIR,—I received in due time by the mail your favor of the 3d inst. I have not written in reply, because I have been absorbed in the discharge of my duties at this place. From the first moment I heard of the bill to re-charter the Farmers Bank, I fixed upon it as furnishing a good opportunity to provide the fifty thousand dollars for our library and apparatus. I mentioned my views to Mr. Garrett when he was in town; and was actuated by these views when I wrote you for your opinion as to a suitable sum for those purposes. I kept my secret, even from the Visitors, and even my brother and most intimate friends, till about the time the bill passed the House of Delegates. The bankers called on me and requested my co-operation in getting the Bank re-chartered, which I promised in the event of being satisfied as to the terms. The House of Delegates passed the bill without demanding any bonus. When I announced my views in the Senate, seventeen Senators declared themselves on my side. But, as I expected, I instantly found myself in the midst of a hornet's nest. What, with the active opposition of stockholders, debtors, directors and officers, a prodigious ferment was excited and still prevails; and I have lost the majority in the Senate. I have made, and am still making, every exertion in my power to compel the bankers to unite with us; and I have still hopes of success. But defeat is not improbable. Yet what a victory would not this be! At such a time—for such an object—against such a host of opponents! Col. Randolph, Mr. Gordon, Gen. Breckenridge, and others, are breasting the storm below. I have a decided majority of the Senate in favor of the measure; but some are afraid of losing the bill by our amendments. Perhaps the struggle will not be over before the return of the mail; and I should be extremely glad to receive from you a few lines to animate our friends and re-kindle their zeal. Probably your letter would get here before the final vote on our amendments in the House of Delegates. I have seen the Governor on the subject of the next meeting, and shall make suitable arrangements with the other Visitors.

I am, dear sir, faithfully yours,

JOS. C. CABELL.

Mr. Jefferson.

P. S. We shall probably carry a bonus in the Senate. If the appropriation to the University fails in the Senate, I still hope it will be carried below, as an amendment to our amendment.

CLXVII.

J. C. C. TO T. J.

RICHMOND, 7th March, 1824.

DEAR SIR,—I presume you have already been informed, by Col. Randolph, of the result of our long continued struggles for the bonus of the Farmers Bank. We have been compelled to relinquish it to the improvement fund, and to accept an equivalent out of the balance of the debt due from the General Government. Never have I known so obstinate a struggle between the two Houses of Assembly. Mr. Johnson has shewn himself, throughout this affair, the sincere friend of the University. He has risen greatly in my esteem. Colonel Randolph and Mr. Gordon, in the House of Delegates, did every thing that could be expected of them. Nearly every other delegate from my district stood against us, at the most critical period of our contest. You can hardly imagine the obloquy to which this business subjected me. I have been abused all around the town, and by a great portion of the Assembly. But I held my onward course, regardless of the efforts of every description made by friends and foes to arrest me. I resolved to ride through on the back of the Farmers Bank, and would never be dismounted. Since the contest has terminated, public opinion and feeling towards me have greatly changed, except among the ******, who are sorely vexed at our success. I refer you to Colonel Randolph for a more particular history of this contest. For my part, I have scarcely seen the earth on which I walked for a month past; and I feel tired and greatly anxious to return to my family.

The claim on the General Government is of two descriptions, viz: for principal advanced and interest paid on that principal. As to the first, the vouchers have been lost, and I apprehend the debt is desperate. The second, Mr. Johnson considers as principal, although it is called interest; and he thinks the claim irresistible. I have this evening held a long conversation with the Governor on this subject. Some month or two ago, Col. Barbour wrote on to the Governor for a statement of the interest paid by Virginia, on account of the United States. The Auditor, after a laborious research, has recently finished the account, and it is now in the hands of the Governor. He could not readily turn to it, so as to let me see the amount, but I presume it exceeds our appropriation. On this foundation repose our hopes of success. Early in the session of Congress, Col. Barbour introduced a bill giving authority to some officer of the Government to settle our claim on equitable principles, but it failed. If Mr. Johnson's opinion be correct, I presume an act of Congress would not be necessary. But whether an act be proper and necessary or not, I am considering of the best means of securing the payment of the claim. I wished Mr. Johnson to undertake to go as agent to Washington, but this he positively refuses, on the ground of his determination never to fill an office which he has assisted in creating. It has occurred to my mind, that a memorial from yourself to the Government would have a powerful effect, and especially if a resort to Congress should be necessary. But I hope you will consider of the matter and suggest whatever you may think for the best. I have written to Mr. Hay to inform him of our success, and with the hope that such an annunciation would make powerful friends at Washington. You and Mr. Madison, and the President, I trust, will prevent the defeat of our hopes. This appropriation will place us beyond the reach of pretended friendship and open hostility. This hope has induced me to run the risk of an entire overthrow of my standing in my district. A faction was eagerly preparing for the sacrifice. But our success here has defeated them there.

Our session is so protracted, that the Governor and the Visitors in town have thought it best to have our next meeting on the first Monday in April.

I leave this for Williamsburg on the 10th instant.

I enclose two schemes of Professorships by Mr. Gilmer, who drew them up without knowing of the one you enclosed me. He wished me to erase the last salary in each scheme, as he might be thought interested; but I send you the paper as I received it. He has been expecting to hear from you.

From my not receiving a reply to my last, I presume you are unwilling to promote the re-establishment of any bank.

I am, dear sir, faithfully yours,

JOSEPH C. CABELL.

Mr. Jefferson.

CLXVIII.

J. C. C. TO T. J.

WILLIAMSBURG, 17th March, 1824.

DEAR SIR,—On the 21st instant I shall take passage in the steamboat for the city of Washington. My stay there will be short, but I will endeavor to collect and bring you all the information I can obtain relative to the claim of the University. You are the best judge of the measures proper to ensure the recovery of this just debt; but I beg leave to urge the importance of letters addressed by yourself and Mr. Madison to such persons as you may think best calculated to promote your views. I shall probably come directly from Washington to Monticello. I hope you will excuse my delay in returning you Russell's tract on the Universities of Great Britain. I ran over the book hastily and handed it to General Breckenridge, accompanied by your message. His engagements in the Assembly caused it to remain long in his possession. At length I obtained it from him, and next delivered it to Mr. Johnson, in whose hands it was when I left town. Mr. Loyall has never seen it. Mr. Johnson will forward or bring it to you. Great excitement was produced by our proceedings at the last session. It is very important that we should succeed at Washington. We have exhausted the favor of the Assembly, and we must not ask for a cent at the next session; if we do, we shall be turned off by a large majority. Such is the general impression. I was very much blamed by inconsiderate friends for asking for the bonus; many invidious remarks were made around the town, even by some of the judges who had formerly been our staunch friends; and both town and Assembly were in universal uproar. Except Col. Randolph and Mr. Gordon, I believe, the whole delegation from my district were in full outcry against me. These gentlemen could not originate the measure in the House of Delegates; if they had done so, the bonus would have gone, of course, to the improvement fund. I waited for that House to commit itself to a relinquishment of the bonus to the bank, so as to clear away the claim of the fund, and then I set up the claim of the University. I mentioned my views to Mr. Garrett, as he was leaving town, subsequently to Mr. Bowyer; and with these exceptions I was silent till the bill was passing the House of Delegates. I knew the game was hazardous, especially to my personal popularity in my district. But the University, James river and Bank interests, I thought, would bear us through. After the bank was secured, we were on the eve of overthrow by the James river interest. They wanted the bonus to pay the interest of their intended loans, and set up the doctrine of pledges against us. It was with difficulty we adjusted the matter by the compromise which took place. I believed, and it was afterwards admitted, that we might have got the bonus, if the Senate had stood out—but there were six senators swayed by the position of the branches of the bank with respect to their districts. They wished us success, but they could not venture beyond a certain point. I knew every mind and every thought. Johnson and myself, therefore, determined to give up the bonus for an equivalent out of the debt. At that period we should certainly have been defeated in the Senate, had we attempted to persist in the original scheme. Ultimately we made strong appeals to the pride of the Senate, and with the aid of the excitement produced by the opposition, screwed them up to an adherence, so as to throw the responsibility of the last vote on the House of Delegates. I was amused at the exultation with which certain persons from my district anticipated my downfall. I was to be an object of universal detestation for bringing ruin on the district, and was to be hurled from the Senate at the next election. I refer you to Col. Randolph and Mr. Gordon for evidence on this subject. After the bill passed, there was, indeed, a change of scene. Shame and discomfiture were hurled upon the heads of our opponents. Many of those who had been most illiberal in their judgments and strictures on my course, came forward and frankly acknowledged their errors, and did us ample justice. I beg to be excused for these egotisms, which a sense of past injury has wrung from me. Mr. Johnson thinks the claim a good one. In one week from this time I will know the impression at Washington. What little I can do, shall be done to benefit the scheme. But one line from yourself and Mr. Madison will do more than all the members of Assembly could say on this subject.

Of the importance of this appropriation, ample evidence is furnished by the conduct of the professors of this college. Opposition is extinct. The tone is totally changed. They have not said it, but I can see distinctly that they regard the condition and prospects of this college as highly perilous. The situation of these professors is calculated to excite sympathy. I think the President would gladly accept a professorship in the University, as would also Campbell and Rogers. If they were sure of their fixed salaries, they would be better reconciled to the course of events. But there are now but thirty-two students, and on the opening of the University a further reduction may be anticipated. I know your liberal feelings to all men of letters; and if justice to the public (which is the polar star) will allow anything to be done, it should be done in favor of these men. I merely mention the subject with the feelings it is calculated to excite, but make no definite proposition. I fear nothing can be done.

I am, dear sir, ever faithfully yours,

JOSEPH C. CABELL.

Mr. Jefferson.

CLXIX.

J. C. C. TO T. J.

CITY OF WASHINGTON, April 1, 1824.

DEAR SIR,—My plan was to leave the city to-day, so as to get to Monticello on Saturday. But finding I cannot reach the point I desired in time to do so, I must now defer my departure till Saturday or Sunday, when I expect to set out on my return, and taking the Monday's stage from Fredericksburg arrive at Monticello on Tuesday. Should I not come myself, you may expect to receive a letter from me. But it is my intention at this time to come; and my object is to endeavor to procure *ad interim* such a recognition of our claim by the Cabinet as will be satisfactory to the Board of Public Works in Virginia. The President and Mr. Wirt are both very friendly, and have received me in the kindest manner. Mr. Crawford was very decisive in our favor. And all the other members probably are well disposed. When I came here, the business was at a stand. An abortive movement had been made by Col. Barbour in the Senate. Such was Mr. Mercer's statement, who was under the impression that the delegation should first have been called together, concert ensured, and an Executive recommendation procured, before any movement was made in Congress. He advised me to try the Cabinet, although he thought I should not succeed. I had spoken with all the Secretaries, except Mr. Adams, and had a formal interview with Mr. Calhoun, at his office, who recognized the justice of the claim, but said that the usage of the department on the subject of interest could only be changed by an act of Congress. I had commenced a letter to the Secretary of War, at the private instance of Mr. Monroe and Mr. Wirt, when the communication of our Governor, covering an able exposition of our claim by Mr. Johnson, arrived. A meeting of the delegation was next had, at the instance of Colonel Barbour, and he was authorized to bring the subject before the Executive through the Department of War. I confess I was surprised at so unexpected a movement; and I still think, that when the subject of the appropriation is discussed in Congress, this intermediate appeal to the Executive, by the delegation, will be of no service with the delegations of the other States. To prevent any misapprehensions of my motives and course, I waited on Col. Barbour, and explained to him my particular views, which were, pending the delays of legislation, to get the Cabinet, if possible, to say, that under the existing laws of the United States the claim stands on the same footing as would a claim for principal, and that nothing but an act of Congress making the appropriation is necessary. He appeared to be entirely satisfied. I think the board ought to be satisfied with such a recognition, and lend us the bonus. The steps which I have taken, and am taking, spring from a desire to promote the views of all the Visitors. If you will adjourn over for one day, perhaps I may be able to bring you the decision of the Cabinet. They will not meet before to-morrow, and I know not how long it will take to make up their decision. I enclose a paper which Col. Monroe requested me to shew you. He says that Percival and Torrey were considered very able men, and Torrey he regards as the best appointment for the chemical chair in our University. He requested me to state to you, that he regarded it as all important to get as many of the professors as possible from this country. He appears to be very friendly to all your views.

If I should not come by the stage on Tuesday, you would oblige me by directing my servant to return home with my horses, on Wednesday morning; and in the interim after his arrival to wait for me at the tavern in Charlottesville.

My best respects attend Mr. Madison and all the Visitors.

I remain, dear sir, faithfully yours,

JOSEPH C. CABELL.

Mr. Jefferson.

P. S. I have opened my letter to inform you that Colonel Barbour, of the Senate, has just called, and indicates every disposition to aid me in the accomplishment of my object. He seems to approve of the ground I have taken, and of the letter, which I *now* propose to address *to the President.** This business has engaged nearly all my time. I hope, to-morrow, to pay more attention to my private claim.

CLXX.

J. C. C. TO T. J.

EDGEWOOD, 8th April, 1824.

DEAR SIR,—This will be delivered to you by my servant Archer, who comes down with the horse you were so good as to lend me. I took the liberty to keep him longer than I promised, because, on getting to Col. John Coles's, I found both

---

* See Appendix, N.

himself and his brother Tucker, together with their families, were setting out to see Lady Skipwith, and all their riding horses seemed to be in requisition. I shall remain at home but a few days, and then return to the lower country. It will be some time in the month of May before I arrive here with my family.

I am, dear sir, ever faithfully yours,

JOSEPH C. CABELL.

Mr. Jefferson.

P. S. I will write to Mr. Maclure from Williamsburg.

CLXXI.

(CIRCULAR.) T. J. TO J. C. C.

MONTICELLO, April 9, 1824.

DEAR SIR,—Notwithstanding the reduction which was made in the rents proposed, it appears that that on the salaries will so much enlarge our surplus, that we may very safely engage eight professors and still have a surplus this year of $6000, and annually after of $5,024. The opportunity of procuring the anatomical professor is so advantageous, that I propose to make the *provisional* instruction for his engagement *absolute*. On this subject I ask your opinion, to be given to me without delay, that it may be in time to be acted on. The statements below will enable you to form your opinion.

Accept assurances of my esteem and respect.

TH: JEFFERSON.

Joseph C. Cabell, Esq.

Estimated Account for 1824.

Current expenses of the institution for this year,	4,500
Expense of procuring professors,	1,500
Salaries of eight professors, for October, November, December,	3,000
Surplus for apparatus, books, contingencies,	6,000
To be paid by the annuity of 1824,	$15,000

Annual Account after 1824, *as may be now estimated.*

Income annuity,	15,000	
Rent of six hotels, at $150,	900	
One hundred dormitories, at $16,	1,600	
Nine smaller dormitories, at $12,	108	
University rent on 218 students, at $12,	$2,616	
		$20,224
Expenditure, current expenses of the institution,	3,000	
Eight professors, at $1,500 each,	12,000	
A military instructor,	200	
Surplus for apparatus, books, contingencies,	$5,024	
		$20,224

This year's surplus of $6,000 will afford for text books $1,000. Apparatus: Chemical, $1,000; Anatomical, $1,000; Astronomical, Physical, Mathematical, $3,000.

CLXXII.

J. C. C. TO T. J.

BREMO, April 16, 1824.

DEAR SIR,—Your favor of the 9th instant was delivered to me by my servant on the 11th. I deferred writing till now, because I thought my answer would not reach you as soon by the mail from Warminster, as by that from Columbia, which place I shall pass in a few hours from this time, on my journey to the lower country. I was very much pleased at the limitation of the foreign professors to a moiety of the whole number. I thought I could see advantages in this limitation, which I attempted to explain to the Board of Visitors. I need not repeat what I said upon this subject. The Professor of Anatomy is not, like the Professor of Law and Politics, and the Professor of Ethics, connected with a science calculated to give tone and direction to the public mind, on the most important subjects that can occupy the human understanding. It is of the class of Professorships which may be prudently filled by foreigners. For this reason, and because the difference between five and six is but one; and above all, because you are an infinitely better judge of the subject than I am, and it is my greatest happiness to give you pleasure upon any and upon all occasions, you may consider me as yielding my assent to your proposition to instruct the agent to engage the Anatomical Professor in Europe. I am hurrying on to rejoin my family, and write in great haste.

I am, dear sir,

Ever faithfully yours,

JOSEPH C. CABELL.

Mr. Jefferson.

I concur with Mr. Cabell in the above.

JOHN H. COCKE.

CLXXIII.

[A new subject is brought before us in the following letter. The ancient college of William & Mary, which, during the interregnum that followed the decease of Bishop Madison, its former President, had much declined, and which had for some years, under the auspices and management of President Smith, happily revived, was again in a depressed condition. This gentleman seeing no immediate prospect of a change in its fortunes for the better, conceived the project of its removal to the city of Richmond, and of uniting therewith a medical school. While this was favored by most of the Faculty, and certain other friends of the institution, as the only probable method of restoring its efficiency, it was warmly resisted by a greater number in the vicinity and the lower counties generally, who could not look calmly on a scheme which, if successful, would have been productive of injury to personal and vested interests, and the occasion of a violent disruption of cherished local and historical associations. Nevertheless, the plan was persisted in; a petition for leave to carry it out was presented to the Legislature, and was advocated by the President at the bar of the House. The proposition was favored by a portion of that body and by the powerful influence of the city of Richmond. Having been previously much canvassed in the newspapers, it here underwent a second discussion, which called forth the most powerful efforts of friends and opponents.

Among the latter were Mr. Cabell and other friends of the University, who thought they saw in its success a dangerous rival to that institution which had cost them so much time and labor, and who honestly believed that Virginia did not need, as she could not maintain more than one such, as they were still endeavoring to establish. This, with its collateral topics, is the theme and burden of many of the subsequent letters. His opposition was based, not on hostility to William & Mary or its existing authorities, but, proceeding on a principle analogous to self-defence, he felt justified in resorting to a weapon, the use of which, under other circumstances, might have been regarded as ungenerous, and which was abandoned by him on the failure of the petition. This college was viewed by him not as a private corporation, but as a public charity. Its endowment having been principally contributed by the authorities of Virginia when a colony, its control was thought to devolve as of right on Virginia as a State. If the college, no longer able to retain its rank as such, must descend to the scale of an academy, what should hinder the State—sufficient funds being reserved for the discharge of this lower function—from reclaiming the surplus and appropriating it to the support of education in other parts of the State where it was most needed. But these and other matters are fully set forth in the letters themselves, and certain papers in the Appendix.]

J. C. C. TO T. J.

WILLIAMSBURG, 5th May, 1824.

DEAR SIR,—A scheme is now in agitation at this place, the object of which is to remove the college of William & Mary to the city of Richmond. All the Professors of the college, except the Professor of Law, are decidedly in favor of it. Chancellor Brown and others, of the Board of Visitors, will give it their support. What number of the Visitors will come into it, I am not informed; but the friends of the measure expect a majority. The plan, as yet, is a topic of private conversation at this place, but it is coming out, as Mr. Brown has publicly spoken of it at the post-office, as an expedient measure, greatly approved, and publicly advocated by all parties in Richmond. Mr. Loyall called here a few days ago on his way from Richmond to Norfolk, and informed me that Mr. Ritchie, Mr. Nicholas, and others, spoke to him warmly in favor of the scheme. It will most unquestionably be attempted, and will be powerfully supported. Bishop Moore is one of the Visitors. The clergy, the Federal party, the metropolis, and probably the faculty of medicine throughout the State, will advocate the removal. The motives of the three first are obvious. The medical faculty are seeking to establish a medical school at the seat of government, and probably a part of the scheme will be to give the college a direction that way, and profit of their extended influence. The scheme will be much opposed by the inhabitants of Williamsburg, headed by Judge Semple and Col. Bassett, who will create a hot party in this section of the State. But knowing, as I do, the powerful influences that will be brought to bear in its favor, I should not be surprised if the Board of Visitors should be brought over to sign a petition to the Assembly to authorize a removal, especially as the impression is general that the college will otherwise certainly fall. I think they calculate largely on the support of Mr. Johnson in the Senate, whom I expect the party for removal will endeavor to run into the Senate from this district in place of Mr. Clopton, at the end of his present term. I expect they also count on Mr. Garnett and others recently elected to the House of Delegates. The loss of the buildings here would probably be compensated by donations from the corporation of Richmond, or from the General Assembly. The capital of the college is upwards of $100,000. I see that this subject is to occupy much of the attention of the State, and I consider it a duty to give you information of the existence of the scheme. What part the friends of the University ought to take on this question, it becomes us promptly to decide. The situation in which we are placed, calls for the exercise of more than ordinary discretion. We have always avowed that we sought not, and would not interfere with the capital of the college. We have said, "keep your college and your endowments; we want not to meddle with you; but you shall not prevent the improvement of the State." The college now will say we cannot flourish in a sickly site. If you will move us to the seat of government, we shall be able to do more public good. The medical faculty, too, may say, the State wants a medical school, and there can be no hospitals at the University. Let us turn the college into a medical school at Richmond, where we can give clinical lectures. Some difficulties to this latter plan would grow out of the private interests of the present professors, particularly those of the Professor of Mathematics. But as the Professor of Law would of course remain here, and two of the Professors are physicians, some provision would probably be made for the Mathematical Professor, so as to accommodate his interests to the plan. My present opinion is decidedly opposed to the plan; because I know that the college would be made a rival to the University, and we should lose in that institution more than we should gain in the college. If a new destination is to be given to the capital of the college, why not endow academies therewith over the whole face of the Commonwealth. We were told some winters ago, by the college party, we do not want an University—we want academies. Now we may say to the State, we do not want a college at Richmond—we want preparatory seminaries over the whole face of the country. But to oppose an institution struggling to save itself, and to thwart the natural endeavors of literary men to advance their fortunes, is truly painful. Yet are we to suffer the labors of so many years to be blasted by an unnecessary and destructive competition? Most assuredly we must not. But can the subjects be reconciled? Would it be prudent to co-operate in the plan of a medical seminary at Richmond? Some winters back my respect for your better judgment restrained me from active support to my medical friends at Richmond. I am pretty confident that whatever plans may be avowed of giving to the college a preparatory character, or that of a medical school, rivalry must still be the object and end of the scheme. Mr. Loyall concurs in these views, but his opinion is not finally made up; and I wish the advice of yourself and Mr. Madison. It is now time to look into the charter, and ascertain what may be done, consistently, with the decision of the Supreme Court in the case of the Dartmouth College. From private conferences with a professor of the college, there is reason to *conjecture* that the Board of Visitors will divide as follows on the question of removal:

For Removal.—Bishop Moore, Mr. Scott of the Council, Col.

Macon of New Kent, Mr. Saunders of Williamsburg, Chancellor Brown, Dr. Charles Everett, Mr. Hugh Nelson, Mr. L. W. Tazewell.

Against Removal.—Col. Bassett, Major Griffin of York, Dr. Galt of Williamsburg, Mr. John W. Sowell of Gloucester.

Doubtful.—Major Prior of Elizabeth City, Mr. John Tyler, Mr. Wm. Armistead of King William, Mr. N. Faulcon.

There are three vacancies to be filled, the whole number being nineteen. I shall leave this to-morrow for Corrottoman. I shall be in Richmond from 20th to 28th of the month; and after that at Warminster.

I am, dear sir,
Faithfully yours,
JOSEPH C. CABELL.

Mr. Jefferson.

CLXXIV.

T. J. TO J. C. C.

MONTICELLO, May 16, 1824.

DEAR SIR,—Your favor of the 5th from Williamsburg has been duly received, and presents to us a case of pregnant character, admitting important issues, and requiring serious consideration and conduct. Yet I am more inclined to view it with hope than dismay. It involves two questions. 1. Shall the college of William & Mary be removed? 2d. To what place? As to the first, I never doubted the lawful authority of the Legislature over the college, as being a public institution, endowed from the public property, by the public agents for that function, and for public purposes. Some have doubted this authority without a relinquishment of what they call a vested right, by the body corporate; but as their voluntary relinquishment is a circumstance of the case, it is relieved from that doubt. I certainly never wished that my venerable

Alma Mater should be disturbed. I considered it as an actual possession of that ancient and earliest settlement of our forefathers, and was disposed to see it yielded as a courtesy, rather than taken as a right. They, however, are free to renounce a benefit, and we to receive it. Had we dissolved it on the principle of right, to give a direction to its funds more useful to the public, the professors, although their chartered tenure is during pleasure only, might have reasonably expected a vote of a year or two's salary, as an intermediate support until they could find other employment for their talents. And, notwithstanding that their abandonment is voluntary, this should still be given them. On this first question, I think we should be absolutely silent and passive, taking no part in it until the old institution is loosened from its foundation, and fairly placed on its wheels.

2. On the second question, to what place shall it be removed? we may take the field boldly. Richmond, it seems, claims it, but on what ground of advantage to the public? When the professors, their charter and funds shall be translated to Richmond, will they become more enlightened there than at the old place? Will they possess more science? be more capable of communicating it, or more competent to raise it from the dead, in a new seat, than to keep it alive in the ancient one? Or has Richmond any peculiarities more favorable for the communication of the sciences generally, than the place which the Legislature has preferred and fixed on for that purpose? This will not be pretended. But it seems they possess advantages for a medical school. Let us scan them. Anatomy may be as completely taught at the University as at Richmond. The only subjects of dissection which either place can count on, are equally acquirable at both. And as to medicine, whatever can be learnt from lectures or books, may be taught at the University of Virginia as well as at Richmond, or even at Baltimore, Philadelphia, New York, or Boston, with the inestimable additional advantage of acquiring at the same time the kindred sciences by attending the other schools. But Rich-

mond thinks it can have a hospital which will furnish subjects for the clinical branch of medicine. The classes of people which furnish subjects for the hospitals of Baltimore, Philadelphia, New York, and Boston, do not exist at Richmond. The shipping constantly present at those places furnish many patients. Is there a ship at Richmond? The class of white servants in those cities, which is numerous and pennyless, and whose regular resource in sickness is always the hospital, constitutes the great body of their patients. This class does not exist at Richmond. The servants there are slaves, whose masters are, by law, obliged to take care of them in sickness, as in health, and who could not be admitted into a hospital. These resources then being null, the free inhabitants alone remain for a hospital at Richmond. And I will ask how many families in Richmond would send their husbands, wives, or children to a hospital, in sickness? to be attended by nurses hardened by habit against the feelings of pity, to lie in public rooms, harrassed by the cries and sufferings of disease under every form, alarmed by the groans of the dying, exposed as a corpse, to be lectured over by a clinical professor, to be crowded and handled by his students, to hear their case learnedly explained to them, its threatening symptoms developed, and its probable termination foreboded? In vindication of Richmond, I may surely answer, that there is not in the place a family so heartless, as relinquishing their own tender cares of a child or parent, to abandon them in sickness to this last resource of poverty. For it is poverty alone which peoples hospitals; and those alone who are on the charities of their parish would go to their hospital. Have they paupers enough to fill a hospital? and sickness enough among these? One reason alleged for the removal of the college to Richmond is, that Williamsburg is sickly and Richmond healthy. The latter then being little sickly, is happily little apt for the situation of a hospital. No, sir, Richmond is no place to furnish subjects for clinical lectures. I have always had Norfolk in view for this purpose. The climate and Pontine country around Norfolk render it truly sickly in itself. It is moreover the rendezvous not only of the shipping of commerce, but of the vessels of the public navy. The United States have there a hospital already established, and supplied with subjects from these local circumstances. I had thought, and have mentioned to yourself and our colleagues, that when our medical school has got well under way, we should propose to the federal government the association with that establishment, and at our own expense, of the clinical branch of our medical school, so that our students after qualifying themselves with the other branches of the science here, might complete their course of preparation by attending clinical lectures for six or twelve months at Norfolk.

But that Richmond has a claim, as *being the seat of government*. The indisposition of Richmond towards our University has not been unfelt. But would it not be wiser in them to rest satisfied with the government and their local academy? Can they afford, on the question of a change of the seat of government, by hostilizing the middle counties, to transfer them from the Eastern to the Western interest? To make it their interest to withdraw from the former that ground of claim, if used for adversary purposes? With things as they are, let both parties remain content and united.

If, then, William & Mary is to be removed, and not to Richmond, can there be two opinions how its funds may be directed to the best advantage for the public? When it was found that that seminary was entirely ineffectual towards the object of public education, and that one on a better plan, and in a better situation, must be provided, what was so obvious as to employ for that purpose the funds of the one abandoned, with what more would be necessary to raise the new establishment? And what so obvious as to do now what might reasonably have been done then by consolidating together the institutions and their funds? The plan sanctioned by the Legislature required for our University ten professors; but the funds appropriated will maintain but eight, and some of these are consequently overburdened with duties. The hundred thousand dollars of principal which you say still remains to William & Mary, by its interest of $6,000, would give us the two deficient professors, with an annual surplus for the purchase of books. And certainly the Legislature will see no public interest, after the expense incurred on the new establishment, in setting up a rival in the city of Richmond; they cannot think it better to have two institutions crippling one another, than one of healthy powers, competent to that highest grade of instruction, which neither with a divided support could expect to attain.

Another argument may eventually arise in favor of consolidation. The contingent gift, at the late session, of $50,000 for books and apparatus, shews a sense in the Legislature that those objects are still to be provided. If we fail in obtaining that sum, they will feel an incumbency to provide it otherwise. What so ready as the derelict capital of William & Mary, and the large library they uselessly possess? Should that college, then, be removed, I cannot doubt that the Legislature, keeping in view its original object, will consolidate it with the University.

But it will not be removed. Richmond is doubtless in earnest; but that the Visitors should concur is impossible. * *
* * * * * * * * * * *

I will only add to this long letter an opinion that we had better say as little as we can on this whole subject. Give them no alarm. Let them petition for the removal; let them get the old structure completely on wheels, and not till then put in our claim to its reception. I shall communicate your letter, as you request, to Mr. Madison, and with it this answer. Why can you not call on us, on your way to Warminster, and make this a subject of conversation? With my devoted respects to Mrs. Cabell, assure her that she can no where be more cordially received than by the family at Monticello; and the deviation from your direct road is too small to merit consideration.

Ever and affectionately your friend and servant,

TH: JEFFERSON.

P. S. *May* 23.—Your letter and this answer have been communicated to Mr. Madison. I enclose you his answer, which be so good as to return to me.

Mr. Madison to Mr. Jefferson. (Copy—the original having been returned, as requested.)

MONTPELIER, May 20, 1824.

DEAR SIR,—I return the letter from Mr. Cabell, with your answer to it, enclosed in yours of the 16th, just come to hand.

It is not probable that a removal of the College from Williamsburg will be espoused by a majority of the Visitors, controled as they will be by the popular voice in that quarter. If it should, Richmond will not be without competitors. The pretensions of Petersburg have already been brought forward. And if, in its new position, it is to be co-ordinate with the present University, there will be a bold claim by the ultramontane country. After all, is the climate of Richmond so different in the public eye from that of Williamsburg, as to make it a satisfactory substitute? Is not Richmond also becoming too much of a city to be an eligible site for such an institution? The most extensive and flourishing of our learned institutions are not in the most populous towns. That in Philadelphia is eclipsed by rising seminaries in other parts of the State. In New York the case is not dissimilar. Be all this as it may, I concur entirely in your opinion, that the best counsel for us is to be passive during the experiment, and turn the result to the best account for the interest of science and of the State.

I wish Mr. Cabell may comply with your invitation to a conversation-interview, on his way to Warminster; with an understanding that mine is included, and that we should be much gratified in welcoming him and his lady over our threshold.

Yours, with affectionate esteem,

JAMES MADISON.

Mr. Jefferson.

CLXXV.

J. C. C. TO T. J.

WARMINSTER, June 13, 1824.

DEAR SIR,—Your favor of the 16th ult., covering Mr. Madison's letter to you of the 20th, was handed to me by Capt. Peyton in Richmond, in the latter part of the month. I have heretofore declined writing in reply, because I have entertained the hope of visiting you as desired, in which event a written answer would be unnecessary. Nothing, I assure you, could have been more agreeable to Mrs. Cabell and myself, than to visit Monticello and Montpelier. But the unfortunate situation of Mrs. Tucker * has deprived us of that pleasure. It demands all our attention, and I fear will eventuate in the loss of her; an affliction which can only be appreciated by those who know her, as I do, to be one of the most perfect of the human race. May Heaven, in its mercy, avert this blow from my family! She has been in bad health and rather declining for upwards of a twelve-month. But when we set out from Williamsburg, her attending physician expressed no serious apprehensions about her case; and the family certainly felt none. But on her arrival in Richmond, she was much injured by the journey, and her physician expressed an opinion very unfavorable to her ultimate recovery. It was agreed in the family that Mrs. Cabell and myself should hurry on, and prepare our domestic affairs for setting out with Mr. and Mrs. Tucker to the White Sulphur Springs in a few days after their arrival at this place. Mrs. Tucker stood the fatigues of the journey from Richmond better than I had expected, and at first we indulged the hope that the air of this upper country would prove very serviceable. But she begins to look again very badly, and all our fears are again revived. We are now

* Mrs. Cabell's mother.

hurrying our preparations for departure, and hope to set out in three days from this time. I go in the morning to Buckingham Courthouse, to make enquiries as to the best stages along the route to New London and Johnson's Springs in Botetourt. If I find it admissible, I shall return home and attend to my harvest. In this situation I must, for the present, decline the kind invitation of yourself and Mr. Madison, to whom I beg you will be good enough to make my apology. I am very thankful to you both for your prompt attention to my letter from Williamsburg. I have shown your letters confidentially to a few friends. When I see you, I will re-state more at large my reasons for thinking that the funds of William & Mary should, if the college falls, receive a different direction from the one you seem disposed to give them. Such of my Assembly friends as I have met with, concur warmly in favor of the academical appropriation. I entirely concur in your views as to the impropriety of the Richmond scheme. It will be warmly supported, and will give us a good deal of trouble; but it can and ought to be defeated. Already I was drawn into some discussions about it. But from the receipt of your letter, I have pursued your advice, and shall inculcate it on my friends. Our course is simple and easy, till the meeting of the next Legislature. In the mean time, I will have the pleasure (and as soon as possible) to see you and Mr. Madison. I write in great haste, and must conclude with the most heartfelt respect and esteem.

Your friend and servant,

JOSEPH C. CABELL.

Mr. Jefferson.

CXLVI.

J. C. C. TO T. J.

RICHMOND, 17th December, 1824.

DEAR SIR,—I reached this place on the 12th instant, and have employed the interval in taking lodgings and in occasional conferences on the interests of my district and of the State. My delay in getting to town, was owing to the failure of an overseer to come to one of my farms at the time I expected him, and partly to the desire of Mrs. Tucker to prolong her stay in the mountain air. I wished and intended to proceed and settle my business at Corrottoman, during the recess of the Senate, which commences to-morrow, and will continue for ten days. But the state of affairs here has induced me to remain in town, and postpone my Corrottoman trip till the close of the session. Our University friends were waiting for my arrival, expecting that I could give them your views and those of the Board, as to the course most expedient to be pursued, both in regard to the University and to the removal of the College. As I did not receive the letter you gave me reason to expect from you about the 20th of November, I am not as fully informed upon all points, as was expected and desired. Our situation is one that gives me great anxiety, more especially as regards the removal of the college. After the best consideration I could give the subject, I have determined to vote for the measure, provided the college will consent to be subject to the control of the General Assembly. I confess that this disposition of the subject leaves me great cause of uneasiness as to the future, and yet it seems to me the best ground to take under the circumstances of the case. Our friends in the Lower House appear disposed to oppose the removal altogether. All seem to regret the prospect before us. Col. Randolph, Mr. Loyall, and Mr. Bowyer, seem doubtful as to the best course to be taken. I shall struggle hard to bring the college under the power of the Assembly. Mr.

Johnson and the friends of removal will oppose it with much zeal. I shall probably explain the use I would feel disposed to make of the power of the Assembly, which is to reduce the capital of the college, leaving a moiety here, and transferring the residue to Winchester and Hampden Sidney, or other points in the State, connected with the general system. It would be utterly impracticable to procure any portion for the University; and I still most earnestly recommend the abandonment of every such idea, if any plan of the kind has ever been formed. The hostile party in Richmond and the college aim decidedly at a great institution connected with a medical school. They are very averse to Legislative control; but if they cannot get the removal on other terms, they will come under the power of the Assembly, and struggle for influence hereafter. The republicans in Richmond, including the high officers of government, only want a preparatory college, and would be disposed to come into any reasonable measures to prevent pernicious competition. I rely greatly on them; and on the interests of the other points referred to above; but I confess I am uneasy about the future, knowing, as I do, the vast influence of the metropolis. The delegation from the country about Williamsburg, oppose the measure with great zeal. They will probably use, as a last resort, the proposition to keep half the capital in Williamsburg, and send half here. Mr. Hay is here, and advises very strongly that the University party should not oppose the removal. Judges Brooke, Green, Coalter, Brockenbrough, &c., who have been powerful friends of the University, are decidedly in favor of the removal, but will all be for legislative control. I will write you more fully from time to time. I have advised our friends in the other House to move immediately the reference of the report of the Rector and Visitors to the Committee of Schools and Colleges, with a view of reporting a resolution in favor of an advance on the part of the State of the $50,000, on the credit of the debt due from the General Government. I fear we shall not succeed, particularly as the college question has got the start of us. But we will do every thing in our power. Mr. Blatterman's arrival here gives a favorable impulse to public opinion. It is suggested, however, that if the friends of the University should oppose the removal of the college, every effort will be made by its friends and by the metropolis, to defeat every measure brought forward for the University. My amendment excites great heat in the higher circles of the opposition. The friends of the other colleges will be greatly opposed to it. Yet I shall make it a *sine quâ non* of my vote. Gen. Taylor is here, entering most earnestly into the interest of the college party. Mr. Leigh, Mr. Johnson, Judge Marshall, Mr. Garnett, &c., &c., join heartily in his zeal. I speak from report; for with the most of these gentlemen I am in no habits of intercourse. I should be truly happy to have the advice of yourself and Mr. Madison, as I am surrounded by powerful adversaries, and have lost the disinterested aid of the great leaders of the republican party. Rest assured of my unabated fidelity, and never ceasing anxiety for the prosperity of the University.

I am, dear sir,

Most truly and in great haste your friend,

JOSEPH C. CABELL.

Mr. Jefferson.

CLXXVII.

J. C. C. TO T. J.

RICHMOND, 21st December, 1824.

DEAR SIR,—Since the date of my last I have been enabled to settle my opinions as to the course which we ought to pursue. My views have undergone a material change. On my first arrival here, I was assailed by old and powerful friends of the University, with all the weapons of reason and persuasion; and wishing to avoid the appearance of illiberality, I for a short time contemplated a compromise, and proposed to vote for the removal of the college, provided its friends would consent to place it under the control of the General Assembly. But subsequent reflection has convinced me that I ought to vote altogether against the removal. Accordingly I have called on my friends on the other side, apprised them of my adherence to my first impression, and am now doing every thing in my power to prevent the removal. In taking this course, I oppose the wishes of my nearest and dearest relatives and friends, and bring upon myself the powerful resentment of the metropolis. But my judgment is satisfied, and I shall brave every consequence. I fear the influence of the metropolis, headed by so many able men, will be too strong for us. Still I have hopes that we may succeed. All the strong friends of the University will do their utmost to put down the scheme. We have had a conference and perfectly agree, with the exception of Mr. Johnson, who will support the Richmond interest. Col. Randolph will be up at Christmas, and will give you all the news. A powerful weapon used by the President of the College is that of a medical college at this place by the voluntary annexation of a medical faculty to William & Mary on its removal. He says it is as impossible to make doctors at the University of Virginia as it is to have ships without sails or waves; and asserts that he will teach here what cannot be taught there. I should wish to be informed precisely how far you propose to carry medical education at the University; and if you only propose a preparatory school, to be furnished with arguments to shew that this place also would be merely preparatory. A former letter of yours, which I have among my papers, throws out lights on this subject; but I should be thankful for anything additional that may enable me to defend the University policy in the departments of medicine and law, which are the points chiefly assailed. You can scarcely form an idea of the immense influence of this town on the General Assembly. Now, as last winter, I have to contend with a powerful interest in the town, which seems to threaten our total overthrow. I will write you from time to time, and should be grateful for any assistance in your power. I have sent my carriage home, and shall not leave the city till the end of the session.

I am, dear sir, ever faithfully yours,

JOSEPH C. CABELL.

Mr. Jefferson.

CXXLVIII.

T. J. TO J. C. C.

MONTICELLO, December 22, 1824.

DEAR SIR,—The proposition to remove William & Mary College to Richmond, with all its present funds, and to add to it a medical school, is nothing more nor less than to remove the University also to that place; because, if both remain, there will not be students enough to make either worthy the acceptance of men of the first order of science. They must each fall down to the level of our present academies, under the direction of common teachers, and our state of education must stand exactly where it now is. Few of the States have been able to maintain one University, none two. Surely the Legisture, after such an expense incurred for a real University, and just as it is prepared to go into action under hopeful auspices, will not consent to destroy it by this side wind. As to the best course to be taken with William & Mary, I am not so good a judge as our colleagues on the spot. They have under their eyes the workings of the enemies of the University, masked and unmasked, and the intrigues of Richmond, * * * * * * * * * * * and they can best see what measures are most likely to counteract these insidious designs.

On the question of the removal I think our particular friends had better take no active part, but vote silently for or against it, according to their own judgment as to the public utility; and if they divide on the question, so much the better, perhaps.

I am glad the Visitors and Professors have invoked the interference of the Legislature, because it is an acknowledgment of its authority, on behalf of the State, to superintend and control it, of which I never had a doubt. It is an institution established for the public good, and not for the personal emolument of the professors, endowed from the public lands, and organized by the Executive functionary, whose legal office it was. The acquiescence of both corporations, under the authority of the Legislature, removes what might otherwise have been a difficulty with some. If the question of removal be decided affirmatively, the next is, how shall their funds be disposed of most advantageously for the State in general? These are about $100,000—too much for a secondary or local institution. The giving a part of them to a school at Winchester, and part to Hampden Sidney is well, as far as it goes; but does not go far enough. Why should not every part of the State participate equally of the benefit of this reversion of right which accrues to the whole equally? This would be no more a violation of law than the giving part to a few. You know that the Rockfish report proposed an intermediate grade of schools between the primary and the University. In that report the objects of the middle schools are stated. See page 10 of the copy I now enclose you. In these schools should be taught Latin and Greek to a good degree. French, also, numerical arithmetic, the elements of geometry, surveying, navigation, geography, the use of the globes, the outlines of the solar system, and the elements of natural philosophy. Two professors would suffice for these, to wit, one for languages, the other for so much of mathematics and natural philosophy as is here proposed. This degree of education would be adapted to the circumstances of a very great number of our citizens, who being intended for lives of business, would not aim at an University education. It would give us a body of yeomanry, too, of substantial information, well prepared to become a firm and steady support to the government. As schools of ancient languages, too, they would be preparatories for the University.

You have now an happy opportunity of carrying this intermediate establishment into execution, without laying a cent of tax on the people, or taking one from the treasury. Divide the State into college districts of about eighty miles square each; there would be about eight such districts below the Alleghany, and two beyond it, which would be necessarily of larger extent, because of the sparseness of their population. The only advance these colleges would call for, would be for a dwelling house for the teacher, of about $1,200 cost, and a boarding house with four or five bed rooms and a school room, for probably about twenty or thirty boys. The whole should not cost more than $5,000; but the funds of William & Mary would enable you to give them $10,000 each. The districts might be so laid off that the principal towns and the academies now existing, might form convenient sites for their colleges, as for example, Williamsburg, Richmond, Fredericksburg, Hampden Sidney, Lynchburg, or Lexington, Staunton, Winchester, &c. Thus, of William & Mary, you will make ten colleges, each as useful as she ever was, leaving one in Williamsburg itself, placing as good a one within a day's ride of every man in the State, and yet our whole scheme of education completely established. I have said that no advance is necessary but for the erection of buildings for these schools, because the boys sent to them would be exclusively of a class of parents in competent circumstances to pay teachers for the education of their own children. The $10,000 given to each would afford a surplus to maintain by its interest one or two persons, duly selected, for their genius, from the primary schools, of those too poor to proceed further of their own means. You will remember, that of the three bills I originally gave you, one was for these district colleges, and going into the necessary details. Will you not have every member in favor of this proposition except those who are for gobbling up the whole funds themselves? The present professors might all be employed in the college of Richmond or Williamsburg, or any other they would prefer, with reasonable salaries in the meantime, until the system should get under way. This occasion of completing our system of education is a God-send, which ought not to pass away neglected. Many may be startled at the first idea, but reflection on the justice and advantage of the measure will produce converts daily and hourly to it. I certainly would not propose that the University should claim a cent of these funds, in competition with the district colleges.

Would it not be better to say nothing about the last donation of $50,000, and endeavor to get the money from Congress, and to press for it immediately? I cannot doubt their allowing it, and it would be much better to get it from them than to revive the displeasure of our own Legislature.

You are aware that we have yet two professors to appoint, to wit: of natural history and moral philosophy, and that we have no time to lose. I propose that such of our colleagues as are of the Legislature, should name a day of meeting convenient to themselves, and give notice of it, by mail, to Mr. Madison, General Cocke and myself; but it should not be till the arrival of the three professors expected at Norfolk. On their arrival only can we publish the day of opening. Our Richmond mail-stage arrives here on Sunday and departs on Wednesday, and arrives again on Thursday and departs on Sunday, each affording two spare intervening days, and requiring from you an absence of six days.

Mr. Long, professor of ancient languages, is located in his apartments at the University. He drew, by lot, Pavilion No. V. He appears to be a most amiable man, of fine understanding, well qualified for his department, and acquiring esteem as fast as he becomes known. Indeed, I have great hopes that the whole selection will fulfill our wishes.

Ever and affectionately yours,

TH: JEFFERSON.

Mr. Cabell.

CLXXIX.

(PRIVATE.)—T. J. TO J. C. C.

MONTICELLO, December 22, 1824.

DEAR SIR,—Let the contents of this letter be known to you and myself only. We want a professor of Ethics. Mr. Madison and myself think with predilection, of George Tucker, our member of Congress. You know him, however, better than we do. Can we get a better? Will he serve? You know the emoluments, and that the tenure is in fact for life, the lodgings comfortable, the society select, &c. If you approve of him, you may venture to propose it to him, and ask him if he will accept. I say "you may venture," because three of us could then be counted on, and we should surely get one, if not more, or all, of the other four gentlemen.

You will probably think it due and proper to shew my other letter of this date to Col. Randolph and Mr. Gordon, under recommendation of due caution. For our colleagues with you, it is intended equally as for yourself. The measure of the district colleges, if approved, had better be brought on by some one having no relations with the University.

Affectionately yours,

TH: JEFFERSON.

Mr. Cabell.

CLXXX.

J. C. C. TO T. J.

RICHMOND, 31st December, 1824.

DEAR SIR,—Your two letters of 22d instant, one of them covering the report from Rockfish Gap, have safely arrived, and both of them have received my most attentive consideration. Your private letter has been seen and will be seen only by myself. On 29th inst. I wrote Mr. Geo. Tucker a letter in conformity to your desire, of which the enclosed is a copy. After the most attentive perusal of the other letter, I took the liberty to blot, so as to render illegible, the following passage: "As to the best course to be taken with William & Mary, I am not so good a judge as our colleagues, on the spot; they have under their eyes the workings of the enemies of the University, masked and unmasked, and the intrigues of Richmond * * * * * * * *. And they can best see what measures are most likely to counteract these insidious designs." I thought this passage calculated to wound the feelings of some of the persons to whom I wished to shew the letter, and to relinquish the defensive posture which I wished to preserve in the eyes of the General Assembly. The residue of the letter was just such a paper as I had a strong desire to receive from you, and one calculated to produce a powerful effect. Some days before your letter arrived, Dr. Smith called in my absence, and mentioned to Mrs. Cabell that there was a letter in town from Mr. Madison, approving of the removal of the college, but did not mention the name of the person to whom it was addressed. I called the next morning on Doctor Smith, with the hope of being able to obtain a copy of the letter; but he was not at his lodgings, and afterwards left town before I could see him; nor have I been able to hear any thing further of this letter. From the conversation between Mr. Madison and myself, at the last meeting of our board, I thought it not improbable that such a letter had been written. Its effect on the opinion of members would be very great, unless counteracted by an opposite letter from yourself. However disagreeable it would be for such a collision of opinion to appear before the public, yet, in the present case, the public weal would render its disclosure unavoidable. Mr. Madison's views had a great influence on my own mind, and favoring my sincere wish to avoid the collision in which I am engaged with so many friends, for a long time, they shook my previous conclusions, and were instrumental in inducing me to suggest the compromise contemplated when I first arrived in this place.

Dr. Smith's disclosure of his plans before the Committee of Schools and Colleges, and some other disclosures, drove me back to my first impressions on the subject; and have neutralized my brother, Mr. Nicholas, Judge Carr, Mr. Gilmer, and Governor Pleasants. I believe I am correct in saying that these gentlemen are all now in *heart* with us, after having been very zealous on the other side. I shewed your letter to Mr. Johnson, with a copy of the passage which I had erased, with a suitable explanation of my motives. His determined support of the removal made me feel some hesitation in opening to him all our views on this occasion. Yet this candid course seemed preferable to one of reserve and caution, towards one who has so often co-operated ably and zealously in our cause; and, moreover, your letter required it. He objected to the course recommended on general grounds of inexpediency, and particularly on that of its incompatibility with the charter. I differed with him, and we separated in a friendly manner. I have since shewn your letter to Mr. Gordon and Col. Randolph, Mr. Loyall and Mr. Bowyer. Col. R. has had it for two days, and has shewn it to many friends, as he assures me, and as I have had some occasion to perceive, with powerful effect. By our exertions we had previously changed the current in some degree; but since the arrival of your letter, I hear a great change has taken place. The bold step of laying hold of, and of dividing the funds of the college, is one perhaps which we shall be unable to take at the present session. The legal difficulties about the charter, and those connected with any division of the State into districts, will probably throw the subject to some future session. But the scheme makes a great impression. I doubt whether the fact of your opinion on this subject being known, will not do us much more good than harm, and am so much disposed to think so that I authorized Col. Randolph, to-day, to shew your letter at his discretion. You can scarcely form an idea of the powerful influence which this town had exerted on this subject, and of the excitement which prevails among the warm advocates of the measure. Our leading officers and judges acted without due reflection in the commencement of the business, and many of them hold on in their career. I trust in God we shall be able to break down this measure, the ruinous consequences of which I now see in lively colors. The hatred and abuse which I bring on myself you can scarcely imagine. But I know and appreciate your great and good views, and will support you at every sacrifice. Sometimes I sink on my bed, exhausted by my reflections and feelings; then, animated by the prospect of the future, I spring up with renovated life and vigor. * * * * * * * * * The 5th January is fixed for the committee to take up the subject. In the interim, Mr. Gordon and myself have agreed upon a resolution relative to the property of the college, in which the object is to shew the injustice of giving all to this place. Judge Semple is summoned to appear before the committee when it meets again, and I anticipate some benefit from his presence. Mr. **** says if the measure should be rejected, the board will try the effect of a new organization—they will set up their table in college, and re-establish their grammar school—and if they do not succeed in a few years, they will lay their charter on the table of the House of Delegates. This is what I, for years past, have advised them to do; but of this I could not convince them. Your hand-writing and your letters have great effect here. Were you to reinforce your letter to me by another to Mr. Loyall, however short, it would have considerable influence. As soon as I hear from Mr. Tucker I will write to you. I need not say that the greater part of this is of a confidential character.

Ever and faithfully yours,

JOS. C. CABELL.

Mr. Jefferson.

CLXXXI.

J. C. C. TO T. J.

RICHMOND, 6th January, 1825.

DEAR SIR,—The enclosed letter from Mr. Tucker, in reply to mine, of which you have a copy, I send for the perusal of yourself and Mr. Madison alone. I can see no objection to its communication thus far, although I expect Mr. Tucker wrote it with an expectation that it would not go beyond me. I expected he would hesitate about accepting a situation which would cut him off from all prospect of future promotion. This very objection furnishes one of the strongest proofs of the propriety of sending to Europe for a large proportion of the professors. I am quite uncertain what Mr. Tucker's decision will be; when I get his final answer I will communicate it to you. I know not what to say to him as to the length of time to be allowed him; and would wish to be governed by your instructions on that head.

We hear nothing of the Competitor. When that ship arrives I will call on the other members of the board to fix a time for meeting, as you propose. It will be very inconvenient for some of the members to come up in the winter. I presume you will not call us together, unless there should be a prospect of filling the vacant professorships, or other good cause.

A Mr. Kidd, of this place, lately an editor of a paper, now a teacher, has, through his friends, made some advances with a view to induce me to propose him as Professor of Ethics. I replied that I had reason to believe the place was about to be engaged to another. Mr. Kidd is a Scotchman by birth; he has traveled in Europe; and seems to be a man of talents and learning. But I know too little of him to recommend him. Colonel Randolph and Mr. Madison, I expect, know much of him.

The petition of William & Mary has lost much ground since I last wrote you. I think it will be rejected by a large vote. The resolution proposed by Mr. Gordon, * * * * * * has had even a greater effect than I expected. The members of the corporation are divided as to the course to be pursued. Judge Semple is now before the committee, and refuses to answer the enquiries. Doctor Smith was willing to give general answers. The Visitors in town, or the greater part of them, approved of Judge Semple's course. This happened in the committee yesterday. They are now acting on the same subject. The college party will try to get the committee discharged from the resolution; the friends of the University, to get them discharged from the whole subject. The measure proposed in your letter is too bold for the present state of the public mind. We will not bring it forward as an original proposition; but, should there be occasion, as a substitute for the measure of removal to this place. The letter has had a considerable effect. The hostile party, apprised of this, endeavor to destroy its influence, by reporting that you have sent orders to the Assembly to plunder the college, and bribe the different parts of the State. I shall hereafter shew the letter to very few.

I yesterday received a letter from Mr. Barbour, of the Senate, under date of the 3d instant, saying, "I had an interview with the chairman, and one of the private members of the Committee of Claims, on yesterday, who presented me with the report and bill which will be presented to-day to the House of Representatives. They are so far favorable as to accord to us the whole amount of the interest actually paid by Virginia on the loans negotiated by her. Indeed, this is all we think prudent to ask for, as interest on all the advances would be a question of great difficulty, as in the actual state of opinion here it might jeopardize the whole."

Thus we have our hopes kindled up again. Should this money be paid, I hope we will proceed directly to invest the whole amount in books and apparatus, trusting to the Legislature to finish the rotunda.

I remain, dear sir, ever faithfully yours,

JOSEPH C. CABELL.

Mr. Jefferson.

CLXXXII.

[It will have been observed that the parties to this correspondence have had their gaze so intently fixed on the great object before them, or on circumstances and current events as they rose, and which seemed to favor or impede its attainment, that there was but little time to dwell on the motives which either did or should have actuated those who were engaged in the enterprise. This, and a few of the preceding letters, may afford an agreeable relief to their general argumentative or matter-of-fact character. We refer particularly to its closing paragraph, the strain of which is resumed and prolonged in another near the close of the series. See No. 207, below. Such sentiments, not put forth for the nonce, but uttered in all sincerity, as between friends and coadjutors in the same cause, may be pondered with profit by the rising generation of statesmen.]

T. J. TO J. C. C.

MONTICELLO, January 11, 1825.

DEAR SIR,—We are dreadfully non-plussed here by the non-arrival of our three professors. We apprehend that the idea of our opening on the 1st of February prevails so much abroad (although we have always mentioned it doubtfully,) as that students will assemble on that day, without awaiting the further notice promised. To send them back, will be discouraging, and to open an University without Mathematics or Natural Philosophy, would bring on us ridicule and disgrace. We therefore publish an advertisement, stating that *on the arrival of these Professors*, notice will be given of the day of opening the institution.

Governor Barbour writes me hopefully of getting our fifty thousand dollars from Congress. The proposition has been originated in the House of Representatives, referred to the Committee of Claims, the chairman of which has prepared a very favorable report, and a bill conformable, assuming the re-payment of all interest which the State has actually paid. The Legislature will certainly owe to us the recovery of this money; for had they not given it in some measure, the reverenced character of a donation for the promotion of learning, it would never have been paid. It is to be hoped, therefore, that the displeasure incurred by wringing it from them at the last session, will now give way to a contrary feeling, and even place us on a ground of some merit. Should this sentiment take place, and the arrival of our professors and filling of our dormitories with students on the 1st of February, encourage them to look more favorably to us, perhaps it might dispose them to enlarge somewhat their order on the same fund. You observe the Proctor has stated in a letter accompanying our report, that it will take about twenty-five thousand dollars more than we have, to finish the rotunda. Besides this, an anatomical theatre (costing about as much as one of our hotels, say about five thousand dollars,) is indispensable to the school of anatomy. There cannot be a single dissection until a proper theatre is prepared, giving an advantageous view of the operation to those within, and effectually excluding observation from without. Either the additional sums therefore of twenty-five and five thousand dollars will be wanting, or we must be permitted to apply five of the fifty thousand dollars to a theatre, leaving the rotunda unfinished for the present. Yet I should think neither object an equivalent for renewing the displeasure of the Legislature. Unless we can carry their hearty patronage with us, the institution can never flourish. I would not, therefore, hint at this additional aid, unless it were agreeable to our friends generally, and tolerably sure of being carried without irritation.

In your letter of December 31, you say my hand-writing and my letters have great effect there, *i. e.*, at Richmond. I am sensible, my dear sir, of the kindness with which this encouragement is held up to me; but my views of their effect are very different. When I retired from the administration of public affairs, I thought I saw some evidence that I retired with a good degree of public favor, and that my conduct in office had been considered, by the one party at least, with approbation, and with acquiescence by the other. But the attempt in which I have embarked so earnestly to procure an improvement in the moral condition of my native State, although in other States it may have strengthened good dispositions, it has certainly weakened them in our own. The attempt ran foul of so many local interests, of so many personal views, and of so much ignorance, and I have been considered as so particularly its promoter, that I see evidently a great change of sentiment towards myself. I cannot doubt its having dissatisfied with myself a respectable minority, if not a majority of the House of Delegates. I feel it deeply and very discouragingly, yet I shall not give way. I have ever found in my progress through life, that, acting for the public, if we do always what is right, the approbation denied in the beginning will surely follow us in the end. It is from posterity, we are to expect remuneration for the sacrifice we are making for their service, of time, quiet, and present good will. And I fear not the appeal. The multitude of fine young men who will feel that they owe to us the elevation of mind, of character, and station, they shall be able to attain from the result of our efforts, will ensure us their remembrance with gratitude. We will not then "be weary in well doing." *Usque ad aras amicus tuus.*

TH: JEFFERSON.

Mr. Cabell.

P. S. Since writing the above I received yours of the 6th.

CLXXXIII.

J. C. C. TO T. J.

RICHMOND, January 16, 1825.

DEAR SIR,—I thank you sincerely for your favor of 11th instant. I have but little time now to answer you. I am sorry to inform you that the party in favor of the removal of the college have gained ground very much since the date of my last; insomuch that I now have the greatest apprehensions of their success. * * * * *
Yet I will not despair. I will contend to the last moment,

and if we are vanquished, my skirts will be clear of all blame. There is one plan by which they may yet be defeated. It is to bring forward a bill to divide the funds of William & Mary, on the plan you propose, as a substitute for their bill for removing the college, towards the latter readings of the bill in the House of Delegates. On the passage, the substitute would probably prevail; or a majority would agree to let both bills lie over till another session. Delay is all we want, so as to get the representatives of the people out of the Richmond parties, and to give the people power to act. I, therefore, my dear sir, invoke your aid in drawing such a bill as will suit the purpose. *You alone* can prepare a bill that will enable us to vanquish the host opposed to us. If you wish me not to make you known as the author, I will not do so. But I am very sure that so far from its doing you or your friends injury, it is the only way to save the State. I beseech you to prepare one immediately, and send it as quickly as possible by the mail. We will keep the subject on the carpet long enough for the bill to get here. It is known that you prefer a division to removal; and no injury can arise to you, in any way, for drawing the bill. It is all important that you should furnish us this weapon on this occasion. I send you a printed copy of your bill for public instruction, to enable you to execute the draft with less trouble. Let the funds be equally divided among the districts, whatever they may be, to be augmented from the literary fund; the donations to old colleges to be revocable at the pleasure of the Legislature, if they will not surrender their old and take new charters. Let the number of districts be as small as due regard to localities will admit. As to details, you will be the best judge of them. I think the representatives will pause before they give away the rights and interests of their constituents. Great excitement prevails. No wonder, when * * * * * * are all united. Give me but this bill, and I think I will yet defeat them.

Yours faithfully,

JOSEPH C. CABELL.

Mr. Jefferson.

CLXXXIV.

T. J. TO J. C. C.

MONTICELLO, January 19, 1825.

DEAR SIR,—You know that the arrearages of our subscriptions were appropriated particularly to the works of the rotunda, but they come in most tardily, and will never be received but on suits, which we determine to commence against every man in arrears in time for the March courts. But this will be a chase of a couple of years, and in the mean time Mr. Brockenbrough is in the utmost distress for about $5,000 due on account of the rotunda. The bank is willing to lend us this sum for two years, and to receive the gradual payments as they come in by collection, if such a measure is sanctioned by the Board of Visitors. But the money is wanting immediately, and the Board cannot meet immediately. Mr. Garrett goes down on this business, and thinks that if the Visitors now in Richmond will sign a note assuring the bank that they will sanction the transaction by a vote at our first meeting, the bank will, on this assurance, advance the money. I wish you to explain this to our colleagues; and if they approve of it, that they will enable Mr. Garrett to effect the negotiation. Should our professors not arrive before the Legislature rises, it is indispensable then to have a meeting, as well for the appointment of two or perhaps three professors, still wanting to make up our complement, as for other objects. Of the particular day, you will, of course, have to give timely notice by mail to Mr. Madison and Gen. Cocke.

Affectionately yours,

TH: JEFFERSON.

Mr. Cabell.

CLXXXV.

T. J. TO J. C. C.

MONTICELLO, January 22, 1825.

DEAR Sir,—I received your favor of the 16th yesterday at noon, and immediately turned in on the task it prescribed to me, in order that I might get it into the mail which is made up this evening. I am so worn down by the drudgery, that I can write little now. The bill is most hastily drawn, and will need your severe amendment.* I have said nothing of the manner of obtaining an account of the funds of the college, because I believe a committee has that subject before them; nor yet of the manner of disposing of these funds, whether by keeping them in their present form, or converting them into stock or cash, because I know too little of them. I have not meddled with the Lexington academy, because it is a mere private institution, founded by Gen. Washington with property made completely his own. Its case is therefore totally different from the public institution of William & Mary. Foreseeing that Hampden Sidney will not consent to accept of the new character proposed for her, I have provided for a substitute in Nottoway, as more equally distant from the colleges of Richmond and Lynchburg, and reasonably so from Hampden Sidney. I have avoided laying off districts as unnecessary and liable to contest. I am quite exhausted, but ever yours.

TH: JEFFERSON.

Mr. Cabell.

---

* For this bill see Appendix O, (a.)

CLXXXVI.

J. C. C. TO T. J.

RICHMOND, 28th January, 1825.

DEAR SIR,—Yours of 22d covering your bill is received, and I beg you to accept my most heartfelt thanks. I have held a conference on it with some of our friends, and I think it will be a powerful instrument in our hands. Our friends in the other House were committed to the Williamsburg party to vote, *in the first instance*, for the postponement. Then they will be free. If that question should not be carried, your bill will be ready. I shall keep it as private as possible. The opposite party are triumphing in anticipation, but I think we will yet defeat them. In the Whig of the 18th and 21st, you will see the funds of William & Mary, and the decision of the Court of Appeals, in the case of Bracken and the College, published by myself, with explanatory remarks. In one of the Tuesday's papers, I shall publish again. Doctor Smith is to appear at the bar of the House on Monday. I send you a copy of the college documents which have just appeared. I refer you to Mr. Garrett for news.

Faithfully yours,

JOSEPH C. CABELL.

Mr. Jefferson.

CLXXXVII.

J. C. C. TO T. J.

RICHMOND, 30th January, 1825.

DEAR SIR,—I have been greatly relieved by finding from a Norfolk paper that the ship Competitor was at Plymouth on the 5th December. I had given them up as lost in the gale of the last of October, and myself almost to despair. I now hope all is safe. I think there is a majority for moving the college; but I am confident the plan of splitting up the funds will succeed, if the opposite party should not be able to put down entirely the idea of our power. I have long foreseen the direction this subject would finally take, and I have sought to bring it to this. It will turn on the principles of the Dartmouth decision. All the leading lawyers of both houses are against us. I fear we shall be unable to get up any thing like a law argument. Here is now our greatest danger. The college party will endeavor to show that donations from the crown stand on the footing of donations from individuals. If you can suggest any authorities or ideas that would aid us on this subject, it would render a great service, as the discussion will perhaps last long enough. I have the pleasure to inform you that three of the Judges of the Court of Appeals are with us.

Faithfully yours,

JOSEPH C. CABELL.

Mr. Jefferson.

CLXXXVIII.

J. C. C. TO T. J.

RICHMOND, 3d February, 1825.

DEAR SIR,—I have taken the liberty in my publication under the signature of "*A Friend of Science,*"* in the Constitutional Whig of Tuesday, more correctly printed in the Enquirer of to-day, to give to the public your letter to me from Poplar Forest, in the year 1817, and in doing so, I hope I have taken no improper liberty. I saw the gathering necessity of setting up the colleges against the Richmond party, and it was requisite to show your former plans, and our efforts to sustain them. I am inclined to think the course will produce a

---

* This paper and the correspondence with President Smith, which grew out of it, as forming a part of the history of the subject, are re-printed in the Appendix O, (b) (c.) Mr. Jefferson's opinion of the validity of the argument is given in Letter 210.

considerable effect. The public mind is scarcely prepared for so bold a measure; but if I am not mistaken, it will enable us to defeat the scheme of removal to this place. The discussion on the substitute of Mr. Jones from York, has been progressing for some days. To-day Mr. Morris, of Hanover, spoke for some hours, and exerted his utmost power to carry the removal. Mr. Upshur, of the Eastern Shore, followed, and half finished a speech of great power and ability. He will conclude to-morrow. He attacked the administration of the college as the real cause of its present situation. He dwelt on the tyranny of the statute compelling the students to give evidence against their fellows, with very great effect. I am of opinion that he will settle the question, and that we shall have no opportunity to bring in our bill. I am told Mr. Gilmer has a third time declined the appointment to the law chair. I wish you would make enquiries (if you have not otherwise made up your mind,) relative to the qualifications of Chancellor Tucker. From the best sources of information, I am inclined to think he has prepared himself very ably to lecture on law, and upon the whole, I suspect he would make a popular and good appointment. There is nothing in my private relations with him, that would induce me to wish him appointed, if he is not the best that could be chosen. Perhaps you have made up your mind. If you have not, I would be glad if you would make enquiries. It will be difficult to fill the law chair well, unless perhaps a judicial station were combined with it; and yet an interference should be, as far as possible, avoided. Suppose a small chancery district, consisting of the counties of Albemarle, Orange, Louisa, Fluvanna, and Nelson, were created, and the Professor of Law made Chancellor of this district. The combination would be enticing to the first order of men. I throw these hints out for consideration.

Ever faithfully yours,

JOSEPH C. CABELL.

Mr. Jefferson.

CLXXXIX.

T. J. TO J. C. C.

MONTICELLO, February 3, 1825.

DEAR SIR,—Although our professors were on the 5th of December still in an English port, that they were safe raises me from the dead; for I was almost ready to give up the ship. That was eight weeks ago, and they may therefore be daily expected.

In most public seminaries, text-books are prescribed to each of the several schools, as the *norma docendi* in that school; and this is generally done by authority of the trustees. I should not propose this generally in our University, because, I believe none of us are so much at the heights of science in the several branches as to undertake this; and therefore that it will be better left to the professors, until occasion of interference shall be given. But there is one branch in which we are the best judges, in which heresies may be taught, of so interesting a character to our own State, and to the United States, as to make it a duty in us to lay down the principles which shall be taught. It is that of government. Mr. Gilmer being withdrawn, we know not who his successor may be. He may be a Richmond lawyer, or one of that school of quondam federalism, now consolidation. It is our duty to guard against the dissemination of such principles among our youth, and the diffusion of that poison, by a previous prescription of the texts to be followed in their discourses. I therefore inclose you a resolution which I think of proposing at our next meeting; strictly confiding it to your own knowledge alone and to that of Mr. Loyall, to whom you may communicate it, as I am sure it harmonizes with his principles. I wish it kept to ourselves, because I have always found that the less such things are spoken of before hand, the less obstruction is contrived to be thrown in their way. I have communicated it to Mr. Madison.

Should the bill for district colleges pass in the end, our

scheme of education will be complete. But the branch of primary schools may need attention, and should be brought, like the rest, to the forum of the Legislature. The Governor, in his annual message, gives a favorable account of them in the lump. But this is not sufficient. We should know the operation of the law establishing these schools more in detail. We should know how much money is furnished to each county every year, and how much education it distributes every year; and such a statement should be laid before the Legislature every year. The sum of education rendered in each county in every year should be estimated by adding together the number of months which each scholar attended, and stating the sum total of the months which all of them together attended. *E. g.*, if in any county one scholar attended two months, three others four months each, eight others six months each, then the sum of these added together will make sixty-two months of schooling afforded in the county that year, and the number of sixty-two months entered in a table opposite to the name of the county gives a satisfactory idea of the sum or quantum of education it rendered in that year. This will enable us to take many interesting and important views of the sufficiency of the plan established, and of the amendments necessary to produce the greatest effect. I enclose a form of the table which should be required, in which you will, of course, be sensible that the numbers entered are at hap-hazard, and *exempli gratiâ*, as I know nothing of the sums furnished or quantum of education rendered in each or any county. I send also the form of such a resolution as should be passed by the one or the other House, perhaps better by the lower one, and to be moved by some member in nowise connected with us; for the less we appear before the House, the less we shall excite dissatisfaction.

I mentioned to you formerly our want of an anatomical hall for dissection. But if we get the $50,000 from Congress, we can charge to that as the library fund the $6,000 of the building fund which we have advanced for it in books and apparatus, and re-paying from the former the $6,000 due to the latter, apply so much of it as is necessary to the anatomical building. No application on the subject need, therefore, be made to our Legislature; but I hear nothing of our prospects before Congress.

Yours, affectionately,

TH: JEFFERSON.

Mr. Cabell.

CXC.

J. C. C. TO T. J.

RICHMOND, 7th February, 1825.

DEAR SIR,—I am happy to inform you that our efforts have eventuated in success, and that the College party have been defeated in the House of Delegates by a majority of 24. You need not give yourself any further trouble on this subject. Our friends and myself concur in thinking that it would be improper to bring in the bill for dividing the funds of the college. The public mind is not prepared for so bold a measure. It is my impression, however, that the division must take place sooner or later. * * * * * * * * * * * * I think of making up a pamphlet on this subject, with the view of preparing the public mind, and of publishing your bill for consideration, without naming you as the author. It is necessary now to provide for another contest. * * * * * * * * * We shall want funds next winter, and must shake off this opposition. My friends assure me that the essay under the signature of "*A Friend of Science*," with the extracts from your letter and bill, had all the effect I could possibly desire. It broke the ranks of the opposition completely. The delegates made a pretext of tyranny at the college, but the real truth is, they found there was a master at home, who would call them to account. Rest assured, my dear sir, that Richmond is now

hors de combat. * * * * * * *
* * * We have the country completely on our side. The idea of the country colleges will bear down all opposition.
* * * * * * * * * * *
In order to counteract the opposition of Richmond, it is necessary to dispose the public mind more and more towards the general system. This will be my object during the remainder of the year.

I write in great haste, and under the influence of that lassitude which I always feel for some days after a contest like this.*

Faithfully yours,

JOSEPH C. CABELL.

Mr. Jefferson.

---

* The Virginia reader needs not to be told that with the defeat of this proposition before the Legislature, it fell not again to be revived. The College of William & Mary remains at the old "Middle Plantation," the site of our ancient metropolis, and is still the principal link which unites our modern history and associations with those of Colonial times. With the improved agriculture of lower Virginia, and some modifications in its government and curriculum of studies, it has again flourished. And none, we are confident, felt more satisfaction in this renewed prosperity of his venerable Alma Mater, or more sincerely wished that it might long continue to diffuse the blessings of education through that quarter of the State, than did Mr. Cabell. A highly respectable Collegiate Institution, under the auspices of the Baptist denomination, and a Medical School—which, though a voluntary association, has received material aid from the State—have both been established at or in the vicinity of Richmond. The two former, like the other colleges of Virginia, have been auxiliaries to, rather than rivals of, the University; and the last has attained a creditable position, without preventing the Medical School of the State from receiving that patronage to which she would seem to be entitled by the advantages of her alliance with other schools of science—the want of which must continue to be felt by any isolated institution. These gratifying results indicate a decided advance in the wealth of the State, or an increased disposition to expend a part of it for purposes of education, or both.

CXCI.

[Retrospective. Mention of the Faithful, as in Letters 88, 118, 138, 149.]

J. C. C. TO T. J.

RICHMOND, 11th February, 1825

DEAR SIR,—Your favor of 3d inst. has been duly received, and your requests attended to. Both the letter and the enclosed resolutions have been shewn to Mr. Loyall, and to him alone. He will unite in supporting the resolution relative to the text-books on government. It would be very agreeable to us to know the time of our next meeting; but I suppose it is impossible to place it on a footing of greater certainty than was done by your former letter on this subject. I fear the Competitor will not arrive before the rising of the Assembly, which will be some time next week. In that event, we shall all disperse, and a regular call will be necessary. If the Competitor arrives before the Assembly rises, Mr. Loyall and myself will come up from this place, probably in the Friday's stage, by the way of New Canton. Since I last wrote you, I have abandoned the idea of publishing a pamphlet on the subject of William & Mary, as my friends here have persuaded me that so much activity on the part of a friend of the University, would be injurious to that institution. Having defeated the college party on the question relative to Jones' substitute, no opportunity was afforded of offering your bill as a substitute; and I am advised that it would be injudicious to press the subject in the form of a separate and independent bill at this time, and that it would be best to hold up your bill till another session. Perhaps we had better suffer the subject to sleep; the country scheme will be carried against the town at any time. I will bring the bill with me to Monticello. Your resolution relative to the primary schools, calling for information for anterior years, could not be complied with, the school commissioners not having reported in a form to enable the Board to make such a report for the years gone by. On conversation with Mr. Brown, the Second Auditor, I amended the resolution so as to make it apply to the current and future years, and to compel the county commissioners to report. These alterations, I supposed, would be desired by yourself, were you apprised of the difficulties as to past years. Thus amended, the resolution was yesterday handed to Mr. Loyall, who will bring it in to-day.

Judge Brooke has, throughout the discussions on the College question, discovered the utmost anxiety to sustain your views, and to accomplish your desires. He has been a powerful friend. On the College question, Goochland, Nelson and Amherst were divided. Fluvanna and Albemarle voted on opposite sides. Our most active friends (besides the College party from below opposed to removal) were Col. Randolph, Mr. Gordon, Mr. Loyall, Mr. Bowyer and Col. Benjamin Cabell, from Pittsylvania. The last is a very popular young man, and by his influence we obtained a much stronger vote on the southern side of the State than we have ever had before. I am now excommunicated in Richmond.

I fear my vote relative to the Convention question will be injurious to me in my district. The subject has cost me much uneasiness. I do not entertain those extensive apprehensions which some discover upon this subject. Yet I cannot see any great inconveniences existing under the present form of our government. The public mind is greatly divided upon many other subjects, and I do not see the prudence or propriety of adding at this time to the causes of agitation. The majority of my district, I really believe, would, upon a full discussion of the question, vote against a Convention. As a representative, I hold myself under the control of the will of my constituents. Should I continue in the Senate, and be satisfied that the people would desire a Convention, I would vote for one.

Faithfully yours,

Jos. C. Cabell.

Mr. Jefferson.

P. S. Since the preceding was written, I am informed that ****** and certain other delegates from my district are consulting together with the view of having me turned out of the Senate. Probably Richmond has something to do in this business. I shall be able to shew that I had reason to believe that the sense of the counties of Nelson and Fluvanna was not fairly taken on the subject of a Convention. I would not wish to remain in the Senate one moment against the wishes of my constituents. I should have left it long ago, but from my desire to support your views relative to our literary institutions. I was consulting with my friends, Gen. Cocke and my brother, relative to the expediency of my withdrawing, when the information above referred to was communicated to me. Should ****** set up opposition to me, and more especially if he should be the opponent, I will certainly not withdraw. I never have, and never will, disobey the settled wishes of my constituents. In the case of the bill subjecting students of seminaries to militia duty, I publicly in the Senate preferred the opinion of my district to my own, and in that case there was no instruction. The question of a Convention is one in which I regarded my district as feeling little or no interest. My whole time and all my faculties have been devoted to the defeat of our enemies in another quarter. Believe me, that enemy will rise again, and harass us for years to come. Should opposition be set up, the disadvantage of my vote on the Convention may be obviated, if my friends should desire it, by having the vote of the freeholders taken at the polls in the spring, and I would certainly obey the instructions of my constituents.

Faithfully yours,

JOSEPH C. CABELL.

CXCII.

J. C. C. TO T. J.

RICHMOND, 11th February, 1825.

DEAR SIR,—In my letter of this morning I forgot to mention that I had sent you by the mail an extra copy of the documents relative to our interest claim, transmitted by the Governor to the Assembly at the commencement of the session. Mr. Loyall strongly recommends that you should send these documents to Mr. Tazewell, with a note of request that he would pay particular attention to the subject. It is now of the utmost importance that we should succeed at Washington; as by the rejection of the College measure we have added some very strong and active enemies to the opposition.

I am, dear sir, faithfully yours,

JOSEPH C. CABELL.

Mr. Jefferson.

CXCIII.

J. C. C. TO T. J.

RICHMOND, 18th February, 1825.

DEAR SIR,—You have no doubt already been informed of the arrival of the three additional professors at this place. I have had a short interview, and am much pleased with them. Mr. Gilmer's selection thus far gives me great satisfaction.

Mr. Johnson, Mr. Loyall and myself, in conformity to your instructions, have fixed on a day for the meeting of the Board, and for that purpose have selected the fourth of March, which I hope will be agreeable to yourself and the other gentlemen. I shall call on Gen. Cocke on my way home, which will render it unnecessary for you to write to him.

The professors will leave this for Charlottesville in the Wednesday's stage.

I am, dear sir, faithfully yours,

JOSEPH C. CABELL.

Mr. Jefferson.

CXCIV.

J. C. C. TO T. J.

RICHMOND, 21st February, 1825.

DEAR SIR,—In adverting in a late letter to Mr. Gilmer's determination not to accept the Law chair, I requested you to make enquiries relative to Gen. Tucker, of whose lectures at Winchester I had received so favorable an account as to induce me to think he would be a suitable and popular appointment. It is incumbent on me now to withdraw the suggestion, as Judge Tucker, to whom I wrote on the subject, informs me that his son would be unwilling to leave Winchester, where he has property, family ties, and a valuable office, which he would be compelled to relinquish. No other communication, direct or indirect, has transpired between myself and Gen. Tucker, to whom I have not written, nor from whom have I received, a line on the subject. I confidentially communicated to Mr. Coalter the purport of my letter to you, who I have reason to believe wrote to General Tucker at the time I wrote to Judge Tucker. The letter which I have received from Judge Tucker induces me to believe that he is correctly informed of his son's views, and it would therefore be improper in me to use his name after the intimation I have received. I have written to Mr. Geo. Tucker that the Board would meet on the 4th March, and requesting him to communicate his final determination to you by that time.

I am, dear sir, faithfully yours,

JOSEPH C. CABELL.

Mr. Jefferson.

CXCV.

T. J. TO J. C. C.

MONTICELLO, April 15, 1825.

DEAR SIR,—I have received a proposition from Mr. Perry, the owner of the lands which separate the two tracts of the University, which I think of so much importance to that institution as to communicate to the Visitors by letter in their separate situations. The University tract of 100 acres is $\frac{3}{4}$ths of a mile distant from that of the observatory of 153 acres. The water which supplies the cisterns of the University by pipes, arises in the mountain a little without this last tract, and the pipes pass on Perry's side of the line, and through his interjacent lands till they enter the University tract. On his side of the line also is a very bold spring, which might be brought by a small ditch so near the buildings of the University as to be of common use. It is in his power at any time to cut off our pipes, and deprive us of that indispensable supply of water. We have always been anxious to purchase this interjacent parcel, not only to consolidate our two tracts, but to secure the supply of water; but we have never more than intimated a willingness to purchase, without pressing him, lest it might induce him to ask an unreasonable price. He is under (as I believe) some pressure which obliges him now to sell it. He gives us the refusal, which if we do not accept, he will sell in lots, as he can readily do. We gave him, about four years ago, $45 an acre for the fifty acres adjacent to it. Since that lands around the University have got to $100 and $130 the acre. He offered the parcel in question to the University for $60. I refused to treat with him at that, and told him that at $50 I would lay it before the Visitors for consideration. He at length agreed, stipulating for $3,000 in hand, one-half of the balance at the end of one year, and the other half at the end of the second, with interest from the date. On these terms, I cannot but strongly recommend its purchase. If once it is sold out in lots, we shall never be able to buy again, but at exorbitant rates, if at all; and our supply of water will assuredly be cut off from us. What passes through our present pipes, with the additional spring, will give us the most abundant supply of that element forever. That you may judge of our means of paying for it, I send you a statement of our income and expenditure for the present and the two next years, drawn up on consultation with Mr. Brockenbrough. You will perceive that I propose to borrow the first payment of $3,000 from the library fund, which can be re-paid from our general funds the next year, in addition to our second payment of $2,067 to Perry, and still leaving a surplus of $2,679 for contingencies that year; and that the same funds will make our third and last payment of $2,184 in 1827, leaving a contingent surplus for that year of $3,094. The library fund can well spare the money for a while, as we need not use of it, for a year or two, more than $40,000, leaving $10,000 for mineralogical and geological collections, which may be deferred without inconvenience. My own opinion is, therefore, that we can make the purchase without any danger of embarrassment, and that if not made now it will be forever lost. The part which I think indispensable contains about 100 acres, but it would be better to take in also the 37 acres, as it squares our lines, and the timber on it is worth the price.

Although the subject is of great and permanent interest to the University, I have not thought of proposing a meeting on it, of the great inconvenience of which to the gentlemen I am sensible; and the rather as the sketch of the ground which I send you, and the prospect of payment can be considered as well separately as together. The only article in the statement of our finances which does not rest on certainty, is the number of students calculated on for the next year. For this year, I have calculated only on the number now entered, 68; and they are coming in nearly every day; and at the summer vacation of the other schools, when they will be disengaged, we know that a large number will come, and that in the course of the year we shall be over 100. That we shall have as many the next year as our dormitories will lodge, all information assures us, and probably as many additional to that as Charlottesville can accommodate, which is expected to be about 100, and would add $1,500 more to our income. As far as we can judge, not one will go to Charlottesville, as long as a dormitory is to be had. As yet there has not been a single application to that place, although several house-keepers there had prepared themselves to take boarders. If this purchase is approved by your separate letters, I will undertake to act on them as if regularly ordered by the Board, as you can pass a vote of confirmation at our first meeting. Perry is pressing (as I believe he is pressed) for an immediate answer.

All our professors are in place except Mr. Tucker, daily expected, and the Professor of Law, whom we have yet to name. We await Mr. Tucker's arrival to form a board of faculty, that the professors may enter on their functions of order and discipline, which some incipient irregularities of the students begin to call for. From a view which I took of their ages when the whole number was 61, I found 6 of 21 and upwards, 9 of 20, 23 of 19, 10 of 18, 10 of 17, and 3 of 16. Two-thirds, therefore, being of 19 and upwards, we may hope are of sufficient discretion to govern themselves, and that the younger third, by their example, as well as by moderate coercion, will not be very difficult to keep in order.

I enclose you a printed copy of our regulations, which appear to give satisfaction to both professors and students.

Ever and affectionately yours,

TH: JEFFERSON.

Mr. Cabell.

CXCVI.

J. C. C. TO T. J.

NORFOLK, May 6, 1825.

DEAR SIR,—Your favor of April 15th, reached me on yesterday at this place. It had gone on to Warminster, when I last had the pleasure of seeing you at Monticello, and was forwarded thence by the mail to Norfolk. I cannot perceive any good ground of objection to the purchase of Mr. Perry's land, in the manner you propose. On the contrary, I give to the measure my most hearty approbation. I am very confident that when the subject is properly explained, it will meet with the support and countenance of the General Assembly. I am very thankful for the fullness of your communication, and for the printed copy of the regulations of the University.

I am, dear sir,

Faithfully yours,

JOSEPH C. CABELL.

Mr. Jefferson.

CXCVII.

(CIRCULAR.)—T. J. TO J. C. C.

MONTICELLO, May 13, 1825.

DEAR SIR,—Every offer of our law chair has been declined, and a late renewal of pressure on Mr. Gilmer has proved him inflexibly decided against undertaking it. What are we to do? The clamor is high for some appointment. We are informed, too, of many students who do not come because that school is not opened, and some now with us think of leaving us for the same reason. You may remember that among those who were the subjects of conversation at our last meeting, Judge Dade was one; but the minds of the Board were so much turned to two particular characters, that little was said of any others.

An idea has got abroad, I know not from what source, that we have appointed Judge Dade, and that he has accepted. This has spread extensively, perhaps from a general sense of his fitness, and I learn that it has been received with much favor, and particularly among the students of the University. I know no more myself of Judge Dade than what I saw of him at our Rockfish meeting, and a short visit he made me in returning from that place. As far as that cpportunity enabled me to form an opinion, I certainly thought very highly of the strength of his mind, and the soundness of his judgment. I happened to receive Mr. Gilmer's ultimate and peremptory refusal while Judge Stuart and Mr. Howe Peyton of Staunton were with me. The former, you know, is his colleague on the bench of the General Court; the latter has been more particularly intimate with him, as having been brought up with him at the same school. I asked from them information respecting Mr. Dade; and they spoke of him in terms of high commendation. They state him to be an excellent Latin and Greek scholar, of clear and sound ideas, lucid in communicating them, equal as a lawyer to any one of the judiciary corps, and superior to all as a writer; and that his character is perfectly correct, his mind liberal and accommodating, yet firm and of sound republican principles. * * * * * * * * This is the substance, and these, I may say, the terms in which they spoke of him; and when I considered the character of these two gentlemen, and their opportunities of knowing what they attested, I could not but be strongly impressed. It happened, very much to my gratification, that Gen. Cocke was here at the same time, received the same information and impression, and authorizes me to add his concurrence in proposing the appointment to our colleagues; and to say, moreover, that if on such further enquiry as they may make, they should approve the choice, and express it by letter, in preference to a meeting for a conference on this subject, I might write to Judge Dade; and, on his acceptance, issue his commission. I should add that the gentlemen above named, were confident he would accept, as well from other circumstances, as from his having three sons to educate. Of course, this would put an end to the anxieties we have all had on this subject. The public impatience for some appointment to this school, renders desirable as early an answer as your convenience admits. Accept the assurance of my great esteem and respect.

TH: JEFFERSON.

Mr. Cabell.

CXCVIII.

J. C. C. TO T. J.

NORFOLK, May 25, 1825.

DEAR SIR,—I arrived at this place yesterday, on my return from Lancaster, and have to-day had an interview with Mr. Loyall, in the course of which he showed me the copy which he had received of your circular of the 13th instant, relative to the nomination of Judge Dade as Professor of Law in the University. Considering it unnecessary to defer writing till my return home some two or three weeks hence, and believing that a prompt communication of my vote will be most acceptable to you, I now beg leave to convey to you the assurance of my sincere and entire approbation of the selection of Judge Dade. Having served with the Judge in the Senate of the State, I have had ample opportunities of forming an opinion of his character, talents and information, and I view them very much in the light in which they are represented in your circular. In the course of a few years, he will be an ornament to the institution. Indeed, I doubt whether, upon the whole, we should have done better in any of the appointments which we have successively contemplated. I am truly gratified to think that we shall have so faithful an expositor of the admirable text books on government selected by yourself and Mr. Madison.

I cannot describe the satisfaction which I feel in reflecting on the present prospects of the University. Our corps of Professors is full of youth, and talent, and energy. What will not such men accomplish, with such advantages? Like a fine steamboat on our noble Chesapeake, cutting her way at the rate of ten knots per hour, and leaving on the horizon all other vessels on the waters, the University will advance with rapid strides, and throw into the rear all the other seminaries of this vast continent. How can this State and nation ever repay you, my dear sir, for this great and good work! What must be your feelings in contemplating this precious work of your hands! How much more pure is the delight of having performed such deeds than that which Napoleon felt at Austerlitz or Marengo!*

I am happy to inform you that I have received at this place a long letter from my old friend Maclure,† written at Paris in the month of March, in which he expresses himself in terms of the highest respect and esteem for you, and desires to be particularly remembered to you. I am happy to find that he is at length coming home to spend the balance of his days on this and the Southern Continent. He will probably be a valuable friend to our mineralogical and geological collections. I shall not fail to enlist him heartily in the interests of the institution.

Faithfully yours,

JOSEPH C. CABELL.

Mr. Jefferson.

---

* This peculiar style of gratulation may be pardoned in one who had participated in the struggle without claiming any share of the triumph, and who had an abiding confidence that the wisdom of their policy would become more and more manifest with the lapse of years.

† This gentleman did return to the United States, and after a sojourn of some years, principally in the North Western States, retired to Mexico, in whose capital city he died in 184—. The University of Virginia received no aid from him; nor did Mr. C. ever again meet with the friend of his early years; but the latter sent him, as a memorial of other days, two volumes of his "Opinions" on various topics of Political Economy, Popular Education, &c., all strongly illustrative of the amiable and philanthropical character of the author.

CXCIX.

(CIRCULAR.)—T. J. TO J. C. C.

MONTICELLO, August 4, 1825.

DEAR SIR,—Chancellor Tucker, Mr. Barbour, Judge Carr, as you know, had declined accepting the law chair of the University, and yesterday I received a letter from Judge Dade, finally declining also. Mr. Gilmer, our first choice, had declined on account of his health, very much deranged by his voyage to Europe. That is now in a great degree re-established, and he is willing to accept. What shall we do? Shall we venture to our first choice, and be done with this difficulty? Or have a meeting and look out for some other? Or do nothing till October? The vacancy of this chair is very disadvantageous, being thought by many more wanting than all the others. If we agree to the re-appointment of Mr. Gilmer, perhaps you will signify it by letter, as in preceding cases, as discussion can promise nothing new on his subject.

Our last $50,000 were placed by the Treasurer in the Virginia Bank, and have been disposed of as follows:

$7,626 to replace so much advanced for books and apparatus by the General Fund.
6,000 to finish library room.
18,000 advanced to Hilliard to complete the library.
6,000 remitted to Mr. King, our minister in London, for philosophical apparatus.
3,000 do. do. do. do. anatomical. do.
500 paid to Dr. Emmet for chemical apparatus.
8,874 balance remaining.
50,000

Accept the assurance of my highest respect and esteem.

TH: JEFFERSON.

Mr. Cabell.

CC.

J. C. C. TO T. J.

EDGEWOOD, 19th August, 1825.

DEAR SIR,—Your favor of 4th instant reached me by the mail of last week. Shortly after it came to hand, I was called to Bremo on business, where I authorized Gen. Cocke, if he should reach Monticello before my regular written reply, to inform you that I should vote for the immediate appointment of Mr. Gilmer, as the Professor of Law. I am confident he would be appointed at the meeting in October, and the anticipation by your circular will give him a longer interval for preparation.

I am, dear sir,

Most respectfully and truly yours,

JOSEPH C. CABELL.

Mr. Jefferson.

CCI.

(CIRCULAR.)—T. J. TO J. C. C.

MONTICELLO, September 10, 1825.

DEAR SIR,—The state of my health renders it perfectly certain that I shall not be able to attend the next meeting of the Visitors (October 3) *at the University*. Yet I think there is no one but myself to whom the matters to be acted on are sufficiently known for communication to them. This adds a reason the more for inducing the members to meet at Monticello the day before, which has been heretofore found to facilitate and shorten our business. If you could be here then on the Sunday to dinner, that afternoon and evening and the morning of Monday, will suffice for all our business, and the Board will only have to ride to the University pro formâ for attesting the proceedings. Permit me, therefore, to expect you to dinner on that day, (October 2) which as it is ever grateful to me, seems on this occasion to be peculiarly urgent. Accept, I pray you, the assurance of my high and friendly esteem and respect.

TH: JEFFERSON.

Mr. Cabell.

CCII.

J. C. C. TO T. J.

RICHMOND, December 7, 1825.

DEAR SIR,—This will be presented to you by our frend Gen. Cocke, whom I am truly sorry not to accompany on his journey to Monticello. My brother-in-law, Dr. Carter, having departed this life on the 30th ultimo, leaving his affairs in a very embarrassed situation, it becomes necessary for some one of his surviving friends to attend at Lancaster court on the third Monday in this month, to qualify as his administrator, and forthwith to adopt measures to prevent the sacrifice of the property of his child. The estate would probably sustain great and irreparable injury from the want of immediate attention. I am called immediately to Williamsburg, to agree with his mother and Mr. Tucker, upon the selection of a suitable agent, and probably to hasten over to Lancaster to engage personally in these new and troublesome duties. I hope these circumstances will justify my absence from the meeting of the Visitors on Monday next. Believe me, that nothing but the strongest motives could induce me to be an absentee on this occasion; and I throw myself on the liberal and indulgent goodness of yourself and the other members of the board, well persuaded that you will excuse me on account of the urgent private duties by which I am called away. There will doubtless be a meeting without me.

I hope Mr. Johnson will not call up his resolution respecting the vacation in the lectures, as I would be glad to have further time to observe the practical operation of the present arrangement. Were I called on to vote on the question at this time I should be compelled to vote against the change, as calculated to jeopardize the interests of the institution in Eastern Virginia, and in the Southern States. But I would prefer further time to enquire and to reflect. I believe Mr. Loyall concurs in these views.

I return you thanks for the three copies of the enactments which I have just received. They are sought after with avidity and will doubtless be printed. I saw Dr. Cooper here on my way down the country. He seems to entertain great doubts of the practicability of establishing with success such a tribunal as Mr. Johnson contemplates. He suggested the expediency of enquiring into the legal powers of the civil magistrate to bind over or commit a man for refusing to give evidence against another charged upon mere suspicion. He expressed, however, the greatest interest in the experiment. I think the character of the University has risen exceedingly in the public estimation since the new regulations were adopted. From the short and hasty view which I have taken of the scene of legislation, I am of opinion that we may obtain, at this session, the money necessary to finish the buildings. If others will not ask for it, I will do it myself. I would be obliged to you for the requisite estimates, so as that I may be able to use them by the 1st January. In every thing which I may do on the subject, I should be happy to have your advice. You expressed the opinion, at the last meeting, that *we* (the Visitors) ought to ask for nothing, but should leave it to others to ask for us. But as we have asked so freely heretofore, perhaps others will wait for us; and if they should take this course, I think they should be gratified. I leave here this morning, and shall return by the 27th instant.

I remain, dear sir,

Faithfully your friend,

JOSEPH C. CABELL.

Mr. Jefferson.

CCIII.

[The few remaining letters of the series relate not solely to the great subject of Education, but in some measure to Mr. J.'s private affairs, which had now become hopelessly embarrassed—a liability from which no citizen can claim entire exemption under our peculiar institutions. The reflections to which this gives rise would be too painful, had not the facts been already given to the public through other channels. That under such pressure he should have been able to continue his efforts and counsels in behalf of the public interests with which he had been charged, must excite our admiration; and still more when we observe the dignity with which he bore up under reverses that would have crushed the spirit of many a younger and stouter man.]

T. J. TO J. C. C.

MONTICELLO, January 20, 1826.

DEAR SIR,—Under a different cover I send a circular on the subject of our Law Professor; and to save writing, which is laborious to me, I must pray my colleagues, on the Assembly, to consider the single copy as addressed equally to all.

My grandson, Thomas J. Randolph, attends the Legislature on a subject of ultimate importance to my future happiness. My own debts were considerable, and a loss was added to them of $20,000, by endorsement for a friend. My application to the Legislature is for permission to dispose of property for payment, in a way which, bringing a fair price for it, may pay my debts, and leave a living for myself in my old age, and leave something for my family. Their consent is necessary. It will injure no man, and few sessions pass without similar exercises of the same power in their discretion. But I refer you to my grandson for particular explanations. I think it just myself; and if it should appear so to you, I am sure, your friendship, as well as justice, will induce you to pay to it the attention which you may think the case will justify. To me it is almost a question of life or death.

Accept my friendly and respectful salutations,

TH: JEFFERSON.

Joseph C. Cabell, Esq.

CCIV.

J. C. C. TO T. J.

RICHMOND, 30th January, 1826.

DEAR SIR,—Your circular to Mr. Johnson, Mr. Loyall and myself, relative to the appointment of a successor to Mr. Gilmer, and your favor of 20th instant by your grandson, respecting the sale of your property, have both come safely to hand, and both commanded much of my attention.

Mr. Johnson was requested to write a reply in conformity to the results of a conference between himself, Mr. Loyall, Gen. Cocke and myself, on the subject of your circular. To that letter I will add one or two remarks. Were we now to appoint a Professor of Law, he would be unable to deliver a course of lectures during the present year; and yet the public would expect him to do so. He would be subject to the lash of public censure, either for not lecturing at all, or for delivering an imperfect course. If the appointment should not be made till the spring, the professor will not be expected to lecture till the end of the year. It is better to keep the place vacant for another year than to make a bad appointment, or to commence with inadequate preparation. I think I am duly sensible of the chief source of your apprehensions from delay; and will do my utmost to avert any appointment that would be disagreeable to you. I shall endeavor to secure the requisite co-operation. Such of the persons named in the list of names which you were good enough to forward, as are not predetermined not to accept, would not probably procure a majority of votes. Such is the impression which I have received from what I have seen and heard from the Visitors in town. I have conversed very freely with Judges Carr and Green, and find both inflexible. Mr. John T. Lomax, of Fredericksburg, is very strongly recommended by Judge Brooke and others. * * * * * * * * * I will give you further information as soon as possible.

You have probably heard of the repulse which Mr. Taylor has met with in the House of Delegates. I hope it will not have a very injurious effect. I confess I was this time very much deceived—which is ascribable to my having been drawn from town by the death of my brother-in-law. All sorts of opposition were introduced on this occasion. The business was not conducted with entire prudence. The college interest is now strong and importunate. The bill respecting William & Mary was sent by me to all the proposed sites, and it has had a great effect over the country. It has alarmed certain interests and awakened new energy. The general interests will ultimately triumph. Probably nothing can be done this session; but a year or two will bring all to rights. There is already a considerable re-action; but it is uncertain whether any new effort ought to be made this session. Some think we could succeed by combining with the colleges, but I will not consent to any compromise that will commit us to a bad system. We all think that the subject of the University should lie till your other subject is disposed of.

I assure you I was truly distressed to receive your letter of the 20th, and to hear the embarrassed state of your affairs. You may rely on my utmost exertions. Your grandson proposed that the first conference should be held at the Eagle. I prevailed on him to remove the scene to Judge Carr's, and to invite all the Judges of the Court of Appeals. Mr. Coalter and my brother were unable to attend; but all the court is with you. Mr. Johnson agreed to draw the bill. I am cooperating as far as lies in my power. I wish complete justice could be done on this occasion; but we have to deal with men as they are. Your grandson will no doubt give you the fullest information. I will occasionally inform you how matters are progressing. In the meantime,

I remain very truly and sincerely yours,

JOSEPH C. CABELL.

Mr. Jefferson.

CCV.

J. C. C. TO T. J.

RICHMOND, 3d February, 1826.

DEAR SIR,—Your intended application to the Legislature has excited much discussion in private circles in Richmond. Your grandson will doubtless give you a full account of passing occurrences. A second conference was held at Mr. Baker's last evening; at which were four of the Judges of the Court of Appeals, and several members of the Legislature. Finding considerable opposition in some of your political friends to the lottery, and feeling mortified myself that the State should stop short at so limited a measure, I suggested the idea of a loan of $80,000, free of interest, from the State, during the remainder of your life. On consultation, our friends decided that it would be impracticable. At the conference of last evening, it was unanimously decided to bring forward and support the lottery. I hear there will be considerable opposition; but I hope it is exaggerated. I do not think that delay would be injurious, as in every case I have found the first impression the worst. Would to God that I had the power to raise the mind of the Legislature to a just conception of its duties on the present occasion. Knowing, so well as I do, how much you have done for us, I have some idea of what we ought to do for you.

Mr. Garland has started a project of dispersing our college funds over the twenty-four senatorial districts. It will have many advocates. I hope, however, it may be rejected or amended. We had better lose the $25,000 for the University, than waste all our college funds on an improper system.

I am, dear sir, very truly yours,

JOSEPH C. CABELL.

Mr. Jefferson.

CCVI.

T. J. TO J. C. C.

MONTICELLO, February 4, 1826.

DEAR SIR,—I received yesterday the joint letter of our colleagues of January 26, and your separate one of the 30th. The vote of the House of Delegates was too decisive to leave any further expectations from that quarter, or doubt of the necessity of winding up our affairs, and ascertaining their ground. I went immediately to the University, and advised the proctor to engage in no new matter which could be done without; to stop every thing unessential in hand; and to reserve all his funds for the book-room of the rotunda, and the anatomical theatre. Till the latter is in a condition for use there can never be a dissection of a single subject; nor until the book-room and cases be completely done can we open another box of books. We have now five boxes on hand from Paris, unopened, five more from the same place are supposed to be arrived in Richmond, seven from London are arrived at Boston, and a part of those from Germany are now in Boston. All these, and others still to arrive, must remain unopened until the room is ready, which unfortunately cannot be till the season will admit of plastering; and the joiner's work goes on so slow that it is doubtful if that will be ready as soon. The arresting all avoidable expense is the more necessary, as our application to Congress for a remission of duties ($3,000) has passed the Committee of Claims by a majority of a single vote only, and has still a long gauntlet to run. We have, however, one certain supplementary resource for present purposes, in the rents for dormitories and the other buildings. I learnt yesterday, from the proctor, that about 130 students were arrived, of which two-thirds were new comers, that there are still about 60 old ones to arrive, who had engaged for another year; and if the same proportion of new comers should still come in, it would make upwards of 300, whose rents, with those of the hotels, would amount to $7,444. I doubt, however, whether Charlottesville can accommodate the 84 in addition to our 216. They seem confident they can, and are making great exertions.

Whatever fund may be contemplated for the intermediate colleges, I should be sorry to see any of it diverted from the impartial and general object. I know no principle of distribution which can be adopted for the second grade of schools, but that of placing one within a day's ride of every man—say in districts of about 80 miles square below the North mountain, which would give them seven, and leave three for the sparse population beyond that, which would be done by your bill. If the $155,000 remaining of the payment by Congress be applied to this object, it will give $10,000 to each of these; one-third of which will be enough for their buildings, and an interest of $400 a year will remain for two tutors, in aid of the tuition fees. I do not think these colleges will have more than 30 pupils each. Twenty-four such schools as proposed by Mr. Garland, with $5000 each, would not have enough to do more than maintain one Connecticut teacher. On our plan there would remain $55,000 to enlarge the University accommodations, and put that by its increased rents on a footing to carry itself on forever, without ever needing the aid of another dollar from the public.

I hope you have not lost sight of the annual tabular report of the primary schools, necessary as a preliminary to perfect that branch of the general system of education.

Ever and affectionately yours,

TH: JEFFERSON.

Mr. Cabell.

CCVII.

T. J. TO J. C. C.

MONTICELLO, February 7, 1826.

DEAR SIR,—I received yesterday your kind letter of the 2d, and am truly sensible of the interest you are so good as to take in my affairs. I had hoped the length and character of my servies might have prevented the fear in the Legislature of the indulgence asked being quoted as a precedent in future cases. But I find no fault with their strict adherence to a rule generally useful, although relaxable in some cases under their discretion, of which they are the proper judges. If it can be yielded in my case, I can save the house of Monticello and a farm adjoining to end my days in and bury my bones. If not, I must sell house and all here, and carry my family to Bedford, where I have not even a log hut to put my head into. In any case, I wish nothing from the treasury. The pecuniary compensations I have received for my services, from time to time, have been fully to my own satisfaction.

I have been very much mortified by the publication, in the Enquirer of the 4th, of two letters from some person called an "American Citizen," who seems to have visited Mr. Madison and myself, and has undertaken to state private conversations with us. In one of these he makes me declare that I had intentionally proceeded in a course of dupery of our Legislature, teazing them, as he makes me say, for six or seven sessions, for successive aids to the University, and asking a part only at a time, and intentionally concealing the ultimate cost, and gives an inexact statement of a story of Obrian. Now, our annual reports will shew that we constantly gave full and candid accounts of the money expended, and statements of what might still be wanting, founded on the Proctor's estimates. No man ever heard me speak of the grants of the Legislature, but with acknowledgments of their liberality, which I have always declared had gone far beyond what I could have expected in the beginning. Yet the letter-writer has given to my expressions an aspect disrespectful of the Legislature, and calculated to give them offence, which I do absolutely disavow. The writer is called an American Citizen. It is evident, if he be so, that he is an adopted one only, who, after calling on us in his travels through the country, as a stranger, may have obtained naturalization and settled in Philadelphia, where he is enjoying the society of the Bonapartes, &c. The familiar style of his letter to his friend in England, and the communication of it to the Literary Gazette there, indicate sufficiently his foreign birth and connections. I can not express to you the pain which this unfaithful version and betrayment of private conversation has given me. I feel what it will add to the disfavor I had incurred with a large portion of the Legislature by my strenuous labors for the establishment of the University, to which they were opposed, insomuch as to let it overweigh whatever of satisfaction former services had given them. I have been long sensible that while I was endeavoring to render our country the greatest of all services, that of regenerating the public education, and placing our rising generation on the level of our sister States (which they have proudly held heretofore), I was discharging the odious function of a physician pouring medicine down the throat of a patient insensible of needing it. I am so sure of the future approbation of posterity, and of the inestimable effect we shall have produced in the elevation of our country by what we have done, as that I cannot repent of the part I have borne in co-operation with my colleagues. I disclaim the honors which this writer (among the other errors he has interlarded with the truths of his letters) has ascribed to me, of having made liberal donations of timber and stone from my own estate, and of having paid all the contracts for materials myself, and I restore them to their true source, the liberal legislators of our country. My pain at these false praises and representations should merit with them an acquittal of any supposed approbation of them by myself.

Ever and affectionately yours,

TH: JEFFERSON.

Mr. Cabell.

CCVIII.

J. C. C. TO T. J.

RICHMOND, 8th February, 1826.

DEAR SIR,—Your favor of the 4th instant has arrived, and has been read with the greatest interest by myself and the friends to whom I have shewn it. Mr. Garland's scheme of twenty-four colleges, in my view, is pregnant with mischief. The only way to defeat it is to present to the House a better plan in lieu of it. My mind has been on the wing for some days, and a view of this most important subject has occurred to me, which I beg to lay before you for your immediate consideration. If you should approve it, I must solicit your immediate co-operation. It appears to me that the plan of location and distribution of the colleges, presented by your bill of 1817–18, is decidedly preferable to that of the bill of last winter. In that first bill you looked only to the people of Virginia, without taking any notice of the old colleges. Experience and reflection convinced me that this was the wisest course that you could have adopted. It is almost impossible to weave them into any good system; and they will never consent to give up their charters. Why, then, should we embarrass ourselves with them? Let us let them alone, and ask them to let us alone. In departing from William & Mary as the pivot, we were led into errors. The arrangement then proposed left the South-west and South-east too naked, and gave the Valley too much; it also threw the colleges into the towns instead of the country. As the funds were to come out of the old college, we were fettered in the system for the whole

State. Looking now to the literary fund as the source of our means, can we not consistently revert to your first arrangement? I think we can. The college party will not wait for William & Mary to come again; they will act and drive the country into action; and we must provide the means with as small a draft as possible on our funds, with a view both to the University and the elementary schools. We must adapt our means to the prevailing opinions respecting the literary fund, which are opposed to the expenditure of the capital. The question draws near to us, and we are expected to present a plan for the consideration and support of our friends. Probably there is yet time for me to hear from you before the decision is called for. I propose that we should unite in support of your first bill of 1817–18, with this alteration, that the local districts shall be required to contribute the necessary lands and buildings, as a condition of the public contribution, and that the latter should be an annual sum out of the surplus revenue of the literary fund, and limited to the support of professors, of whom there should be eventually at least two, one of languages, the other of philosophy. The details of the bill should be altered so as to suit this outline. A salary of $500 each is universally admitted to be adequate to the object. The complete establishment of the nine colleges would cost the State $9,000 only. The institutions might, however, commence with only one salary, viz: $4,500 in the whole, or even with a smaller amount. I am perfectly convinced that the requisite lands and buildings would be contributed by the local population *in every instance.* We would only have to prescribe some reasonable limit to the discretion of the commissioners in departing from the exact central situations. The competition that would arise between the two or three central counties would ensure success. By this process we should double our funds without oppressing any one. We might now commence the whole system, and give 25 or 32,000 to the University. The estimated surplus for the ensuing year is $6,000, and the fund is fast increasing. What a scene of glorious enterprise would not this exhibit? The country gentlemen, to whom I have mentioned it, seem greatly pleased with it, and think there is no inherent difficulty. There will be great opposition, and probably we cannot carry it now; but in many points of view the effort would, in my opinion, be prudent. * * * * * * * * * * * Some wish to keep the whole subject back for another session, and then to push the college question foremost. We have only one plain object, the good of the whole, by the shortest possible route; and we owe it to ourselves and the country to suggest the most perfect plan, and only to submit to compromise when it becomes unavoidable. The influence of this town is prodigious. I would prefer to conciliate it, if possible; but, if it be necessary, we must have its opposition. If you should approve these views, I would be extremely thankful to you if you would change your first bill in the manner proposed and send me the new bill with as little delay as possible. Lest you may not have a copy at hand, I send you a copy of my pamphlet, in which you will find both the bills. Any provisions in the last bill, or which further reflection may suggest to you as coming under the class of improvements on the original, would be acceptable, provided they should leave the outline proposed. If you should disapprove the scheme, you will be good enough to inform me to that effect. The state of things at the University is enough to awaken the renewed patronage of the Legislature; but the sources of hostility to the institution are not to be dried up by success. On the contrary, success inflames the opposition of certain classes. The march of the system of public instruction is hateful to your enemies.

Mr. Loyall made a motion on the subject of your lottery bill to-day. It was laid on the table by a vote of 95 to 94. This vote is not at all indicative of the sense of the House on the main question. I have no doubt the bill will pass.

I am, dear sir, most sincerely yours,

JOSEPH C. CABELL.

Mr. Jefferson.

CCIX.

J. C. C. TO T. J.

RICHMOND, February 10th, 1826.

DEAR SIR,—Your favor of 7th inst. has this moment been received. I was already sitting down to add to my last letter. I am distressed to inform you that leave was given on yesterday to bring in your bill by a majority of only four. I was out among my friends last evening, and I learn from them that there is no doubt of its passage, but that the majority will be considerably less than we lately expected. I think the discussion in the House will be favorable to the measure. I wished to bring forward a stronger measure; not because you wished it, but because a regard to ourselves required it; in this I was assured I could not succeed, and I reluctantly abandoned the plan. I blush for my country, and am humiliated to think how we shall appear on the page of history. As I suppose your grandson writes you very often and very fully on this subject, I will pass to the main subject of my last—the best collegiate system for the State.

My continued reflections confirm me in the views expressed in my last letter, insomuch that I earnestly beseech you to alter the bill in the manner proposed, and to send it down as soon as possible. From conversations held on yesterday with the members of the Senate, I am disposed to think two-thirds of the body would support the scheme. It will be necessary to adopt guards in the bill against imposition in regard to the lands and buildings. Every little academy in the State will desire to be selected. We can get new and good buildings, and as much land as we could desire. I leave to your better judgment what quantity of land should be required, or whether a discretion in this respect should be reposed in the Literary Board. Near towns and villages, the same quantity as in rural sites would perhaps be an oppressive requisition. I would fix in the bill the maximum appropriation to each and all the colleges; I think $1,000 each, or $9,000 to all, per annum, would be enough. This would give two salaries of $500 to two professors; these, with the fees, would be competent, I should suppose. A simple provision that the surplus revenue of the literary fund should be appropriated and equally divided among the nine colleges till it should reach the sum of $9,000 per annum, would be sufficient. The surplus revenue is now appropriated to colleges generally till it reaches $20,000 per annum. The plan proposed would relieve the fund to the amount of $11,000 per annum in future times. The College of Hampden Sidney might apply for the location in the district where it is situated. Or, perhaps it would be better to legislate specially, by separate bill, as to that college, giving it an annuity revocable at the will of the Legislature, and leaving its charter as it is. The other two colleges want nothing. I think we ought to take no notice of them in our bill; and their open avowal not to come under the control of the State, is a sufficient justification. If the friends of Hampden Sidney should be strong enough to force it into the bill, we must make the best terms we can. I would wish to do something for that institution; it has been and will be useful; and is supported by a most respectable population. But we should never lose sight of the whole State, and do nothing for a part that will mar the entire scheme. I would recommend that no notice be taken of any particular institution in the bill, except the University. To that I would propose an appropriation of $32,000, viz: the $25,000 mentioned in our report to the Legislature, and $6,000 added thereto to replace the sum borrowed from the library fund to finish the library room. Or, if you think it better, we might ask for the exact sum mentioned in our report, saying nothing of the $6,000. Taking out the $25,000, there would remain a sufficient surplus to start all the colleges with one salary of $450—the local population giving the lands and buildings, and the students the fees. These colleges would all, upon this plan, be fully endowed in five years from this time. They would be the best friends of the University. The old colleges would be left unmolested. As to William & Mary, we might, if the country should so desire, give her a roving commission. But upon that question we need not give any opinion, but leave it for future adjustment. What is to prevent the success of this scheme! Nothing but private and local interests in the House of Delegates. Perhaps this will be the result. But we should not lose by the suggestion; for the people would every where see that we were looking home to them, and moving towards them with a firm and consistent march. We would get the intelligent farmers on our side. And the friends of the primary schools would see an end speedily approaching to the appropriations to the higher seminaries, and that our system would soon embrace the whole body of the people. Some have thought that the Governor and Council would be a better body to decide on the locations and grants than the Literary Board. Great and powerful interests in the State will co-operate with local and selfish interests to break down this project. But I am in hopes we may be able to carry it sooner or later. I have not time to write to both yourself and Mr. Madison; but presume that you and he understand each other's views. Until I hear from you, I shall be entirely engaged in endeavoring to prepare the necessary support for the bill. I enclose Mr. Pictet's letter, which I have received from Mr. Madison and shewn to Mr. Johnson and Mr. Loyall. Your last letter will have a considerable effect. I shall confer with your friends as to the best mode of using it.

Faithfully your friend,

JOSEPH C. CABELL.

Mr. Jefferson

CCX.

T. J. TO J. C. C.

MONTICELLO, February 14, 1826.

DEAR SIR,—Your two favors of the 8th and 10th were received yesterday, and I will endeavor to get this into the mail which is to be closed this evening. If they have not cheered me in all things, they greatly do it in the prospect they hold up of succeeding in our intermediate plan of schools. But I am sorry you waited a moment to consult me on the subject, and the more so as it finds me under a severe relapse, and during a paroxysm of pain, rendering impossible all attention of the mind to any thing but aggravated suffering. This, however, occurs to me at once, that I always considered the first plan as far the best, but the second the only one which could be obtained from the local interests it enlisted. I remember, too, that the second bill was copied from the first *verbatim;* except in the mutations of place, and the changes which these called for. Obvious as these are, they are still such as under my present pain are beyond my powers, but you can make them yourself in a few minutes. Lay them side by side, and comparing section by section, the changes in the second will present themselves at once for rejection. The remaining sections of both will be found *verbatim* the same; unless here and there a word may have occurred in the second, or a phrase or idea better than had occurred in the first. Other changes for the better may also occur to yourself. Some, indeed, are specified in your letter, and in general I approve of all your new suggestions. Pray then do not wait a moment, but drive at once the nail which you find will go. As to the quantity of ground necessary, if each professor and the steward has a curtilage, garden, pasture, and orchard, it is enough. The printing your pamphlet was all-important. The reasoning of the "Friend of Science" cannot be answered. My letter too of September 17, must be felt. Equal right, the principle of the first bill, is the polar star to be followed.

Whatever may be the sentence to be pronounced in my particular case, the efforts of my friends are so visible, the impressions so profoundly sunk to the bottom of my heart, that they can never be obliterated. They plant there a consolation which countervails whatever other indications might seem to import. The report of the Committee of Finance, particularly, is balm to my soul. Thanks to you all, and warm and affectionate acknowledgments. I count on nothing now. I am taught to know my standard, and have to meet with no further disappointment.

TH: JEFFERSON.

Mr. Cabell.

CCXI.

J. C. C. TO T. J.

RICHMOND, February 15, 1826.

DEAR SIR,—The publication of the extract from your last letter to me, was made with the approbation of Judge Carr, and I hope will not be disagreeable to you, as I am sure it will produce a very good effect. The Lottery Bill was not taken up to-day. It has gained ground for some days past, and I have no doubt will pass, but not without a large minority. We have a wayward house to deal with, but I hope you will not suffer these things to depress you; for *we* are to be injured by them, not yourself. If it be in your power, I wish you would alter your bill in the mode proposed, and send it to me. The idea of making the districts give the lands is very popular. On this plan we can now give $25,000 to finish the University, and a salary of $500 to each of the nine colleges. The Senator from the S. W. corner of the State is much dissatisfied with his district, as the centre is in high mountains. But what is to be done? We cannot give the trans-Alleghany country three, and the Kanawha Valley must be postponed for the present. I think there is judgment in proposing *now* the same arrangement you did formerly. I like much the idea of having one near the University, as a preparatory school.

Yours, most sincerely,

JOSEPH C. CABELL.

Mr. Jefferson.

J. C. C. TO T. J.

CCXII.

SENATE CHAMBER, 20th February, 1826.

DEAR SIR,—On the next page you will find the vote of the Senate on the passage of your bill. Of the four Senators who voted against it, two were carried off by their aversion to lotteries. The bill was committed at 12. I asked leave for the Committee to sit during the session of the House. We reported at 1, and passed the bill *instanter*. If the House of Delegates had not adjourned on account of the death of a member, the passage of the bill would have been communicated by special message. It is now a law of the land.* I sin-

---

* [The General Assembly having granted the lottery for the better disposition of Mr. Jefferson's property, measures for carrying it promptly into effect were initiated in Richmond, at a public meeting of citizens favorable to the object, who also recommended similar meetings in the different counties. Resolutions were drawn up with this view by Mr. Cabell in Nelson; but owing to a present indisposition in the author, were offered by another and adopted at a conference of citizens in Lovingston, June 26, 1826. A Committee to obtain subscriptions was appointed, and the members were moving with an activity that promised success, when, in a few days, intelligence of the death of Mr. Jefferson reached them, and suspended their proceedings. The preamble of that paper is given here, to show that the efforts of Mr. Cabell to serve his revered friend were continued to the last.]

The undersigned citizens of Nelson county, concurring cordially in the views lately expressed by their fellow-citizens at the seat of government, and heartily sympathising in the sentiments of grateful respect and affectionate regard recently evinced both there and elsewhere, for their countryman, Thomas Jefferson, cannot disguise the sincere satisfaction which they derive from the prospect of a general co-operation to relieve this aged and distinguished patriot. The important services for which we are indebted to Mr. Jefferson, from the days of his youth, when he drew upon himself the resent-

cerely wish your health may be better than it was when you last wrote me. I have prepared, as you suggested in your last, an Amendatory Act relative to the colleges, which has been approved by all to whom I have shown it. In this number are included four out of five of the Judges of the Court of Appeals. I shall wait on Mr. Taylor to-morrow, and ask him to introduce it. Your former collegiate bill is the basis of the plan. I fear it is too late in the session to carry it. I will, however, get it printed, and pave the way for future success, should we fail now.*

I am, dear sir, ever faithfully yours,

JOSEPH C. CABELL.

Mr. Jefferson.

Ayes.—Johnson of Petersburg, Goodwyn, Allen, Brown, Dade, Fry, Tom, Sharp, Cabell, Martin, Saunders, Jones, Holt—13.

Noes.—Ruffin, McCarty, Morgan, Armistead—4.

---

ment of Dunmore, to the present time, when, at the close of a long life, he is laboring to enlighten the nation which he has contributed to make free, place him in the highest rank of national benefactors, and eminently entitle him to the character of the people's friend. Whether considered as the servant of the State, or of the United States; whether regarded as an advocate or a statesman; whether as a patriot, a legislator, a philosopher, or a friend of liberty and republican government, he is the unquestioned ornament of his country, and unites in himself every title to our respect, our veneration and gratitude. His services are written in the hearts of a grateful people; they are identified with the fundamental institutions of his country; they entitle him to "the fairest page of faithful history;" and will be remembered as long as liberty and science are respected on earth. Profoundly impressed with these sentiments, the undersigned citizens of Nelson county consider it compatible with neither the national character nor with the gratitude of the Republic, that this aged patriot should be deprived of his estate, or abridged in his comforts, at the close of a long life so ably spent in the service of his country. Therefore,

1. *Resolved,* That the resolutions relative to Thomas Jefferson, recently adopted by the citizens of Richmond and Manchester, meet the cordial approbation of the undersigned citizens of Nelson county, &c.

* A copy of this proposed bill is given in Appendix P. It was presented to the House, but failed this session, partly through the opposition of the professed friends of the Primary Schools, partly on the alleged ground that Mr.

CCXIII.

(CIRCULAR.)—T. J. TO J. C. C.

MONTICELLO, April 21, 1826.

DEAR SIR,—Mr. Wirt declined the offices proposed to him.* Mr. Lomax has accepted the Professorship of Law, and will open his school on the first of July. He has paid us a visit, and his appointment appears to have given the highest degree of satisfaction to every body, professors, students, neighbors, and to none more than myself. We have now 166 students; and, on the opening of the law school, we expect to have all our dormitories filled. Order and industry nearly complete, and sensibly improving every day.

Affectionately yours,

TH: JEFFERSON.

Mr. Cabell.

Cabell's estimates of the cost of erecting and maintaining such an establishment was much too low. To rebut this argument, he devoted a part of his leisure to drawing a "Plan for a small college." Such as was contemplated by the bill. This was elaborated with great care and in minute detail, and when examined convinced many who had doubted before. It was Mr. C's. wish that an experiment should be tried with a single one, which, if successful, might serve as a model for others in those parts of the State where they were most required. But the plan was loaned to a friend, and in passing from his hands to others was lost. Frequent applications were made to him afterwards for the loan of it, and by several with a view of again trying its fortune before the Legislature; but after diligent enquiry he was unable to recover it, and never found leisure for its re-production, before his attention became absorbed by another great public interest—the uniting of the Eastern and Western waters of the State. The subsequent multiplication of colleges and academies in Virginia has also superseded the necessity of such an establishment.

* These were the *Presidency* of the University united with the Professorship of Law. (See Kennedy's Life of Wirt, II. 207–9.) The former post having been created as an additional inducement to his acceptance of the other, and declined by him, the arrangement was rescinded; and the institution has never had any permanent head, the ordinary duties of a President devolving on the "Chairman of the Faculty" for the time-being, who is annually re elected.

APPENDIX.

A.

We, John Harris, John Nicholas, John Kelly, Peter Carr and John Carr, five of those appointed trustees by the act of the General Assembly entitled "an act to establish an academy in the county of Albemarle, and for other purposes," having met at the house of Triplett T. Estes, in the town of Charlottesville, on the 25th day of March, 1814, for the purpose of taking into consideration the said recited act, and there not appearing a majority, as by the said act is required, have agreed, in order to fill such vacancies as have occurred by deaths, resignations and removals, to nominate the following citizens, to wit: Thomas Jefferson, Jonathan B. Carr, Robert B. Streshley, James Leitch, Edmund Anderson, Thomas Wells, Nicholas M. Lewis, Frank Carr, John Winn, Alexander Garrett, Dabney Minor, Samuel Carr and Thomas Jameson, to fill such vacancies; and whenever the concurrence of one other of the trustees named in the said recited act shall concur in the said nomination, they shall be considered as duly appointed as trustees for the purpose of carrying the said recited act into execution, and a general meeting is recommended at the house of Triplett T. Estes, in the town of Charlottesville, on the fifth day of the next month.

(Signed,)

JOHN HARRIS,
JOHN NICHOLAS,
JOHN KELLY,
P. CARR,
JOHN CARR,
EDWARD GARLAND.

Agreeable to the recommendation of the 25th of March last past, on this 5th day of April, 1814, appeared at the place appointed, Thomas Jefferson, Jonathan B. Carr, Robert B. Streshley, James Leitch, Edmund Anderson, Thomas Wells, Nicholas M. Lewis, Frank Carr, John Winn, Alexander Garrett, Peter Carr, Edward Garland, John Kelly, John Nicholas, Rice Garland, Samuel Carr, Thomas Jameson and John Carr, and the nomination made on the 25th of March last having been duly approved of by Edward Garland, making a majority of the remaining Trustees under the act aforesaid—

Whereupon, the said Trustees proceeded to elect their President and Secretary. Peter Carr was chosen President and John Carr Secretary.

On motion to designate the place where the proposed establishment shall be made, the determination thereof is postponed until the 15th day of the present month.

A committee, consisting of the following members, to wit: Thomas Jefferson, Peter Carr, Frank Carr, John Nicholas and Alexander Garrett, were chosen to draft rules and regulations for the government of the proposed institution.

The same committee are instructed to report to the next meeting a plan for raising funds for the erection and support of the said institution; and thereupon the meeting is adjourned till the 15th instant, at the house of Triplett T. Estes.

(Signed,) P. CARR.

At a meeting of the Trustees of the Albemarle Academy, held at the house of Triplett T. Estes, Charlottesville, the 15th day of April, 1814, agreeable to adjournment:

Present—Peter Carr, President, Thomas Jameson, Frank Carr, Jonathan B. Carr, Robert B. Streshley, James Leitch, John Kelly, John Nicholas, John Winn, John Carr and Edmund Anderson. The number present consisting of a bare majority, and it being desirable that a full Board should be had to take into consideration the important subjects submitted to the committee appointed at the last meeting: It is therefore ordered, that the sitting be adjourned till Tuesday, the 3d day of May next.

P. CARR, *Pres't.*

At a meetlng of the Trustees of the Albemarle Academy, held at the house of Triplett T. Estes, the 3d day of May, 1814, agreeable to adjournment:

Present—Peter Carr, President, John Harris, Dabney Minor, Thomas Wells, Samuel Carr, John Kelly, John Winn, Rice Garland, John Nicholas, Robert B. Streshley, Jonathan B. Carr, Frank Carr, Thomas Jameson, James Leitch and Edmund Anderson.

Wilson C. Nicholas, by letter dated 2d May, 1814, declines acting as a trustee of the Academy. Nimrod Bramham was chosen to fill the vacancy occasioned by the resignation of the said Wilson C. Nicholas, and the Secretary is ordered to inform the said Bramham of his appointment.

The committee appointed by an order of the Board made the 5th day of April, 1814, to draft rules and regulations for the government of the proposed Academy, and who were directed also to report on the ways and means of raising funds for the establishment and support of the institution, this day made a report in these words, to wit: "The committee appointed," &c., which, being submitted to the consideration of the Board, was unanimously adopted.

The Board then proceeded to appoint a committee to carry into effect that article of the report which relates to the management of the lottery, when John Winn, John Kelly, James Leitch, Frank Carr and Alexander Garrett were elected for that purpose.

The Board then proceeded to elect a Treasurer and President of the Board of Managers of the Lottery, when John Kelly was chosen.

Dabney Minor, Thomas Wells and Edmund Anderson were elected a committee to open subscriptions agreeable to that article of the report of the committee on this subject.

Thomas Jefferson, Thomas M. Randolph and Peter Carr were elected a committee to draft petitions to the next Assembly asking an appropriation of the money arising from the sale of the glebe lands for the benefit of the institution.

Adjourned till the third Friday in June next.

P. CARR, *Pres't.*

Teste—JNO. CARR, *Sec'y.*

At a meeting of the Board of Trustees of the Albemarle Academy, at Charlottesville, the 17th June, 1814:

In the absence of the Secretary, Frank Carr was nominated and appointed as Secretary.

On motion made and seconded, the scheme of a lottery heretofore reported to the Board was amended by the adoption of the following substitute:

Resolved, That a committee of five, to wit: John Winn, James Leitch, John Nicholas, Frank Carr and Alexander Garrett be appointed to view the different situations in the county of Albemarle for the purpose of locating the Albemarle Academy, and to enquire into the relative expense of building on the best and most economical plan, and of purchasing a situation already improved; and that they report their reasons at large in favor of the situation to which they give the preference.

Ordered, that the Board adjourn till the meeting in course.

P. CARR, *Pres't.*

At a stated meeting of the Trustees of the Albemarle Academy, held at the house of Triplett T. Estes, in Charlottesville, the 19th day of August, 1814:

Present—Peter Carr, President, Thomas Jefferson, Dabney Minor, John Winn, Thomas Wells, Rice Garland, Alexander Garrett, Jonathan B. Carr, Robert B. Streshley, Nicholas M. Lewis, James Leitch, Edward Garland, John Nicholas, John Kelly, Samuel Carr and John Carr.

The committee to whom was referred the subject of location, made a report in these words, to wit:

"The committee to whom was referred the resolution of the Board of Trustees of the Albemarle Academy of the 17th of June, 1814, relative to the location of said Academy, have had the same under consideration, and thereupon agreed to the following report:

"Your committee have viewed the different sites on which it would be advisable to locate the Academy in the town of Charlottesville and its vicinity, and in their opinion it would be most advisable to locate the same in the vicinity of the town, distant not more than one-half mile, provided such location, building, &c. would not cost the institution more than a situation in town already improved suitable to the purpose. To form some idea of the probable cost of improving a site in the vicinity of the town, your committee beg leave to submit the annexed plan, and recommend its adoption by the Board as one best suited to the purpose, provided the work can be completed according to the terms of the estimate.

"Your committee have in vain attempted to ascertain the cost of a site unimproved in the vicinity of town, not being able to propose any particular terms of purchase, there being no funds at present at command of the Board of Trustees; they therefore beg of the Board to indulge the committee in a report on this part of the said resolution until a fund shall have been raised necessary to the purchase of such site. When this shall be accomplished, your committee will then be enabled to propose the terms of purchase with certainty, and the proprietors of the sites enabled to make proposals of sale accordingly.

"All of which is respectfully submitted.

"John Winn,
"James Leitch,
"John Nicholas,
"Alex. Garrett.

"19*th August*, 1814."

Which report is ordered to be recorded.

It is ordered and directed, that the President of the Board cause notice to be given in the public prints, according to law, that a petition will be presented to the next General Assembly praying an appropriation of the money arising from the sale of the glebes to the benefit of the Academy.

The meeting is now adjourned till the third Friday in November next.

P. Carr.

B.

A LETTER FROM THOMAS JEFFERSON TO THE LATE PETER CARR,

Originally published in the Enquirer.

MONTICELLO, September 7th, 1814.

DEAR SIR,—On the subject of the academy or college proposed to be established in our neighborhood, I promised the trustees that I would prepare for them a plan, adapted, in the first instance, to our slender funds, but susceptible of being enlarged, either by their own growth or by accession from other quarters.

I have long entertained the hope that this, our native State, would take up the subject of education, and make an establishment, either with or without incorporation into that of William & Mary, where every branch of science, deemed useful at this day, should be taught in its highest degree. With this view, I have lost no occasion of making myself acquainted with the organization of the best seminaries in other countries, and with the opinions of the most enlightened individuals, on the subject of the sciences worthy of a place in such an institution. In order to prepare what I have promised our trustees, I have lately revised these several plans with attention; and I am struck with the diversity of arrangement observable in them—no two alike. Yet, I have no doubt that these several arrangements have been the subject of mature reflection, by wise and learned men, who, contemplating local circumstances, have adapted them to the condition of the section of society for which they have been framed. I am strengthened in this conclusion by an examination of each separately, and a conviction that no one of them, if adopted without change, would be suited to the circumstances and pursuit of our country. The example they have set, then, is authority for us to select from their different institutions the materials which are good *for us*, and, with them, to erect a structure, whose arrangement shall correspond with our own social condition, and shall admit of enlargement in proportion to the encouragement it may merit and receive. As I may not be able to attend the meetings of the trustees, I will make you the depository of my ideas on the subject, which may be corrected, as you proceed, by the better view of others, and adapted, from time to time, to the prospects which open upon us, and which cannot be specifically seen and provided for.

In the first place, we must ascertain with precision the object of our institution, by taking a survey of the general field of science, and marking out the portion we mean to occupy at first, and the ultimate extension of our views beyond that, should we be enabled to render it, in the end, as comprehensive as we would wish.

1. Elementary Schools.

It is highly interesting to our country, and it is the duty of its functionaries, to provide that every citizen in it should receive an education proportioned to the condition and pursuits of his life. The mass of our citizens may be divided into two classes—the laboring and the learned. The laboring will need the first grade of education to qualify them for their pursuits and duties; the learned will need it as a foundation for further acquirements. A plan was formerly proposed to the Legislature of this State for laying off every county into hundreds or wards of five or six miles square, within each of which should be a school for the education of the children of the ward, wherein they should receive three years' instruction gratis, in reading, writing, arithmetic, as far as fractions, the roots and ratios, and geography. The Legislature, at one time, tried an ineffectual expedient for introducing this plan, which having failed, it is hoped they will some day resume it in a more promising form.

2. General Schools.

At the discharging of the pupils from the elementary schools, the two classes separate—those destined for labor will engage in the business of agriculture, or enter into apprenticeships to such handicraft art as may be their choice; their companions, destined to the pursuits of science, will proceed to the college, which will consist, 1st, of General Schools; and 2d, of Professional Schools. The General Schools will constitute the second grade of education.

The learned class may still be subdivided into two sections; 1, Those who are destined for learned professions, as a means of livelihood; and 2, The wealthy, who, possessing independent fortunes, may aspire to share in conducting the affairs of the nation, or to live with usefulness and respect in the private ranks of life. Both of these sections will require instruction in all the higher branches of science; the wealthy to qualify them for either public or private life; the professional section will need those branches, especially, which are the basis of their future profession, and a general knowledge of the others, as auxiliary to that, and necessary to their standing and associating with the scientific class. All the branches, then, of useful science, ought to be taught in the general schools, to a competent extent, in the first instance. These sciences may be arranged into three departments, not rigorously scientific, indeed, but sufficiently so for our purposes. These are, I, Language; II, Mathematics; III, Philosophy.

I. *Language.* In the first department, I would arrange a distinct science. 1, Languages and History, ancient and modern; 2, Grammar; 3, Belles Lettres; 4, Rhetoric and Oratory; 5, A school for the deaf, dumb and blind. History is here associated with languages, not as a kindred subject, but on a principle of economy, because both may be attained by the same course of reading, if books are selected with that view.

II. *Mathematics.* In the department of mathematics, I should give place distinctly, 1, Mathematics pure; 2, Physico-Mathematics; 3, Physic; 4, Chemistry; 5, Natural History, *to wit:* Mineralogy; 6, Botany; and 7, Zoology; 8. Anatomy; 9, the Theory of Medicine.

III. *Philosophy.* In the Philosophical department, I should distinguish, 1, Ideology; 2, Ethics; 3, the Law of Nature and Nations; 4, Government; 5, Political Economy.

But, some of these terms being used by different writers, in different degrees of extension, I shall define exactly what I mean to comprehend in each of them.

I. 3. Within the term of Belles Lettres I include poetry and composition generally, and Criticism.

II. 1. I consider pure Mathematics as the science of, I, Numbers, and II, Measure in the abstract; that of numbers comprehending Arithmetic, Algebra and Fluxions; that of Measure (under the general appellation of Geometry) comprehending Trigonometry, plane and spherical, conic sections, and transcendental curves.

II. 2. Physico-Mathematics treat of physical subjects by the aid of mathematical calculation. These are Mechanics, Statics, Hydrostatics, Hydrodynamics, Navigation, Astronomy, Geography, Optics, Pneumatics, Acoustics.

II. 3. Physics, or Natural Philosophy, (not entering the limits of

Chemistry,) treat of natural substances, their properties, mutual relations and action. They particularly examine the subjects of motion, action, magnetism, electricity, galvanism, light, meteorology, with an &c. not easily enumerated. These definitions and specifications render immaterial the question whether I use the Generic terms in the exact degree of comprehension in which others use them; to be understood is all that is necessary to the present object.

3. Professional Schools.

At the close of this course the students separate; the wealthy retiring, with a sufficient stock of knowledge, to improve themselves to any degree to which their views may lead them, and the professional section to the professional schools, constituting the third grade of education, and teaching the particular sciences which the individuals of this section mean to pursue, with more minuteness and detail than was within the scope of the general schools for the second grade of instruction. In these professional schools each science is to be taught in the highest degree it has yet attained. They are to be the

1st *Department*, the fine arts, to wit: Civil Architecture, Gardening, Painting, Sculpture, and the theory of Music; the

2d *Department*, Architecture, Military and Naval; Projectiles, Rural Economy, (comprehending Agriculture, Horticulture and Veterinary,) Technical Philosophy, the practice of Medicine, Materia Medica, Pharmacy and Surgery. In the

3d *Department*, Theology and Ecclesiastical History; Law, Municipal and Foreign.

To these professional schools will come those who separated at the close of their first elementary course, to wit:

The lawyer to the school of law.

The ecclesiastic to that of theology and ecclesiastical history.

The physician to those of the practice of medicine, materia medica, pharmacy and surgery.

The military man to that of military and naval architecture and projectiles.

The agricultor to that of rural economy.

The gentleman, the architect, the pleasure gardener, painter and musician to the school of fine arts.

And to that of technical philosophy will come the mariner, carpenter, ship-wright, pump maker, clock maker, machinist, optician, metallurgist, founder, cutler, druggist, brewer, vintner, distiller, dyer, painter, bleecher, soap maker, tanner, powder maker, salt maker, glass maker, to learn as much as shall be necessary to pursue their art understandingly, of the sciences of geometry, mechanics, statics, hydrostatics, hydraulics, hydrodynamics, navigation, astronomy, geography, optics, pneumatics, acoustics, physics, chemistry, natural history, botany, mineralogy and pharmacy.

The school of technical philosophy will differ essentially in its functions from the other professional schools. The others are instituted to ramify and dilate the particular sciences taught in the schools of the second grade on a general scale only. The technical school is to abridge those which were taught there too much *in extenso* for the limited wants of the artificer or practical man. These artificers must be grouped together, according to the particular branch of science in which they need elementary and practical instruction; and a special lecture or lectures should be prepared for each group—and these lectures should be given in the evening, so as not to interrupt the labors of the day. The school, particularly, should be maintained wholly at the public expense, on the same principles with that of the ward schools. Through the whole of the collegiate course, at the hours of recreation on certain days, all the students should be taught the manual exercise, military evolutions and manœuvres, should be under a standing organization as a military corps, and with proper officers to train and command them.

A tabular statement of this distribution of the sciences will place the system of instruction more purticularly in view:

1st or Elementary Grade in the Ward Schools.

Reading, Writing, Arithmetic, Geography.

2d, or General Grade.

1. Language and History, ancient and modern.
2. Mathematics, viz:

Mathematics pure,	Anatomy,
Physico-Mathematics,	Theory of Medicine,
Physics,	Zoology,
Chemistry,	Botany and Mineralogy.

3. Philosophy, viz:

Ideology, and Ethics,	Government,
Law of Nature and Nations,	Political Economy.

3d, or Professional Grades.

Theology and Ecclesiastical History.
Law, Municipal and Foreign.
Practice of Medicine.
Materia Medica and Pharmacy.
Surgery.
Architecture, Military and Naval, and Projectiles.
Technical Philosophy.
Rural Economy.
Fine Arts.

On this survey of the field of science, I recur to the question, what portion of it we mark out for the occupation of our institution? With the first grade of education we shall have nothing to do. The sciences of the second grade are our first object; and, to adapt them to our slender beginnings, we must separate them into groups, comprehending many sciences each, and greatly more, in the first instance, than ought to be imposed on, or can be competently conducted by a single professor permanently. They must be subdivided from time to time, as our means increase, until each professor shall have no more under his care than he can attend to with advantage to his pupils and ease to himself. In the further advance of our resources, the professional schools must be introduced, and professorships established for them also. For the present, we may group the sciences into professorships, as follows, subject, however, to be changed, according to the qualifications of the persons we may be able to engage.

I. *Professorship.*

Language and History, ancient and modern.
Belles Lettres, Rhetoric and Oratory.

II. *Professorship.*

Mathematics pure—Physico-Mathematics.
Physics—Anatomy—Medicine—Theory.

III. *Professorship.*

Chemistry—Zoology—Botany—Mineralogy.

IV. *Professorship.*

Philosophy.

The organization of the branch of the institution which respects its government, police and economy, depending on principles which have no affinity with those of its institution, may be the subject of separate and subsequent consideration.

With this tribute of duty to the Board of Trustees, accept the assurance of my great esteem and consideration.

TH: JEFFERSON.

C.

A PETITION of the Trustees of Albemarle Academy, praying to be authorized by law to demand and receive certain moneys which have arisen on the sale of the two glebes of the parishes of St. Ann and Fredericksville in the said county, with the interest or profits thereon; and also, annually, from the President and Directors of the Literary Fund, a dividend of the interest or profits of that fund, proportioned every year to the ratio which the contributions of the said county shall have borne to those of the rest of the State in the preceding year; praying, also, the General Assembly to reduce the number of visitors, to provide for their appointment and succession, and for that of such other officers as they may think necessary; to define their powers and duties, to lay down such fixed principles for the government and administration of the said institution as may give it stability; to change its name to that of the *Central College;* and to make such amendments to the act for the establishment of public schools, passed on the 22d day December, 1796, as may facilitate its commencement and lighten its execution in the said county.

Ordered, That the said petition be referred to the Committee of Propositions and Grievances; that they do examine the matter thereof, and report the same, with their opinion thereupon, to the House.

Resolved, As the opinion of this Committee, that so much of the petition of the Trustees of the Albemarle Academy as prays for certain amendments to the act establishing the same, is reasonable.

Resolved, As the opinion of this Committee, that so much of the said petition as prays that all moneys now appropriated to the literary fund, within the said county, may hereafter be vested in the said Trustees, for the use of the said Academy, be rejected.

The said resolutions being twice read, were, on questions severally put thereupon, agreed to by the House.—*Journal of House of Delegates for* 1815-6, *pp.* 23, 38, 56.

D.

AN ACT FOR ESTABLISHING A COLLEGE IN THE COUNTY OF ALBEMARLE.

1. *Be it enacted by the General Assembly*, That there shall be established in the county of Albemarle, at the place which has been, or shall be elected by the Trustees of Albemarle Academy, and in lieu of such academy, an institution for the education of youth, to be called "The Central College," which shall be established, governed, and administered as follows:

2. The Governor of this Commonwealth for the time-being, shall be the Patron of the said college, and shall have power to appoint the Visitors thereof in the first instance, and to fill up such vacancies in the Board of Visitors as may exist afterwards, from time to time.

3. There shall be six Visitors, who shall hold their offices each for the term of three years, if he shall so long demean himself well; of which the Chancellor of the district shall be the competent judge.

4. The said Board of Visitors shall have two stated meetings in every year, in the said college, to wit: on the day of the commencement of the spring term of the Albemarle Circuit Court, and on the day of the commencement of the fall term of the said Circuit Court; and such occasional meetings as may be called from time to time by any three members, giving effectual and timely notice to the others; and if, from any cause, the said Visitors do not attend the said stated meetings, or such occasional meetings as may be called from time to time, the said meetings may be adjourned from day to day, until a general meeting shall be had.

5. They, or a majority of them, shall have power to appoint a Treasurer and Proctor; to establish professorships, prescribe their duties, and the course of education to be pursued; determine the

salaries, and accommodations they shall receive from the college, and the perquisites from their pupils; to lay down rules for the government and discipline of the students; for their subsistence, board and accommodation, and the charges to which they shall be subject for these and for tuition; to prescribe and control the duties and proceedings of all officers, servants and others, with respect to the buildings, lands, and other property of the college, and to the providing subsistence, board, accommodations, and all necessaries for the students and others appertaining to the same; and to fix the allowance and emoluments for their salaries; and, in general, to direct and do all matters and things which to them shall seem best for promoting the purposes of the institution, and for securing, improving, and employing its property; which several functions may be exercised by them in the form of by-laws, rules, orders, instructions, or otherwise as they shall deem proper.

6. There shall be a Treasurer, to be appointed by the Visitors, to hold his office during their pleasure; whose duty it shall be to receive all moneys which shall become due or accrue to the college; to pay all moneys which shall be due from it, according to such directions, general or special, as shall be given by the Board of Visitors; and to render his account at such times, in such forms, and to such persons, as they shall require, or to themselves.

7. There shall be a Proctor, to be appointed by the Visitors, to hold his office during their pleasure. In him, in trust for the college, shall be vested, transmissible to his successors, the legal estate in all property of the college, whether in possession, in interest, or in action; and he shall have authority to maintain the same in all suits, as plaintiff or defendant; which suits shall not abate by the determination of his office, but shall stand revived in the name of his successor; he shall be capable in law, and in trust for the college, of receiving subscriptions and donations, real and personal, of purchasing, receiving, and holding, transmissible to his successor, all property, real and personal, in possession, interest, or action.

8. It shall be his duty to superintend, manage, preserve, and improve all the property of the college, in possession, interest, or action; to erect, preserve, and repair the buildings, improvements, and possessions; to provide subsistence and other necessaries, and to direct and control the due and economical dispensation of them; to employ and control all agents, servants, and others necessary for the

works or the services prædial or menial of the institution; and in all those functions he shall act conformably with the provisions and principles established by the Visitors, of whose laws, regulations, and orders, he shall have the general execution, when not addressed to any other person.

9. *And be it further enacted*, That the rights and claims, now existing in the said Albemarle Academy and its Trustees, shall by this act become vested in the said Central College and its proper officers, so soon as they shall be appointed; and that, in aid of the subscriptions and donations obtained, and of the proceeds of the lottery authorized by the act for establishing the Albemarle Academy, the said college shall, by its proper officers, when appointed, be authorized to demand and receive the moneys which arose from the sales of the glebe lands of the parishes of St. Ann and Fredericksville, in the county of Albemarle, or such part thereof as belongs to the county of Albemarle or its citizens, or in whatever hands they may be, to be employed for the purposes of the said college.

10. *And be it further enacted*, That the act passed in the year one thousand eight hundred and three, for establishing the said Albemarle Academy, that of the same year amending the said act, and all other provisions of other acts contrary to the purview of this act, shall be repealed from and after the appointment of Visitors, as therein provided.

11. This act shall commence and be in force from and after the passing thereof.

E.

At a meeting of the Visitors of the Central College, held at Charlottesville on the 5th day of May, 1817, on a call by three members, to wit: John Hartwell Cocke, Jos. C. Cabell, and Thomas Jefferson.

Present—James Monroe, James Madison, John H. Cocke, and Thomas Jefferson.

The records of the Trustees of the Albemarle Academy, in lieu of which the Central College is established, were received from their Secretary by the hands of Alexander Garrett, one of the said Trustees.

Resolved, That Valentine W. Southall be appointed Secretary to the Board, and that the said records be delivered to him.

The Board proceeded to the appointment of a Proctor, and the said Alexander Garrett was appointed, with a request that he will act as Treasurer also, until a special appointment can be made.

The Board being informed that at a meeting which had been proposed for the 8th day of April last at Charlottesville, and at which the three members only who called this present meeting had attended, the said members had visited and examined the different sites for the college within a convenient distance around Charlottesville, had deemed the one offered them by John Perry, a mile above the town, to be the most suitable, and offered on the most reasonable terms, and had provisionally authorized a purchase of certain parcels thereof for the site of the said college and its appendages, and the members now present having themselves proceeded to the said grounds, examined them, and considered the terms of the said provisional purchase, do now approve of said grounds as a site for the said college and its appendages, and of the terms of purchase, which they hereby confirm and ratify, and they accordingly authorize their Proctor above named to proceed to obtain a regular conveyance thereof to himself and his successors in trust for the said college.

The act establishing the Central College, having transferred to the same all the rights and claims existing in the Albemarle Academy and its Trustees; and having in aid of the subscriptions and donations obtained or to be obtained, and of the proceeds of the lottery authorized by law, specially empowered this college by its officers, to demand and receive the moneys which arose from the sales of the glebe lands of the parishes of St. Ann and Fredericksville, or such part thereof as belongs to the county of Albemarle or its citizens, in whatever hands they may be, to be employed for the purposes of this college. Ordered that the Proctor enquire into the state of the said property, and report the same to this Board; and that in the mean time he be authorized to demand and receive so much of the said moneys as may be requisite to pay for the lands purchased from the said John Perry, and to make payment accordingly.

On view of a plan presented to the Trustees of the Albemarle Academy, for erecting a distinct pavilion or building for each separate professorship, and for arranging these around a square, each pavilion containing a school room and two apartments for the accommodation of the professor, with other reasonable conveniencies, the Board determines that one of those pavilions shall now be erected, and they request the Proctor, so soon as the funds are at his command, to agree with proper workmen for the building of one, of stone or brick below ground, and of brick above, of substantial work, of regular architecture, well executed, and to be completed, if possible, during the ensuing summer and winter; that the lot for the said pavilions be delineated on the ground of the breadth of — feet, with two parallel sides of indefinite length, and that the pavilion first to be erected be placed on one of the lines so delineated, with its floor on such degree of elevation from the ground as may correspond with the regular inclined plane to which it may admit of being reduced hereafter.

And it is further resolved, that so far as the funds may admit, the Proctor be requested to proceed to the erection of dormitories for the students adjacent to the said pavilion, not exceeding ten on each side, of brick, and of regular architecture, according to the same plan proposed.

The Board proceeding to consider the plan of a lottery prepared by the Trustees of Albemarle Academy, approve of the same, and resolve that it be carried into execution, and without delay, by the Proctor and by such agents as he shall appoint, and that the moneys to be received for tickets by those entrusted with the sale of them, be, from time to time, and at short periods, paid into the hands of the Proctor, and by him deposited in the Bank of Virginia in Richmond, with which Bank it is thought expedient that an account should be opened with him in trust for the Central College.

Resolved, That a subscription paper be prepared, and placed in such hands as the Proctor shall deem will be the most likely to promote it with energy and success, in which shall be different columns, to wit: one for those who may be willing to give a donation in gross, another for those who may be willing to give a certain sum annually for the term of four years, and a third for donations in any other form; and that the moneys subscribed be disposed of as they are received by the Proctor, in the manner above prescribed for those received on the lottery.

Resolved, That Thomas Jefferson and John H. Cocke be a Committee on the part of the Visitors, with authority jointly or severally, to advise and sanction all plans and the application of moneys for executing them, which may be within the purview and functions of the Proctor for the time being.

TH: JEFFERSON,
JAMES MONROE,
JAMES MADISON,
J. H. COCKE.

May 5, 1817.

July 28, 1817.

At a called meeting of the Visitors of the Central College, held at the house of Mr. Madison, in Orange, Thomas Jefferson, James Madison, John Hartwell Cocke and Joseph C. Cabell, being present:

The plan of the first pavilion to be erected, and the proceedings thereupon, having been stated and agreed to,

It is agreed that application be made to Doctor Knox, of Baltimore, to accept the Professorship of Languages, Belles Lettres, Rhetoric, History and Geography; and that an independent salary of five hundred dollars, with a perquisite of twenty-five dollars from each pupil, together with chambers for his accommodation, be allowed him as a compensation for his services, he finding the necessary assistant ushers.

Alexander Garrett requesting to resign the office of Proctor, it is agreed that Nelson Barksdale, of the county of Albemarle, be appointed his successor.

It is also agreed, that it be expedient to import a stone-cutter from Italy, and that Mr. Jefferson be authorized and requested to take the requisite measures to effect that object.

JAMES MADISON,
J. H. COCKE,
JOSEPH C. CABELL,
TH: JEFFERSON.

At a meeting of the Visitors, &c., held at Charlottesville, 7th October, 1817:

On information of the amount of the subscriptions to the Central College, known to be made, and others understood to be so, the Board resolves, that the pavilion now erecting be completed as heretofore directed, with the twenty dormitories attached to it, and that two other pavilions be contracted for and executed the next year, with the same number of dormitories to each; that one of these be appropriated to the Professor of Languages, Belles Lettres, Rhetoric, Oratory, History and Geography; one other to the Professor of Chemistry, Zoology, Botany, Anatomy; and the third, until otherwise wanted, for a boarding-house, to be kept by some French family of good character, wherein it is proposed that the boarders shall be permitted to speak French only, with a view to their becoming familiarized to conversation in that language.

The Board is of opinion, that the ground for these buildings should be previously reduced to a plain or to terraces, as it shall be found to admit, with due regard to expense; that the pavilions be correct in their architecture and execution; and that, where the family of a professor requires it, two additional rooms shall be added for their accommodation.

On information that the Rev. Mr. Knox, formerly thought of for a professor of languages, is withdrawn from business, the order of July the 28th is rescinded, and it is resolved to offer, in the first place, the professorship of chemistry, &c. to Doct. Thomas Cooper, of Pennsylvania, adding to it that of law, with a fixed salary of $1,000, and tuition fees of $20 from each of his students, to be paid by them, and to accede also to the conditions stated in his letter of September 16, to Th: Jefferson, and that he be advised with as to a qualified professor of languages, or such other measures be taken to obtain one as shall be found most advisable; that the professor of languages should be engaged to take place on the first of April, and Doctor Cooper as soon as the pavilion for him can be erected, or as he can otherwise accommodate himself with lodgings.

Resolved, That every student shall be required to pay $60 per annum tuition fees, of which $20 shall be paid to each professor he attends, and the surplus thereof, if any, to remain for the use of the College, and that $15 be paid moreover for each dormitory by the students occupying them.

Resolved, That any deficiency in the moneys paid or payable by subscription or otherwise, in or before April next, to pay for the pavilions and dormitories, the first year's salaries to the two professors aforesaid, and other necessary expenses, shall be obtained, if practicable, by negotiation with the banks, or a pledge of the future installments of subscriptions, and of the College property, as security; and that of the latter installments the sum of $25,000 shall be disposed of as shall hereafter be directed, either to the Commonwealth or the banks, or some other safe monied institution, on an interest sufficient to pay the annual salaries of the two professors aforesaid forever.

Resolved, That the Proctor be authorized to hire laborers for leveling the grounds and performing necessary services for the works or other purposes.

JAMES MADISON,
JAMES MONROE,
DAVID WATSON,
J. H. COCKE,
JOS. C. CABELL,
TH: JEFFERSON.

October 7th, 1817.

At a meeting of the Visitors, &c., 8th October, 1817:

Certain letters from Dr. Cooper to Th: Jefferson, dated September 17 and 19, received since the meeting of yesterday, being communicated to the Board of Visitors, and taken into consideration with his former letter of September 16, they are of opinion that it will be for the interest of the College to modify the terms of agreement which might be generally proper, so as to accommodate them to the particular circumstances of Dr. Cooper, and to reconcile his interests to an acceptance of the professorship before proposed to him. They therefore resolve:

1. That the expenses of transporting his library and collection of minerals to the College shall be re-imbursed to him.

2. That however disposed they would be to purchase for the College his collection of mineral subjects, his philosophical and chemical apparatus, the extent of their funds is as yet too little ascertained to authorize engagements for them; but that an interest of 6 per cent. per annum on a fair valuation should be paid for the use of them in his own hands, until it can be seen that the other more indispensable calls on the funds of the College will leave them competent to the purchase.

And, ultimately, should nothing short of the immediate purchase of these articles be sufficient, then we are of opinion that their purchase be made, and that the ready money, if required, be obtained from the banks, as proposed in the resolution of yesterday for other pecuniary deficiencies.

3. That the expense of articles consumed necessarily in a course of chemical lectures, shall be defrayed by the College.

4. That the branches of science proposed for Dr. Cooper be varied and accommodated in his case, as it is expected they must be in others, to the particular qualifications of the professor.

5. That the committee of superintendence of the proceedings of the Proctor in the execution of his functions, heretofore appointed, are authorized to take such measures as they think best for providing the necessary apartments for the use of the chemical and mineralogical purposes.

Resolved, That Alexander Garrett be appointed Treasurer for the College.

JOSEPH C. CABELL,
J. H. COCKE,
JAMES MONROE,
TH: JEFFERSON, for
himself and for James Madison, who assented to all the articles, but was obliged to depart before they could be copied and signed.

CHARLOTTESVILLE, 11th May, 1818.

At a regular meeting of the Visitors of the Central College, on 11th May, 1818, at which Thomas Jefferson, James Madison, John H. Cocke and Joseph C. Cabell were present, it was agreed, that it being ascertained whether Thomas Cooper would accept the professorship of chemistry, in the event of his not doing so, it would be expedient to procure a professor of mathematics.

It was also agreed to allow the Proctor of the College the sum of two hundred dollars for the present year.

JAMES MADISON,
TH: JEFFERSON,
J. H. COCKE,
JOSEPH C. CABELL.

May 11*th*, 1818.

January 6, 1818.

The Honorable, the Speaker of the House of Delegates:

SIR,—The late Governor of the Commonwealth having thought proper to confide to us the office of Visitors of the Central College near Charlottesville, under an act of the Legislature, establishing as its patron the Governor for the time being, we deem it our duty to report to you our proceedings under that appointment, with the progress and prospects of that institution.

The want of a seminary of general science in a healthy part of our country, and nearly central to its population, so long felt by our citizens, and so earnestly and extensively desired, produced an expectation that an establishment, so located, and with views entirely general, might meet the wishes of the different parts of the State, and be carried into effect, in an useful degree, by individual and voluntary contributions. The neighborhood of Charlottesville was thought to unite prominent advantages for such an establishment. That situation was therefore proposed; and in order to divest it of all local character and control, and to place its direction under the will of those who represent us, the Legislature was petitioned to vest its patronage in the Governor of the Commonwealth, annually elected by themselves, and to commit to Visitors, to be named by him from time to time, its entire and exclusive direction.

These functions having been accordingly accepted, the subscribers were named as Visitors, to carrry into execution the views so contemplated. Papers for voluntary subscriptions were circulated in different parts of the State, and with more or less success, in proportion, it would seem, as the object and government were correctly seen to be of a general character, or erroneously viewed as merely local. For it is not to be supposed that, on the abstract proposition of a general and central establishment for finishing the instruction of youth, begun in local institutions, the contributions of any one part of the State, would have been less liberal than those of others.

As soon as it was perceived that the contributions, although partial, would be sufficient for an establishment which should embrace the most useful sciences, to a desirable extent, the Visitors assembled and commenced their duties. They adopted a scale, accommodated, in the first instance, to the present prospect of funds, but capable of being enlarged indefinitely to any extent, to which more general efforts may hereafter advance them. They purchased, at a distance of a mile from Charlottesville, and for the sum of one thousand five hundred and eighteen dollars and seventy-five cents, two hundred acres of land, on which was an eligible site for the college, high, dry, open, furnished with good water, and nothing in its vicinity which could threaten the health of the students.

Instead of constructing a single and large edifice, which might have exhausted their funds, and left nothing, or too little, for other essential expenses, they thought it better to erect a small and separate building, or pavilion, for each professor they should be able to employ, with an apartment for his lectures, and others for his own accommodation, connecting these pavilions by a range of dormitories, capable each of lodging two students only, a provision equally friendly to study as to morals and order.

This plan offered the further advantages of greater security against fire and infection, of extending the buildings in equal pace with the funds, and of adding to them indefinitely hereafter, with the indefinite progress of contributions, private or public; and it gave to the whole, in form and effect, the character of an academical village.

Workmen were immediately engaged to commence the first pavilion; but the season being advanced, it will not be finished till the ensuing spring, when one or two others will be begun, together with the contiguous ranges of dormitories, two or three sets of twenty for each pavilion, and sufficient consequently for the accommodation of from eighty to one hundred students. These we count on finishing in the course of the ensuing summer and autumn, and to provide, within the same period, professors of distinction in their respective lines of science, such as may give eminence to the character of the institution, and offer to our youth the instruction for which few have been able to send them abroad, and many could have afforded to give them at home.

We cannot, however, expect from private contributions, to look beyond a single professor for each of the four great departments; of Language, Mathematical, Physiological, and Ideological sciences. The subscription papers already returned, amount to thirty-five thousand one hundred and two dollars, to which are to be added three thousand one hundred and ninety-five dollars eighty-six cents, the proceeds of the sales of glebes in the county of Albemarle; this application of these ancient acquisitions being thought most analogous to their original objects, and equally for the benefit of all interested in them. To these sums, making together thirty-eight thousand two hundred and ninety-seven dollars eighty-six cents, particular papers of which we have information, although not returned, will add about eight thousand dollars, enabling us to count with safety on forty-six or forty-seven thousand dollars. Other papers are still out, of which we have no information, but which we trust will make further and sensible addition to our stock. These moneys, however, being payable in four annual installments only, and the nature of the institution recommending its being brought into effect at once, as far as the funds will go, they will be lessened by the discounts requisite for that purpose.

In proceeding to apply our funds, we suppose that each pavilion for a professor, with its appendage of twenty dormitories, will cost about $7,000; that, for a salary of $500 to a professor of languages, besides his tuition fees, a deposit must be made in the funds of the State, or in some other safe funds, of $8,333⅓, and for a salary of $1,000, besides tuition fees, to each of the other professors, a deposit of $16,666⅔. From the interest of which sums the salaries of the professors may be permanently secured; so that whatever our funds enable us once to establish, may be established forever, and securely guarded from the danger of future deficiencies; and we cherish the hope that, with the progress of time, and of the sense of the value of such an institution, progressive liberalities may make further additions equally permanent, until the institution shall become worthy the station of our State in the scale of its confederates and of the nations of the world.

The premises shew, that our funds, already certain, will enable us to establish, during the ensuing season, two professorships only, with their necessary buildings, and to erect the pavilion, and, if the outstanding subscription papers fulfill our hopes, the dormitories also for a third; depending for this salary, as well as for the salary and buildings for a fourth, on future and unassured donations.

And even with four professorships, there must be on each such an accumulation of sciences, branches of the same department, as cannot be sufficiently taught by a single professor. To do this as it should be done, to give all its developments to every useful branch of all the departments, and in the highest degree, to which each has been already carried, would require a greatly increased number of professors, and funds far beyond what can be expected from individual contributions.

To this the resources at the command of the Legislature would alone be adequate. And we are happy to see, that among the cares for the general good, which their station and the confidence of their fellow-citizens have made incumbent on them, this great political and moral want has not been overlooked. By a bill of the last session, passed by one branch, and printed by the other for public consideration, a disposition appears to go into a system of general education, of which a single University for the use of the whole State is to be a component part. A purpose so auspicious to the future destinies of our country, which would bring such a mass of mind into activity for its welfare, cannot be contemplated without kindling the warmest affections for the land of our birth, with an animating prospect into its future history. Well directed education improves the morals, enlarges the minds, enlightens the councils, instructs the industry, and advances the power, the prosperity and the happiness of a nation. But it is not for us to suggest the high considerations, which their peculiar situation will naturally present to the minds of our law-givers, encouraging a pursuit of such incalculable effect; nor would it be within the limits of our dutiful respect to them, to add reasonings or inducements to their better understanding of what will be wise and profitable for our country. But observing that in the bill presented to public consideration a combination of private and public contributions has been contemplated; and considering such an incorporation as completely fulfilling the view of our institution, we undertake to declare, that if the Legislature shall think proper to proceed to the establishment of an University, and to adopt for its location the site of the Central College, we are so certain of the approbation of those for whom we act, that we may give safe assurance of the ready transfer to the State of all the property and rights of the Central College, in possession or in action, towards the establishment of such an University, and under such laws and provisions as the Legislature shall be pleased to establish; and that we ourselves shall be ready to deliver over our charge to such successors, or such other organization, as the Legislature shall be pleased to ordain, and with increased confidence of its success under their care.

If the relations, sir, in which you stand with the Legislature of our country, and with this institution, shall, in your judgment, render it proper, we request that this declaration may be placed before that honorable body, in such form as you think best, and with the assurance of our entire and respectful submission to their will.

To your Excellency we tender the particular and high respect and consideration with which we have the honor to be

Your most obedient
And most humble servants,

James Monroe,
James Madison,
David Watson,
J. H. Cocke,
Th: Jefferson,
Joseph C. Cabell.

F.

Subscriptions to the Central College from persons residing in the county of Albemarle and in other counties and places.

Names.	Sum subscribed.		No. of installments.
Albemarle county.			
Nathaniel Anderson,	$100 00		4 installments.
Benjamin Austin,	100 00		"
Nelson Barksdale,	200 00		"
Joseph Bishop,	200 00		"
Nimrod Bramham,	500 00		"
Achillis Broadhead,	75 00		"
Charles Brown,	100 00		"
William Brown,	20 00		"
Elijah Brown,	100 00		"
William Brown,	25 00		"
Samuel Carr,	500 00		
Frank Carr,	400 00		
Daniel F. Carr,	200 00		
James O. Carr,	300 00	2,820 00	
Amount carried forward,		$2,820 00	

Names.	Sum subscribed.		No. of installments.
Amount brought forward,		$2,820 00	
John F. Carr,	50 00		
Henry Chiles,	100 00		
Hugh Chisholm,	100 00		
James Clarke,	200 00		
Joseph Coffman,	50 00		
Charles Cocke,	500 00		
Robert L. Coleman,	100 00		
Tucker Coles,	500 00		
John Coles,	500 00		
Isaac A. Coles,	200 00		
Walter Coles,	200 00		
John H. Craven,	500 00		
Isaac Curd,	100 00		
Cash,	20 00		
Allen Dawson,	100 00		
Martin Dawson,	200 00		
James Dinsmore,	200 00		
Dixon Deadman,	50 00		
George Divers,	1,000 00		
Charles Day,	50 00		
William Dunkum,	100 00		
John Dunkum,	100 00		
Thomas Draffen,	60 00		
Samuel Dyer, sr.,	400 00		
Samuel Dyer, jr.,	200 00		
Francis B. Dyer,	100 00		
Archibald B. Duke,	50 00		
Richard Duke,	200 00		
Charles Everitte,	333 33		
John Fagg,	100 00		
John Fretwell,	100 00		
Jesse W. Garth,	200 00		
Jesse Garth, sr.,	150 00		
William Garth,	150 00		
Garland Garth,	300 00	7,263 33	
Amount carried forward,		$10,083 33	

Names.	Sum subscribed.		No. of installments.
Amount bro't forward,		$10,083 33	
Willis D. Garth,	80 00		
Alexander Garrett,	500 00		4 installments
Ira Garrett,	100 00		
James Garnett,	50 00		
Robert Gentry,	100 00		
Jeremiah A. Goodman,	50 00		
William F. Gordon,	200 00		
John Goss,	200 00		
Clifton Harris,	100 00		
Ira Harris,	100 00		
John Harris,	1,000 00		
Benjamin Harden,	100 00		
Charles Harper,	200 00		
William Hamner,	20 00		
Andrew Hart,	100 00		
Samuel L. Hart,	100 00		
John Hudson,	100 00		
Thomas Jefferson,	1,000 00		
John Jones,	75 00		
David Isaacs,	200 00		
James Kinsolving, sr.,	50 00		
George W. Kinsolving,	50 00		
James Leitch,	500 00		
William Leitch,	100 00		
Nicholas H. Lewis,	300 00		
Howell Lewis,	200 00		
Jesse Lewis,	100 00		4 installments.
Reuben Lindsay, sr.,	1,000 00		
James Lindsay,	100 00		
Reuben Maury,	100 00		
Thomas W. Maury,	100 00		
John H. Marks,	100 00		
Francis McGehee,	40 00		
William H. Merewether,	200 00		
James Minor,	300 00		
Dabney Minor,	400 00	8,015 00	
Amount carried forward,		$18,098 33	

Names.	Sum subscribed.		No. of installments.
Amount bro't forward,		$18,098 33	
Peter Minor,	500 00		5 installments.
James Monroe,	1,000 00		4 "
William Morris,	20 00		
Wilson C. Nicholas,	1,000 00		
Opie Norris,	300 00		
Mann Page,	400 00		
John Patterson,	1,000 00		
John M. Perry,	200 00		
Moses Perrygory,	25 00		
John Pollock,	200 00		
Peter Porter,	20 00		
Thomas J. Randolph,	500 00		4 installments.
Thomas E. Randolph,	200 00		
John C. Ragland,	200 00		
Daniel M. Railey,	100 00		
William J. Robertson,	100 00		
John Rogers,	200 00		
William Ragland,	25 00		1 installment.
John W. Saunders,	50 00		
John Scott, jr.,	500 00		
Zachariah Shackleford,	200 00		
Nelson T. Shelton,	100 00		
William A. Shelton,	100 00		
John Slaughter,	50 00		
Valentine W. Southall,	200 00		
Lewis Teel,	100 00		
James H. Terrell,	200 00		
Martin Thacker,	60 00		
John L. Thomas,	100 00		
John Thomas, jr.,	40 00		
William Watson,	100 00		
John Watson, L. M.,	150 00		
John Walker,	20 00		
James G. Waddle,	160 00		
Christian Wertenbaker,	25 00	8,145 00	
Amount carried forward,		$26,243 33	

Names.	Sum subscribed.		No. of installments.
Amount bro't forward,		$26,243 33	
John Winn,	300 00		
Arthur Whitehurst,	50 00		
Micajah Woods,	200 00		
Drury Wood,	100 00		
William Woods, S.,	200 00		
Richard Woods,	100 00		
James Wood,	50 00		
George M. Woods,	100 00		
Thomas Wood,	100 00	1,200 00	
		$27,443 33	
Amherst county.			
Richard S. Ellis,	100 00		
		100 00	
Buckingham county.			
John W. Eppes,	200 00		
		200 00	
Cumberland county.			
William Bondurant,	100 00		
George W. Bondurant,	50 00		
Jerman Baker,	100 00		
Alex. Cheatwood,	60 00		
F. B. Deane,	100 00		4 installments.
William Daniel,	100 00		
G. H. Fitzgerald,	40 00		
Randolph Harrison,	500 00		
Carter E. Harrison,	100 00		
Thomas H. Harrison,	200 00		
Jesse Hughes,	50 00		
James Jennings,	40 00		
Richard P. James,	50 00		
John Miller,	80 00		
John Page,	100 00		
William Skipwith,	50 00		
George N. Skipwith,	100 00	1,820 00	
Amount carried forward,		$1,820 00	

Names.	Sum subscribed.		No. of installments.
Amount bro't forward,		$1,820 00	
Stephen W. Trent,	100 00		
Wm. M. Thornton,	100 00		
Thomas N. Walton,	10 00		
Hugh Watson,	50 00		
William H. Watkins,	40 00		
D. A. Wilson,	20 00		
J. B. Woodson,	20 00		
Charles Woodson,	30 00	370 00	
		2,190 00	
Fluvanna county.			
Wilson J. Cary,	200 00		
Miles Cary,	100 00		
John H. Cocke,	1,000 00		
John Dyer,	100 00		
John Fuqua,	40 00		
George Holeman,	200 00		
Wm. B. Johnson,	100 00		
Joshua Key,	40 00		
Jacob Myers,	100 00		
John R. Perkins,	40 00		
Wm. Pasture,	80 00		
Charles A. Scott,	500 00		
Horatio Wills,	40 00		
John Winn,	50 00		
		2,590 00	
Goochland county.			
Benjamin Anderson,	100 00		4 installments.
William Bolling,	100 00		
Archibald Bryce, jr.	50 00		
William F. Carter,	5 00		
John G. Crouch,	20 00		
W. Campbell,	25 00		
Edward Garland,	100 00		
Thomas Miller,	100 00	500 00	
Amount carried forward,		500 00	

Names.	Sum subscribed.	No. of installments.
Amount bro't forward,		500 00
Thomas Pemberton,	100 00	
George C. Pickett,	50 00	
James Pleasants, jr.	100 00	
Wm. G. Pendleton,	100 00	
Thomas M. Randolph,	100 00	
Wm. Salmon,	5 00	
Richard Sampson,	50 00	
George S. Smith,	20 00	
Joseph S. Watkins,	100 00	
Thomas B. Watkins,	20 00	
Benjamin P. Watkins,	20 00	
Tarlton Woodson,	20 00	
		685 00
		1,185 00
Loudoun county.		
Armstead T. Mason,	200 00	200 00
Louisa county.		
Frederick Harris,	400 00	
William Morris, jr.	200 00	
James Minor,	200 00	
George W. Trueheart,	200 00	
James Watson,	200 00	
David Watson,	200 00	
		1,400 00
Lynchburg.		
S. J. Harrison,	200 00	
Charles Johnston,	200 00	
William Mitchell,	200 00	
Robert Morris,	200 00	
Richard Pollard,	100 00	
Thomas Wells,	200 00	
Joel Yancey,	200 00	
		1,300 00

Names.	Sum subscribed.	No. of installments.
Nelson county.		
Joseph C. Cabell,	1,000 00	
William Cabell, sen'r,	100 00	
Landon Cabell,	200 00	
George Calloway,	100 00	
John P. Cobbs,	200 00	
John Digges,	50 00	
Henry Dawson,	24 00	
Spottswood Garland,	100 00	
William B. Hare,	100 00	
Robert J. Kincaid,	50 00	
Samuel Loving,	50 00	
Thomas S. McClelland,	100 00	
John Mosby,	28 00	
Zachariah Nevil,	50 00	
Robert Rives,	500 00	
William C. Rives,	200 00	
Joseph Shelton,	50 00	
Michael Woods,	50 00	
		2,952 00
Orange county.		
Samuel Hardesty,	30 00	
James Madison,	1,000 00	
		1,030 00
Richmond city.		
Edmund Anderson,	200 00	
William Carter,	500 00	
John Coalter,	100 00	
F. W. Gilmer,	100 00	
Jacqueline B. Harvie,	500 00	
Jesse B. Key,	200 00	
Hall Neilson,	30 00	
Bernard Peyton,	200 00	
B. Roddy,	20 00	
Norborne K. Thomas,	175 00	
St. George Tucker,	200 00	
		2,225 00

Names.	Sum subscribed.		No. of Installments.
Spottsylvania county.			
Francis W. Taliaferro,	400 00		
		400 00	
Stafford county.			
William Brent, Jr.	100 00		
		100 00	
Winchester.			
Dabney Carr,	100 00		
Hugh Holmes,	300 00		
Henry Lee, Jr.	200 00		
Henry St. George Tucker,	200 00		
		800 00	
Albemarle,			27,443 33
Amherst,			100 00
Buckingham,			200 00
Cumberland,			2,190 00
Fluvanna,			2,590 00
Goochland,			1,185 00
Loudoun,			200 00
Louisa,			1,400 00
Lynchburg,			1,300 00
Nelson,			2,952 00
Orange,			1,030 00
Richmond city,			2,225 00
Spottsylvania,			400 00
Stafford,			100 00
Winchester,			800 00
			$44,115 33

G.

A BILL FOR ESTABLISHING A SYSTEM OF PUBLIC EDUCATION.

1. For establishing schools at which the children of all the citizens of this Commonwealth may receive a primary grade of education at the common expense.

Be it enacted by the General Assembly of Virginia as follows: At the first session of the Superior Court in every county within this Commonwealth, next ensuing the passage of this act, the Judge thereof shall appoint three discreet and well informed persons, residents of the county, to serve as Visitors of the primary schools in the said county, of which appointment the sheriff shall, within fifteen days thereafter, deliver a certificate under the hand of the clerk of the said court to each of the persons so appointed.

2.* The said Visitors shall meet at the courthouse of their county on the first county court day after they shall have received notice of their appointment, and afterwards at such times and places as they, or any two of them, with reasonable notice to the third, shall have agreed, and shall proceed to divide their county into wards, by metes and bounds so designated, as to comprehend each about the number of militia sufficient for a company, and so also as not to divide and place in different wards the lands of any one person held in one body,

---

* This designation of the size of a ward is founded upon these considerations:

1. That the population which furnishes a company of militia, will generally about furnish children enough for a school.

2. That in most instances at present the militia captaincies being laid off compactly by known and convenient metes and bounds, many will be adopted without change, and others will furnish a canvass to work on and to reform.

3. That these wards once established, will be found convenient and salutary aids in the administration of government, of which they will constitute the organic elements, and the first integral members in the composition of the military.

The prohibition to parcel among different wards the lands of a single individual, held in a body, is 1st, to save the proprietor from the perplexity of multiplied responsibilities; and 2d, to prevent arbitrary and inconsistent apportionments by different Wardens of the comparative values of the different portions of his lands in their respective wards.

which division into wards shall, within six months from the date of their appointment, be completely designated, published and reported, by their metes and bounds, to the office of the clerk of the Superior Court, there to be recorded; subject, however, to such alterations from time to time afterwards, as changes of circumstances shall, in the opinion of the said Visitors, or their successors, with the approbation of the said court, render expedient.

3. The said original division into wards being made, the Visitors shall appoint days for the first meeting of every ward at such place as they shall name within the same; of which appointment notice shall be given at least two weeks before the day of meeting, by advertisement at some place within the ward, requiring every free white male citizen of full age, resident within the ward, to meet at the place, and by the hour of 12 of the day so appointed; at which meeting some one of the Visitors shall also attend; and, a majority of the said Warders being in attendance, the Visitors present shall propose to them to decide, by a majority of their votes, the location of a school house for the ward, and of a dwelling house for the teacher, (the owner of the ground consenting thereto,) the size and structure of the said houses, and whether the same shall be built by the joint labor of the Warders, or by their pecuniary contributions; and also to elect, by a plurality of their votes, a Warden resident, who shall direct and superintend the said buildings, and be charged with their future care.

4.* And if they decide that the said buildings shall be erected by the joint labor of the Warders, then all persons within the said ward, liable to work on the highways, shall attend at the order of the Warden, and, under his direction, shall labor thereon until completed, under the same penalties as provided by law to enforce labor on the highways; and, if they decide on erection by pecuniary contributions, the residents and owners of property within the ward, shall

---

* It is presumed that the wards will generally build such log houses for the school and teacher, as they now do, and will join force and build them themselves, experience proving them to be as comfortable as they are cheap. Nor would it be advisable to build expensive houses in the country wards, which, from changes in their population, will be liable to changes of their boundaries and consequent displacements of their centres, and drawing with it a removal of their school house. In towns better houses may be more safely built or rented, for both purposes.

contribute towards the cost, each in proportion to the taxes they last paid to the State for their persons and for the same property, of which the sheriff shall furnish a statement to the Warden, who, according to the ratio of that statement, shall apportion and assess the quota of contribution for each, and be authorized to demand, receive, and apply the same to the purposes of the contribution, and to render account thereof, as in all other of his pecuniary transactions for the school to the Visitors; and on failure of payment by any contributor, the sheriff, on the order of the Warden, first approved by the Visitors, shall collect and render the same, under like powers and regulations as provided for the collection of the public taxes. And in every case it shall be the duty of the Warden to have the buildings completed within six months from the date of his election.

5.* It shall be the duty of the said Visitors to seek and employ for every ward, whenever the number and ages of its children require it,

---

* Estimating 800 militia to a county, there will be twelve captaincies or wards in a county on an average. Suppose each of these, three years in every six, to have children enough for a school who have not yet had three years' schooling, such a county will employ six teachers, each serving two wards by alternate terms. These teachers will be taken from the laboring class, as they are now, to wit: from that which furnishes mechanics, overseers, and tillers of the earth; and they will chiefly be the cripples, the weakly, and the old of that class, who will have been qualified for these functions by the ward schools themselves; if put on a footing then for wages and subsistence, with the young and the able of their class, they will be liberally compensated, say with $150 wages, and the usual allowance of meat and bread. The subsistence will probably be contributed in kind by the Warders out of their family stock; the wages alone will be a pecuniary tax of about $900 to a county. This addition would be of about one-fifth of the taxes we now pay to the State, or about one-fifth of one per cent. on every man's taxable property, if tax can be called that which we give to our children in the most valuable of all forms, that of instruction. Were these schools to be established on the public funds, and to be managed by the Governor and Council, or the Commissioners of the Literary Fund, brick houses to be built for the schools and teachers, high wages and subsistence given them, they would be badly managed, depraved by abuses, and would exhaust the whole literary fund. While under the eye and animadversion of the wards, and the control of the Warden and Visitors, economy, diligence, and correctness of conduct will be enforced, and the whole literary fund will be spared to complete the general system of education by colleges in every district for instruction in the languages, and an University for the whole of the higher sciences; and this by an addition to our contributions almost insensible, and which in fact will not be felt as a burthen, because applied immediately and visibly to the good of our children.

a person of good moral character, qualified to teach reading, writing, numeral arithmetic, and the elements of geography, whose subsistence shall be furnished by the residents and proprietors of the ward, either in money or in kind, at the choice of each contributor, and in the ratio of their public taxes, to be apportioned and levied as on the failures before provided for. The teacher shall also have the use of the house and accommodations provided for him, and shall moreover receive annually such standing wages as the Visitors shall have determined, to be proportioned on the residents and proprietors of the ward, and to be paid, levied, and applied as before provided in other cases of pecuniary contribution.

6. At this school shall be received and instructed gratis, every infant in the ward, of competent age, who has not already had three years' schooling.

7. And to keep up a constant succession of Visitors, the Judge of the Superior Court of every county shall, at his first session in every bissextile year, appoint Visitors, as before characterized, either the same or others, at his discretion, and, in case of the death or resignation of any Visitor, during the term of his appointment, or of his removal from the county, or by the said Judge for good cause, moral or physical, he shall appoint another to serve until the next bissextile appointment; which Visitors shall have their first meeting at their courthouse, on the county court day next ensuing their appointment; and afterwards at such times and places as themselves or any two of them, with reasonable notice to the third, shall agree; but the election of Wardens shall be annually at the first meeting of the ward, after the month of March, until which election the Warden last elected shall continue in office.

8. All ward meetings shall be at their school house, and on failure of the meeting of a majority of the Warders on the call of a Visitor, or of their Warden, such Visitor or Warden may call another meeting.

9. At all times when repairs or alterations of the buildings before provided for shall be wanting, it shall be the duty of the Warden, or of a Visitor, to call a ward meeting, and to take the same measures towards such repairs or alterations as herein before authorized for the original buildings.

10. Where, on the application of any Warden, authorized thereto by the vote of his ward, the Judge of the Superior Court shall be of

opinion that the contributors of any particular ward are disproportionately and oppressively over-burthened with an unusual number of children of non-contributors of their ward, he may direct an order to the county court to assess in their next county levy the whole or such part of the extra burthen as he shall think excessive and unreasonable, to be paid to the Warden, for its proper use, to which order the said county court is required to conform.

11. The said teachers shall, in all things relating to the education and government of their pupils, be under the direction and control of the Visitors.

12. Some one of the Visitors, once in every year at least, shall visit the school, shall enquire into the proceedings and practices thereat, shall examine the progress of the pupils, and give to those who excel in reading, in writing, in arithmetic, or in geography, such honorary marks and testimonies of approbation as may encourage and excite to industry and emulation.

13. All decisions and proceedings of the Visitors, relative to the original designation of wards, at any time before the buildings are begun, or to the changes of wards at any time after, to the quantum of subsistence or wages allowed to the teacher, and to the rules prescribed to him for the education and government of his pupils, shall be subject to control and correction by the Judge of the Superior Court of the county on the complaint of any individual aggrieved or interested.

And for the establishment of colleges whereat the youth of the Commonwealth may, within convenient distances from their homes, receive a higher grade of education,

14. *Be it further enacted as follows:* The several counties of this Commonwealth shall be distributed into nine collegiate districts, whereof one shall be composed of the counties of Accomac, Northampton, Northumberland, Lancaster, Richmond, Westmoreland, Middlesex, Essex, Matthews, Gloucester, King & Queen, King William, Elizabeth City, Warwick, York, James City, New Kent, and Charles City; one other of the counties of Princess Anne, Norfolk, Norfolk borough, Nansemond, Isle of Wight, Southampton, Surry, Prince George, Sussex, and Greensville; one other of the counties of Fairfax, Loudoun, King George, Stafford, Prince William, Fauquier, Culpeper, Madison, Caroline, and Spotsylvania; one other of the counties of Hanover, City of Richmond, Goochland, Louisa, Flu-

vanna, Powhatan, Cumberland, Buckingham, Orange, Albemarle, Nelson, Amherst, Augusta, and Rockbridge; one other of the counties of Chesterfield, town of Petersburg, Dinwiddie, Brunswick, Amelia, Nottoway, Lunenburg, Mecklenburg, Prince Edward, Charlotte, and Halifax; one other of the counties of Campbell, Pittsylvania, Bedford, Franklin, Henry, Patrick, Botetourt, and Montgomery; one other of the counties of Frederick, Jefferson, Berkeley, Hampshire, Shenandoah, Hardy, Rockingham, and Pendleton; one other of the counties of Monongalia, Brooke, Ohio, Randolph, Harrison, Wood, and Mason; and one other of the counties of Bath, Greenbrier, Kanawha, Cabell, Giles, Monroe, Tazewell, Wythe, Grayson, Washington, Russell, and Lee.

15. Within three months after the passing of this act, the President and Directors of the Literary Fund, who shall henceforward be called the Board of Public Instruction, shall appoint one fit person in every county, in each of the districts, who, with those appointed in the other counties of the same district, shall compose the Board of Visitors for the College of that district; and shall, within four months after passing this act, cause notice to be given to each individual so appointed, prescribing to them a day, within one month thereafter, and a place within their district, for their first meeting, with supplementary instructions for procuring a meeting subsequently, in the event of failure at the time first appointed.

16. The said Visitors, or so many of them as, being a majority, shall attend, shall appoint a rector, of their own body, who shall preside at their meetings, and a secretary to record and preserve their proceedings; and shall proceed to consider of the site for a college most convenient for their district, having regard to the extent, population and other circumstances, and within the term of six months from the passing of this act shall report the same to the Board of Public Instruction, with the reasons on which each site is preferred; and if any minority of two or more members prefer any other place, the same shall be reported, with the reasons for and against the same.

17. Within seven months after the passing of this act the said Board of Public Instruction shall determine on such of the sites reported as they shall think most eligible for the college of each district, shall notify the same to the said Visitors, and shall charge them with the office of obtaining from the proprietor, with his consent, the proper grounds for the building, and its appurtenances, either by dona-

tion or purchase; or if his consent, on reasonable terms, cannot be obtained, the clerk of the county, wherein the site is, shall, on their request, issue and direct to the sheriff of the same county a writ of *ad quod damnum*, to ascertain by a jury the value of the grounds selected, and to fix their extent by metes and bounds, so, however, as not to include the dwelling house, or buildings appurtenant, the curtilage, gardens or orchards of the owner; which writ shall be executed according to the ordinary forms prescribed by the laws in such cases; and shall be returned to the same clerk to be recorded: *Provided*, that in no case, either of purchase or valuation by a jury, shall more grounds be located than of the value of $500; which grounds, if by donation or purchase, shall, by the deed of the owner, or if by valuation of a jury, shall, by their inquest, become vested in the said Board of Public Instruction, as trustees for the Commonwealth, and for the uses and purposes of a college of instruction.

18. On each of the sites so located shall be erected one or more substantial buildings—the walls of which shall be of brick or stone, with two school rooms, and four rooms for the accommodation of the professors, and with sixteen dormitories in or adjacent to the same, each sufficient for two pupils, and in which no more than two shall be permitted to lodge, with a fire place in each, and the whole in a comfortable and decent style, suitable to their purpose.

19. The plan of the said buildings, and their appurtenances, shall be furnished or approved by the said Board of Public Instruction, and that of the dormitories shall be such as may conveniently receive additions from time to time. The Visitors shall have all the powers which are necessary and proper for carrying them into execution, and shall proceed in their execution accordingly. Provided, that in no case shall the whole cost of the said buildings and appurtenances of any one college exceed the sum of $7,500.

20. The college of the district first in this act described, to wit: of Accomac, &c. shall be called the Wythe College, or the College of the District of Wythe; that of the second description, to wit: Princess Anne, &c. shall be called the ——; that of the third description, to wit: Fairfax, &c. shall be called the ——; that of the fourth description, to wit: Hanover, &c. shall be called the ——; that of the fifth description, to wit: Chesterfield, &c. shall be called the ——; that of the sixth description, to wit: Campbell, &c. shall be called the ——; that of the seventh description, to wit: Frederick, &c.

shall be called the ——; that of the eighth description, to wit: Monongalia, &c. shall be called the ——; and that of the ninth description, to wit: Bath, &c. shall be called the ——.

21. In the said colleges shall be taught the Greek, Latin, French, Spanish, Italian and German languages, English grammar, geography, ancient and modern, the higher branches of numerical arithmetic, the mensuration of land, the use of the globes, and the ordinary elements of navigation.

22. To each of the said colleges shall be appointed two professors, the one for teaching Greek, Latin, and such other branches of learning, before described, as he may be qualified to teach, and the other for the remaining branches thereof, who shall each be allowed the use of the apartments provided for him, and a standing salary of $500 yearly, to be drawn from the literary fund, with such tuition fee from each pupil as the Visitors shall establish.

23. The said Visitors shall be charged with the preservation and repair of the buildings, the care of the ground and appurtenances for which, and other necessary purposes, they may employ a steward and competent laborers; they shall have power to appoint and remove the professors, to prescribe their duties, and the course of education to be pursued; they shall establish rules for the government and discipline of the pupils, for their subsistence and board, if boarded in the college, and for their accommodation, and the charges to which they shall be subject for the same, as well as the rent for the dormitories they occupy. They may draw from the literary fund such moneys as are hereby charged on it for their institution. And, in general, they shall direct and do all matters and things which, not being inconsistent with the laws of the land, to them shall seem most expedient for promoting the purposes of the said institution; which several functions may be exercised by them in the form of by-laws, resolutions, orders, instructions, or otherwise, as they shall deem proper.

24. The rents of the dormitories, the profits of boarding the pupils, donations and other occasional resources shall constitute the fund, and shall be at their disposal for the necessary purposes of the said institution, and not otherwise provided for; and they shall have authority to draw on the said Board of Public Instruction for the purchase or valuation money of the site of their college, for the cost of the buildings and improvements authorized by law, and for the standing salaries of the professors herein allowed—for the administration of all which they may appoint a bursar.

25. They shall have two stated meetings in the year, at their colleges, on the first Mondays of April and October, and occasional meetings at the same place, and at such other times, as they shall appoint; giving due notice thereof to every individual of their board.

26. A majority of them shall constitute a quorum for business, and on the death or resignation of a member, or on his removal by the Board of Public Instruction, or out of the county from which he was appointed, the said Board shall appoint a successor, resident in the same county.

27. The Visitors of every collegiate district shall be a body politic and corporate, to be called the Visitors of the College, by name, for which they are appointed, with capacity to plead, or be impleaded, in all courts of justice, and in all cases interesting to their college, which may be the subject of legal cognizance and jurisdiction, which pleas shall not abate by the determination of the office of all or any of them, but shall stand revived in the name of their successors; and they shall be capable in law, and in trust for their college, of receiving subscriptions and donations, real and personal, as well from bodies corporate, or persons associated, as from private individuals.

28. Some member, or members, of the Board of Visitors, to be nominated by the said Board, or such other persons as they shall nominate, shall, once in every year, at least, visit the college of their district, enquire into the proceedings and practices thereat, examine the progress of the pupils, and give to those who excel in any branch of learning prescribed for the said college, such honorary marks and testimonies of approbation as may encourage or excite to industry and emulation.

29. The decisions and proceedings of the said Visitors shall be subject to control and correction by the Board of Public Instruction, either on the complaint of any individual, aggrieved or interested, or on the proper motion of the said board.

30. On every 29th day of February, or, if that be Sunday, then on the next or earliest day thereafter, on which a meeting can be effected, the Board of Public Instruction shall be in session, and shall appoint, in every county of each district, a Visitor, resident therein, either the same before appointed, or another, at their discretion, to serve until the ensuing 29th day of February, duly and timely notifying to them their appointment, and prescribing a day for their first

meeting at the college of their district, after which, their stated meetings shall be at their college, on the first Mondays of April and October, annually; and their occasional meetings at the same place, and at such times as themselves shall appoint, due notice thereof being given to every member of their board.

Utrum horum?

And for establishing in a central and healthy part of the State an University wherein all the branches of useful science may be taught, Be it enacted as follows:

31. Within the limits of the county of —— there shall be established an University, to be called the University of Virginia; and so soon as may be after the passage of this act the board of public instruction shall appoint eight fit persons to constitute the Board of Visitors for the said University; and shall forthwith give notice to each individual so appointed, prescribing to them a day for their first meeting at the Court-house of the said county, with supplementary instructions for procuring a meeting subsequently in the event of failure at the time first appointed.

And for establishing in a central and healthy part of the State an University wherein all the branches of useful science may be taught, Be it further enacted as follows:

31. Whensoever the Visitors of the Central College in Albemarle, authorized thereto by the consent in writing of the subscribers of the major part of the amount subscribed to that institution, shall convey or cause to be conveyed to the Board of Public Instruction, for the use of this Commonwealth, all the lands, buildings, property and rights of the said College, in possession, in interest, or in action, (save only so much as may discharge their engagements then existing,) the same shall be thereupon vested in this Commonwealth, and shall be appropriated to the institution of an University to be called the University of Virginia, which shall be established on the said lands. The said Board of Public Instruction shall thereupon forthwith appoint eight fit persons who shall compose the Board of Visitors for the government of the said University, notifying thereof the persons so appointed, and prescribing to them a day for their first meeting at Charlottesville, with supplementary instructions for procuring a meeting subsequently, in the event of failure at the time first appointed.

32. The said Visitors, or so many of them as, being a majority, shall attend, shall appoint a Rector of their own body, who shall preside at their meetings, and a Secretary to record and preserve their proceedings, and shall proceed to enquire into and select the most eligible site for the University, and to obtain from the proprietor, with his consent, the proper grounds for the buildings and appurtenances, either by donation or purchase, or, if his consent on reasonable terms cannot be obtained, the clerk of the county shall, on their request, issue and direct to the sheriff of the county a writ of *ad quod damnum* to ascertain by a jury the value of the grounds selected, and to fix their extent by metes and bounds, so however as not to include the dwelling house or buildings appurtenant, the curtilage, gardens or orchards of the owner; which writ shall be executed according to the ordinary forms prescribed by the laws in such cases, and shall be returned to the same clerk to be recorded: *Provided*, That in no case, either of purchase or valuation by a jury, shall more grounds be located than of the value of $2,000; which grounds, if by donation or purchase, shall, by the deed of the owner, or if by valuation of a jury, shall, by their inquest, become vested in the Board of Public Instruction aforesaid, as trustees for the Commonwealth, for the uses and purposes of an University.

32. The said Visitors, or so many of them as, being a majority, shall attend, shall appoint a Rector of their own body to preside at their meetings, and a Secretary to record and preserve their proceedings, and shall proceed to examine into the state of the property conveyed as aforesaid, shall make an inventory of the same, specifying the items whereof it consists, shall notice the buildings and other improvements already made, and those which are in progress, shall take measures for their completion, shall consider what others may be necessary in addition, and of the best plan for effecting the same, with estimates of the probable cost, and shall make report of the whole to the said Board of Public Instruction, which is authorized to approve, negative or modify any of the measures so proposed by the said Visitors.

33. A plan of the buildings and appurtenances necessary and proper for an University being furnished or approved by the Board of Public Instruction, in which

33. The said measures being approved or modified, the Visitors shall have all the powers relative thereto which shall be necessary or proper for carrying them into

that of the dormitories shall be such as may conveniently admit additions from time to time, the Visitors shall have all the powers which shall be necessary and proper for carrying them into execution, and shall proceed in their execution accordingly.

execution, and shall proceed in their execution accordingly.

34. In the said University shall be taught history and geography, ancient and modern; natural philosophy, agriculture, chemistry and the theories of medicine; anatomy, zoology, botany, mineralogy and geology; mathematics, pure and mixed; military and naval science; ideology, ethics, the law of nature and of nations; law, municipal and foreign; the science of civil government and political economy; languages, rhetoric, belles lettres, and the fine arts generally; which branches of science shall be so distributed and under so many professorships, not exceeding ten, as the Visitors shall think most proper.

35. Each professor shall be allowed the use of the apartments and accommodations provided for him, and such standing salary, not exceeding $1,000 yearly, as the Visitors shall think proper, to be drawn from the literary fund, with such tuition fees from the students as the Visitors shall establish.

36. The said Visitors shall be charged with the erection, preservation and repair of the buildings, the care of the grounds and appurtenances, and of the interests of the University generally; they shall have power to appoint a bursar, employ a steward and all other necessary agents; to appoint and remove professors; to prescribe their duties, and the course of education to be pursued; to establish rules for the government and discipline of the students, for their subsistence, board and accommodation, if boarded by the University, and the charges to which they shall be subject for the same, as well as for the dormitories they occupy; to provide and control the duties and proceedings of all officers, servants and others, with respect to the buildings, lands, appurtenances, and other property and interests of the University; to draw from the literary fund such moneys as are hereby charged on it for this institution; and in general to direct and do all matters and things which, not being inconsistent with the laws of the land, to them shall seem most expedient for promoting the purposes of the said institution; which several functions may be ex-

ercised by them in the form of by-laws, rules, resolutions, orders, instructions, or otherwise, as they shall deem proper.

37. They shall have two stated meetings in the year, to wit: on the first Mondays of April and October, and occasional meetings at such other times as they shall appoint, due notice thereof being given to every individual of their Board, which meetings shall be at the said University; a majority of them shall constitute a quorum for business; and on the death or resignation of a member, or on his removal by the Board of Public Instruction, or change of habitation to a greater than his former distance from the University, the said Board shall appoint a successor.

38. The Visitors of the said University shall be a body politic and corporate under the style and title of the Visitors of the University of Virginia, with capacity to plead or be impleaded in all courts of justice, and in all cases interesting to their College, which may be the subjects of legal cognizance and jurisdiction, which pleas shall not abate by the determination of their office, but shall stand revived in the name of their successors; and they shall be capable in law, and in trust for their College, of receiving subscriptions and donations, real and personal, as well from bodies coporate or persons associated, as from private individuals.

39. Some member or members of the Board of Visitors, to be nominated by the said Board, or such other person as they shall nominate, shall, once in every year at least, visit the said University, enquire into the proceeding and practices thereat, examine the progress of the students, and give to those who excel in any branch of science there taught such honorary marks and testimonies of approbation as may encourage and excite to industry and emulation.

40. All decisions and proceedings of the Visitors shall be subject to control and direction by the Board of Public Instruction, either on the complaint of any individual aggrieved or interested, or on the proper motion of the said Board.

41. On every 29th day of February, or, if that be Sunday, then on the next or earliest day thereafter on which a meeting can be effected, the said Board of Public Instruction shall be in session, and shall appoint Visitors for the said University, either the same or others, at their discretion, to serve until the 29th day of February next ensuing, duly and timely notifying to them their appointment, and prescribing a day for their first meeting at the University, after

which their stated meetings shall be on the first Mondays of April and October annually, and their occasional meetings at the same place, and at such times as themselves shall appoint, due notice thereof being given to every member of their Board.

[NOTE.—If the Central College be adopted for the University, the following section may be added: "Provided, that nothing in this act contained shall suspend the proceedings of the Visitors of the said Central College of Albemarle; but, for the purpose of expediting the objects of the said institution, they shall be authorized, under the control of the Board of Public Instruction, to continue the exercise of their functions until the first meeting of the Visitors of the University."]

And to avail the Commonwealth of those talents and virtues which nature has sown as liberally among the poor as rich, and which are lost to their country by the want of means for their cultivation, Be it further enacted as follows:

42. On every 29th day of February, or, if that be Sunday, then on the next day, the Visitors of the Ward-schools in every county shall meet at the Court-House of their county, and after the most diligent and impartial observation and enquiry of the boys who have been three years at the Ward-schools, and whose parents are too poor to give them a collegiate education, shall select from among them some one of the most promising and sound understanding, who shall be sent to the first meeting of the Visitors of their collegiate district, with such proofs as the case requires and admits, for the examination and information of that Board; who, from among the candidates so offered from the several counties of their district, shall select two of the most sound and promising understanding, who shall be admitted to their College, and there be maintained and educated five years at the public expense, under such rules and limitations as the Board of Public Instruction shall prescribe; and at the end of the said five years the said Collegiate Visitors shall select that one of the two who shall, on their most diligent and impartial enquiry and best information, be adjudged by them to be of the most sound and promising understanding and character, and most improved by their course of education, who shall be sent on immediately thereafter to the University, there to be maintained and educated in such branches of the sciences taught

there as are most proper to qualify him for the calling to which his parents or guardians may destine him; and to continue at the said University three years at the public expense, under such rules and limitations as the Board of Public Instruction shall prescribe. And the expenses of the persons so to be publicly maintained and educated at the Colleges and University shall be drawn by their respective Visitors from the literary fund.

H.

AN ACT APPROPRIATING PART OF THE REVENUE OF THE LITERARY FUND, AND FOR OTHER PURPOSES.

(Passed 21st February, 1818.)

1. *Be it enacted by the General Assembly*, That for the purpose of duly applying a part of the income of the literary fund to the *primary* object of its institution, it shall be the duty of the courts of the several counties, cities, and corporate towns represented in the General Assembly and of the borough of Norfolk, as soon as may be in the present year, and annually thereafter in the month of October, to appoint not less than five nor more than fifteen discreet persons, to be called School Commissioners, for the counties, cities, the said corporate towns and borough of Norfolk respectively, who, or a majority of them, shall hold their first meeting at the courthouses of their respective counties and corporations, on the first day of the court of the county or corporation next after that at which they shall have been appointed, or as soon thereafter as may be; they shall afterwards, in every year, hold a meeting at the places aforesaid, on the first day of the court of their county or corporation which shall be holden in the month of November; and they shall hold such extra meetings at the places aforesaid, as they may deem necessary, to be convened at any time on the application of any number of the said Commissioners, not less than a third part of the whole, reasonable notice thereof having been first given by advertisement, at the door of the courthouse, on some court day; a majority of the whole number of Commissioners shall be, at all times, necessary to form a board for the transaction of business, or to adjourn, except from day to day; but any smaller

number may adjourn from day to day; the board may adjourn from time to time, as they may think proper. The said Commissioners shall annually appoint one of their own body Treasurer, who, before he shall be entitled to receive any money by virtue of his office, shall give bond and good security in the court of the county, city, corporate town, or borough in which he may be appointed, payable to the President and Directors of the Literary Fund, in the penalty of two thousand dollars, conditioned for the faithful application and accounting for all moneys which may come to his hands by virtue of his office; which bond shall be filed and recorded in the office of such court. The said Commissioners shall have power to determine what number of poor children they will educate, what sum shall be paid for their education, to authorize each of themselves to select so many poor children as they may deem expedient, and to draw orders upon their Treasurer for the payment of the expense of tuition, and of furnishing such children with proper books and materials for writing and cyphering. The poor children, selected in manner aforesaid, shall, (with the assent of the father, or if no father, of the mother of such children respectively, or if no mother, with the assent of the guardian,) be sent to such school as may be convenient, to be taught reading, writing, and arithmetic.

2. *And be it enacted*, That the said Treasurer shall pay all moneys which may come to his hands in virtue of his office, to the order of the said Commissioners, or of such of them as shall have been authorized at their lawful meeting to draw upon him, and shall annually render an account of his receipts and disbursements, supported by proper vouchers, to the said Commissioners, who shall examine the same, and after correcting all errors which may be found therein, shall return the same to the clerks of the courts of their counties, corporate towns, cities, and borough of Norfolk respectively; and the said clerks shall certify a copy of such account to the President and Directors of the Literary Fund; for which copy and certificate the said clerks respectively shall be allowed by the said Commissioners such a fee as they may deem reasonable, to be paid by order on the said Treasurer; and whenever such Treasurer shall go out of office, he shall pay over any balance which may be in his hands to his successor in office.

3. *And be it enacted*, That it shall and may be lawful for the said Commissioners to appoint one of their own body as clerk, to fill all

vacancies created by death, resignation, or removal; to make such allowance to their Treasurer as they may deem reasonable for his services, and to authorize their Treasurer to pay their own reasonable expenses incurred in attending their meeting.

4. *And be it enacted,* That the President and Directors of the Literary Fund shall annually pay to each of the said Treasurers, or order, upon the production of a certificate from the proper clerk, that he has given the bond required by this act, such proportion of the sum of forty-five thousand dollars as the free white population of the county, city, corporate town, or borough, in which such Treasurers may respectively have been appointed, bears to the whole free white population of the Commonwealth, according to the last and every future census taken under the authority of the United States.

5. *And be it enacted,* That the bonds given by the Treasurers may be put in suit in the name of the President and Directors of the Literary Fund for their benefit, or for the benefit, and at the costs, of any person or persons who may sustain injury by a breach of the condition thereof. And if any Treasurer appointed under the authority of this act, or his executors, administrators, or other personal representative, shall, at any time, when duly required thereto, fail to pay any money received by such Treasurer by virtue of his office, it shall be lawful for the Commissioners of Schools, in the name of the President and Directors of the Literary Fund, or for the said President and Directors in their own name, by motion, on ten days previous notice, in any court of record having jurisdiction thereof, to recover a a judgment and have execution for such money, with ten per centum per annum damages thereon, from the time of such failure till payment, together with cost, against the said Treasurer and his securities, jointly or severally, or against the executors, administrators, or personal representative, of such Treasurer or his securities, or any of them; and the money made upon such judgment or execution shall be paid to the order of the Board of Commissioners, or of such person as they shall have authorized to receive it, pursuant to the provisions of this act.

6. *And be it further enacted,* That all money, funds, debts, or property now held by the overseers of the poor of any county or corporation, and derived from or acquired by the sale or forfeiture of glebe lands, and which shall be unappropriated by the citizens of such county or corporation, shall, after the passage of this act, be vested in

the said School Commissioners, the revenue or income of such money, funds, debts, or other property, to be used and applied by the said Commissioners to the education of the poor youth of their county or corporation, in the same manner as they are directed by this act to apply that portion of the revenue of the literary fund to which their county or corporation may be entitled; *provided*, that before any such funds, money, or other property shall be thus invested in the said Commissioners, the citizens of such county or corporation, or a majority of them, shall assent to the said investment.

7. *And be it enacted*, That the School Commissioners shall annually present a statement to the President and Directors of the Literary Fund, exhibiting the number of schools and indigent children in their county or corporation; the price paid for their tuition; the number of children educated in such schools; and what farther appropriation from the literary fund will, in their opinion, be sufficient to furnish the means of education to all the indigent children in their county or corporation.

8. *Be it further enacted*, That there shall be established in some convenient and proper part of the State, a University, to be called "The University of Virginia," wherein all the branches of useful science shall be taught. In order to aid the Legislature in ascertaining the permanent site of the said University, and in organizing it, there shall be appointed, without delay, by the Executive of this Commonwealth, twenty-four discreet and intelligent persons, who shall constitute a Board to be called "The Board of Commissioners for the University." One member of the said Board shall be appointed from each of the senatorial districts, as they were arranged by an act of the last session of the Legislature. If any person so appointed shall fail or refuse to act, his place shall be supplied from the same district, by appointment of the President and Directors of the Literary Fund. The said Board shall meet on the first day of August next, at the tavern in Rockfish Gap on the Blue Ridge, for the purpose of performing the duties hereby assigned to them. At least three-fourths of the whole number shall be necessary to form a Board for the transaction of business; but any smaller number may adjourn from day to day, until a quorum shall attend. The said Board, when assembled, shall have power to adjourn from time to time, and from place to place, until their duties shall have been per-

formed. It shall be their duty to enquire and report to the Legislature at their next session:

First—A proper site for the University.

Secondly—A plan for the building thereof.

Thirdly—The branches of learning which should be taught therein.

Fourthly—The number and description of professorships; and

Fifthly—Such general provisions as might properly be enacted by the Legislature, for the better organizing and governing the University.

The said Board are also authorized and required to receive any voluntary contributions, whether conditional or absolute, whether in land, money, or other property, which may be offered, through them, to the President and Directors of the Literary Fund, for the benefit of the University; and to report the same to the Legislature at their next session. The members of the said Board of Commissioners shall be allowed for their services the same pay and traveling expenses, as are allowed to members of the General Assembly, to be ascertained and certified by the Board, and paid out of the literary fund.

9. *Be it further enacted*, That as soon as the site of the said University shall be ascertained by law, there shall be appropriated out of the revenue of the literary fund, the sum of fifteen thousand dollars per annum, for the purpose of defraying the expenses of procuring the land and erecting the buildings, and for the permanent endowment of the said University; *provided, however*, that the appropriation hereby made to the University, shall in no manner impair or diminish the appropriations hereinbefore made to the education of the poor in the several counties or corporations.

10. *Be it further enacted*, That the University aforesaid shall be under the government of thirteen Visitors, to be appointed by the President and Directors of the Literary Fund, and to hold their offices for seven years, and until their successors shall be appointed, unless sooner displaced by the said President and Directors. All vacancies in the office of Visitor, by death, resignation, or removal out of the Commonwealth, or failure to act, for the space of one year, shall be supplied by the said President and Directors.

11. The said Visitors shall appoint one of their own body to be Rector, and they shall be a body corporate, under the name and style of "The Rector and Visitors of the University of Virginia;" and, as such, they may have and use a common seal, receive and hold pro-

perty for the benefit of the University, sue and be sued, implead and be impleaded. They shall have power to appoint a clerk for their own body, and allow him a reasonable compensation for his services; to appoint and remove the professors and teachers, and all other officers of the University; to regulate their salaries and fees, and to make all such by-laws and regulations as may be necessary to the good government of the University, and not contrary to the laws of the land. But the said Rector and Visitors shall at all times conform to such laws as the Legislature may from time to time think proper to enact for their government; and the said University shall in all things, at all times, be subject to the control of the Legislature.

12. This act shall commence and be in force from and after the 1st day of March.

I.

REPORT OF THE COMMISSIONERS APPOINTED TO FIX THE SITE OF THE UNIVERSITY OF VIRGINIA, &c.

The Commissioners for the University of Virginia, having met, as by law required, at the tavern, in Rockfish Gap, on the Blue Ridge, on the first day of August, of this present year, 1818; and having formed a board, proceeded on that day to the discharge of the duties assigned to them by the act of the Legislature, entitled "An act, appropriating part of the revenue of the literary fund, and for other purposes;" and having continued their proceedings by adjournment, from day to day, to Tuesday, the 4th day of August, have agreed to a report on the several matters with which they were charged, which report they now respectfully address and submit to the Legislature of the State.

The first duty enjoined on them, was to enquire and report a site, in some convenient and proper part of the State, for an university, to be called the "University of Virginia." In this enquiry, they supposed that the governing considerations should be the healthiness of the site, the fertility of the neighboring country, and its centrality to the white population of the whole State. For, although the act authorized and required them to receive any voluntary contributions, whether conditional or absolute, which might be offered through them to the President and Directors of the Literary Fund, for the benefit of the University, yet they did not consider this as establishing an auction, or as pledging the location to the highest bidder.

Three places were proposed, to wit: Lexington, in the county of Rockbridge, Staunton, in the county of Augusta, and the Central College, in the county of Albemarle. Each of these was unexceptionable as to healthiness and fertility. It was the degree of centrality to the white population of the State which alone then constituted the important point of comparison between these places; and the Board, after full enquiry, and impartial and mature consideration, are of opinion, that the central point of the white population of the State is nearer to the Central College than to either Lexington or Staunton, by great and important differences; and all other circumstances of the place in general being favorable to it, as a position for an university, they do report the Central College, in Albemarle, to be a convenient and proper part of the State for the University of Virginia.

2. The Board having thus agreed on a proper site for the University, to be reported to the Legislature, proceed to the second of the duties assigned to them—that of proposing a plan for its buildings—and they are of opinion that it should consist of distinct houses or pavilions, arranged at proper distances on each side of a lawn of a proper breadth, and of indefinite extent, in one direction, at least; in each of which should be a lecturing room, with from two to four apartments, for the accommodation of a professor and his family; that these pavilions should be united by a range of dormitories, sufficient each for the accommodation of two students only, this provision being deemed advantageous to morals, to order, and to uninterrupted study; and that a passage of some kind, under cover from the weather, should give a communication along the whole range. It is supposed that such pavilions, on an average of the larger and smaller, will cost each about $5,000; each dormitory about $350, and hotels of a single room, for a refectory, and two rooms for the tenant, necessary for dieting the students, will cost about $3500 each. The number of these pavilions will depend on the number of professors, and that of the dormitories and hotels on the number of students to be lodged and dieted. The advantages of this plan are: greater security against fire and infection; tranquillity and comfort to the professors and their families thus insulated; retirement to the students; and the admission of enlargement to any degree to which the institution may extend

28

in future times. It is supposed probable, that a building of somewhat more size in the middle of the grounds may be called for in time, in which may be rooms for religious worship, under such impartial regulations as the Visitors shall prescribe, for public examinations, for a library, for the schools of music, drawing, and other associated purposes.

3, 4. In proceeding to the third and fourth duties prescribed by the Legislature, of reporting "the branches of learning, which should be taught in the University, and the number and description of the professorships they will require," the Commissioners were first to consider at what point it was understood that university education should commence? Certainly not with the alphabet, for reasons of expediency and impracticability, as well from the obvious sense of the Legislature, who, in the same act, make other provision for the primary instruction of the poor children, expecting, doubtless, that in other cases it would be provided by the parent, or become, perhaps, subject of future and further attention of the Legislature. The objects of this primary education determine its character and limits. These objects would be,

To give to every citizen the information he needs for the transaction of his own business;

To enable him to calculate for himself, and to express and preserve his ideas, his contracts and accounts, in writing;

To improve, by reading, his morals and faculties;

To understand his duties to his neighbors and country, and to discharge with competence the functions confided to him by either;

To know his rights; to exercise with order and justice those he retains; to choose with discretion the fiduciary of those he delegates; and to notice their conduct with diligence, with candor, and judgment;

And, in general, to observe with intelligence and faithfulness all the social relations under which he shall be placed.

To instruct the mass of our citizens in these, their rights, interests and duties, as men and citizens, being then the objects of education in the primary schools, whether private or public, in them should be taught reading, writing and numerical arithmetic, the elements of mensuration, (useful in so many callings,) and the outlines of geography and history. And this brings us to the point at which are to commence the higher branches of education, of which the Legislature require the development; those, for example, which are,

To form the statesmen, legislators and judges, on whom public prosperity and individual happiness are so much to depend;

To expound the principles and structure of government, the laws which regulate the intercourse of nations, those formed municipally for our own government, and a sound spirit of legislation, which, banishing all arbitrary and unnecessary restraint on individual action, shall leave us free to do whatever does not violate the equal rights of another;

To harmonize and promote the interests of agriculture, manufactures and commerce, and by well informed views of political economy to give a free scope to the public industry;

To develop the reasoning faculties of our youth, enlarge their minds, cultivate their morals, and instill into them the precepts of virtue and order;

To enlighten them with mathematical and physical sciences, which advance the arts, and administer to the health, the subsistence, and comforts of human life;

And, generally, to form them to habits of reflection and correct action, rendering them examples of virtue to others, and of happiness within themselves.

These are the objects of that higher grade of education, the benefits and blessings of which the Legislature now propose to provide for the good and ornament of their country, the gratification and happiness of their fellow-citizens, of the parent especially, and his progeny, on which all his affections are concentrated.

In entering on this field, the Commissioners are aware that they have to encounter much difference of opinion as to the extent which it is expedient that this institution should occupy. Some good men, and even of respectable information, consider the learned sciences as useless acquirements; some think that they do not better the condition of man; and others that education, like private and individual concerns, should be left to private individual effort; not reflecting that an establishment embracing all the sciences which may be useful and even necessary in the various vocations of life, with the buildings and apparatus belonging to each, are far beyond the reach of individual means, and must either derive existence from public patronage, or not exist at all. This would leave us, then, without those callings which depend on education, or send us to other countries to seek the instruction they require. But the Commissioners are happy in considering the statute under which they are assembled as proof that the Legislature is far from the abandonment of objects so interesting. They are sensible that the advantages of well-directed education, moral, political and economical, are truly above all estimate. Education generates habits of application, of order, and the love of virtue; and controls, by the force of habit, any innate obliquities in our moral organization. We should be far, too, from the discouraging persuasion that man is fixed, by the law of his nature, at a given point; that his improvement is a chimera, and the hope delusive of rendering ourselves wiser, happier or better than our forefathers were. As well might it be urged that the wild and uncultivated tree, hitherto yielding sour and bitter fruit only, can never be made to yield better; yet we know that the grafting art implants a new tree on the savage stock, producing what is most estimable both in kind and degree. Education, in like manner, engrafts a new man on the native stock, and improves what in his nature was vicious and perverse into qualties of virtue and social worth. And it cannot be but that each generation succeeding to the knowledge acquired by all those who preceded it, adding to it their own acqusitions and discoveries, and handing the mass down for successive and constant accumulation, must advance the knowledge and well-being of mankind, not *infinitely*, as some have said, but *indefinitely*, and to a term which no one can fix and foresee. Indeed, we need look back half a century, to times which many now living remember well, and see the wonderful advances in the sciences and arts which have been made within that period. Some of these have rendered the elements themselves subservient to the purposes of man, have harnessed them to the yoke of his labors, and effected the great blessings of moderating his own, of accomplishing what was beyond his feeble force, and extending the comforts of life to a much enlarged circle, to those who had before known its necessaries only. That these are not the vain dreams of sanguine hope, we have before our eyes real and living examples. What, but education, has advanced us beyond the condition of our indigenous neighbors? And what chains them to their present state of barbarism and wretchedness, but a bigotted veneration for the supposed superlative wisdom of their fathers, and the preposterous idea that they are to look backward for better things, and not forward, longing, as it should seem, to return to the days of eating acorns and roots, rather than indulge in the degeneracies of civilization? And how much more encouraging to the achievements of science and improvement is this, than the desponding view that the condition of man cannot be ameliorated, that what has been must ever be, and that to secure ourselves where we are, we must tread with awful reverence in the footsteps of our fathers. This doctrine is the genuine fruit of the alliance between Church and State; the tenants of which, finding themselves but too well in their present condition, oppose all advances which might unmask their usurpations, and monopolies of honors, wealth, and power, and fear every change, as endangering the comforts they now hold. Nor must we omit to mention, among the benefits of education, the incalculable advantage of training up able counsellors to administer the affairs of our country in all its departments, legislative, executive and judiciary, and to bear their proper share in the councils of our national government; nothing more than education advancing the prosperity, the power, and the happiness of a nation.

Encouraged, therefore, by the sentiments of the Legislature, manifested in this statute, we present the following tabular statement of the branches of learning which we think should be taught in the University, forming them into groups, each of which are within the powers of a single professor:

I. Languages, ancient:
- Latin,
- Greek,
- Hebrew.

II. Languages, modern:
- French,
- Spanish,
- Italian,
- German,
- Anglo-Saxon.

III. Mathematics, pure:
- Algebra,
- Fluxions,
- Geometry, Elementary, Transcendental.
- Architecture, Military, Naval.

IV. Physico-Mathematics:
- Mechanics,
- Statics,
- Dynamics,
- Pneumatics,
- Acoustics,
- Optics,
- Astronomy,
- Geography.

V. Physics, or Natural Philosophy:
- Chemistry,
- Mineralogy.

VI. Botany,
- Zoology.

VII. Anatomy,
- Medicine.

VIII. Government,
Political Economy,
Law of Nature and Nations,
History, being interwoven with Politics and Law.

IX. Law, municipal.

X. Ideology,
General Grammar,
Ethics,
Rhetoric,
Belles Lettres, and the fine arts.

Some of the terms used in this table being subject to a difference of acceptation, it is proper to define the meaning and comprehension intended to be given them here:

Geometry, Elementary, is that of straight lines and of the circle.
Transcendental, is that of all other curves; it includes, of course, *Projectiles*, a leading branch of the military art.

Military Architecture includes Fortification, another branch of that art.

Statics respect matter generally, in a state of rest, and include Hydrostatics, or the laws of fluids particularly, at rest or in equilibrio.

Dynamics, used as a general term, include
Dynamics proper, or the laws of *solids* in motion; and
Hydrodynamics, or Hydraulics, those of *fluids* in motion.

Pneumatics teach the theory of air, its weight, motion, condensation, rarefaction, &c.

Acoustics, or Phonics, the theory of sound.

Optics, the laws of light and vision.

Physics, or Physiology, in a general sense, mean the doctrine of the physical objects of our senses.

Chemistry is meant, with its other usual branches, to comprehend the theory of agriculture.

Mineralogy, in addition to its peculiar subjects, is here understood to embrace what is real in geology.

Ideology is the doctrine of thought.

General Grammar explains the construction of language.

Some articles in this distribution of sciences will need observation. A professor is proposed for ancient languages, the Latin, Greek, and Hebrew, particularly; but these languages being the foundation common to all the sciences, it is difficult to foresee what may be the extent of this school. At the same time, no greater obstruction to industrious study could be proposed than the presence, the intrusions and the noisy turbulence of a multitude of small boys; and if they are to be placed here for the rudiments of the languages, they may be so numerous that its character and value as an University will be merged in those of a Grammar school. It is, therefore, greatly to be wished, that preliminary schools, either on private or public establishment, could be distributed in districts through the State, as preparatory to the entrance of students into the University. The tender age at which this part of education commences, generally about the tenth year, would weigh heavily with parents in sending their sons to a school so distant as the central establishment would be from most of them. Districts of such extent as that every parent should be within a day's journey of his son at school, would be desirable in cases of sickness, and convenient for supplying their ordinary wants, and might be made to lessen sensibly the expense of this part of their education. And where a sparse population would not, within such a compass, furnish subjects sufficient to maintain a school, a competent enlargement of district must, of necessity, there be submitted to. At these district schools or colleges, boys should be rendered able to read the easier authors, Latin and Greek. This would be useful and sufficient for many not intended for an University education. At these, too, might be taught English grammar, the higher branches of numerical arithmetic, the geometry of straight lines and of the circle, the elements of navigation, and geography to a sufficient degree, and thus afford to greater numbers the means of being qualified for the various vocations of life, needing more instruction than merely menial or prædial labor, and the same advantages to youths whose education may have been neglected until too late to lay a foundation in the learned languages. These institutions, intermediate between the primary schools and University, might then be the passage of entrance for youths into the University, where their classical learning might be critically completed, by a study of the authors of highest degree; and it is at this stage only that they should be received at the University. Giving then a portion of their time to a finished knowledge of the Latin and Greek, the rest might be appropriated to the modern languages, or to the commencement of the course of science for which they should be destined. This would generally be about the fifteenth year of their age, when they might go with more safety and contentment to that distance from their parents. Until this preparatory provision shall be made, either the University will be overwhelmed with the grammar school, or a separate establishment, under one or more ushers, for its lower classes, will be advisable, at a mile or two distant from the general one; where, too, may be exercised the stricter government necessary for young boys, but unsuitable for youths arrived at years of discretion.

The considerations which have governed the specification of languages to be taught by the professor of modern languages were, that the French is the language of general intercourse among nations, and as a depository of human science, is unsurpassed by any other language, living or dead; that the Spanish is highly interesting to us, as the language spoken by so great a portion of the inhabitants of our continents, with whom we shall probably have great intercourse ere long, and is that also in which is written the greater part of the earlier history of America. The Italian abounds with works of very superior order, valuable for their matter, and still more distinguished as models of the finest taste in style and composition. And the German now stands in a line with that of the most learned nations in richness of erudition and advance in the sciences. It is too of common descent with the language of our own country, a branch of the same original Gothic stock, and furnishes valuable illustrations for us. But in this point of view, the Anglo-Saxon is of peculiar value. We have placed it among the modern languages, because it is in fact that which we speak, in the earliest form in which we have knowledge of it. It has been undergoing, with time, those gradual changes which all languages, ancient and modern, have experienced; and even now needs only to be printed in the modern character and orthography to be intelligible, in a considerable degree, to an English reader. It has this value, too, above the Greek and Latin, that while it gives the radix of the mass of our language, they explain its innovations only. Obvious proofs of this have been presented to the modern reader in the disquisitions of Horn Tooke; and Fortescue Aland has well explained the great instruction which may be derived from it to a full understanding of our ancient common law, on which, as a stock, our whole system of law is engrafted. It will form the first link in the chain of an historical review of our language through all its successive changes to the present day, will constitute the foundation of that critical instruction in it which ought to be found in a seminary of general learning, and thus reward amply the few weeks of attention which would alone be requisite for its attainment; a language already fraught with all the eminent science of our parent country, the future vehicle of whatever we may ourselves achieve, and destined to occupy so much space on the globe, claims distinguished attention in American education.

Medicine, where fully taught, is usually subdivided into several professorships, but this cannot well be without the accessory of an hospital, where the student can have the benefit of attending clinical lectures, and of assisting at operations of surgery. With this accessory, the seat of our University is not yet prepared, either by its population or by the numbers of poor who would leave their own houses, and accept of the charities of an hospital. For the present, therefore, we propose but a single professor for both medicine and anatomy. By him the medical science may be taught, with a history and explanations of all its successive theories from Hippocrates to the present day; and anatomy may be fully treated. Vegetable pharmacy will make a part of the botanical course, and mineral and chemical pharmacy of those of mineralogy and chemistry. This degree of medical information is such as the mass of scientific students would wish to possess, as enabling them in their course through life, to estimate with satisfaction the extent and limits of the aid to human life and health, which they may understandingly expect from that art; and it constitutes such a foundation for those intended for the profession, that the finishing course of practice at the bed-sides of the sick, and at the operations of surgery in a hospital, can neither be long nor expensive. To seek this finishing elsewhere, must therefore be submitted to for a while.

In conformity with the principles of our Constitution, which places all sects of religion on an equal footing, with the jealousies of the different sects in guarding that equality from encroachment and surprise, and with the sentiments of the Legislature in favor of freedom of religion, manifested on former occasions, we have proposed no professor of divinity; and the rather as the proofs of the being of a God, the creator, preserver, and supreme ruler of the universe, the author of all the relations of morality, and of the laws and obligations these infer, will be within the province of the professor of ethics; to which adding the developments of these moral obligations, of those in which all sects agree, with a knowledge of the languages, Hebrew, Greek, and Latin, a basis will be formed common to all sects. Proceeding thus far without offence to the Constitution, we have thought it proper at this point to leave every sect to provide, as they think fittest, the means of further instruction in their own peculiar tenets.

We are further of opinion, that after declaring by law that certain sciences shall be taught in the University, fixing the number of professors they require, which we think should, at present, be ten, limiting (except as to the professors who shall be first engaged in each branch,) a maximum for their salaries, (which should be a certain but moderate subsistence, to be made up by liberal tuition fees, as an excitement to assiduity,) it will be best to leave to the discretion of the visitors, the grouping of these sciences together, according to the accidental qualifications of the professors; and the introduction also of other branches of science, when enabled by private donations, or by public provision, and called for by the increase of population, or other change of circumstances; to establish beginnings, in short, to be developed by time, as those who come after us shall find expedient. They will be more advanced than we are in science and in useful arts, and will know best what will suit the circumstances of their day.

We have proposed no formal provision for the gymnastics of the school, although a proper object of attention for every institution of youth. These exercises with ancient nations, constituted the principal part of the education of their youth. Their arms and mode of warfare rendered them severe in the extreme; ours, on the same correct principle, should be adapted to our arms and warfare; and the manual exercise, military manœuvres, and tactics generally, should be the frequent exercises of the students, in their hours of recreation. It is at that age of aptness, docility, and emulation of the practices of manhood, that such things are soonest learnt and longest remembered. The use of tools too in the manual arts is worthy of encouragement, by facilitating to such as choose it, an admission into the neighboring workshops. To these should be added the arts which embellish life, dancing, music, and drawing; the last more especially, as an important part of military education. These innocent arts furnish amusement and happiness to those who, having time on their hands, might less inoffensively employ it. Needing, at the same time, no regular incorporation with the institution, they may be left to accessory teachers, who will be paid by the individuals employing them, the University only providing proper apartments for their exercise.

The fifth duty prescribed to the Commissioners, is to propose such general provisions as may be properly enacted by the Legislature, for the better organizing and governing the University.

In the education of youth, provision is to be made for, 1, tuition; 2, diet; 3, lodging; 4, government; and 5, honorary excitements. The first of these constitutes the proper functions of the professors; 2, the dieting of the students should be left to private boarding houses of their own choice, and at their own expense; to be regulated by the Visitors from time to time, the house only being provided by the University within its own precincts, and thereby of course subjected to the general regimen, moral or sumptuary, which they shall prescribe. 3. They should be lodged in dormitories, making a part of the general system of buildings. 4. The best mode of government for youth, in large collections, is certainly a desideratum not yet attained with us. It may be well questioned whether *fear* after a certain age, is a motive to which we should have ordinary recourse. The human character is susceptible of other incitements to correct conduct, more worthy of employ, and of better effect. Pride of character, laudable ambition, and moral dispositions are innate correctives of the indiscretions of that lively age; and when strengthened by habitual appeal and exercise, have a happier effect on future character than the degrading motive of fear. Hardening them to disgrace, to corporal punishments, and servile humiliations cannot be the best process for producing erect character. The affectionate deportment between father and son, offers in truth the best example for that of tutor and pupil; and the experience and practice of other* countries, in this respect, may be worthy of enquiry and consideration with us. It will then be for the wisdom and discretion of the Visitors to devise and perfect a proper system of government, which, if it be founded in reason and comity, will be more likely to nourish in the minds of our youth the combined spirit of order and self-respect, so congenial with our political institutions, and so important to be woven into the American character. 5. What qualifications shall be required to entitle to entrance into the University, the arrangement of the days and hours of lecturing for the different schools, so as to facilitate to the students the circle of attendance on them; the establishment of periodical and public examinations, the premiums to be given for distinguished merit; whether honorary degrees shall be

---

* A police exercised by the students themselves, under proper discretion, has been tried with success in some countries, and the rather as forming them for initiation into the duties and practices of civil life.

conferred, and by what appellations; whether the title to these shall depend on the time the candidate has been at the University, or, where nature has given a greater share of understanding, attention, and application; whether he shall not be allowed the advantages resulting from these endowments, with other minor items of government, we are of opinion should be entrusted to the Visitors; and the statute under which we act having provided for the appointment of these, we think they should moreover be charged with

The erection, preservation, and repair of the buildings, the care of the grounds and appurtenances, and of the interest of the University generally.

That they should have power to appoint a bursar, employ a proctor, and all other necessary agents.

To appoint and remove professors, two-thirds of the whole number of Visitors voting for the removal.

To prescribe their duties and the course of education, in conformity with the law.

To establish rules for the government and discipline of the students, not contrary to the laws of the land.

To regulate the tuition fees, and the rent of the dormitories they occupy.

To prescribe and control the duties and proceedings of all officers, servants, and others, with respect to the buildings, lands, appurtenances, and other property and interests of the University.

To draw from the literary fund such moneys as are by law charged on it for this institution; and in general

To direct and do all matters and things which, not being inconsistent with the laws of the land, to them shall seem most expedient for promoting the purposes of the said institution; which several functions they should be free to exercise in the form of by-laws, rules, resolutions, orders, instructions, or otherwise, as they should deem proper.

That they should have two stated meetings in the year, and occasional meetings at such times as they should appoint, or on a special call with such notice as themselves shall prescribe by a general rule; which meetings should be at the Univresity, a majority of them constituting a quorum for business; and that on the death or resignation of a member, or on his removal by the President and Directors of the Literary Fund, or the Executive, or such other authority as the Legislature shall think best, such President and Directors, or the Executive, or other authority, shall appoint a successor.

That the said Visitors should appoint one of their own body to be Rector, and with him be a body corporate, under the style and title of the Rector and Visitors of the University of Virginia, with the right, as such, to use a common seal; that they should have capacity to plead and be impleaded in all courts of justice, and in all cases interesting to the University, which may be the subjects of legal cognizance and jurisdiction; which pleas should not abate by the determination of their office, but should stand revived in the name of their successors, and they should be capable in law and in trust for the University, of receiving subscriptions and donations, real and personal, as well from bodies corporate, or persons associated, as from private individuals.

And that the said Rector and Visitors should, at all times, conform to such laws as the Legislature may, from time to time, think proper to enact for their government; and the said University should, in all things, and at all times, be subject to the control of the Legislature.

And lastly, the Commissioners report to the Legislature the following conditional offers to the President and Directors of the Literary Fund, for the benefit of the University:

On the condition that Lexington, or its vicinity, shall be selected as the site of the University, and that the same be permanently established there within two years from the date, John Robinson, of Rockbridge county, has executed a deed to the President and Directors of the Literary Fund, to take effect at his death, for the following tracts of land, to wit:

400 acres on the North fork of James river, known by the name of Hart's bottom, purchased of the late Gen. Bowyer.

171 acres adjoining the same, purchased of James Griggsby.

203 acres joining the last mentioned tract, purchased of William Paxton.

112 acres lying on the North river, above the lands of Arthur Glasgow, conveyed to him by William Paxton's heirs.

500 acres adjoining the lands of Arthur Glasgow, Benjamin Camden and David Edmonson.

545 acres lying in Pryor's gap, conveyed to him by the heirs of William Paxton, deceased.

260 acres lying in Childer's gap, purchased of Wm. Mitchell.

300 acres lying, also, in Childer's gap, purchased of Nicholas Jones.

500 acres lying on Buffalo, joining the lands of Jas. Johnston.

340 acres on the Cowpasture river, conveyed to him by General James Breckenridge—reserving the right of selling the two last mentioned tracts, and converting them into other lands contiguous to Hart's bottom, for the benefit of the University; also, the whole of his slaves, amounting to 57 in number; one lot of 22 acres, joining the town of Lexington, to pass immediately on the establishment of the University, together with all the personal estate of every kind, subject only to the payment of his debts and fulfillment of his contracts.

It has not escaped the attention of the Commissioners, that the deed referred to is insufficient to pass the estate in the lands intended to be conveyed, and may be otherwise defective; but, if necessary, this defect may be remedied before the meeting of the Legislature, which the Commissioners are advised will be done.

The Board of Trustees of Washington College have also proposed to transfer the whole of their funds, viz: 100 shares in the funds of the James River Company, 31 acres of land upon which their buildings stand, their philosophical apparatus, their expected interest in the funds of the Cincinnati Society, the libraries of the Graham and Washington Societies, and $3,000 in cash, on condition that a reasonable provision be made for the present professors. A subscription has also been offered by the people of Lexington and its vicinity, amounting to $17,878, all which will appear from the deed and other documents, reference thereto being had.

In this case, also, it has not escaped the attention of the Commissioners, that questions may arise as to the power of the trustees to make the above transfers.

On the condition that the Central College shall be made the site of the University, its whole property, real and personal, in possession or in action, is offered. This consists of a parcel of land of 47 acres, whereon the buildings of the college are begun, one pavilion and its appendix of dormitories being already far advanced, and with one other pavilion, and equal annexation of dormitories, being expected to be completed during the present season—of another parcel of 153 acres, near the former, and including a considerable eminence very favorable for the erection of a future observatory; of the proceeds of the sales of two glebes, amounting to $3,280 86 cents; and of a subscription of $41,248, on papers in hand, besides what is on outstanding papers of unknown amount, not yet returned—out of these sums are to be taken, however, the cost of the lands, of the buildings, and other works done, and for existing contracts. For the conditional transfer of these to the President and Directors of the Literary Fund, a regular power, signed by the subscribers and founders of the Central College generally, has been given to its Visitors and Proctor, and a deed conveying the said property accordingly to the President and Directors of the Literary Fund, has been duly executed by the said Proctor, and acknowledged for record in the office of the clerk of the county court of Albemarle.

Signed and certified by the members present, each in his proper hand-writing, this 4th day of August, 1818.

TH: JEFFERSON,
CREED TAYLOR,
PETER RANDOLPH,
WM. BROCKENBROUGH,
ARCH'D RUTHERFORD,
ARDH'D STUART,
JAMES BRECKENRIDGE,
HENRY E. WATKINS,
JAMES MADISON,
A. T. MASON,
HUGH HOLMES,
PHIL. C. PENDLETON,
SPENCER ROANE,
JOHN M. C. TAYLOR,
J. G. JACKSON,
PHIL. SLAUGHTER,
WM. H. CABELL,
NAT. H. CLAIBORNE,
WM. A. C. DADE,
WILLIAM JONES,
THOMAS WILSON.

K.

AN ACT ESTABLISHING THE UNIVERSITY,

(Passed January 25th, 1819.)

1. Be it declared, by the General Assembly of Virginia, that the conveyance of the lands, and other property appertaining to the Central College, in the county of Albemarle, which has been executed by the Proctor thereof, under authority of the subscribers and founders, to the President and Directors of the Literary Fund, is hereby

accepted, for the use, and on the conditions in the said deed of conveyance expressed.

2. And be it enacted, that there shall be established, on the site provided for the said college, an University, to be called, "*The University of Virginia;*" that it shall be under the government of seven Visitors, to be appointed forthwith by the Governor, with the advice of the Council, notifying thereof the persons so appointed, and prescribing to them a day for their first meeting at the said University, with supplementary instructions for procuring a meeting subsequently, in the event of failure at the time first appointed.

3. The said Visitors, or so many of them as, being a majority, shall attend, shall appoint a Rector of their own body, to preside at their meetings, and a secretary to record, attest and preserve their proceedings, and shall proceed to examine into the state of the property conveyed as aforesaid; and shall make an inventory of the same, specifying the items whereof it consists; shall notice the buildings and other improvements already made, and those which are in progress; and shall take measures for their completion, and for the addition of such others, from time to time, as may be necessary.

4. In the said University shall be taught the Latin, Greek and Hebrew languages, French, Spanish, Italian, German and Anglo-Saxon, the different branches of Mathematics, pure and physical; natural philosophy; the principles of agriculture; chemistry; mineralogy, including geology; botany; zoology; anatomy; medicine; civil government; political economy; the law of nature and nations; municipal law; history; ideology; general grammar; ethics; rhetoric; and belles lettres; which branches of science shall be so distributed, and under so many professors, not exceeding ten, as the Visitors shall think proper and expedient.

5. Each professor shall be allowed the use of the apartment and accommodations provided for him, and those first employed, such standing salary as the Visitors shall think proper and sufficient, and their successors such standing salary, not exceeding $1,000, as the Visitors shall think proper and sufficient, with such tuition fees from each student as the Visitors shall, from time to time, establish.

6. The said Visitors shall be charged with the erection, preservation and repair of the buildings, the care of the grounds and appurtenances, and of the interests of the University generally; they shall have power to appoint a Bursar, employ a Proctor, and all other

necessary agents; to appoint and remove professors, two-thirds of the whole number of Visitors voting for the removal; to prescribe their duties, and the course of education, in conformity with the law; to establish rules for the government and discipline of the students, not contrary to the laws of the land; to regulate the tuition fees, and the rent of the dormitories occupied; to prescribe and control the duties and proceedings of all officers, servants and others, with respect to the buildings, lands, appurtenances and other property and interests of the University; to draw from the literary fund such moneys as are by law charged on it for this institution; and, in general, to direct and do all matters and things which, not being inconsistent with the laws of the land, to them shall seem most expedient for promoting the purposes of the said institution; which several functions they shall be free to exercise in the form of by-laws, rules, resolutions, orders, instructions, or otherwise, as they shall deem proper.

7. They shall have two stated meetings in every year, to wit: on the first Mondays of April and October; and occasional meetings at such other times as they shall appoint, or on a special call, with such notice as they themselves shall prescribe by a general rule; which meetings shall be at the University; a majority of them constituting a quorum for business; and on the death, resignation of a member, or failure to act for the space of one year, or on his removal out of the Commonwealth, or by the Governor, with the advice of council, the Governor, with like advice, shall appoint a successor.

8. The said Rector and Visitors shall be a body corporate, under the style and title of *The Rector and Visitors of the University of Virginia*, with the right, as such, to use a common seal; they shall have capacity to plead and be impleaded in all courts of justice, and in all cases interesting to the University, which may be subjects of legal cognizance and jurisdiction; which pleas shall not abate by the determination of their office, but shall stand revived in the name of their successors; and they shall be capable in law, and in trust, for the University, of receiving subscriptions and donations, real and personal, as well from bodies corporate, or persons associated, as from private individuals.

9. The said Rector and Visitors shall, at all times, conform to such laws as the Legislature may, from time to time, think proper to enact for their government; and the said University shall, in all things, and at all times, be subject to the control of the Legislature. And

the said Rector and Visitors of the University of Virginia, shall be, and they are hereby required to make report, annually, to the President and Directors of the Literary Fund, (to be laid before the Legislature at their next succeeding session,) embracing a full account of the disbursements, the funds on hand, and a general statement of the condition of the said University.

10. The said Board of Visitors, or a majority thereof, by nomination of the Board, shall, once in every year, at least, visit the said University; enquire into the proceedings and practices thereat; examine the progress of the students, and give to those who excel in any branch of science, there taught, such honorary marks and testimonies of approbation as may encourage and excite to industry and emulation.

11. On every 29th of February, or, if that be Sunday, then on the next or earliest day thereafter, on which a meeting can be effected, the Governor and Council shall be in session, and shall appoint Visitors of the University, either the same or others, at their discretion, to serve until the 29th day of February next ensuing, duly and timely notifying to them their appointment, and prescribing a day for their first meeting at the University; after which, their meetings, stated and occasional, shall be as hereinbefore provided: *Provided*, that nothing in this act contained shall suspend the proceedings of the Visitors of the said Central College of Albemarle; but, for the purpose of expediting the objects of said institution, they shall be authorized, under the control of the Governor and Council, to continue the exercise of their functions, and fulfill those of their successors, until the first actual meeting of their said successors.

L.

We, the subscribers, Visitors of the Central College, having been specially called to meet on 26th of February, 1819, and authorized by the act of the Legislature, now in session, for establishing the University of Virginia, to continue the exercise of our former functions, and to fulfill the duties of our successors, Visitors of the said University, until their first actual meeting, have unanimously agreed on the following opinions and proceedings:

That it is expedient that all the funds of the University, applicable to the services of the present year, which shall remain after meeting all the other current and necessary purposes, shall be applied to the providing additional buildings for the accommodation of the professors, and for dieting and lodging the students of the University.

That the urgency of the advancing season, and the importance of procuring workmen before they become generally otherwise engaged for the season, render it necessary for expediting the objects of the University, that certain measures be forthwith taken, which, if delayed until the first actual meeting of our successors, would materially retard those objects.

That taking into view the balance remaining of the funds of the last year, to wit: of the proceeds of the glebes and of the first and second installments of subscriptions, after payment shall have been made of the expenditures of the same year: as also the third installment of subscriptions payable in April, 1820, and the public endowment of $15,000 for the present year; engagements may be entered into for building, in the approaching season, two more pavilions for the professors, one hotel for dieting the students, and as many additional dormitories for their lodging, with the necessary appendages, as the said funds shall be competent to accomplish; that we approve of the propositions for covering with tin sheets the pavilions and hotels hereafter to be covered, and for bringing water to them by wooden pipes from the neighboring highlands.

That Alexander Garrett, Treasurer of the Central College, be continued as the depository of the funds of the institution, with authority to exercise the powers and perform the duties of the Bursar of the University until otherwise provided.

That to meet the immediate and pressing calls for money, he be authorized to receive from the Treasury of the State the sum of fifteen hundred dollars for the present year.

That a copy of these proceedings be laid before the Governor and Council, for the exercise of the power of control committed to them by the same act of the Legislature, should they think proper to exercise that power on any part of these proceedings.

(Signed,) TH: JEFFERSON,
JAMES MADISON,
J. H. COCKE,
DAVID WATSON.

At a meeting of the Visitors of the University of Virginia, at the said University on the 29th day of March, 1819, being the day prescribed by the Governor for their first meeting, James Madison, Joseph C. Cabell, Chapman Johnson, James Breckenridge, Robert Taylor, John H. Cocke, and Thomas Jefferson, attended.

The Board proceeding to the duties prescribed to them by the act of the General Assembly, entitled "An act establishing an University," appointed Thomas Jefferson their Rector, and Peter Minor their Secretary.

Resolved, That Alexander Garrett be appointed Bursar of the University, and that he be allowed as a compensation for the duties of his said office, the sum of $250 a year; and that the Committee of Superintendence, hereafter to be named, be authorized to engage Arthur Brockenbrough as Proctor of the University, with an allowacce not exceeding $2,000 a year, or if he cannot be engaged, then any other person on such terms as they find necessary.

Resolved, That the acting Proctor be instructed to examine into the state of the property, real and personal, (moneys and credits excepted,) formerly appertaining to the Central College, and conveyed to the President and Directors of the Literary Fund; that he make an inventory of the same, as it stands at this day, specifying the items whereof it consists, and noticing the buildings and other improvements already made, and those which are in progress, and that the late Treasurer of the College, now the Bursar, be instructed to make a statement of the funds in money and credits which appertained to the said College, and were conveyed to the said President and Directors; specifying how much of the said moneys have been received, how much have been paid away, to whom and for what purposes, what debts, to whom, and for what purposes are due on settled accounts, to whom and for what purposes debts are due on unsettled accounts; what part of the annual donation by the Commonwealth has been received, and how much thereof has been paid away, to whom, and for what purposes; all referring to the present date; and that the said inventory and statement be returned to this Board, to be preserved among its records.

Resolved, That the Proctor be required to provide a common seal for the University, in the field of which shall be engraved a Minerva enrobed in her peplum and characteristic habiliments as inventress and protectress of the arts, and that the verge be "University of Virginia," and at the bottom the date of "1819."

It is the opinion of the Board that each of the professors of the University be allowed a standing salary of $1,500 a year, and to receive also $30 annually from every student attending him for instruction in any or all of the branches of science which constitute the department of which he is professor; and that he be allowed for his accommodation the use of one of the pavilions, built or to be built, clear of rent; it being understood that a professor of one department holding temporarily another may receive tuition fees from students attending him in each department, but only one salary, unless it be otherwise specially provided.

That the dormitories be rented to the students at a rent of $20 a year for each dormitory, to be paid by the occupant or occupants; not more than two being permitted to lodge in the same dormitory.

Resolved, That a committee of advice, superintendence and control be appointed to direct the proceedings of the several agents of the Board during the intervals of its sessions, and to call a special meeting of the Board whenever in their opinion the good of the institution indispensably requires it; that notice of such call be addressed by the committee themselves, or by the Secretary on their order, to each member of the Board, and be forwarded to their respective residences by mail, and be also published in the Richmond Enquirer at least fifteen days before the time appointed for such meeting.

The Board hereby authorize their Bursar, with the advice of a member of the committee of superintendence, to draw on the President and Directors of the Literary Fund for the whole or any part of the public donation charged on that fund, either for immediate payment to those to whom moneys may be due, or to deposit the same in the Bank of Virginia, and thence, with the same advice, countersigned by a member of the committee, to draw it occasionally as may be requisite.

Resolved, That the Board concurs in the opinion of the Visitors of the Central College, as expressed in their resolution of February 26, that it is expedient that the funds of the University be diverted as little as possible to the general engagement of the professors required for the institution, until provision be made of buildings for their accommodation, and for dieting and lodging the students; and that the measures adopted by them for the buildings of the present year be approved and pursued.

That Doct. Thomas Cooper, of Philadelphia, heretofore appointed professor of chemistry and of law for the Central College, be confirmed and appointed for the University, as professor of chemistry, mineralogy and natural philosophy, and as professor of law also, until the advance of the institution, and the increase of the number of students, shall render necessary a separate appointment to the professorship of law; that in addition to his permanent salary of one thousand five hundred dollars, he shall receive such sum during the first and second years as, with his salary and tuition fees, shall amount on the whole to not less than $3,500 a year, to commence on the first Monday of April of the ensuing year, or so soon thereafter as he shall arrive at the University.

That the expense of removing his philosophical apparatus, his library and collection of minerals to the University be re-imbursed to him; that until he shall have fifty students of chemistry, the expense in articles consumed necessarily in the courses of chemical lectures be defrayed by the University, not exceeding $250 in any course.

That the offer of his philosophical apparatus, at the price it cost him, be accepted, and that also of 2,500 specimens of his collection of minerals, labelled and arranged in pasteboard cases, to be selected from his whole collection for the use of the University, at the price of fifty cents each, by John Vaughan, Prof. Patterson and Zacheus Collins; with a suspension of payment, however, of the principal of these purchases until the more urgent provisions for the accommodation of the professors and students shall enable the schools of the University to be opened generally, and with the payment in the mean time of interest at the rate of six per centum per annum on their amount.

Considering the importance and the difficulty also at this time of procuring American citizens of the first order of science in their respective lines to be professors in the University, the committee of superintendence are hereby jointly instructed and authorized, should any such offer, not to lose the opportunity of securing them to the University by any provisional arrangement they can make within the limits of the salary and tuition fees before stated, and even with such reasonable accommodations as the case may require; suspending, however, the actual engagement until a meeting of the Visitors, and reserving to them the right of approval or rejection.

Resolved, That the said committee be authorized to purchase, at a fair valuation or reasonable price, of John Perry, if a fit occasion occur, such portion of his land lying between the two parcels heretofore purchased of him, as may conveniently unite the whole in one body, provided the payment be deferred until it can be received of the fourth installment of subscriptions, or of the public endowment for the third year of the institution.

The Board proceeded to the appointment of the committee of superintendence, and John H. Cocke and Th: Jefferson were appointed, with authority jointly or severally to direct the proceedings of the agents of the institution, but jointly only to call a special meeting of the Board.

Resolved, That the course of authenticating the proceedings of the Board be by the signature of the Secretary, and counter signature of the Rector; or, if there be no Secretary, or none present, then by that of the Rector alone.

And the Board adjourned.

TH: JEFFERSON, *Rector.*

March 29, 1819.

M.

At a meeting of the Visitors of the University of Virginia, at the said University, on Monday, the 4th October, 1819: Present—Thos. Jefferson, Rob't Taylor, James Madison, Chapman Johnson and John Hartwell Cocke.

Resolved, That instead of the hotel which had been directed to be built in this present year by the Visitors of the Central College, at their meeting of the 29th of March last, the erection of an additional pavilion, by the committee of superintendence, is approved; as also their engagement for two other additional pavilions and dormitories, in anticipation of the funds of the ensuing year.

Resolved, That for the accomplishment of the buildings commenced, and for all other lawful expenses and disbursements on behalf of the University, the Bursar be authorized, with the approbation of a member of the committee of superintendence, to draw on the President and Directors of the Literary Fund for the whole, or any part, of the public donation charged on that fund for the ensuing year (1820), so soon as the same shall become payable.

It is the opinion of the Board, that at least three other pavilions, making ten with those in hand, five hotels, and additional dormitories, in number depending on that of the students who shall apply for admission into the University, with their appendages, will be necessary for the proper accommodation of the whole number of professors contemplated by the Legislature; and that the Proctor, under the direction of the committee of superintendence, be required to make an estimate of the whole expense of completing such buildings, distinguishing the expense of each, and that such estimate should accompany the report of this Board to the President and Directors of the Literary Fund.

Resolved, That as the stone in the neighborhood of the University is found not capable of being wrought into capitals for the columns of some of the pavilions, and it may be necessary to procure elsewhere proper stone or marble, and to have such capitals executed here or elsewhere, the Proctor be authorized to take such measures relative thereto, and to make such arrangements for their execution, either by the two Italian artists engaged for that purpose, or by others, and to make such compromise with them, as the committee of superintendence shall approve.

It appearing to the Board that the buildings and the funds of the University will not be in a condition to justify the commencement of any of its schools during the next spring, and that, therefore, the duties of the professorship to which Dr. Thos. Cooper was appointed must be deferred, the committee of superintendence is instructed to communicate that fact to Dr. Cooper, to arrange with him the terms on which the delay may be made consistent with his convenience and conformable to an honorable fulfillment of our engagements with him, and to report their proceedings to the Board at their next meeting.

An inventory of the property conveyed by the Proctor of the Central College to the President and Directors of the Literary Fund, a statement of the funds in money and credits of the said College conveyed for the use of the University, with accounts of the disbursements, and of the funds in hand, from the close of the preceding accounts to the last day of September in this present year, as furnished by the Bursar and Proctor, and a draught of a *Report* of the same, and of the condition of the University, being proposed to the Board, the same, after consideration and amendment, is agreed to in the following words, to wit:

[NO. I.]

To the President and Directors of the Literary Fund:

In obedience to the act of the Legislature of Virginia entitled "an act establishing an University," and enjoining on the Rector and Visitors thereof, "to make report annually to the President and Directors of the Literary Fund (to be laid before the Legislature at their next succeeding session), embracing a full account of the disbursements, the funds on hand, and a general statement of the condition of the University," the said Rector and Visitors make the following report:

The Governor having been pleased, with the advice of the Council, to appoint James Breckenridge, Joseph C. Cabell, John H. Cocke, Thomas Jefferson, Chapman Johnson, James Madison and Robert Taylor to be Visitors of the University of Virginia, and prescribed for their first meeting the last Monday in March of the present year, the Visitors so appointed met accordingly at the site provided for the Central College, and adopted by the Legislature for that of the University, and proceeded to the duties prescribed to them by the said act of the Legislature. They appointed Thomas Jefferson, one of their body, to be Rector, Alexander Garrett, Bursar, Arthur S. Brockenbrough, Proctor, and Peter Minor their Secretary. They examined into the state of the property conveyed by the Proctor of the Central College to the President and Directors of the Literary Fund; had an inventory thereof made by the Proctor, as it stood at that day, specifying the items whereof it consisted, and noticing the buildings and other improvements made or in progress, a copy of which inventory is hereto annexed; and they required and received from the late Treasurer of the Central College, now Bursar of the University, a statement of the funds in money and credits of the said College conveyed for the use of the University, specifying the moneys received, those paid away, to whom and for what purposes; what debts, to whom and for what purposes, were due, and what part of the annual donation by the Commonwealth had been received; a copy of which statement is hereto also annexed; and to these is added an account of the disbursements, and of the funds in hand, prepared by the Bursar and Proctor, from the close of the preceding accounts to the last day of September of the present year, as required by law; and also an estimate of the probable cost of the buildings still necessary for the accommodation of the whole number of professors contemplated by the Legislature, and of the students.

The Visitors of the Central College having been in treaty with Dr. Thomas Cooper to be a professor in the said College, those of the University confirmed his appointment as professor of chemistry, mineralogy and natural philosophy, and agreed with him for the purchase of his valuable collection of minerals, and of his philosophical apparatus. The time, however, for the commencement of his functions is not yet ultimately fixed, but they deemed it inexpedient to make any further appointments of professors until accommodations for their reception, and for that of the students, should be provided; and the rather as the salaries of the professors, whenever they commence, by absorbing the funds of the University, will leave little to be employed in buildings for their accommodation. They therefore concurred in the opinion of the Visitors of the Central College, expressed in their resolution of February 26, that it was expedient that the funds of the University should be diverted as little as possible to the general employment of professors until provision should be made for their accommodation, and for boarding-houses and lodgings for the students; and for this purpose they gave directions under which one of the pavilions and fifteen of the dormitories, in the inventory mentioned, have been as nearly finished as is deemed expedient until wanted for occupation; and the other pavilion, therein also mentioned, will be completed this winter; five others are more or less advanced, each sufficient to accommodate one professor, and about twenty other dormitories are in progress. These will probably have their walls completed and covered in during the present season, but will not be otherwise finished but in the course of another. And in order to effect this much, the Visitors have been obliged to enter into engagements which will not only exhaust the funds of the present year, but pledge those of the ensuing one also; for, two seasons being generally requisite for the accomplishment of good buildings, the one for their walls and covering, the other for inner finishings, had the commencement of these been postponed to the ensuing season, another year would have been added to the delays of the institution.

The Visitors would have had sincere pleasure in announcing to the President and Directors that they should be able to open the University in time and manner to meet the public expectations, but the sum necessary for the preliminary measure of providing accommodations will leave the funds of the institution in a condition which does not enable them to do this. If an early commencement, however, should be deemed of importance enough to justify an additional and competent aid from the funds over which your Board presides, for effecting the residuary buildings, the Visitors trust that they could have in place, by the autumn or winter of the ensuing year, the complement of professors contemplated by the law, and open the institution at that epoch with the distinction called for by the interests and character of the State; and were they to indulge their own judgment, it would be, that the annual tribute we are paying to other countries for the education of our youth, the retention of that sum at home, and receipt of a greater from abroad, which might flow to an University on an approved scale, would make it a gainful employment of the money advanced, were even dollars and cents to mingle themselves with the considerations of an higher order urging the accomplishment of this institution. But this urgency they leave with confidence, as in duty bound, to the wiser judgment of the Legislature, with assurances on the part of the Visitors that, whether with the present or additional funds, they will omit nothing which may hasten the desirable moment when the youth of their country may find at home those resources of instruction which they have so long been in the habit of seeking elsewhere; and when, by a sound education, a wholesome direction may be given to *public opinion*, the safest guide and guardian of the public morals and welfare, the arbitress in every age of its destinies to happiness or wretchedness, and the source to which, as either pure or corrupted, the changes of condition in every country on earth may be traced and ascribed.

And the Rector is instructed to authenticate and transmit the same, with the documents therein referred to, to the President and Directors of the Literary Fund, according to law.

And the Board adjourned itself indefinitely.

TH: JEFFERSON, *Rector*.

October 4, 1819.

At an adjourned meeting of the Visitors of the University of Virginia, held on 3d October, 1820: Present—Thomas Jefferson, James Madison, Robert B. Taylor, John H. Cocke and Joseph C. Cabell.

The Board approved the arrangement made by the committee of superintendence relative to the annulment of the contract with Dr. Thomas Cooper.

Resolved, From and after the first day of October, 1820, the compensation of the Bursar of the University for his services shall be at the rate of one per cent. on the amount of his disbursements.

Resolved, That Joseph C. Cabell be and he is hereby desired and authorized to examine and verify the accounts of the preceding year, not already examined and verified.

Resolved, That the committee of superintendence be authorized to enter into negotiations with the following persons, with the view of engaging them as professors of the University, viz: Mr. Bowditch, of Salem, and Mr. Ticknor, of Boston.

Resolved, That in the negotiations with Mr. Bowditch and Mr. Ticknor, the committee be authorized to offer the compensation hereinafter specified, viz:

1. Apartments.
2. A salary of $2,000 per annum.

3. A fee of $10 for each student engaged to attend the lectures of the professor.

4. If the aggregate amount of the salary and of the fees of tuition should fall short of $2,500, in either the first, second, or third year, the deficiency to be paid out of the funds of the University.

The following *report* was agreed to:

[NO. II.]

To the President and Directors of the Literary Fund:

In obedience to the act of the General Assembly of Virginia, requiring that the Rector and Visitors of the University of Virginia should make report annually to the President and Directors of the Literary Fund, (to be laid before the Legislature at their next succeeding session,) embracing a full account of the disbursements, the funds on hand, and a general statement of the condition of the said University, the said Visitors make the following report:

The General Assembly at their last session of 1819–20, having passed an act authorising the said Visitors, for the purpose of finishing the buildings of the University, to borrow the sum of $60,000, and to pledge for re-payment of the said sum and interest, any part of the annual appropriation of $15,000, heretofore made by law, the Board of Visitors at their semi-annual meeting of April last proceeded to the consideration of the said act, and of the authorities therein permitted to them, they were of opinion, in the first place, that it would be most expedient to complete all the buildings necessary for the accommodation of the professors and students before opening the institution, as the maintenance of that, when opened, by absorbing all its funds, would leave nothing to complete what might yet be requisite for the full estatablishment called for by law.

On view of the accounts rendered by the Bursar and Proctor, they found that with the aid of the loan authorised, (if the commencement of its installment for re-payment could be suspended four years,) and of their annuity during the same time, they might accomplish the whole of the buildings of accommodation for the professors and students, according to the estimates heretofore made of their probable cost, of which the following statement presents a summary view.

1820.		
April—	The existing debts are - - -	$10,000
	To complete the 7 pavilions and 31 dormitories on hand, - - - - -	18,000
	To build 3 more pavilions and 31 dormitories, to complete the lawn, - - - -	27,600
	To build 3 hotels and 25 dormitories, completing the east back street, - - -	19,000
1821.		
	To build 2 hotels and Proctor's house, and 25 dormitories, completing west back street, -	19,000
		$93,600

MEANS.

1820.		
April—	Loan from the literary fund of - -	$40,000
1821.		
Jan. 1—	Annuity of $15,000, $2,400 int'st of $40,000	12,600
	Additional loan of - - - - -	20,000
1822.		
Jan 1—	Annuity of $15,000, $3,600 int'st of $60,000,	11,400
1823.		
Jan. 1—	Annuity of $15,000, $3,600 int'st of $60,000,	11,400
		$95,400

They therefore proceeded to negotiate a loan of $40,000 from the President and Directors of the Literary Fund, reimbursable by five installments if $14,244 a year, beginning on the — day of April, 1824, and afterwards a second loan of $20,000, reimbursable by like annual installments, commencing from the day when the others should end.

On this view of their resources, the Board proceeded to authorize their Proctor to enter into contracts for the completion of the buildings already begun, and for the erection of those still wanting, so as to provide in the whole, 10 pavilions for the professors, required by law, 5 hotels for dieting the students, and a 6th for the use of the Proctor, with 104 dormitories, sufficient for lodging 208 students;

and they instructed him to make, in his contracts, effectual provision that the whole shall be completed in the autumn of the ensuing year 1821. At that time, therefore, the buildings of accommodation for the professors and students are expected to be all ready for their reception, and the institution might then be opened, but that the remaining engagements for the buildings, and the reimbursment of the sums borrowed from the literary fund will require the whole revenue of the University for 7 years to come, that is to say, until the — day of April, 1828.

In the statement of expenditures and means of the University, it will be perceived that we have not taken the private subscriptions into account, of these $2,079 33 of the first installment, $3,914 13 of the second, and $8,217 09 of the third, are still due; and the last amounting to $10,666 50, will become due on the 1st day of April next; but of these some loss will be occasioned by the distresses of the times; and the residue, from the same cause, will be so tardy and uncertain in the times of its receipt, that the Visitors have not thought it safe to found on it any stipulations requiring punctuality in their fulfillment; they have thought it more advisable to reserve it as a supplementary and contingent fund, to aid the general revenue, as it shall be received, and to meet casualties unforeseen, errors of estimate, and expenses other than those of mere building.

In the report of the Commissioners who met at Rockfish Gap on the 1st day of August, 1818, it was stated that "a building of somewhat more size in the middle of the grounds, may be called for in time, in which may be rooms for religious worship under such impartial regulations as the Visitors shall prescribe, for public examinations, for a library, for the schools of music, drawing, and other associated purposes." The expenses of this building are not embraced in the estimates hereinbefore stated. Its cost will probably be of about $40,000, and its want will be felt as soon as the University shall open; but the building is beyond the reach of the present funds; nor are these, indeed, adequate to the maintenance of the University on the full scale enacted by the Legislature. That body, aware that professors of desirable eminence could not be expected to relinquish the situations in which they might be found, for others new, untried, and unknown, without a certainty of adequate compensation, confided to the discretion of the Visitors the salaries which should be stipulated to the professors first employed; but the annuity heretofore appropriated to the maintenance of the University, cannot furnish sufficient inducement to ten professors, of high degree each in his respective line of science; and yet to employ inferior persons, would be to stand where we are in science, unavailed of the higher advances already made elsewhere, and of the advantages contemplated by the statute under which we act.

If the Legislature shall be of opinion that the annuity already apportioned to the establishment and maintenance of an institution for instruction in all the useful sciences, is its proper part of the whole fund, the Visitors will faithfully see that it shall be punctually applied to the remaining engagements for the buildings, and to the reimbursement of the extra sum lately received from the general fund; that during the term of its exclusive application to these objects, due care shall be taken to preserve the buildings erected from ruin or injury, and at the end of that term, they will provide for opening the institution in the partial degree to which its present annuity shall be adequate.

If, on the other hand, the Legislature shall be of opinion that the sums so advanced in the name of a loan, from the general fund of education, were legitimately applicable to the purposes of an University, that its early commencement will promote the public good by offering to our youth now ready and waiting for it, an early and near resource for instruction, and by arresting the heavy tribute we are annually paying to other States and countries for the article of education, and shall think proper to liberate the present annuity from its engagements, the Visitors trust it will be in their power, by the autumn of the ensuing year 1821, to engage and bring into place that portion of the Professors designated by the law, to which the present annuity may be found competent; or, by the same epoch, to carry into full execution the whole objects of the law, if an enlargement be made of its participation in the general fund, adequate to the full establishment contemplated by the law.

The accounts, receipts, disbursements, and funds on hand for the year ending with the present date, as rendered by the Bursar and Proctor of the University, are given with this report, as is required by law.

TH: JEFFERSON, *Rector.*

October 3, 1820.

At a meeting of the Visitors of the University of Virginia, by special call, on Thursday, the 29th of November, 1821, at the University, two members only attending, to wit: Thomas Jefferson and Chapman Johnson, they adjourned to the next day.

November 30.—Present: Thomas Jefferson, Chapman Johnson, James Madison and John Hartwell Cocke.

The Board being informed that of the $60,000 permitted to be borrowed from the literary fund, by the act of the last General Assembly, the sum of $29,100 only has as yet been obtained, and that there is uncertainty as to the time when the balance may be obtained, they deem it expedient that the annuity of $15,000, receivable on the 1st of January next, be applied to the accomplishment of the buildings and other current purposes, in the first place, and that, should further sums be wanted before the receipt of the balance of the said loan, the committee of superintendence be authorized to borrow from the banks to the amount of that balance, to be replaced by the said balance when received.

Resolved, That the superintending committee be authorized to have an engraving made of the ground-plat of the buildings of the University, including the library, and so many copies struck off for sale as they shall think proper, and also to engage a good painter to draw a perspective view of the upper level of buildings, to be engraved, yielding to him, for his trouble, the patent right, and paying his reasonable expenses, coming, staying and returning, should it be required.

A proposition having been received to join with other seminaries in a petition to Congress for a repeal of the duty on imported books,

Resolved, That this Board will concur in such a petition, and a form being prepared and approved, and a form also of a letter to our Senators and Representatives in Congress, requesting them to present and advocate the said petition, the Rector is desired to authenticate and forward the same.

A form of *a report,* as annually required to be made to the President and Directors of the Literary Fund, on the funds and condition of the University, was then proposed, amended and agreed to, in the following words:

[NO. III.]

To the President and Directors of the Literary Fund:

In obedience to the act of the General Assembly of Virginia, requiring that the Rector and Visitors of the University of Virginia should make report annually to the President and Directors of the Literary Fund, to be laid before the Legislature at their next succeeding session, embracing a full account of the disbursements, the funds on hand, and a general statement of the condition of the said University, the said Rector and Visitors make the following report:

At their meeting in April last, the attention of the Visitors was first drawn to the consideration of the act of the late General Assembly, which authorized the Literary Board to lend, for the use of the University, a further sum of $60,000, from such moneys as should thereafter come to their hands, and taking such view as could then be obtained of the expenses already incurred for the land, buildings, and accessory purposes for the accommodation of the professors and students of the University, so far as already completed, or in a state of advancement, and the further expenses still to be incurred, necessarily, to complete those accommodations, they concluded it to be for the benefit of the institution to obtain the said loan. Application was accordingly made to the Literary Board, a sum of $29,100 obtained, and the further sum of $30,900 is expected, so soon as the receipts of that Board shall enable them to furnish it.

In the meantime, the Board deemed it incumbent to obtain, as early as possible, a correct statement of the actual cost of what was already done, and a probable one of that still to be done, estimated according to the experience now obtained. They therefore instructed their Proctor to apply himself assiduously to the completion of the buildings generally, to a settlement of all accounts of the actual cost of those finished, and an estimate, according to that, of what would be the cost of those still to be finished. The completion of the buildings of accommodation, which are in four rows of about 600 feet in length each, as may be seen by the plan accompanying this report, has been pressed with as much effect as could be expected; insomuch that there are now completed, and in readiness for occupation, six pavilions for the accommodation of the professors, eighty-two dormitories for that of the students, and two hotels for their dieting; and the others will all be completed in the ensuing summer. The accounts for the construction of those already finished have been actually settled; and the probable cost of the unfinished has been estimated according to the rates which the others have been found to cost.

The following is a summary view of the actual expenditures of the institution from the beginning, of those yet to be incurred to its completion, and of the funds received and still receivable, as nearly as can at present be stated:

6 pavilions, finished, have cost -	$52,713 76	
17 capitals, for them expected from Italy, are to cost, by contract, - -	2,052 00	
2 hotels, finished, have cost - -	8,215 82	
82 dormitories, finished, have cost -	52,997 74	
		$113,927 32

The following are nearly finished, and are estimated at the rates the others have cost, or at prices actually contracted for:

4 pavilions, - - - - - -	$33,563 15	
4 hotels, - - - - - -	16,000 00	
27 dormitories, - - - - -	11,952 21	
		$61,515 36
Back yards and gardens, - - - - - -		1,500 00
Making the whole cost, of the four rows of accommodation, - - - - - - -		$176,942 68
The purchase of 245½ acres of land, and the buildings on them, past compensations to the Bursar and Proctor, hire and maintenance of laborers, and all other accessory and contingent expenses, - -		24,607 77
Making a total for the lands, buildings, &c. complete,		$201,550 43
To which add for interest on the loans, calculated to December 31st, 1821, - - - - - -		6,160 25
		$207,710 70

The funds applied and applicable to these expenditures, are

The sale of glebe lands, - - - -	$3,104 09	
A State certificate No. 32, bearing interest,	176 77	
Annuities of 1819–20–21, - - - -	45,000 00	
Loan of 1820, - - - - - -	60,000 00	
Subscriptions received to Nov. 27, 1821,	24,676 37	
Balance of subscriptions (due $19,668 91, of which suppose $3,000 lost,) - -	16,668 95	
		$209,626 18
From this would result a small surplus of - -		$1,915 48
		$207,710 70

According to the Rector's accounts for the present year, (which, with the Bursar's, are herewith enclosed,) and which contain minuter specifications of the expenditures :

To finish and pay for the whole of the buildings of accommodation not yet finished and paid for, will require a further sum to be placed at his command of - - - -		$53,494 79
The resources for this are,		
The balance of the loan of 1821, still to be received, - - - - - -	$30,900 00	
The balance still due of subscription moneys separate, - - - - - -	16,668 95	
Cash in the Banks undrawn as per Bursar's account, - - - - - -	2,301 23	
Do. in the Bursar's hands, as per his account,	447 84	
State certificate No. 32, - . . - -	176 77	
From which would result a deficit to be supplied from the annuity of - - -	3,000 00	
		$53,494 79

So far then as can at present be seen, (and we are now so near the end of this work that there is room for little error,) the funds received and receivable will, within a small fraction, pay for the lands purchased for the whole system of buildings of accommodation, and all accessory expenses.

The building for the library, comprehending halls, indispensably necessary for other public purposes, and estimated by the Proctor, according to past experience, to cost $46,847, will remain to be erected from the same fund of the annuity, the anticipations of this by loans, for expediting the other buildings, will have weakened it by nearly one-half its amount by the sums of interest to which it is subject; and will consequently retard the commencement of its application to the discharge of the sums borrowed by annual installments, if such should continue to be the will of the Legislature.

The buildings of accommodation will be finished, as before observed, in the ensuing summer, and will constitute the whole establishment, except that of the library. With the close of these works the accounts of their costs will also be closed. These will be first examined by a committee of the Visitors, that nothing may enter into them not sanctioned by the Board; they will then be finally submitted to the accountant of the Literary Board, for the assurance of the public that the moneys have been correctly and faithfully applied. In the course of these works as is unavoidably, perhaps generally, in those of considerable magnitude, there have occurred instances of moneys paid, not in direct furtherance of the legitimate object. The first was the case of a contract by the Visitors of the Central College, for a professor, while acting for that as a private establishment; but that institution being afterwards merged in this of the University, and the enlargement of the plan occasioning that of the time of its commencement also, it became important that that contract should be rescinded; this was done on a just and reasonable compromise and indemnification of $1,500. Another instance was the importation of a foreign artist, for carving the capitals of the more difficult orders of the buildings. The few persons in this country, capable of that work, were able to obtain elsewhere such high prices for their skill and labor, that we believed it would be economy to procure an artist from some country where skill is more abundant and labor cheaper. We did so; but on trial the stone we had counted on in the neighborhood of the University was found totally insusceptible of delicate work; and some from a very distant, but the nearest other quarry known, besides a heavy expense attending its transportation, was extremely tedious to work, and believed not proof against the influences of the weather. In the meantime we had enquired and learned that the same capitals could be furnished in Italy, and delivered in our own ports for a half or third of the price in marble, which they would have cost us here in doubtful stone. We arrested the work here, therefore, and compromised with our artist at the expense of his past wages, his board and passage hither, amounting to $1,390 56. These are the only instances of false expense which have occurred within our knowledge.

The two pavilions and their adjacent dormitories, begun and considerably advanced by the authorities of the Central College, were contracted for by them, when all things were at their most inflated paper-prices and therefore have been of extraordinary cost; but all the buildings since done on the more enlarged scale of the University, have been at prices of from 25 to 50 per cent. reduction; and it is confidently believed that, with that exception, no considerable system of building, within the United States, has been done on cheaper terms, nor more correctly, faithfully, or solidly executed, according to the nature of the materials used.

That the style or scale of the buildings should have met the approbation of every individual judgment, was impossible from the various structure of various minds. Whether it has satisfied the general judgment, is not known to us. No previous expression of that was manifested, but in the injunctions of the law to provide for the accommodation of ten professors, and a competent number of students; and by the subsequent enactments, implying an approbation of the plan reported by the original commissioners, on the requisition of the law constituting them; which plan was exactly that now carried into execution. We had, therefore, no supplementary guide but our own judgments, which we have exercised conscientiously, in adopting a scale and style of building, believed to be proportioned to the respectability, the means, and the wants of our country, and such as will be approved in any future condition it may attain. We owed to it to do, not what was to perish with ourselves, but what would remain, be respected, and preserved through other ages; and we fondly hope that the instruction which may flow from this institution, kindly cherished, by advancing the minds of our youth with the growing science of the times, and elevating the views of our citizens generally to the practice of the social duties, and the functions of self-government, may ensure to our country the reputation, the safety and prosperity, and all the other blessings which experience proves to result from the cultivation and improvement of the general mind; and, without going into the monitory history of the ancient world, in all its quarters, and at all its periods, that of the soil on which we live, and of its occupants, indigenous and immigrant, teaches the awful lesson, that no nation is permitted to live in ignorance with impunity.

And the Board adjourned without day.

TH: JEFFERSON, *Rector*.

November 29, 1821.

At a meeting of the Visitors of the University of Virginia, at the said University, on Monday, the 7th of October, 1822. Present: Thomas Jefferson, Rector; James Breckenridge, Joseph C. Cabell, John H. Cocke, and James Madison.

Resolved, That the Proctor be instructed to enter into conferences with such skillful and responsible undertakers as he would approve, for the building of the library, on the plan heretofore proposed, and now in his possession, and to procure from them declarations of the smallest sums for which they will undertake the different portions of the work of the said building, each portion to be done as well, in materials, manner, and sufficiency, as the best of the same kind of work already done in the preceding buildings, or as well and sufficiently as shall now be agreed on; that (omitting the capitals of the columns, which would be procured elsewhere,) the several other portions be specified under such general heads and details as may be convenient to show the cost of each, and by whom undertaken, fixing also the time within which each portion shall be completed; and that his agreements be provisional only, and subject to the future acceptance or refusal of the Visitors.

Resolved, That the Committee of Superintendence be authorized to employ a collector, to proceed to the collection of the moneys still due on subscriptions, under such instructions and agreement as they shall approve.

Resolved, That the examination and report of the accounts of the Bursar of the University of Virginia, from the 1st day of October, 1820, to the 31st of March, 1821, and from the 31st of March, 1821, to the 27th day of November, 1821, made by John H. Cocke, at the request of the Rector, by his letter of the 1st December, 1821, be hereby ratified as done under authority of this Board; and that the said John H. Cocke be, and he is hereby appointed, to examine and verify the accounts of the said Bursar, from the 27th November, 1821, to this date, and make report thereof to this Board.

Resolved, That George Loyall, Esq., now a member of this Board, appointed on the resignation of Robert B. Taylor, be added to the Committee for settlement of the Bursar's and Proctor's accounts, with authority to the Committee to act singly or together, as convenience may admit.

The following *report* was then agreed to:

[NO. IV.]

To the President and Directors of the Literary Fund:

In obedience to the act of the General Assembly of Virginia, requiring that the Rector and Visitors of the University of Virginia should make report annually to the President and Directors of the Literary Fund, (to be laid before the Legislature at their next succeeding session,) embracing a full account of the disbursements, the funds on hand, and a general statement of the condition of the University, the said Rector and Visitors make the following report:

The Visitors considering as the law of their duty the report of the Commissioners of 1818, which was made to the Legislature, and acted on by them, from time to time subsequently, have completed all the buildings proposed by that report, except one; that is to say, ten distinct houses or pavilions containing each a lecturing room, with generally four other apartments for the accommodation of a professor and his family, and with a garden and the requisite family offices; six hotels for dieting the students, with a single room in each for a refectory, and two rooms, a garden and offices for the tenant; and an hundred and nine dormitories, sufficient each for the accommodation of two students, arranged in four distinct rows between the pavilions and hotels, and united with them by covered ways; which buildings are all in readiness for occupation, except that there is still some plastering to be done, now on hand, which will be finished early in the present season, the garden grounds and garden walls to be completed, and some columns awaiting their capitals, not yet received from Italy. These buildings are mostly paid for by the moneys which have been received, and it is still expected they would be completely so, by the subscriptions due, were they in hand; but the slowness of their collection will render it necessary to make good their deficiences, in the first instance, out of the annuity of the ensuing years, to be replaced to that fund again by the subscriptions as they come in.

The remaining building, necessary to complete the whole establishment, and called for by the report of 1818, which was to contain rooms for religious worship, for public examinations, for a library, and for other associated purposes, is not yet begun for want of funds. It was estimated heretofore by the Proctor, according to the prices which the other buildings have actually cost, at the sum of $46,847. The Visitors, from the beginning, have considered it indispensable to complete all the buildings before opening the institution; because, from the moment that it shall be opened, the whole income of the University will be absorbed by the salaries of the professors and other incidental and current expenses, and nothing will remain to erect any building still wanting to complete the system. They are still of opinion, therefore, that it is better to postpone, for a while, the commencement of the institution, and then to open it in full and complete system, than to begin prematurely in an unfinished state, and go on, perhaps forever, on the contracted scale of local academies, utterly inadequate to the great purposes which the report of 1818 and the Legislature have hitherto had in contemplation. They believe that, in that imperfect state, it will offer little allurement to other than neighboring students, and that professors of the first eminence in their respective lines of science, will not be induced to attach their reputations to an institution defective in its outset, and offering no pledge of rising to future distinction. Yet the Visitors consider the procuring such characters (and it will certainly be their aim) as the peculiar feature which is to give reputation and value to the institution, and to constitute its desirable and important attractions. But the present state of the funds renders the prospect of finishing this last building indefinitely distant. The interest of the sums advanced to the institution now absorbs nearly half its income. A suspension of interest, indeed, for three or four years, would give time for erecting the building with the established authority; but the subsequent re-payment of the principal from that annuity would remove the opening of the institution to a very remote period.

On this view of the condition of the University, the Visitors think it their duty to state, that if the Legislature shall be of opinion that the sums advanced to the University, in the name of loans, from the general fund for education, have been applied to their legitimate object, and shall think proper to liberate the annuity from their reimbursement, it will suffice in three or four years to complete the last building, and the institution may be opened at the end of that term; and further, that if the requisite sum can be supplied from the same or any other fund, then the University may be put into as full operation as its income will admit in the course of the year ensuing the present date, and while the remaining building will be proceeding on such supplementary fund. This, however, or whatever else their wisdom may devise, is subject to their direction, to which the Visitors will in willing duty conform.

In the same report of the Commissioners of 1818, it was stated by them that "in conformity with the principles of our Constitution, which place all sects of religion on an equal footing, with the jealousies of the different sects in guarding that equality from encroachment or surprise, and with the sentiments of the Legislature in favor of freedom of religion, manifested on former occasions, they had not proposed that any professorship of Divinity should be established in the University; that provision, however, was made for giving instruction in the Hebrew, Greek and Latin languages, the depositories of the originals, and of the earliest and most respected authorities of the faith of every sect, and for courses of ethical lectures, developing those moral obligations in which all sects agree; that proceeding thus far without offence to the Constitution, they had left, at this point, to every sect to take into their own hands the office of further instruction in the peculiar tenets of each."

It was not, however, to be understood that instruction in religious opinions and duties was meant to be precluded by the public authorities as indifferent to the interests of society; on the contrary, the relations which exist between man and his Maker, and the duties resulting from those relations, are the most interesting and important to every human being, and the most incumbent on his study and investigation. The want of instruction in the various creeds of religious faith existing among our citizens presents, therefore, a chasm in a general institution of the useful sciences; but it was thought that this want, and the entrustment to each society of instruction in its own doctrines, were evils of less danger than a permission to the public authorities to dictate modes or principles of religious instruction, or than opportunities furnished them of giving countenance or ascendancy to any one sect over another. A remedy, however, has been suggested, of promising aspect, which, while it excludes the public authorities from the domain of religious freedom, would give to the sectarian schools of divinity the full benefit of the public provisions made for instruction in the other branches of science. These branches are equally necessary to the divine as to the other professional or civil characters, to enable them to fulfill the duties of their calling with understanding and usefulness. It has, therefore, been in contemplation, and suggested by some pious individuals, who perceive the advantages of associating other studies with those of religion, to establish their religious schools on the confines of the University, so as to give to their students ready and convenient access and attendance on the scientific lectures of the University; and to maintain, by that means, those destined for the religious professions on as high a standing of science, and of personal weight and respectability, as may be obtained by others from the benefits of the University. Such establishments would offer the further and great advantage of enabling the students of the University to attend religious exercises with the professor of their particular sect, either in the rooms of the building still to be erected, and destined to that purpose under impartial regulations, as proposed in the same report of the Commissioners, or in the lecturing room of such professor. To such propositions the Visitors are prepared to lend a willing ear, and would think it their duty to give every encouragement, by assuring to those who might choose such a location for their schools that the regulations of the University should be so modified and accommodated as to give every facility of access and attendance to their students, with such regulated use also as may be permitted to the other students of the library which may hereafter be acquired, either by public or private munificence, but always understanding that these schools shall be independent of the University and of each other. Such an arrangement would complete the circle of useful sciences embraced by this institution, and would fill the chasm now existing on principles which would leave inviolate the constitutional freedom of religion, the most unalienable and sacred of all human rights, over which the people and authorities of this State, individually and publicly, have ever manifested the most watchful jealousy; and could this jealousy be now alarmed, in the opinion of the Legislature, by what is here suggested, the idea will be relinquished on any surmise of disapprobation which they might think proper to express.

A committee of the Board was duly appointed to settle finally the accounts of all receipts and disbursements, from the commencement of the Central College to the entire completion of the four ranges of buildings of the University. They found it necessary to employ a skillful accountant to make up a complete set of books, in regular form, wherein all the accounts, general and particular, should be stated, so as that every dollar might be traced from its receipt to its ultimate expenditure, and the clearest view be thus exhibited of the faithful application of the moneys placed under the direction of the Board. This work has taken more time than was expected; and although considerably advanced, is not entirely completed. Until its completion, however, the committee cannot proceed in the final settlement with which they are charged. The Bursar's accounts for the year preceding this date are rendered herewith; as are also the Proctor's for the first six months, but his books and papers being necessarily in the hands of the accountant, his account for the last half year could not as yet be prepared. The settlement of the committee, when made, will be transmitted, or a supplementary document, to the Literary Board, as well for its regular audit by their accountant, as to be laid before the Legislature.

And the Board adjourned without day.

TH: JEFFERSON, *Rector*.

October 7, 1822.

MONTICELLO, December 23, 1822.

SIR,—According to the requisitions of the law, I now transmit to the President and Directors of the Literary Fund, for communication to the Legislature, the annual report of the Visitors of the University of Virginia, bearing date the 7th of October last. At that date the regular books were not yet completed, which were under preparation for the purpose of exhibiting a clear and methodical view of the application of all the moneys which have been received and employed on this institution. From the best view which, before that time, had been taken of the affairs of the University it was expected, as is stated in this report, that the buildings now prepared would be completely paid for by the subscriptions still due. These books have been since completed, and the result (as appears by the certificates herewith inclosed) is, that the institution has received from the beginning to the 23d of last month, on the whole, and from all funds, the sum of

sum of	$199,159 98½
And is still to receive of subscriptions unpaid,	18,343 43½
	$217,503 42
That there has been paid, within the same period, for the purposes of the institution, the same sum of	$199,159 98½
And there remains to be paid of debts settled and unsettled about	27,001 63
	$226,161 61½

An estimate by the Proctor, at an early period, supposed that the last building called for by the report of 1818, and not yet executed, would probably cost the sum of $46,847; but this did not include two considerable appendages necessary to connect it with the other buildings. An estimate including these, now recently made by the principal undertakers and executors of the other buildings, raises its amount to about one-third more.

It is by instruction from the Visitors that I communicate facts which, resulting from investigations not concluded at the date of their report, and consequently not known to them, constitute an important supplement to the matter of their report; to which I add the assurance of my high consideration.

TH: JEFFERSON, *Rector.*

[NO. V.]

To the President and Directors of the Literary Fund:

In obedience to the law requiring that the Rector and Visitors of the University of Virginia should make report annually to the President and Directors of the Literary Fund (to be laid before the Legislature at their next succeeding session), embracing a full account of the disbursement, the funds on hand, and a general statement of the condition of the said University, the said Rector and Visitors make the following report:

In conformity with the act of the General Assembly of February 5th of the present year, requiring that out of the uninvested capital then lying in the literary fund, there should be loaned, by the President and Directors of the said fund, to the Rector and Visitors of the University of Virginia, for the purpose of completing the buildings and making the necessary preparations for putting the said University into operation, any sum required by the said Rector and Visitors, not exceeding that of $60,000, the Visitors, at their meeting on the 7th of April last, deemed it necessary for the institution to require the whole of the said sum, but that it should be drawn in different portions, and at different times, as it should be wanting, so far as the Literary Board should think admissible. There was, accordingly, received by an order of the said Board, in the month of May last, a sum of forty thousand dollars. In consequence hereof the larger building, for a library and other purposes, was commenced, and has been carried on with activity, insomuch that its walls are now ready to receive their roof; but that being of hemispherical form, and pressing outwardly in every direction, it has been thought not advisable to place it on the walls in their present green state; but rather to give them time to settle and dry until the ensuing season, when the roof will be ready, and the walls in a proper condition to receive it. Whether the interior work of the building will be finished within the ensuing year, is doubtful.

The report of the 7th of October, of the last year, stated that the buildings for the accommodation of the professors and students were in readiness for occupation, except as to some small articles of plastering then on hand, the garden walls and grounds, and some columns which awaited their capitals from abroad. These finishings are done, the capitals are received and put up; and the whole of these buildings are now in perfect readiness for putting the institution into operation—and this might be done (taking reasonable time for procuring professors) at the close of the ensuing year, 1824, were its funds liberated from their present incumbrances, but these remove the epoch to a very distant time. The several sums advanced from the literary fund, as loans, when the balance of the last shall have been received, will amount to $180,000, bearing a present interest of $10,800. This, with the cost and necessary care and preservation of the establishment, will leave, of the annual endowment of the University, a surplus of between two and three thousand dollars only. As before mentioned, this loan of $180,000 will be extinguished by the annual payment of a constant sum of $2,500, at the end of twenty-five years, a term too distant for the education of any person already born, or to be born, for some time to come: and within that period a great expense will be incurred in the mere preservation of the buildings and appurtenances. These are views which it is the duty of the Visitors to present, and to leave to the wisdom and paternal consideration of the Legislature, to whose care are confided the instruction and other interests of the present, as well as of the future generations proceeding from us.

That report, with the letter of the 23d accompanying it, stated also that the buildings of accommodation for the professors and students, were so far paid for as that the arrearages of subscriptions still due being $18,343 43½ cents, would, when received, complete their payment to within the sum of $5,658 19½ cents. While there were other funds to which present recourse could be had, it had been deemed reasonable to indulge the convenience of such subscribers as found difficulties in paying their installments rigorously at the periods prescribed, but that these arrears having then become urgently necessary, an active collector had been employed to settle and call for them. In the course of the year he has collected, of these arrearages, the sum of $4,828 77½ cents. He has obtained bonds or promises, verbal or written, for prompt payment, deemed good, to the amount of $10,107 93¾ cents; and as to the remainder, some of the subscribers have not been yet called on, some have removed out of the State, and some become insolvent. Of this remainder, he considers $932.25 cents as sperate, and the residue, between $2,500 and $2,600, as desperate; which, on $43,808, the whole sum subscribed will be an ultimate loss of nearly 6 per cent. This will so far increase the deficit of $8,658 19½, before stated, as falling short of paying for the four rows of buildings, and so far add to the charge on the funds in hand, or still to accrue. This state of things obliges a call for peremptory and prompt payment of these arrearages, which cannot be thought unreasonable by the subscribers, who have been so far indulged already, when it is considered that these works were engaged on the faith of the sums subscribed, so far as their amount; that those who undertook them have accordingly executed them, and are now justly entitled to the compensation stipulated. We trust, therefore, that in the course of the ensuing twelve months these arrearages will be paid up, except such as entervening circumstances may have rendered desperate.

A general statement of the receipts and expenditures, from all funds, and for all purposes, from the beginning of the establishment to the first of October of the last year, was communicated for the Legislature at their last session. Those of the Bursar and Proctor, for the year ending the first day of this present October, are herewith rendered—they have been duly settled and tested by their vouchers, by the same accountant and committee employed on the former occasion, and will be duly submitted by these officers for audit by the accountant of the literary board.

TH: JEFFERSON.

October 6, 1823.

[NO. VI.]

To the President and Directors of the Literary Fund:

In obedience to the law requiring that the Rector and Visitors of the University of Virginia should make report annually to the President and Directors of the Literary Fund, (to be laid before the Legislature at their next succeeding session) embracing a full account of the disbursements, the funds on hand, and a general statement of the condition of the said University, the said Rector and Visitors make the following report:

In that of the preceding year it was stated, that the buildings for the accommodation of the professors and students were in readiness for their occupation, and that the walls of the larger building, intended for a library and other purposes, were completed. In the course of the present season this building has received its roof, and will be put into a condition for preservation and use, although its interior cannot be completed. It was then also stated that, without awaiting that completion, the institution might be put into operation at the close of this present year, were its funds liberated from the incumbrances with which they were charged. This article was removed by the act of the Legislature of January 27th, of the present year, concerning the University of Virginia.

In consequence of this liberation, the Board of Visitors, at their ensuing meeting, on the 5th April last, proceeded to take such preparatory measures as could be taken at that time to carry the views of the Legislature into effect with as little delay as practicable. From the accounts and estimates then rendered by the Bursar and Proctor, it appeared that on the last day of the preceding year, 1823, the funds in hand and due to the University, of the last loan, and of the arrearages of subscriptions, would be sufficient, when received, to pay all debts then existing, on any account, and to leave a sum of about $21,000, applicable to the building of the library; which, with the sum of $19,370 40½, already paid or provided for that edifice, would put it into a state of safety, and of some use, until other and more pressing objects should have been accomplished. They considered the University, therefore, as having had in hand, on the first day of the present year, 1824, the annuity of this year (clear of all prior claims) as a fund for defraying the current expenses of the year, for meeting those necessary towards procuring professors, paying any commence-ments of salaries which might be incurred to the end of the year, and to leave a small surplus for contingencies.

They found, from a view of the future income, consisting of the annuity, and such rents for buildings as may be reasonably required, that it would not be adequate to the full establishment of the ten professorships contemplated by the Legislature in their act of January 28, 1819, for establishing the University; but that it might suffice for instituting eight professorships, for the present, and that the branches of science proposed to be taught in the University might be arranged within the competence of that number, for a time, and until future and favorable circumstances might enable them to add the others, and to lighten duly the professorships thus overcharged with duties.

They proceeded, therefore, to settle the organizations of the schools, and the distribution of the sciences among them, and they concluded on the same as follows:

In the University of Virginia shall be instituted eight professorships, to wit: 1st, of ancient languages; 2d, modern languages; 3d, mathematics; 4th, natural philosophy; 5th, natural history; 6th, anatomy and medicine; 7th, moral philosophy; 8th, law.

In the school of ancient languages are to be taught the higher grade of the Latin and Greek languages, the Hebrew, rhetoric, belles lettres, ancient history and ancient geography.

In the school of modern languages are to be taught French, Spanish, Italian, German, and the English language, in its Anglo-Saxon form; also, modern history and modern geography.

In the school of mathematics are to be taught mathematics generally, including the higher branches of numerical arithmetic, algebra, trigonometry plane and spherical, geometry, mensuration, navigation, conic sections, fluxions or differentials, military and civil architecture.

In the school of natural philosophy, are to be taught the laws and properties of bodies generally, including mechanics, statics, hydrostatics, hydraulics, pneumatics, acoustics, optics and astronomy.

In the school of natural history are to be taught, botany, zoology, mineralogy, chemistry, geology, and rural economy.

In the school of anatomy and medicine are to be taught anatomy, surgery, the history of the progress and theories of medicine, physiology, pathology, materia medica and pharmacy.

In the school of moral philosophy are to be taught mental science generally, including ideology, general grammar and ethics.

In the school of law are to be taught the common and statute law, that of the chancery, the laws feudal, civil, mercatorial, and of nature and nations; and also the principles of government and political economy.

But it was meant that this distribution should give way to occasional interchanges of particular branches of science, among the professors, in accommodation of their respective qualifications.

The Visitors were sensible that there might be found in the different seminaries of the United States, persons qualified to conduct these several schools with entire competence; but it was neither probable that they would leave the situations in which they then were, nor honorable or moral to endeavor to seduce them from their stations; and to have filled the professorial chairs with unemployed and secondary characters, would not have fulfilled the object, or satisfied the expectations of our country in this institution. It was moreover believed that, to advance in science we must avail ourselves of the lights of countries already advanced before us; it was, therefore, deemed most advisable to resort to Europe for some of the professors, and of preference to the countries which speak the same language, in order to obtain characters of the first grade of science in their respective lines; and, to make the selections with proper information, caution and advisement, it was necessary to send an agent of science and confidence. Francis W. Gilmer, a learned and trustworthy citizen of this State, was appointed, and has proceeded on the mission; and should his objects be accomplished as early as expected, we count on opening the institution on the first day of February next.

Could the donation of the last Legislature, out of the debt due to this State from the United States, have been obtained for the purpose of procuring a library, and the apparatus necessary for the several schools, the opportunity would have been highly advantageous of having them chosen by this agent while in Europe, with the advice and assistance of the respective professors; but the application was not in time to be acted on before the adjournment of the late Congress. Yet some books were indispensable, and some apparatus to make even an imperfect commencement. To procure these articles, therefore, and to defray the expenses necessary for the other objects of the mission, the Board was under the necessity of applying to these purposes a sum of $10,500 of the annuity of the present year, and to leave the internal finishing of the library, however much to be regretted, until some opportunity of greater convenience should occur.

There is some reason to doubt, from the information received, whether our agent will be able to effect his objects at as early a day as we had expected; but of this, more will be known in time for its communication, by the Rector, with this report, were it still possible to obtain from the United States a settlement of so much of the claim on them as was appropriated to this institution, in time to find our agent and professors yet in place to invest it, our University would open under auspices highly propitious, in comparison with those to which it will be subjected by this unfortunate delay.

The success of our collector in his applications for the arrearages due from subscribers, has not been as great as it has been in further securing the sums which had not yet been secured. The receipts from this resource, since the date of our last report, have amounted to $2,069 88½, and the sums deemed sperate and still to be received, amount to $7,468 92½.

The accounts of the receipts, disbursements, and funds on hand, for the year ending with the last month of September, as rendered by the Bursar and Proctor, are given with this report, as is required by law.

TH: JEFFERSON, *Rector.*

October 5, 1824.

[NO. VII.]

To the President and Directors of the Literary Fund:

In obedience to the law requiring that the Rector and Visitors of the University of Virginia should make a report annually to the President and Directors of the Literary Fund, (to be laid before the Legislature at their next succeeding session,) embracing a full account of the disbursements, the funds on hand, and a general statement of the condition of the said University, the said Rector and Visitors make the following report:

That which was rendered on the 5th of October of the last year, informed the President and Directors of the Literary Board of the state of preparation to which we were then advanced towards getting the institution into actual operation, of the measures taken for procuring professors for the several schools, for purchasing some books and apparatus, and of the ground of hope, then existing, that it might be actually opened on the 1st day of February then next ensuing. It was not, however, until the 7th of March that, the professors of ancient and modern languages, of mathematics, of natural philosophy, and of anatomy and medicine, being in place, the institution was opened and put into operation. Professors of the schools of moral philosophy and natural history were received at short intervals afterwards; but no satisfactory engagement having been effected, till lately, of a professor for the chair of law, that school has not yet been opened; nor is it decided whether it will be most eligible to put it into operation at this advanced season of the year, or to await the beginning of the term in February next. The commencement on the 7th of March was with about 40 students; others continued to arrive from day to day at first, and from week to week since; and the whole number matriculated on the last day of the last month of September was 116. Few more can be expected during the present term, which closes on the 15th of December next; and the state of the schools on the same day was as follows:

In the school of	ancient languages were	55	scholars,
	modern languages,	64	
	mathematics,	68	
	natural philosophy,	33	
	natural history,	30	
	anatomy and medicine,	20	
	moral philosophy,	14	

From the information received from different quarters, we have reason to expect a large accession to our numbers at the commencement of the next term. The dormitories now provided can accommodate 218 students, the neighboring town of Charlottesville perhaps 50 more; but should more be offered they could not be received. Ex-boarders, too, will labor under serious disadvantages, as, besides increased opportunities of relaxed order, they must lose the use of the library, the books of which cannot be permitted to be carried out of the precincts of the University.

A printed copy of the statutes and regulations enacted by the Board of Visitors for the government of the University is now communicated. We have thought it peculiarly requisite to leave to the civil magistrate the restraint and punishment of all offences which come within the ordinary cognizance of the laws. At the age of 16, the earliest period of admission into the University, habits of obedience to the laws become a proper part of education and practice; the minor provisions and irregularities alone, unnoticed by the laws of the land, are the peculiar subjects of academical authority. No system of these provisions has ever yet prevented all disorder. Those first provided by this Board were founded on the principles of avoiding too much government, of not multiplying occasions of coercion, by erecting indifferent actions into things of offence, and for leaving room to the student for habitually exercising his own discretion; but experience has already proved, that stricter provisions are necessary for the preservation of order; that coercion must be resorted to where confidence has been disappointed. We have, accordingly, at the present session, considerably amended and enlarged the scope of our former system of regulations, and we shall proceed in the duties of tightening or relaxing the reins of government, as experience shall instruct us, in the progress of the institution; and we are not certain that the further aid of the Legislature itself will not be necessary, to enable the authorities of the institution to interpose, in some cases, with more promptitude, energy, and effect, than is permitted by the laws as they stand at present.

The lands heretofore purchased for the use of the University consisted of two parcels, about half a mile distant the one from the other; the one of 153 acres, comprehending a small mountain, peculiarly adapted, and important to be secured, for the purpose of an observatory, whenever the future advance of circumstances may render such an establishment desirable; the other, of $107\frac{8}{10}$ acres, made up of several small purchases, which constitute the site of the University itself. Between these is a parcel of 132 acres, which, besides the consolidation of these possessions, and other and great conveniences offered by it, lies in the way of the water necessary for the supply of the establishment, which is brought in pipes through it, from the high lands to the site of the University. From the benefit of this communication, we were liable to be cut off, at any moment, by the owner of this parcel of lands. It was lately offered to us, and at a price thought reasonable, to wit: at $50 the acre. We had, several years ago, paid $40 for the parcel adjacent on one side; and $100 the acre had been given by an individual for a larger parcel, adjacent on another side. The consideration that the purchase would so far lessen the funds for finishing the rotunda called, certainly, for serious hesitation; but the supply of water indispensable to the establishment, the irrecoverable loss of it if sold out to individuals in lots, as proposed by the proprietor, made it, in our view, an over-ruling duty to secure the University against so irreparable an injury, and we concluded the purchase. This now gives to the institution a tract of nearly 400 acres, beyond the limits of which it has nothing to desire.

The last report stated that, in addition to the sum of $19,370 40, which had been paid or provided towards the building called the rotunda, there were still remaining of the general funds, a sum of about $21,000, applicable to that building, that this sum, although not sufficient to finish it, would put it into a state of safety, and of some use, until other more pressing objects should have been accomplished. It has been indispensable to finish the circular room, destined for the reception of the books; because, once deposited in their places, the removing them for any finishing which might be left to be done hereafter, would be inadmissible. That has therefore been carried on actively, and we trust will be ready for the reception of the books. The other apartments of indispensable use were, two for a chemical laboratory, one for a museum of natural history, and one for examinations, for accessory schools, and other associated purposes. An additional building too for anatomical dissections, and other kindred uses, has become necessary. We are endeavoring to put these into a bare state for use, although with some jeopardy as to the competence of the funds.

On representations to the General Government of the interest which the Legislature of Virginia had given to their University in certain claims then depending between them, of the great disadvantages under which that institution must labor, without the books and apparatus which this donation was to supply, that government did not hesitate to aid us with an advance, on account, of such a sum as might cover that given to the University. A catalogue of books for the library was thereupon prepared, an agent employed to purchase them wherever they could be obtained cheapest and best, and a sum of $18,000 for this purpose was placed at his disposal. A previous sum of $7,677 81 had been advanced by the general fund for the purchase of books and apparatus of immediate necessity, and a sum of $6,000 appropriated on loan towards preparing the room in the rotunda, destined for a library; making together $31,677 81 for the purchase of a philosophical apparatus. A sum of $6,000 was deposited in London, (having cost here $6,300,) a list of the proper articles, and their selection and purchase, were committed to a character there highly qualified for the execution of the charge; and another sum of $3,000 was deposited in London (having cost here $3,157 50,) for the acquisition of articles necessary for the anatomical school, which, with $500 paid for a chemical apparatus, and $289 58 for transportation and other miscellaneous expenses, amount to $41,924 89, leaving a balance of $8,075 11 for defraying incidental expenses, which will be considerable. A good proportion of these articles we are in hopes to receive this autumn, and the residue in the ensuing year. Some donations of mineral collections have already been received, others destined for the University are known of, and it is believed we shall, in this way, be supplied sufficiently for all the purposes of education. Much too may be expected from the future industry of the alumni themselves of the University, when they shall have entered on the active business of life.

The receipts by the collector of arrearages of subscriptions since the date of our last report, have amounted to $2,734 89, and the balance still to be expected is $4,306 53½, leaving a sum of $4,500 desperate, as is believed.

The accounts for the receipts, disbursements, and funds on hand for the year ending with the late month of September, as rendered by the Bursar and Proctor, are given with this report, as is required by law.

TH: JEFFERSON, *Rector*.

October 7, 1825.

N.

WASHINGTON, April 2, 1824.

To James Monroe, President of the United States:

SIR,—In the character of a Visitor of the University of Virginia, I beg leave to submit to your consideration a few remarks, on a subject in which that institution is deeply interested. I allude to the unsatisfied balance still due to the State of Virginia, on account of advances made by that State to the Government of the United States, during the prosecution of the late war.

The Legislature of Virginia, at the session recently terminated, passed an act, whereby it appropriated, for the purpose of procuring the requisite library and apparatus for the University of the State, the sum of $50,000, to be paid out of the first moneys which might be received from the General Government in further discharge of the debt still due to the Commonwealth. The Visitors of the University are required by law to assemble on the first Monday in April; and one of the first objects of the meeting is, to make such preliminary arrangements as may be necessary for procuring suitable professors, and for putting the institution into speedy and successful operation. The importance of the appropriation recently conferred by the Legislature of Virginia, in the dawn of such an establishment, is too apparent to require the support of argument, or the aid of elucidation. Suffice it to say, that it is calculated to excite feelings of the most heartfelt interest, among all the friends of science and literature; and to none can it be an object of more lively solicitude, than the distinguished individuals with whom I have the honor to be associated at the Board of Visitors.

By the act to which we are indebted for this beneficent appropriation, it is provided that, as soon as satisfactory assurances shall reach the Board of Public Works in Virginia, that the claim of the State on the Government of the United States will ultimately be available to the amount of the appropriation, that Board will have authority to anticipate the payment, by lending to the Rector and Visitors of the University an equivalent amount, out of a fund set apart in that State, and consecrated to the purposes of internal improvement.

You must be sensible, sir, that, next to a successful issue, nothing can be more desirable than a prompt decision of this interesting question. I am not informed as to the degree of evidence which will be satisfactory to the Board of Public Works in Virginia, with regard to the ultimate validity of the claim. I take it for granted, however, that a decision of one branch of the General Government, in favor of the justice of the claim, and the want of nothing but an act of appropriation by another department of that government, will be sufficient to satisfy that Board that there is no necessity to postpone the loan, at the expense of the best and dearest interests of Virginia. It is not to be presumed that the requisite appropriation will not be made by the Congress of the United States, to satisfy any fair claim on the justice and good faith of the Federal Government.

My object, therefore, sir, is to invite your attention to this subject, with as little delay as your convenience will permit; and pending the unavoidable delays of legislation, to procure from you such an expression of opinion on the merits of our claim, as will satisfy the Board of Public Works in Virginia, that it will ultimately be established to an amount sufficient to fulfill the appropriation recently made to the University of Virginia.

It is proper that I should state, on the threshold, for your information, that I have no authority to make the present application expressly delegated to me by the Board of Visitors of the University. Nevertheless, I am so thoroughly persuaded that, in so doing, I shall be acting in conformity to the sentiments and views of all its members, that I do not hesitate to take upon myself the responsibility of the measure.

The merits of the claim of Virginia, accompanied by a statement of its present amount, and its details, will probably be presented to your view through the regular organs of the State, with a degree of force and clearness infinitely beyond any thing which I can say upon this subject. Yet, as the question of its ultimate validity is one on which now mainly depends the prosperity of a most beneficent institution, whose interests are partly confided to my care, I trust, sir, that I may venture, without the appearance of officious arrogance, to suggest such arguments as occur to my recollection, in behalf of this claim, tending to recommend it to a favorable reception on the part of the government of the Union.

You are aware, sir, that, with the exception of a small sum of principal, still suspended for the want of regular vouchers, the existing claim of Virginia is a claim for interest on the sums advanced to the

General Government by the State, for and on account of expenditures incurred in its necessary defence, during the progress of the late war. What proportion of this claim consists of interest actually paid by the State on loans negotiated to defray the expenses of the war, I am not exactly informed; but, as I know that the amount is more than sufficient to satisfy the appropriation to the University, and as I consider this part of the claim as standing on higher ground than the residue, I would wish you to regard it as the exclusive subject of my present application.

It appears, then, from the present state of the claim, that the success of the appropriation to the University of Virginia, depends essentially on the recognition by this government of the principle, that, in certain cases, it is bound to refund the interest paid for moneys borrowed and expended for its benefit and accommodation, without previous authority expressly given by the government.

To this principle I understand there are two objections:

First. It is alleged to be contrary to the established usage of the government.

Secondly. The usage is believed to be founded in good policy.

First. In regard to the usage of the government, I beg leave to remark, that it is not an usage to which the government has uniformly and invariably adhered. Probably upon investigation, it would appear that there had been several exceptions. Permit me to invite your attention to some exceptions which, if I am not incorrectly informed, took place in regard to certain western contractors, during the period of time that the present Secretary of the Treasury superintended the department of war. Whether the rule be, or be not, founded in good policy, it would seem, therefore, that there are cases of departure, warranted, in the opinion of the government, by the existing laws of the United States.

Secondly. The usage, it is alleged, is founded on good policy, and ought not to be changed. I have sought for information as to the reasons on which this usage is bottomed; and I understand that the principal, if not the only reason, is, that the government of the United States is supposed to be at all times ready to meet its engagements, and that the payment of interest would furnish an inducement to the public creditors to hold up their claims, and thereby prevent the timely liquidation of accounts, and the regular discharge of the public debts.

It is not my purpose, sir, to discuss the merits of the usage, as a general system of policy; nor attempt to disprove the general verity and soundness of the reasoning by which it is supposed to be justified and supported. My object does not require it; and I would not presumptuously intrude upon discussions not necessarily connected with my subject. My purpose simply is, to endeavor to demonstrate, to your satisfaction, that the reason alleged in support of the existing usage of the government, does not apply to the claim of Virginia; and, consequently, that this claim constitutes a fit subject for an exception to the rule.

There are, sir, various grounds on which I could contend, that the prevailing usage of the Department of War should not be applied to the claim of Virginia, for a reimbursement of the interest actually paid by the State. But the one on which I propose now to rely, is that of the liberal conduct of Virginia towards the government of the United States from the commencement to the conclusion of the war.

I shall not pretend, sir, to enter into a comprehensive and complete history of the situation and conduct of the State of Virginia, throughout the period to which I allude. This subject, in its outline, and most of its details, is already known, and in possession of the government. That part of the conduct of the State, to which I wish particularly to draw your attention, is the course pursued by the General Assembly on the subject of the advances to the General Government, and, more especially, in regard to the very interest which forms the basis of my present application. There are some circumstances connected with the latter branch of the subject, which bear, in my opinion, with direct and peculiar force on the question now under consideration.

The liberal spirit towards the government of the Union, which was always felt, and uniformly displayed by the General Assembly of Virginia, will be best illustrated by reference to some conspicuous and forcible examples.

What, at that time, was the situation of Virginia?

Upwards of a year had elapsed since the enemy's fleet had entered the Chesapeake. Our commerce was cut off; our agriculture benumbed; our resources, both public and private, greatly curtailed. A powerful British squadron rode triumphant in our waters. Our maritime towns were threatened with conflagration. The slave population were instigated to rebellion. In despite of the exertions of a vigilant executive, and a brave militia, ever ready to meet the foe, the enemy having command of our waters, and choosing his points of attack, invaded our shores and extended his ravages along the extensive line of our eastern borders. It was the avowed object of the enemy, to make Virginia feel the worst effects of a war, of which she had been one of the earliest, most steadfast, and decided advocates. Harassed by difficulties, foreign and domestic, the government of the United States was unable to fulfill its own patriotic intentions, and to meet the exigencies of an extended empire. True to herself and faithful to the Union, the State of Virginia, from the first moment of invasion, put forth her resources with a liberal and unsparing hand. From the most remote extremities of her territory, her citizens marched, at the call of the law, to the defence of any and every part of this extensive empire. In addition to the ordinary expenses of her government, the State, by taxes and by loans, augmented her military contingent fund, and, on all occasions, was ready to anticipate, or to support the government of the Union. The experience of the past, and the prospect of the future, equally pointed to the policy of husbanding her peculiar resources, and of providing, by every possible expedient, for the defence of her maritime borders, against a powerful enemy, during a war of indefinite continuance.

This rapid sketch will suffice to recall to your view the position of the State of Virgina at the close of the winter of 1814.

In such a situation, the financial relations of the State filled with inquietude the minds of some of our most respectable citizens. The abortive attempts heretofore made, through the executive branch of the government, for the purpose of effecting an adjustment of our account, produced, as was admitted by all, from a want of neither zeal nor ability in the agency which had been employed, gave rise to the idea of enlisting the weight and authority of the General Assembly of Virginia on the side of an immediate settlement and discharge of the debt.

From these considerations, the accompanying preamble and resolutions,* presenting a lucid view of the claims of the State, and authorising the appointment of Commissioners, and convenient and accommodating terms of payment, were introduced into the House of Dele-

* See Journal of the House of Delegates for session 1813–14.

gates by a distinguished member of the body, passed unanimously, and sent up to the Senate.

In an animated and protracted debate, which arose in the Senate on this occasion, all the bearings of the proposed resolutions, as well upon the interests of the State of Virginia, as upon those of the government of the United States, were fully developed to the view of the body. They were advocated upon the ground, that such a settlement and such terms of payment as those which were authorized by these resolutions, were necessary to the State, and would be advantageous to both the governments. They were opposed upon the ground that, although the terms of payment were accommodating to the government of the United States, and reimbursement was desirable to the State, yet the measure, for various reasons, was not necessary, and might be productive of inconvenience to the General Government.

On this occasion the question of interest upon our advances to the General Government, was brought distinctly into view. And although it was contended, on the side of the advocates of the measure, that the apprehensions entertained of the hostile aspect under which it would exhibit the General Assembly of Virginia, in its relations to the General Government, were not justified by its character or tendency; and although it was attempted to be shown, that the fears were visionary, which were suggested as to the inconvenience that a demand of the interest might bring upon that government, nevertheless, views of a very opposite description were zealously and confidently expressed by those members of the Senate who rose on the side of the opposition. It was stated, most earnestly, by the opponents of the measure, among many other arguments, "that it would have the aspect of arraying the State of Virginia against the General Government, which would produce an injurious impression in the other States and on the enemy; that a distinction ought to be drawn between the ultimate security of our claim, and its immediate discharge; that we should, by moving at this time, move all the creditor States, whose claims might not be as small as they were represented; that although Virginia might be willing to take stock, the other States might insist on immediate payment in full; that even if they should be willing to take stock, the necessity of providing for the interest, *at the existing crisis*, might embarrass the General Government, or call for additional taxes, or affect the success of the loan of $25,000,000; that our peace establishment, and the interest of the public debt, already amounted to $12,000,000, and our revenue only $10,000,000; that the revenue on the side of the customs, would fall off, while the internal revenue could not be augmented without difficulty; and, *that the amount of our claim had been funded, and there was no necessity, at this time, to press for payment on the General Government.*"

In despite of all the efforts of eloquence and argument, the preamble and resolutions were rejected in the Senate. The subject attracted considerable attention at the time; and that the grounds here stated were mainly relied on by the majority of the Senate, reference might be had, if necessary, to the author of the resolutions, now a distinguished member of the House of Representatives, and to the Attorney General of the United States.

In the present prosperous state of the national finances, it is difficult to conceive the state of things which could justify such a course of argument and such vindication. Nevertheless, the history of the times will furnish the defence of the Senate.

Having been a member at this period, and having participated in the rejection of this measure, I have a right to know the motives by which we were governed; and I can confidently affirm that, whatever may be the opinion now entertained of the direction then given to the fiscal concerns of the State, the spirit which guided our deliberations was no other than an affectionate and respectful solicitude for the financial credit of the Union, an anxious desire to avoid every possible appearance of distrust or apprehension on the part of the Legislature of Virginia, and a firm determination to support the National Government to the utmost extent of our ability; never doubting, for a moment, but that, at the first period of convenience, all our accounts would be fairly settled, and all our advances of principal and interest would be amply and honorably reimbursed.

We were aware, sir, it is true, that the Executive of the State had sent, and might again send forward agents to liquidate the accounts; and that our delegation in Congress would not forget the peculiar interests of the State which they represented; nevertheless, we were equally sensible, that in communicating through the ordinary channels of Executive agency, the important point—*the time of reimbursement*—would more completely lie at the discretion of the government; and that our delegation in Congress, constituting, as they did, a part of the National Legislature, could not and would not, by any indiscreet or untimely movement, cripple the credit of the Federal Government, and thereby impair its ability to sustain the war, to the declaration of which they had themselves been mainly instrumental.

Permit me now, sir, to request your attention to that part of the claim of Virginia which is founded on a loan made by the Executive of the State, in the month of September, 1814, and subsequently sanctioned by the General Assembly. It would seem to me, that the interest paid by the State, on the loan which was then negotiated, fastens itself with irresistible force on the justice and good faith of the Government of the Union. The very impressive circumstances under which this loan was effected, deserve well to be recalled to your recollection.

The metropolis of the Union had just fallen under the arm of the invader, and the capitol of the nation had been wrapped in flames. Flushed with victory, and exulting in the trophies recently won at our expense, the British army was descending to the Chesapeake, and threatened to strike at the metropolis of Virginia. The crisis called for vigorous measures. With a promptitude and energy demanded by the occasion, the Governor of Virginia called upon the people of the State to rally to his standard, and meet the expected invaders. An increasing army was rapidly thrown between the metropolis of Virginia and the shores of the Chesapeake. On the 1st September, 1814, this impressive letter is sent to the Governor of Virginia, by Mr. Monroe, then Secretary of War:

"The enemy have embarked on board their vessels on the Patuxent, and will, as I presume, in execution of their desolating system, proceed immediately to some other of our principal towns. Norfolk is known to be one on which they have fixed their attention. Baltimore and Richmond are others. Against which they will move, in the first instance, will not be known till they land their men in a marked direction towards it. Be on your guard, prepared at every point, and in all circumstances, to repel the invaders."

Was it possible for the Federal Government to make a more powerful call upon the forces of the State? Had the Governor of Virginia turned a deaf ear to a warning like this, would he not have acted the part of a traitor? At a crisis like this our State treasury is exhausted, not even a dollar remaining. The United States are unable to furnish either supplies or money to meet the crying emergencies of the moment; funds must be obtained, or the forces disbanded, and the country thrown open to the invader.

It was in this embarrassed situation that I found the Governor of Virginia, in my first interview with him, after my arrival at his headquarters. Unfolding to me the dangers of the State, and pointing my attention to the secretary's letter, he requested my co-operation, as a member of the Senate, in procuring the funds indispensably necessary to prevent the disbandment of the army. In compliance with his wishes, I waited on the principal stockholders of the Farmers Bank of Virginia, and, in the preliminary explanations which I made, in conformity to his instructions, I relied on the contents of the letter recently received from the Secretary of War. A loan of about $200,000 was subsequently effected, through the regular organs of the State, and the bank requiring the individual responsibility of the then Governor and Treasurer of the State, those officers did not hesitate at the condition demanded; relying, for indemnity, on the judgment and magnanimity of their country. The Legislature of Virginia, at its ensuing session, proceeded with promptitude to assume the responsibility of the debt; and the interest which was paid to the bank, for money thus borrowed, as I may say, at the instance of this Government, constitutes a part of the claim of Virginia now submitted to your consideration.

Suffer me now, sir, to invite your attention to the financial services of Virginia in the memorable winter of 1814 and '15. This was a period calculated to test the loyalty of the State to the government of the Union. We then contended, single-handed, against a powerful foe. His fleets covered the Chesapeake. His canvass whitened on all the rivers of Virginia. Strengthened by victorious legions from the continent of Europe, the enemy waged a savage warfare throughout the line of our Eastern frontier. Now spread out into predatory bands, he wasted the shores of the Chesapeake, and steered his course on the midnight wave by the light of our flaming habitations. Next concentrating his forces, he threatened the interior of the State, and menaced our principal towns and fortified positions. A brave militia, whose ranks had been recently thinned by the sultry suns of summer, next were wasted, by marches and counter-marches, through the floods of autumn and through the snows of winter. The second year now hastened to its term, since the British fleet had entered the Chesapeake, and now the war seemed but just beginning, with every prospect of indefinite duration. That I do not charge the picture with fictitious colors, I appeal, in my justification, to your own candid recollections.

At this critical stage of the contest, what was the situation of your military chest in Virginia? There were periods at which it was totally exhausted. Even the most inconsiderable claims were unavoidably postponed, for want of money, by the regular and authorized agents of your government. Instances fell under my own observation.

What, permit me to ask, was the spirit which, at this time, reigned in the General Assembly of Virginia, that leading branch of our government, at once the index to the feelings of the people, and the organ of its will? Did it murmur at the unequal pressure of the war, or the want of adequate protection, or the amount of its advances? Did it forfeit its pledges, or abandon its loyalty, or waver in its counsels, or oscillate in its course? Did it require the re-imbursement of the million in arrears, or demand guarantees against unequal burthens for the future? Turn, I beseech you, to its records, and once more examine its course. No, sir; our coffers were still open to you, and our advances still continued. When your funds fell short, we hastened to supply the deficiency. Wherever you appeared weak, we endeavored to add to your strength; wherever you seemed naked, we sought to draw a veil over your infirmities, and to hide them from the eyes of the enemy. To ensure the defence, to which we were clearly entitled, we again and again went into the market and borrowed money, and funded the debts, and paid the interest, until finally, at the close of the contest, the amount of our advances fell but little short of $2,000,000. All descriptions of politicians, both Houses of Assembly, all departments of the government, enlightened citizens throughout the State, all mingled in joint counsels, to devise the best means to supply the funds necessary to sustain the army, and to maintain the war. The barrier between the two governments appeared, for the time, to be prostrate. One common treasury seemed to exist between us.

In the midst of advances so heavy, and so well calculated to test the genuine feelings of the State, the General Assembly of Virginia continued to hold, to the last hour of the contest, this course of generous confidence, of delicate forbearance, of exalted devotion; turning a deaf ear to every proposition, however demanded by all the suggestions of ordinary prudence, which might be calculated, in the most distant manner, to draw into question the very amicable and liberal relations that always existed between the two governments. As far, sir, as my recollection serves me, (for I write from memory, and without access or reference to all the documents on this subject,) it was not till some time after the storm was over, and your financial troubles at an end, that it adopted any resolutions whatsoever on the subject of its advances.

And I think myself warranted in declaring, that nothing could have been more grateful to the feelings of the people of Virginia, than to discover, in the event, how completely their confidence was justified. It was, I assure you, with the most cordial satisfaction that we received from the present Attorney General of the United States his statement of the very impressive manner in which he was met by the present Secretary of the Treasury, under the auspices of the whole Cabinet at Washington. With a promptitude and decision which did honor to the government, the whole amount of our principal debt (with the exception of a small part not supported by proper vouchers) was unhesitatingly allowed, and immediately discharged. The impression made in the State of Virginia was, I assure you, of the most pleasing and durable character; equally honorable, in my humble estimation, to both the parties concerned.

Nor has anything yet occurred, on the subject of our interest claim, to shake my convictions that it must, and will, eventually, meet with the same liberal reception. This part of the claim, if I am not under a misapprehension, is now, for the first time, brought in regular form before the government; and, perhaps, this furnishes the reason why its concomitant circumstances should heretofore have commanded so little of the public attention.

Having been a member of the General Assembly of Virginia, throughout the period of the late war, I think myself well informed of the genius of its counsels, and the spirit of its measures. Lest, however, I might labor under a delusion, I have made it my business to call on a distinguished member of the Senate, and of the House of Representatives, from Virginia, who bore a conspicuous part in the transactions of the times, and have ascertained that they unite with me in these recollections, and concur in the views which I now present to you.

Having requested your decision on this interesting question, I have considered this narrative due to the character of Virginia and the justice of the Union.

I have the honor, sir, to be,

With the highest consideration,

Your obedient servant,

JOSEPH C. CABELL.

O (a).

A BILL FOR THE DISCONTINUANCE OF THE COLLEGE OF WILLIAM & MARY, AND THE ESTABLISHMENT OF OTHER COLLEGES IN CONVENIENT DISTRIBUTION OVER THE STATE.

[The following bill was intended to be offered as a substitute for any bill which might be brought forward, at the session of 1824–25, for removing the College of William & Mary to the city of Richmond. The rejection of the resolution recommended by the Committee of Schools and Colleges put an end to the discussion, and prevented this bill from being brought forward.]

Whereas, it has been represented to this General Assembly, by the Visitors and Professors of the College of William & Mary, that the said College, from circumstances of climate or other causes unknown, has fallen much into disuse, has generally few students, and no longer answers the purposes of its institution; and whereas the said College was originally established by the public authorities of the country, to which the administration of its affairs was then confided in trust for the public purposes, and was endowed principally by large grants of land, the property of the public, partly also by a duty levied on the public on certain imports of their produce (which continued to be paid until the late revolution), and partly by certain fees and perquisites granted by authority of the laws, and continuing still to be paid, which several endowments were vested in the said College in trust for the use and benefit of the public towards the education of the youth of the country, and now failing to answer that purpose, it has become necessary so to dispose anew of the said endowments as that they may fulfill more effectually their original purpose of education; and on the discontinuance of the said College, the said endowments of property reverting of right to the citizens of the State generally, it is just and expedient that its new disposition be such as by establishing the means of education in different parts of the State, they may be placed more within the reach and convenience of its citizens generally.

1. *Be it therefore enacted by the General Assembly*, That the said College of William & Mary, from and after the first day of November in the ensuing year 1826, shall be discontinued and dissolved, and, instead thereof, there shall be established a college at, or within one mile, respectively, of each of the following places, to wit: at Williamsburg, Hampden Sidney, Lynchburg, Richmond, Fredericksburg, Winchester, Staunton, Fincastle, Lewisburg, and Clarksburg.

2. To the College of Williamsburg shall be appropriated the buildings now existing of the College of William & Mary, the tract of land whereon they are situated, the library, apparatus, furniture and other appurtenances of every kind to the same belonging; and to the same College shall be attached all the foundations and donations for the education of youth heretofore given by private individuals, and now held by the said College of William & Mary, with all the trusts and powers respecting the same which may now be lawfully exercised by the authorities of the said College of William & Mary. Saving, nevertheless, to all persons any rights in the said foundations or donations which, on the discontinuance of the said College of William & Mary, may be legally devolved on them.

3. The residue of the property, real and personal, in possession or in right or action, now belonging to the said College of William & Mary, after paying the just debts of the said College now due, and its reasonable maintenance until the day of its dissolution, shall constitute a fund for procuring grounds and erecting the necessary buildings at the places aforesaid, to each of which shall be allotted an equal portion of the said residuary property.

4. Immediately after the dissolution aforesaid there shall be appointed by the Governor, with the advice and consent of the Council, for each of the said Colleges, seven Visitors, living each of them nearer to that for which he is appointed than to any other of the said Colleges, of which notice shall be given to the persons so appointed, who shall thereupon, on a day to be named by the Governor with advice and consent of the Council, assemble each at the place at or near which their respective College is to be established, or on the first day there-

after at which a full meeting can be obtained, and shall proceed to choose a site for their College within the limits aforesaid, and to report the same to the Governor and Council for their approbation or rejection; and if rejected, a new choice shall be made by the said Visitors until such a site shall be proposed as the same authority shall approve.

[The sections of this bill, from 5 to 16 inclusive, correspond *mutatis mutandis* with sections 17, 18, 21, 22, 23, 25, 26, 27, 28, 30, 42, of Mr. Jefferson's bill for establishing a system of public education, already given. Appendix G.]

17. *And be it further enacted*, That the salaries of the present professors of the College of William & Mary shall be continued to them until the opening of some one or more of the Colleges provided for in this act, they continuing their services in William & Mary until its discontinuance; and, moreover, that if the competent authorities of the present Academy of Hampden Sidney shall not consent that the same shall become a public institution, subject to the laws, regulations, benefits and responsibilities herein provided for the other Colleges, then a site shall be selected in the county of Nottoway by the Visitors to be appointed as provided for the other Colleges, and to the College there to be erected shall be transferred all the provisions and benefits proposed in this act to the said Academy of Hampden Sidney, in like manner as if the said College of Nottoway had been herein named instead of that of Hampden Sidney.

O (b).

TO THE GENERAL ASSEMBLY OF VIRGINIA.

One who feels an interest, in common with his fellow-citizens, in the literary institutions of the State, begs leave most respectfully to submit to your perusal and consideration the subjoined letters and papers, accompanied by a few explanatory observations.

These documents, gentlemen, deserve your serious attention, as well on account of their own intrinsic merit, as of the distinguished source from which they emanated. They shed useful lights on the petitions now preferred from various parts of the Commonwealth for aids to the intermediate seminaries; and exhibit in a striking point of view the long-continued and anxious efforts of one of the greatest of men to improve the moral condition of his countrymen, by the introduction of a general system of public instruction.

The bill from which the subjoined sections are extracted is entitled "A bill for establishing a system of public education," and provides for a whole scheme of national instruction, consisting of three grades—Primary Schools, Colleges, and an University. The failure of a similar bill at the session of 1816–17 gave occasion to a member of the General Assembly, who was friendly to the objects of the measure, to request Mr. Jefferson to disclose his views on the subject, and to make the communication in a form to be readily presented to the Legislature of the State. The bill which grew out of this application, and from which the subjoined sections were taken, was offered by Mr. Samuel Taylor of Chesterfield, to the House of Delegates at the session of 1817–18, and was supported with great zeal and ability by that gentleman, at the head of a numerous and respectable party in the Legislature. The existing provision for the education of the poor, and the University of Virginia, formed the basis of the compromise which then took place between the two houses of Assembly; the former being the favorite measure of the House of Delegates, and the latter being the *sine qua non* of the Senate. The friends of the bill made the utmost exertions to carry it in all its parts; but the primary schools and the colleges were stricken from it in the House of Delegates. Great perplexities were found to attend any system of primary schools, many of which were suggested and discussed; and the parish tax, by which the author of the bill proposed to diminish and soften the financial difficulties of the subject, was by no means acceptable to the representatives of the people. The objects of compromise absorbing all the disposable funds of the State, and it being impracticable to procure the means of carrying the whole system into effect, the colleges were necessarily postponed along with the primary schools.

Since the winter of 1817–18, efforts have been made from session to session towards the endowment of some or more of the existing colleges and academies; but the literary funds of the State being limited, and the drafts for the purpose of completing the University being heavy and pressing, these efforts have consequently proved abortive. A movement in favor of one college has invariably been accompanied by similar movements in favor of many others; and, the funds being insufficient for a general appropriation, all have failed of success.

At the session of 1820–21, a general appropriation was made in favor of the colleges thereafter to be established or patronized, of the surplus revenue of the literary fund, till it should reach the amount of $20,000 per annum, which was partially repealed in favor of the University at the last session of the Assembly. No surplus having yet accrued, no specific appropriation in favor of the colleges has heretofore taken place; and this part of the system lies over awaiting the tardy increase of the literary fund.

In this state of things, the College of William & Mary comes before you; and, upon the ground that it can no longer accomplish the end of its institution at Williamsburg, invites you to give it a different location.

You will doubtless inquire, both impartially and diligently into all the causes of the present reduced situation of this ancient establishment. It is for you to decide what influence is due to the various causes alleged—to the charter; or to the administration under the charter; to the present location of the institution, or to the expected opening of the University of Virginia. It is your province to determine whether the causes of its failure be temporary or permanent; and whether, upon a full and candid inquiry into all the circumstances of the case, the old site or a new location will be most conducive to the interests of literature.

Should you, however, be finally convinced that your duty to the people requires you to give a new disposition to the funds of the college, the question will then arise, whether the petition of the Visitors and professors does not furnish a propitious occasion for hastening the accomplishment of the collegiate part of our system of public instruction, and whether, instead of transporting to the city of Richmond the whole of these extensive endowments, under their present organization, it would not be equally the dictate of justice and of policy to divide and to distribute them over the surface of the State, upon a plan analogous to that recommended by Mr. Jefferson in the year 1817; taking care to select for sites of the new colleges such places as Richmond, Fredericksburg, Lynchburg, Staunton, Lewisburg, Clarksburg, &c., and to support a seminary of equal grade with the others, in the edifice now occupied by the ancient institution.

A proposition which calls for changes so new and so extensive, will doubtless meet with much opposition. I respectfully invite you not hastily to condemn it; to subject it to the test of the most rigid scrutiny; and to compare its results with the advantages of the plan of removal to Richmond.

In regard to the details of the plan exhibited in the subjoined bill, amendments might be made at discretion. It is the outline only, with such of the details as on revision might be approved, that is recommended as a preferable measure on the present occasion.

You will perceive that, according to the estimate of Mr. Jefferson, each college will require an appropriation as follows: for lands $500; for buildings $7,342; for paying the salary of $500 to each of two professors, $16,666 66. In short, each college would require for its necessary lands and buildings an appropriation of $7,842, and for the supply of the salary of its two professors a further advance of $16,666 66, or a total capital of $24,508 66. Consequently the nine colleges would require the following outlay: For lands and buildings $70,578; for the purpose of raising salaries $150,000; or an aggregate amount of $220,578.

But, if the colleges should be distributed and located with a view to the present buildings of William & Mary, as a part of the system, it would probably become necessary to increase the number, and to have ten of these institutions in the State. Let this be supposed for the sake of argument and illustration.

The account would then stand as follows: For lands and buildings for nine new colleges $70,578; for raising the salaries of twenty professors in the ten colleges $166,666 66; making an aggregate amount of $237,244 66.

For the sum then of $237,244 66, the whole State of Virginia could, according to this estimate, be supplied with these collegiate establishments.

It will be said, perhaps, that this estimate is too low, and, in the end, will be found fallacious and deceptive. Does the supposed error lie in the allowance for the lands and buildings, or in that for the salaries of the professors?

It is presumed that no objection will be made to the estimate for the lands. In regard to the buildings, it is proper to remark, that a much cheaper and plainer style of architecture might be adopted for these secondary and subordinate institutions, than that which has been introduced at the University of Virginia. The object there was not merely to accommodate the professors and students, but to present to the world and to transmit to posterity, a monument of the taste and of the genius of the present age.

Let facts be appealed to on the present occasion.

The new college edifice at Washington College, is probably much more extensive than the buildings in question. It has a chapel 47 by 34 feet. A chemical apartment in two parts—one for the apparatus and another for lecturing. A similar apartment for the accommodation of a professor of natural philosophy. Two large society rooms, and fourteen lodging rooms for the professors and students, susceptible each of containing four persons. It is a considerable building, three stories high, and would probably be regarded as a respectable college edifice in any part of the Union. It is understood that it will cost the sum of $9,000.

The writer of this article has not seen the new college edifice at Hampden Sidney, but he has been informed that it is more extensive than the new college at Lexington, and that it will cost about the sum of $15,000. Should it be necessary, the delegates from the respective counties will verify or correct this statement, and furnish all the details which could be desired.

As to the adequacy of the allowance for salaries, let us appeal to the experience of William & Mary. We are informed, on the authority of one of the Visitors who appeared as a witness before the Committee of Schools and Colleges, (see report of the Committee, page 18,) that prior to the year 1815, the salaries of the professors of that college stood as follows:

Professor of Law and Police, - - - -	$500 00
Moral Philosophy, - - - - - -	600 00
Mathematics, - - - - - -	700 00
Natural Philosophy, - - - - - -	500 00
Chemistry, Natural History and Botany, - -	600 00

These salaries were augmented, some of them considerably, in the year 1815. But if the salaries of an institution of high grade, like William & Mary, stood as here stated, as late as the year 1815, does it not furnish the strongest evidence of the correctness of Mr. Jefferson's estimate? It is worthy of remark also, that money has greatly appreciated since the year 1815, and that $500 at the present time would be equal to the average of the salaries of William & Mary prior to the year 1815.

At Hampden Sidney College, now one of the most flourishing literary institutions in the State, it is understood that the professors depend altogether for their support and emoluments on fees of tuition. It is admitted, however, that as a measure of general policy, and especially in new seminaries just going into operation without an established reputation, a portion of fixed salary ought, if possible, to be allowed.

The facts already quoted, might be fortified by similar facts and by reasoning, and appear to establish the correctness and solidity of the estimate in question, in respect to the allowance both for the buildings and for the salaries of the professors.

Indeed it is not an extravagant supposition that the whole item of lands and building might be striken from the account of the public expenditure. Practical and judicious men entertain the opinion, that were the law to designate the proper sites for the colleges, and to make the donation of the salaries from the public funds, to take effect as soon as the requisite and proper lands and buildings should be contributed by individuals, the lands and buildings would forthwith appear at each and every place indicated in your act.

Should this supposition be well founded, and you frame your law in accordance with it, then the estimated amount for the lands and buildings, viz: $70,578 might be deducted from the above mentioned aggregate of $237,244 66, and in that case, the draft upon the public funds for the whole system of colleges would be reduced to the sum of $166,666 66.

Let us next enquire how far the funds of the present college of William & Mary would go towards the accomplishment of this national system of colleges.

From the report of the Committee of Schools and Colleges, it appears that the present moneyed capital of William & Mary amounts to the sum of $132,161 69. This, however, is exclusive of 5,025 acres of land in the county of King William, and 1,582 acres in the county of Sussex. It is represented upon good authority, that the former is worth at the rate of $3 50, and the latter $3 per acre The lands in King William, then, constitute a capital of $17,587, and those in Sussex another capital of $5,537; making together an aggregate of $23,124. This added to the moneyed capital makes the whole available funds of William & Mary, exclusive of the library and apparatus, the buildings and the land on which the buildings are situated, to amount to the sum of $155,285 69.

If the lands and buildings of the colleges be contributed by individuals, then the capital of William & Mary would fall short of the sum to be expended for all the colleges, only $11,380 90.

If these lands and buildings are to be furnished by the public, the capital of the college would fall short of the necessary amount in the sum of $81,958 90.

There is a bill now before the Senate for selling the lands vested in the President and Directors of the Literary Fund. There are also grounds to expect that our interest claim will shortly be paid by the General Government. From these sources we may justly expect that $81,958 90 will soon be added to the capital of the fund. Nay, should experience demonstrate that the estimate here exhibited will prove deficient, or that a third professor ought to be added to each of the colleges, our literary finances will probably be in a situation to answer any such augmented demand. And the further surplus of the revenue of the literary fund would then be unfettered from the claims of the colleges, and might be applied to the third branch of our system of public instruction, upon such enlarged and improved principles as the sages of the land are doubtless competent devise. Thus the march of the entire scheme of national instruction towards its final completion would be greatly accelerated; and consistency of design and unity of action would reign throughout the consecutive labors of succeeding sessions of the General Assembly.

That the diffusion of institutions, such as are here recommended, would be of incalculable advantage to the education of our youth, is a proposition too clear to require that any argument should be urged in its defence. To make the attempt would be to insult the intelligence of your honorable body. Were arguments necessary, they might be found abundantly in the numerous petitions now crowding your table.

What are the advantages of the plan of transferring all the funds of William & Mary to the city of Richmond, compared to the benefits of the scheme of division and diffusion?

The Richmond plan takes every thing from the ancient metropolis, and abandons to utter loss and ruin the present college edifice.

The general scheme leaves Williamsburg and the surrounding country on an equal footing with the other parts of the State, and preserves for useful purposes the college buildings.

The Richmond plan transfers to the metropolis an institution of high grade, the utility of which, in the actual state of things, will, to say the least, be very limited; and concentrates, at one point in the East, all the disposable college funds now held by the State.

The general scheme gives equal participation in those funds to the country beyond the Alleghany, to the Valley, and to all parts of the Commonwealth.

The Richmond plan would promote, in a very limited degree, and in a partial manner, a system of public instruction to the State at large, to which the people of Virginia have so long looked forward with anxious expectation.

The general scheme advances directly and rapidly the system of public instruction in which the State is embarked; and, by carrying home to the doors of our yeomanry facilities of education for their sons, rescues our literary establishment from the imputation of conducing to the instruction only of the paupers and of the nabobs of the land.

By the Richmond plan the lights of science will blaze forth with redundant splendor at two points in the State.

By the general scheme there will be one great luminary in the centre, and lesser lights kindled up over the whole extent of our territory.

By the Richmond plan the surplus revenue of the literary fund will stand mortgaged to the colleges, to the exclusion of the primary schools for an indefinite series of years yet to come.

By the general scheme you will, at once, nearly satisfy the wants of the colleges, and liberate and lay open the surplus to the claims of the primary schools.

Under circumstances such as these, can the General Assembly of Virginia hesitate to make its election?

What, then, are the obstacles to the adoption of a scheme of such wide-spreading and incalculable benefits to the whole people of Virginia?

Is not the money our own? Does not the corporation of the college of William & Mary exist for us, and not we for the corporation? Are the crown lands which the king gave the college to be considered as private donations, when they were held by him as our governor for the time being, and were conferred at the request of our forefathers, who entered the wilderness, drove off the Indians, and conquered those very lands? No. Representatives, tell not your constituents that these royal donations were not the property of the brave forefathers of the people of Virginia!

The objections which are supposed to arise from the charter of the college, and the rights of the corporation cannot be justified in the light of reason, or on the ground of authority.

Were this the case of a private eleemosynary corporation, like Hampden Sydney or Washington College, these objections would be entitled to the highest consideration; but they are believed to be entirely inapplicable to the public corporation of William & Mary, which was chartered at the instance of the General Assembly, and endowed, by the Executive functionary of the time, from the public lands and the public coffers, for public and general objects, and not for private and individual purposes. The small medium of private donations, constituting, perhaps, a tenth or a twentieth part of the college property, should be considered as following rather than leading and stamping the character of this public institution. History proves that the first and greatest of the private donations, that of Governor Nicholson and the Council was intended mainly to give an impulse to the General Assembly, and to enlist the public authorities of the colony in the support of the project, without whose aid, as the historian expressly states, the projectors well knew that nothing efficient could be accomplished. It is worthy of remark, that the Central College originated in a similar manner, after a lapse of upwards of a century from the foundation of the College of William & Mary.

Is there any good reason that an institution thus founded, and thus endowed, should not come within the pale of Legislative control, as much as the corporation of the literary fund or of the University of Virginia?

The experience of the country is rapidly developing how many prejudices have existed on this subject, and how idle are the supposed dangers of giving the representatives of the people an efficient control over our literary institutions? The actual situation of the College of William & Mary, and the petition of the Visitors and professors, furnish the strongest proofs of the absolute necessity of a regulating power in the hands of the representative body. Of this the petitioners seem to be duly sensible, provided you will limit its exercise to the sanction of the plans of policy which they propose to establish; but, if you, gentlemen, should all happen to differ with them in opinion, they will tell you to attend to your appropriate duties; "that you are not qualified to discuss the relations of cause and effect; to settle the controversies of a Hume, a Paine, or a Voltaire; or to pursue the devious comet in his flight through the trackless regions of space;" no, gentlemen, they will then tell you, "thus far shalt thou go, and no farther." When, in your law, creating the University of Virginia, you reserved a paramount control in the last resort, over this literary institution of highest grade in the State, (might I not say in the United States,) was it with the view of intermeddling in the ordinary routine of duties properly appertaining to the Visitors whom you have appointed to conduct it; or was it to step in on great and important occasions, to rectify its organization, and to adopt its frame and its polity to the unavoidable changes which spring from the progress of society? We are not apprised of any attempt, or of any disposition, to repeal that part of the charter of the University, which places this exalted institution, at all times, and in all things, under the control of the General Assembly. Your agent, Mr. Gilmer, found this part of the charter no impediment to the success of his mission; and the philosophers of Great Britain have arrived, or are now crossing the Atlantic, on the faith of a charter which gives you complete authority to put down, to preserve, to alter, or to amend the institution in which they are coming to embark their fortunes.

The fact, that such men as Jefferson, Pendleton and Wythe, did actually, in 1779, report to the Legislature a bill amending the constitution of William & Mary, and that the Judges of the Court of Appeals did, in the two cases of Bracken and the College, in the years 1787 and 1790, upon the fullest and most mature consideration, indicate the opinion that the college was a public and not a private corporation, is surely entitled to the most serious consideration of every candid and dispassionate mind. However heterodoxical these opinions now appear in the circles of the metropolis, the people of Virginia will not fail to hold them in the highest respect and veneration, and will probably regard them as strictly conformable to the most orthodox canons of constitutional law.

What reasons have we to believe, that, were the question now to come before the judiciary of the State, an opinion would exist different from that formerly entertained by the Judges of the Court of Appeals?

But the Supreme Court of the United States, and the decision in the case of the Dartmouth College, are interposed as barriers to the exercise of such a power as that which is now claimed for the Legislature; and that, too, at a time when it is invited to surrender to the Visitors the right of selecting the site of the college, which was confided to the representatives of the people by the very terms of the charter. It is not easily perceived that there is any thing of positive decision or necessary inference, even in this celebrated case, to bind the hands of your honorable body, and to prevent you from legislating with the most perfect freedom and discretion with regard to the College of William & Mary. The cases appear to be widely different. It is believed that no such case as that of William & Mary College has ever come under the consideration of the Supreme Court. In the Dartmouth case, Dr. Wheelock, Mr. Whitiker, the Earl of Dartmouth, and other private persons, were the founders; and the funds were private; and the Chief Justice, in delivering his opinion, laid considerable stress on both these circumstances. The power of the General Assembly of Virginia cannot and ought not to be restrained and limited by doubtful inferences from the decisions of a tribunal which, however able and enlightened, has not heretofore been regarded in Virginia as entertaining views the most limited of the federal judiciary.

Were there better grounds than seem to exist, for the opposition to the powers of the Legislature, is not the question surrendered, and all doubt removed, by the petition of the Visitors and professors, invoking the interposition of the Legislature?

And even if the corporation were confessedly private, and trial and judgment were necessary before you touch the funds, could you not, upon the ground of the facts set forth, in the report of the Committee of Schools and Colleges, instruct the Attorney General to apply for a writ of *quo warranto*, to ascertain and establish the forfeiture of the charter? In the one way, or in the other, you can rightfully reach the subject; and the question is thus reducible to a mere question of discretion and expediency.

When, in the progress of time, the representation in the Senate of the State had become unequal, you construed your powers liberally in favor of the equal rights of the people, and were not withheld from an act of justice by the constitutional difficulties attempted to be thrown in your way.

If you should finally entertain the opinion, that the plan of removal to Richmond would not be as conducive to the interests of literature as that of dividing and diffusing the funds, would there be just ground of opposition to your law from the corporation which asks at your hands the power to select a new location, "with a view to a more extended diffusion of the benefits of the institution?"

If you should doubt your power or condemn the scheme of decision, still would not justice and policy dictate the propriety of leaving the question open for the people to consider and to decide for themselves in an affair in which they are so deeply interested? What are the disadvantages of leaving the funds unproductive for another year, compared to the baleful consequences of a precipitate decision, committing the faith of the State, possibly in opposition to the public judgment and the public feelings? It is a dictate of wisdom, that all great changes should be made with caution, and the utmost practicable latitude given for deliberation and discussion. The scheme of removal was not spoken of till the month of May; was hastily discussed in the public prints in June; was postponed, in favor of a further experiment on the old site, by the Visitors, in July, and was unexpectedly adopted at the convocation in November. The Visitors and professors did not, *themselves*, decide in favor of removal, till the 26th of November, when, from all points of our territory, you had left your constituents, and had already arrived at the seat of government, or were traveling on the high roads leading to it. Should you now decide in favor of removal to Richmond, a large amount of private funds will be invested on the faith of your act, and new and perhaps insurmountable impediments, will spring up, to prevent the adoption of any better plan, which might arise from a conflict of opinions, and from a comparison of views. Would it not be more wise to follow the prudent example of your predecessors at the session of 1816–17, who, instead of adopting the bill on public education, which was then presented, published the bill, together with every kindred document on the subject, for the consideration of the people of Virginia?

No one can respect more highly than the writer of this article the talents and the virtues of the advocates of the contemplated removal. But may it not be asked, whether the plan they recommend, of fixing one of our principal seminaries, in an expensive commercial city, a city in which you yourselves are sitting at an expense of $4 per day, and at the rate of $1,460 per annum, is not, at least, novel and of doubtful propriety? Is it not questionable, whether the good people of this Commonwealth would not prefer to establish subordinate seminaries over the surface of the country?

Will the people around Fredericksburg and Lynchburg, around Winchester and Staunton, around Clarksburg and Lewisburg, and other points yet to be named; will *they* be satisfied to yield up to the city of Richmond, all these munificent funds, the gift of our forefathers for our common good, and unite in condemning a policy which brings science home to their countries, and "makes the desert blossom as the rose?"

Whatever may be thought of the course recommended, the subjoined documents will prove that the measure is not now, for the first time, brought to the view of your honorable body.

During the pendency of the bill submitted by Mr. Taylor, at the session of 1817–18, objections were made, as already stated, to the expense of the primary schools, which drew from the pen of its illustrious author (Mr. Jefferson) the following defence of that part of the system:

"And will the wealthy individual have no retribution? And what will this be? 1. The peopling his neighborhood with honest, useful and enlightened citizens, understanding their own rights, and firm in their perpetuation. 2. When his own descendants become poor, which they generally do within three generations, (no law of primogeniture now perpetuating wealth in the same families,) their children will be educated by the then rich, and the little advance he now makes to poverty, while rich himself, will be repaid by the then rich, to his descendants when they become poor, and thus give them a chance of rising again. This is a solid consideration, and should go home to the bosom of every parent. This will be seed sewed in fertile ground. It is a provision for his family, looking to distant times, and far in duration beyond that he has now in hand for them. Let every man count backward in his own family, and see how many generations he can go before he comes to the ancestor who made the fortune he now holds; most will be stopped at the first generation; many at the second; a few will reach the third; and not one in the State go beyond the fifth.

"A system of general instruction, which shall reach every description of citizens, from the richest to the poorest, as it was the earliest, so will it be the latest of all the public concerns in which I shall permit myself to take an interest. Nor am I tenacious of the form in which it shall be introduced. Be that what it may, our descendants will be as wise as we are, and will know how to amend, and to amend it until it shall suit their circumstances. Give it to us, then, in a shape, and receive for the inestimable boon the thanks of the young and the blessings of the old, who are past all other services but prayers for the prosperity of their country, and blessings to those who promote it."

Permit me, gentlemen, to ask you, if these are the sentiments of a monopolist, devoted exclusively to the aggrandisement of a particular and favorite institution? Where is the man with heart so cold as not to glow at the recital of views so generous and so exalted? The name of this great and good man will descend with his works to the latest times, and will be hailed with rapturous enthusiasm by the friends of liberty and learning in every quarter of the civilized globe.

A Friend of Science.

O (c).

Williamsburg, 7th March, 1825.

Dear Cabell,—When we were in Richmond I told you, that if we lost our cause, which I confess I did not expect, that I should not therefore give up the contest. Accordingly, as soon as I heard the fate of our scheme, I set to work, and have prepared for the press a second edition of my address. I have prefixed an introduction and appended some notes. In these I have spoken of the University party,* and of Mr. Jefferson, in a manner not calculated to gratify his feelings or to advance his reputation. I have, as you know, no personal obligations to Mr. Jefferson, but I assure you I have had no wish to detract from his standing. He is, and has been for years, the most prominent character among us, and, being moreover a Virginian, I had much rather it had fallen to my lot to aid in exalting him than

* I except, of course, those gentlemen who did *not* oppose us, but no name except that of Mr. J. is mentioned.

to assist in lowering him. Such, however, is the course of events, and I cannot avoid it. My performance is drawn up with freedom and with all the force I could throw into it. When printed, it is my intention to send copies to every part of the State, to my literary friends in the large cities to the North, and to all the principal colleges from Maine to Georgia, and westward to the Ohio. The part which these persons and these institutions will take in it, is not difficult to foresee. The professors throughout the country will more or less actively make a common cause of it. Of the effect of this, you can judge as well as I can.

Such are my present plans, but they may be modified, though not, I think, to any great extent.

But to the principal object of this letter, which is to gain information, rather than to communicate it.

The very day on which our proposition was in effect rejected, a piece appeared in the Enquirer, under the signature of "A Friend of Science," written, as I believe, in whole or in part by Mr. Jefferson. In one of my notes I have accordingly stated that such is my conviction; but I do not wish to state even a suspicion which is not founded in fact. If, therefore, you will assure me that Mr. J. had no hand in the composition of the piece in question, I will correct the note; otherwise, it must stand as it is. I do not wish to be told who was the immediate agent in furnishing the piece to the Enquirer. Upon that point my intelligence is satisfactory; but I am not altogether certain as to the authorship of the "Friend of Science."

You need not be in any hurry to answer this letter, as my pamphlet will not go to press for some months to come, according to my present views.

My compliments to Mrs. C., and tell her I lament her good wishes in my behalf were all frustrated.

Respectfully, your ob't serv't,

J. Aug. Smith.

Jos. C. Cabell, Esq.,
Warminster, Nelson county, Va.

EDGEWOOD, 24th March, 1825.

DEAR DOCTOR,—Your favor of the 7th instant reached me by the last mail, and I confess that I am not a little gratified by the compliment you pay me in supposing Mr. Jefferson to be the author of the piece under the signature of "A Friend of Science." Mr. Jefferson did not write that piece, nor any part of it; nor did he furnish the materials; nor did he advise the publication. Nor had any body else except myself any share or agency in the composition of the essay. It was believed in Richmond that it was the production of a party. But this was all mistake. Mr. Jefferson is incapable of writing a piece in which he is himself the object of the highest eulogy; and I am sure you had forgotten the concluding part of the essay, when you suggested the possibility of his being the author. His letter and bill referred to in the essay, were among my public papers which I annually carry to the seat of government. You know that the friends of the University who opposed your scheme were assailed in the newspapers and vilified all over Richmond. I understood that I was myself the object of extensive and bitter obloquy. Under a sense of duty to myself, my friends, and my constituents, I hastily wrote some essays (of which the one you mention was the last), in order that the views of the friends of the University might be fully and fairly before the public, and appreciated according to their intrinsic worth. I availed myself, in my individual character, of the equal right of every citizen, to submit to the public, under a fictitious signature, my views of a great question then pending before the Legislature; and in so doing, I only followed the example of General Tucker on a similar occasion, and of many others who have gone before me. The mail which brought me your letter, was the bearer of a pamphlet prepared for the press and addressed to my constituents, in which I avow myself to be the author of the essays above referred to. The same motives that induced me to publish them in the winter, have urged me to lay them, with other documents, before my constituents; for the principal cause, in my opinion, of almost all the late rumors of opposition to my re-election, grow out of my conduct in regard to the literary institutions of the State during the last two sessions of the General Assembly, on both which occasions I had the misfortune to differ with a large portion of the delegation from this district. Having devoted seventeen winters of my life to the public service, not for a salary, but for the good opinion of the public, I am naturally sensitive to the efforts in progress to deprive me altogether of the public favor. I will send you a copy of my pamphlet when it appears, in which you will perceive, I think, nothing personal or illiberal towards yourself or the other advocates of removal; and I need not remind you of my uniform efforts, throughout our conflicts of opinion, to reconcile the duties of a friend with those of a patriot and a representative. Let me advise you to re-consider your determination to make a deliberate attack on Mr. Jefferson and the University party. That party (if such it may be called) were acknowledged by your friends to have conducted themselves with much moderation and prudence in the debate on the College question; whereas, some of the delegation from your tide-water country handled the faculty with great severity. May I not suggest the expediency of confining your remarks to the arguments and opinions of Mr. Jefferson and the University party, instead of attempting to injure them personally and to lessen them in the public estimation? Those gentlemen have a right to their opinions on public questions; and in nothing that they have done, have they been actuated by the desire of injuring you. Some of them have, in the midst of the late contests, evinced every disposition to conciliate your personal interests with the changes in the literary institutions of the State, which they deemed necessary for the good of the community. You are too liberal, I am sure, to impute this advice to any but the most friendly and correct motives. I should be thankful for a copy of your pamphlet when it appears.

Mrs. Cabell is with her friends in Norfolk, and as I write to her to-day, I convey your message in my letter.

Present me in the kindest terms to Mrs. Smith and your children, and give my best wishes to Mr. Campbell.

Yours, with sincere regard,

JOSEPH C. CABELL.

Doct. John A. Smith, President of William & Mary College.

P.

A BILL FOR THE COMPLETION OF THE BUILDINGS OF THE UNIVERSITY OF VIRGINIA, AND FOR THE ESTABLISHMENT OF COLLEGES IN CONVENIENT DISTRIBUTION OVER THE STATE.

Whereas, it appears that the endowments heretofore conferred upon the University of Virginia have been found insufficient to finish its buildings, and that additional funds are necessary to effect their final completion; and whereas the fostering support of the Legislature, if now extended, in aid of former enactments, will tend to crown with success the early operations of the institution, and to ensure the important ends for which it was founded:

1. *Be it therefore enacted,* That in order to finish the buildings of the University of Virginia, and to pay the debts which, with a view to their advancement and completion, have already been contracted, or may hereafter be incurred, the sum of thirty-two thousand dollars shall be and the same is hereby appropriated; and the President and Directors of the Literary Fund are hereby authorized and required to pay to the Rector and Visitors of the University of Virginia, for the purposes herein specified, the said sum of thirty-two thousand dollars out of the moneys recently received from the Government of the United States on account of interest upon the advances made by this State to that government during the prosecution of the late war, or if previous to this act the said moneys shall have been invested in stocks, in conformity to the provisions of an act passed during the present session entitled, "An act concerning the President and Directors of the Literary Fund," in that case, it shall be the duty of the said President and Directors forthwith to cause to be sold at public auction so much of the said stock as may be necessary to fulfill the object of the present appropriation, and for the establishment of colleges whereat the youth of this Commonwealth may, within convenient distances from their homes, receive a higher grade of education.

[The remaining sections of this bill accord very nearly with the provisions of that part of the bill for establishing a system of public education which relates to colleges. The modifications are such as are suggested in Mr. Cabell's letters of February 8th and 10th, 1826.]

Q.

[The following paper, from the pen of Professor Minor, of the Law Department, will shew the present administration of the University; its general conformity with the original plan, and the very few particulars in which it has been found expedient to deviate therefrom.]

The government, discipline, organization and methods of instruction of the University, retain the impression derived from Mr. Jefferson, and in most respects are eminently characteristic of him.

THE GOVERNMENT.

The government is vested in the Rector and Visitors. The Visitors are appointed by the Governor, for four years, every 29th of February. They are nine in number, two from each grand division of the State, except that in which the University is situated (the Piedmont division), from which three are appointed, with a view to the formation of an Executive Committee to act in the recess of the Board. The Visitors elect a Rector from amongst themselves. Vacancies occurring in the Board are filled by the Governor. They meet at the University, at least once a year, and as much oftener as circumstances require, and make an annual report to the Legislature.

The affairs of the institution are administered under the general direction of this Board, and in pursuance of its enactments, by the Chairman, Faculty, Proctor and other subordinate agents.

The Chairman and Faculty are charged with the immediate control. The Chairman is selected annually from among the members of the Faculty, and discharges most of the functions of President of the University, being, for the time, the executive chief. To this republican feature of rotation, Mr. Jefferson attached not a little importance, insomuch that at the very last meeting of the Board before his death, Mr. Wirt, then Attorney General of the United States, having been appointed Professor of Law and President of the University, Mr. Jefferson, while expressing his hearty concurrence in Mr. Wirt's appointment to the Chair of Law, entered upon the minutes, with his own hand, so strong a protest against the creation of the office of President, that upon Mr. Wirt's declining, the proposition was never renewed. Thirty years experience has served to shew that in respect to the government of men, the founder of the University was in advance of his age in sagacity. The system is not without its disadvantages, but its benefits decidedly preponderate. It makes the institution less dependent on a single man, generates a more lively interest in its fortunes amongst all the members of the Faculty, each of whom feels a due share of responsibility for its success, and by exercising all more or less in administration, fits them, to a greater or less degree, for its duties.

THE DISCIPLINE.

The policy adopted at the beginning, and in general steadily pursued, has been to institute a government of *laws*, and not of *discretion*, and yet to have as few regulations as possible, and none founded on artificial restraints, supposed to be conducive to College order. Nothing is forbidden which is not positively pernicious, nor anything required which is not essential to the successful conduct of the education of young men. Mr. Jefferson's views upon this subject were at first somewhat too liberal, his confidence in the self-governing capacity of young men having betrayed him into providing insufficient restraints for the heady passions incident to their age. He lived long enough, however, to correct this partial error, and readily acquiesced in an increased stringency of the laws.

But no system of espionage is employed. The statements of students are received as on honor, and full credence awarded them, and in all respects manly principles of self-government are appealed to, and an enlightened public sentiment among the young men is cherished. These do not, indeed, dispense with an occasional resort to severer measures, but they make such measures rarely necessary.

THE ORGANIZATION FOR INSTRUCTION.

There is no fixed *curriculum* of study prescribed, but each department is organized into a distinct "school" of itself, with its distinct professor, or professors, and assistants; and in these several schools, which are exclusively under the control of the instructors therein, subject only to the Board of Visitors, degrees are conferred separately; so that the University may be regarded as a collection of schools, each of which is devoted to a special subject.

This plan, it will be perceived, admits of and contemplates an indefinite multiplication of "schools," keeping pace with the demands of society. At present there are nine, with one or more instructors in each, viz:

I. Ancient Languages—With a Professor and two Assistants, called "Assistant Instructors," corresponding to tutors elsewhere.
II. Modern Languages—With a Professor and one Assistant.
III. Mathematics—With a Professor and one Assistant.
IV. Natural Philosophy—With one Professor.
V. Chemistry—With one Professor.
VI. Medicine—With one Professor.
VII. Comparative Anatomy, Physiology, Surgery, Human Anatomy, and Materia Medica—With one Professor, a Lecturer, and a Demonstrator of Anatomy.
VIII. Moral Philosophy—With one Professor.
IX. Law—With two Professors.

Students attend as many of the schools as they think fit, paying a fee for each. But in order to ensure sufficient employment, no one can attend less than three, without leave of the Faculty.

In this feature is seen Mr. Jefferson's characteristic confidence in the capacity of individuals to determine for themselves what is best for them. He thought it safe to submit to the judgment of each student and his friends, the choice of subjects best adapted to the cast of his mind, and to his views in life. The results of the system are not wholly good, but the good preponderates. Custom has begun to prescribe an order of studies which experience has approved as in general to be preferred, whilst those whose circumstances suggest a different course, are free to pursue it. But the chief advantage is found in the effect on the several departments of instruction. As they conduct their operations independently of each other, they are at liberty to advance *ad libitum* the standard of attainment and the extent of knowledge imparted in each; and the instructors are urged in that direction continually, as well by the promptings of interest as by a generous emulation.

In each school, and in each class of every school, if there is more than one, a *semi-annual* examination is had. The examination is conducted in *writing*, and all the students are expected to undergo it. Those who exhibit a certain proficiency are announced to the public as *distinguished* in such a class of such a school—an ill-chosen term, it must be allowed, inferring, as it does, the highest honor of a school, whilst it is, in truth, the lowest.

Degrees, as has been said, are conferred in each school upon those who, upon rigorous examinations, partly in writing and partly oral, manifest a thorough acquaintance with the subjects taught. They carry with them no specific title, except in the School of Law, the graduates of which are styled "Bachelor of Laws." The graduates in the schools which constitute the Medical department, have the title of "Doctor of Medicine." Those who obtain degrees in two of the *literary* schools, (viz: Ancient Languages, Modern Languages, and Moral Philosophy,) and in two of the scientific, (viz: Mathematics, Natural Philosophy, and Chemistry,) and who also reach a certain proficiency in the other two of those six, have the title of "Bachelor of Arts;" whilst upon those who have first gained degrees in all the academic schools (the six above named), and have undergone afterwards a satisfactory examination in the aggregate on all the subjects, is conferred the title of "Master of Arts."

No honorary degrees are bestowed, nor does length of residence constitute, in any case, a part of the consideration in granting testimonials of proficiency.

METHODS OF INSTRUCTION.

Instruction is given partly by text-books, and partly by oral lectures; the system being based on the old observation, that "reading without hearing is dark and irksome, and hearing without reading is slippery and uncertain." Daily recitations upon the text-books and lectures stimulate the diligence, and remove the doubts and embarrassments of the student; whilst written exercises, in those subjects that admit of them, serve to mature and arrange the knowledge which has been gained.

INDEX TO CORRESPONDENCE.

www.ingramcontent.com/pod-product-compliance
Lightning Source LLC
LaVergne TN
LVHW021234110826
845150LV00002B/329

* 9 7 8 1 4 2 5 5 6 2 2 8 1 *